MARIE ANTOINETTE'S DARKEST DAYS

ALSO BY WILL BASHOR

Jean-Baptiste Cléry: Eyewitness to Louis XVI and Marie-Antoinette's Nightmare

Marie Antoinette's Head: The Royal Hairdresser, the Queen, and the Revolution

MARIE ANTOINETTE'S DARKEST DAYS

PRISONER NO. 280 IN THE CONCIERGERIE

Will Bashor

ROWMAN & LITTLEFIELD
Lanham • Boulder • New York • London

Published by Rowman & Littlefield
A wholly owned subsidary of The Rowman & Littlefield Publishing Group, Inc.
4501 Forbes Boulevard, Suite 200, Lanham, Maryland 20706
www.rowman.com

6 Tinworth Street, London SE11 5AL, United Kingdom

Distributed by NATIONAL BOOK NETWORK

British Library Cataloguing in Publication Information Available

Library of Congress Cataloging-in-Publication Data

Names: Bashor, Will, author.
Title: Marie Antoinette's Darkest Days : Prisoner No.280 in the Conciergerie
  / Will Bashor.
Description: Lanham, Maryland : Rowman & Littlefield, 2016. | Includes
  bibliographical references and index.
Identifiers: LCCN 2016000797 (print) | LCCN 2016001206 (ebook) | ISBN
  9781442254992 (cloth : alk. paper) | ISBN 9781538138908 (pbk. : alk. paper) |
  ISBN 9781442255005 (electronic)
Subjects: LCSH: Marie Antoinette, Queen, consort of Louis XVI, King of
  France, 1755–1793—Imprisonment. | Marie Antoinette, Queen, consort of
  Louis XVI, King of France, 1755–1793—Trials, litigation, etc. | Marie
  Antoinette, Queen, consort of Louis XVI, King of France, 1755–1793—Death
  and burial. | France—History—Revolution, 1789-1799.
Classification: LCC DC137.17 .B37 2016 (print) | LCC DC137.17 (ebook) | DDC
  944/.035092—dc23
LC record available at http://lccn.loc.gov/2016000797

As always, for Norma Blanche,
Bertina Faye, and Randall Scott

"I was a queen, and you took away my crown; a wife, and you killed my husband; a mother, and you deprived me of my children. My blood alone remains: take it, but do not make me suffer long."

Marie Antoinette[*]
Revolutionary Tribunal, October 16, 1793

---

[*]Eugêne Pottet, *Histoire de la Conciergerie du Palais de Paris* (Paris: Quantin, 1895), 208. "Non, répondit Marie-Antoinette. J'étais reine et vous m'avez détrônée. J'étais épouse et vous avez fait périr mon mari. J'étais mère et vous m'avez arraché mes enfants. Il ne me reste que mon sang: abreuvez-vous-en; mais ne me faites pas souffrir plus longtemps."

CONTENTS

AUTHOR'S NOTE

My intention in this book is not to defend Marie Antoinette or justify any of her actions as queen of France but rather to document her last days of imprisonment at the Conciergerie prison—when only the guillotine's blade could end her agony. Because prisoners remained incarcerated at the Conciergerie for a very short time before being sentenced in the nearby Tribunal court, the prison was better known as the "antechamber of the guillotine." The queen's incarceration, however, would last for two and a half months in the noisy, moldy dungeon that reeked of rat urine, pipe smoke, and poor sanitation.

Considering the efforts to reconstruct these scenes, readers may find that *Marie Antoinette's Darkest Days* at times reads like a novel. However, with vigorous research and study of archived documents and secondary material from mostly eighteenth- and nineteenth-century sources, every effort has been made to retell this incredible story as accurately as possible. All dialogue in French has been translated verbatim from the most credible of sources, and all translations are my own unless otherwise noted. In many instances the original French has been included in the corresponding notes.

Unfortunately, there are conflicting accounts of Marie Antoinette's imprisonment in the Conciergerie. This, added to the embellishment on the part of royalists and revolutionaries alike for their own political purposes, has not done past narratives of her final days any justice. I will thus chronicle the queen's days in the Conciergerie in greater detail by noting any and all inconsistencies found in prior accounts.

I have striven to maintain a nonjudgmental tone when analyzing the research from this period. It goes without saying that Marie Antoinette was well known for her lavish expenditures and frivolous lifestyle. Not long after furnishing and completing the gardens at the Petit Trianon, for example, Louis XVI purchased the château of St. Cloud for his queen. When Parisians complained about the great expense of her subsequent renovations, she replied with a laugh, "The Parisians are frogs that do nothing but croak."[1]

One could argue, however, that the revolutionary press went too far at times—for instance, when it branded the queen "Madame Deficit" or the "Austrian bitch in heat."[2] And the historian Louis-Marie Prudhomme surely overreacted when he wrote, "All the crimes committed before and after the Revolution are the work of Marie Antoinette. Her impure blood will not suffice to wash out all her wickedness."[3]

In any event, we must take all the malicious sayings that circulated about Marie Antoinette into consideration, whether true or not, to better understand the pretext for her imprisonment in the Conciergerie and the accusations brought against her in the Revolutionary Tribunal.

Will Bashor
Paris, October 2015

PROLOGUE

PRELUDE TO THE REVOLUTION

On June 22, 1775, fourteen years before the start of the French Revolution, Marie Antoinette wrote her mother, Empress Maria Theresa of Austria, describing how moved she was at the coronation of her husband, Louis XVI, at the Cathedral of Reims; the crowd's enthusiasm and "most touching acclamations" had brought her to tears. But the new queen was already aware that problems lurked on the horizon at the onset of her reign: "It is at the same time amazing and wonderful to be so well received two months after the riots and in spite of the high price of bread which unfortunately continues."[1] Marie Antoinette was referring to the Flour Wars, a wave of riots throughout much of France due to the hoarding of grain in the royal reserves. The artificially high cost of grain and, consequently, the high cost of bread resulted in what many historians have called the prelude to the Revolution.[2]

However, there were warning signs much earlier about the troubles to come. On his death bed in 1715, Louis XIV, the "Sun King," cautioned the heir to the throne, his five-year-old great-grandson Louis, about extravagant spending, whether for war or other projects:

> You will soon be king of a great kingdom. What I recommend most strongly is to never forget the obligations you have to God to whom you owe all that

you are. Try to keep peace with your neighbors. I'm too fond of war; do not imitate me in this, nor in the great expenses that I made.[3]

Louis XIV was certainly referring to the numerous wars fought during his reign and the extravagant building projects such as Versailles, with its elaborate decor, gardens, and fountains. But recognizing the needs of his subjects, he continued, "Care for your people as soon as you can and do not as I have had the misfortune to do myself."[4]

Louis XV, the "Well-Beloved" (*Bien-Aimé*), however, did not follow the Sun King's advice, and by his death in 1774 was known as Louis the "Hated" (*Détesté*). His reign was riddled with excessive spending, fragile foreign relations, high taxes, powerful mistresses, and debauchery. Although the aristocracy and bourgeoisie gained power, the people suffered greatly. When on his deathbed, Louis XV reputedly uttered the phrase "After me the deluge" (*Après moi le déluge*).[5] And, indeed, it was a bloody one.

There are many schools of thought with respect to the origins of the French Revolution. Although this book does not focus exclusively on this violent transformation, it is important to understand why the young fairy-tale princess from Austria would one day be so viciously attacked as the "scourge and blood-sucker of all the French."[6]

By the time of the storming of the Bastille in 1789, the French people had lost faith in King Louis XVI and increasingly blamed his spendthrift queen for their hardships. In fact, the press was calling for her—and other royals and aristocrats—to be chopped up like meat for pâté.[7]

A number of factors, ranging from social and political considerations to the weak and irresolute Louis XVI himself, contributed to this rage. At a time of national crisis, when decisive leadership was needed, the king turned to hunting or tinkering with his locks and handiworks to escape the burdens of governing. His inexperienced wife, Marie Antoinette, and his youngest brother, the comte d'Artois, soon filled this policy vacuum, and such a remedy could only lead to disaster:

> Where the monarch is feeble-minded, the courtiers are intriguing, the factions are loud, the populace is daring, good men become timid, the most zealous public servants become discouraged, the men of talent meet only with repulses, and the best counsels lead to no effect.[8]

Storming of the Bastille

Ironically, other than humiliating France's rival, England, Louis XVI's exorbitant financial support for the American Revolution had no effect in weakening the English influence in the American colonies or in strengthening France's position in Europe. As a consequence, however, France's involvement in America did invigorate the French ideals of *liberté, égalité,* and *fraternité.*

It would be a far stretch to consider the American Revolution as a major cause of the French Revolution. The French people knew very little of America and perhaps cared less; they were more concerned with royal absolutism and its encumbering taxes, the system of privileges for the nobles and priests, and the more immediate scarcity of food.[9]

In sum, the years of suffering culminated in the people's march on Versailles on October 5, 1789, and the insurrection on August 10, 1792, a defining event of the Revolution that resulted in the fall of the French monarchy. Subsequently, King Louis XVI and the royal family were arrested and imprisoned in the Temple prison, and ultimately Louis XVI was found guilty of treason and guillotined on January 21, 1793.

Execution of Louis XVI

Marie Antoinette, her two children, and her sister-in-law Élisabeth waited in the Temple prison that morning for a final farewell from the king, but the king failed to keep his promise. Only the shouts of joy of the infuriated people of Paris informed them that the king was no more. In the days to come, nobles, aristocrats, and members of the royal family would share Louis XVI's fate. This period of violence will forever be known as the Reign of Terror.

CHRONOLOGY

1789

May 5	Opening of the Estates-General at Versailles
July 14	Storming of the Bastille
October 1	Royal Body Guards invite regiment of Flanders to feast at Versailles
October 5	March on Versailles and return of the royal family to Paris

1791

June 20	The royal family's late-night flight from Paris
June 21	Royal family arrested in Varennes
June 22	Royal family dispatched back to Paris at dawn
July 17	Champ de Mars massacre

1792

August 9	Overthrow of King Louis XVI and siege of the Tuileries planned
August 10	Tuileries stormed and royal family forced to seek refuge in the assembly; the end of the French monarchy
August 11	Louis and his family transferred to the nearby Feuillants convent

August 13	Louis and his family imprisoned in the tower of the Temple
December 11	Trial of Louis Capet

1793

January 17	Louis Capet convicted of treason and condemned to death
January 21	Louis Capet guillotined at the place de la Révolution
July 2	Marie Antoinette's son, Louis Charles, separated from his family
August 2	Marie Antoinette taken to the Conciergerie prison
August 28	Note concealed in a carnation to help Marie Antoinette escape discovered
September 2	"The head of Antoinette" promised to the French by republican Jacques René Hébert
October 14	First day of Marie Antoinette's trial
October 16	Marie Antoinette found guilty and executed

1794

May 10	Marie Antoinette's sister-in-law, Madame Élisabeth, executed

1795

June 9	Death of Marie Antoinette's son, Louis Charles
December 18	Marie Antoinette's daughter, Marie-Thérèse, liberated from the Temple

1815

January 18	Marie Antoinette's body exhumed by order of King Louis XVIII
January 21	Christian burial of Marie Antoinette's remains at Saint-Denis

HOUSE OF BOURBON
Family Tree of Louis XVI

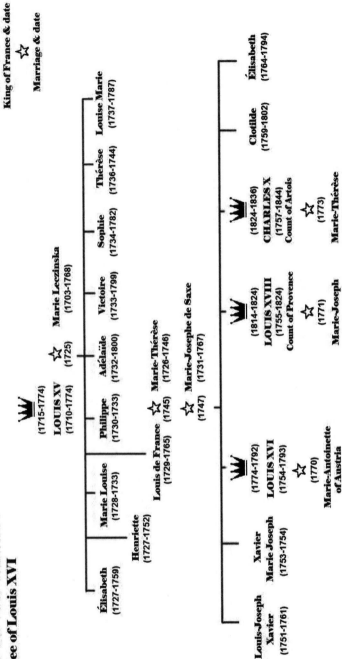

(Will Bashor)

INTRODUCTION

"Is it our forgetfulness of the Austrian woman's crimes and our indifference toward the Capet family that has deceived our enemies? If so, the time has come to eradicate every trace of royalty!"

—Bertrand Barère to the National Convention,
Paris, August 1, 1793

Paris
1793

Gone are the days of extravagant balls, the towering pouf hairstyles, and the lavish court life of Versailles. Queen Marie Antoinette, the daughter of Empress Maria Theresa of Austria, is imprisoned in the Temple prison with her sister-in-law Madame Élisabeth, her daughter Marie-Thérèse, and her eight-year-old son Louis Charles, the uncrowned King Louis XVII of France—uncrowned since the execution of his father Louis XVI on January 21, 1793.

The month after Louis XVI's rendezvous with the guillotine, and unbeknownst to Marie Antoinette, the insurrectionary delegates of the government of Paris asked that the queen be separated from her family. She could then be transported to the Conciergerie prison for a speedy trial by the newly created Revolutionary Tribunal. Amid laughter and murmurs, the delegates were amazed to learn that after the death of Louis XVI the government still provided his widow with valets de chambre to "empty her chamber pot" in the Temple.[1]

Since the king's death, eight cooks still "sumptuously" prepared the queen's table at the Temple, and the young Louis Charles was often found sitting on a cushion at the head of the table and addressed as "sire."[2] Despite her imprisonment, the queen remained optimistic of a better future; she had communicated her wishes to the ex-king's brother, the count of Provence, that he serve as regent of France during her son's minority. The legal majority of a king of France had been fixed at the age of fourteen,* but he could actually begin to govern at thirteen years and a day.[3]

When the queen's sister-in-law less enthusiastically asked her to face reality, the queen responded, "I have great hope in the fickleness of the French people and the outcome of the war; time and the allied powers will be on my side."[4]

Unfortunately, the allied powers' influence was waning, despite the French people's fervor; time was running out for the queen. The National Convention was already proposing that she be accused of treason and brought to justice. Although the initial request to remove Marie Antoinette from the Temple and send her to the Conciergerie for judgment was denied, the government remained apprehensive about the young prince's presumptuous claim to the empty throne.

After the execution of his father, the young heir Louis Charles could now be targeted, but how would the government dispose of an innocent child who could hardly be convicted of any single crime against France? With each day that passed, however, the young heir was becoming increasingly more of a threat to the revolutionaries. King Louis XVI was now out of the picture, but a delegate warned that the young prince was "a hostage that must be preserved carefully." The danger was not what the boy was but what he could become. The delegate reminded the assembly of a similar event in English history: "Charles I died on the scaffold, but his son still ascended to the throne."[5]

The delegates had reason to be concerned. It was no longer just a small group of loyal followers who proclaimed the child King Louis XVII. Support for the Bourbon royal family was gaining not only throughout France but also in England, Russia, and Spain. The world was beginning to acknowl-

---

*King Charles V decreed this ordinance in the fourteenth century.

edge an unavoidable fact: the ragged little child in the Temple prison was rightly the true sovereign of France.

To put such fears to rest, the child was ordered separated from his family by a decree of the National Convention and confined to another cell in the Temple tower.[6] The young heir would not be assassinated; the revolutionary government was farsighted enough to realize such a cruel measure would be a mistake. The execution of a child would likely backfire, only imperiling the new government's popularity.

Instead, the jailers would destroy the child's health by depriving him of fresh air, light, proper exercise, and wholesome food and by keeping him in a state of fear and fever-breeding filth in his cold, dark cell. Then, when necessary, the convention could present a "moping little idiot, whose diseased body and vacant stare of imbecility would make him such a sorry and pathetic choice for a monarch that the people would turn away in horror."[7]

Towers of the Temple prison

On July 3, this infamously cruel order was executed.* Late in the evening Marie Antoinette and Élisabeth were mending the children's clothes, Marie-Thérèse was reading aloud from the book of Psalms, and Louis Charles was sound asleep in his bed when footsteps sounded on the stairs of the Temple tower. Locks and bolts clanked, and half a dozen municipal officers ferociously burst into the royal prisoners' chambers.[8]

"We have come," said one of the municipals coarsely, "to acquaint you with the orders of the committee." And then he proceeded to read, "The Committee of Public Safety decrees that the son of Capet† be separated from his mother and committed to the charge of a mentor."[9]

Marie Antoinette stood up. "Take my child away from me?" she asked. Pale and terrified, she threw herself between the municipals and the shawl she had hung up in front of Louis Charles's bed to screen the light from his eyes.

"No, no, you cannot mean that—it's impossible!" she cried. "He is too young and too weak; he needs my care so much."

"The order has been given," said the officer, "and it is our duty to immediately carry it out."

Marie-Thérèse rushed to her mother's side while Élisabeth stood frozen nearby. Both had at first been too horrified to speak, but they soon joined the queen with tears and pleas.

"In the name of heaven, gentlemen, do not lay this terrible trial upon us!" cried Élisabeth.

"What's the use of all this noise and disturbance?" said another officer. "We're not going to kill the child. Come, give him up quietly or we shall take him by force."

Someone leaned against the shawl suspended as a curtain, and it fell upon the young prince's head, waking him up. When he realized what

---

*This decree also ordered that other members of the royal family be exiled from France, that those in custody be exiled only if found innocent, that the two children, Marie-Thérèse and Louis Charles, be furnished only what was necessary for food and lodging, and that Élisabeth be held in the Temple until after the trial of the queen—to discover evidence of any complicity.

†After the end of the monarchy, when the French Republic was declared on September 22, 1792, the king was simply referred to as "Citizen Capet," being the descendent of Hugh Capet, the king of Franks of the House of Capet from 987 to 996. All titles of nobility had been abolished since June 17, 1790.

was happening, the hapless child sprang up and threw himself into his mother's arms.

"Mamma, mamma!" he shrieked. "Save me! Do not leave me!"

Pressing him closely to her bosom, she clung with all her strength to the bedpost. "You may slay me if you wish, but for as long as I am alive, you shall not rob me of my child!"

"No use fighting with women," said one of the officers. "Citizens, call in the guard!"

There was a moment's hesitation before Élisabeth begged them to delay until the next day, to no avail. She then implored them to allow the mother at least to see her child from time to time, but her passionate appeals met only with rude rebuffs.

Meanwhile, the boy was still buried in his mother's bosom, shivering with terror. After an hour of stalemate, the officers finally managed to pull the child from his mother's clutches through a devious trick. Two officers seized Marie-Thérèse and swore that they would slaughter her and her brother then and there unless the boy was handed over to them at once.[10]

The queen had no choice but to give in. Slowly she began to dress the prince. Marie-Thérèse and Élisabeth passed article after article of clothing to her, taking as much time as possible for the family to smother the child in kisses. The officers began to lose patience, and the inevitable moment of parting arrived.[11]

The queen stopped weeping and calmly pulled her son toward her as she seated herself on a chair. She laid her hands upon his tiny shoulders. "My child," she solemnly said, "we are about to part. Remember your duty when I am no longer present to remind you of it.

"Never forget the good God who tries your faith nor your mother who loves you," she continued. "Be good, patient and truthful, and your Father in heaven will bless you from the heights above."[12]

After kissing him on his forehead, she tried to turn him over to the officers, but the terrified child still clung tightly to his mother.

"My son, you must obey," she said, resigned to his fate.

"Come, come!" said one of the officers. "No more preaching to the child."

"He must do without it henceforth," said a second officer, who grabbed the child and dragged him toward the door.

Separation of Louis Charles from his family
(Bibliothèque Nationale Française)

"No need of it," added a third. "The nation, always great and generous, will provide for his education."

The door was pulled shut with such force that the vaulted chamber echoed. Only locks and bolts separated the widowed mother from her only son in the Temple prison. The rest of that night was never recorded; there were no witnesses to narrate what passed between the young, uncrowned king of France and his new jailer, Antoine Simon. We know only that the child was still crouching in the darkest corner of his dimly lit cell when day broke.[13] Still weeping, the only words that interrupted his sobs were the pitiful cries of "Mamma, mamma."[14]

If Marie Antoinette's Christian principles had helped her endure all the pain and sacrifices in her life, her queenly pride helped her bear all the humiliation. But now any illusion that she would never be separated from her children was dispelled. Perhaps she realized that things might never return to normal.

Young Louis Charles, his jailer Antoine Simon, and Madame Simon
(Bibliothèque Nationale Française)

The following day the queen requested that her son be cared for by the king's former valet, the faithful Jean-Baptiste Cléry, who had been removed from service at the Temple after the king's death, or perhaps Cléry could be permitted to serve the child his meals, as he was accustomed to receive them, at the table.* If necessary, she argued, Cléry could even be prohibited from speaking to the child or showing any sign of tenderness or sympathy. But the convention found the request irrelevant and promptly ignored it.[15]

In the days to follow, the child was occasionally allowed to take a short walk on a ledge of the Temple tower, and Marie Antoinette would sit for hours just to catch a quick glimpse of him through a small slit in the wall— but even this flash of solace did not last long.[16]

When the convention received the shocking news that a European conspiracy threatened French liberty on August 1, Bertrand Barère of the revolutionary Committee of Public Safety reported that the time had come "to eradicate every trace of royalty." He called for the convention to adopt

---

*Jean-Baptiste Cléry was Louis XVI's valet in the Temple. After the king's death, Cléry was removed from the Temple, but he remained a loyal supporter in exile until his death in 1809.

violent measures, including the immediate transfer of Marie Antoinette to the Conciergerie prison to appear before the Revolutionary Tribunal.[17]

Widow Capet, Prisoner No. 280 in the Conciergerie. Marie Antoinette's destiny was soon to be a cruel mixture of grandeur, humiliation, and terror. Generations of authors have reveled in reliving the queen's reign amid the splendors of the court of Versailles and the Petit Trianon, but few have ever found the space (or perhaps the courage) in their voluminous biographies to narrate her final imprisonment in a fetid dungeon cell at the Conciergerie. The queen surely understood that her days might be numbered, but she could never have known that two and a half months would pass before she would finally stand trial for the most ungodly charges.

I

THE CONCIERGERIE

Marie Antoinette taken to the Conciergerie
(Bibliothèque Nationale Française)

1

TRANSFER FROM THE TEMPLE PRISON

*"The most infected dungeon with a few trusses of straw for a
bed is all that is necessary."*

—Prison guard to Warden Toussaint Richard,
Paris, August 2, 1793

Paris
August 1793

During the afternoon of August 1, 1793, Commander François Hanriot
of the Parisian forces visited the Temple prison, where Marie Antoinette, her daughter Marie-Thérèse, her son Louis Charles, and her sister-in-
law Madame Élisabeth had been imprisoned for almost a year.*

After inspecting all the prison gates, Hanriot reported the lack of artillery
and immediately took new measures to increase security at the centuries-old
fortress. In fact, the guards were soon supplied with such an arsenal of ammunition that it appeared the Temple was in a state of siege. By eight o'clock
in the evening Hanriot was convinced that the Temple was well fortified.[1]

The coarse and gruff Hanriot then inspected the royal prisoners' quarters. "From the time he came into the room until the moment he left it, he
did nothing but swear," Marie-Thérèse wrote in her memoirs.[2]

---

*The daughters of the king of France, his sisters, and the eldest daughter of the dauphin
were all called "Madame." Marie-Thérèse was also known as "Madame Royale."

At a quarter past one in the morning, police commissioners Jean-Baptiste Michonis, Nicholas Froidure, Jean-Baptiste Marino, and Etienne Michel arrived on the scene, armed with a decree drawn up the previous day. It ordered Marie Antoinette's immediate transfer from the Temple to the Conciergerie. Michonis had already stationed over a dozen gendarmes in the Temple courtyard to receive the dethroned queen of France.

At two o'clock in the morning, Marie Antoinette was brutally awakened—if indeed she had ever slept—and armed men read the solemn decree: "Marie Antoinette is being sent to the special Tribunal; she will be transported at once to the Conciergerie."[3]

Years later Princess Marie-Thérèse remarked that her mother showed no emotion and did not speak a word when the commissioners arrived to take her away. The queen embraced her daughter and her sister-in-law, who both begged for permission to join her at the Conciergerie, but their pleas were denied.[4]

Marie Antoinette silently prepared a small packet of personal items as the officials stood watching. The half-naked queen, at one time clothed only in the finest raiment by her ladies-in-waiting, was now forced to dress in front of complete strangers. The officials also ransacked the chamber and asked her to empty her pockets. When she complied, they confiscated the contents and informed her that the items would be produced as evidence in her trial. In all, they took a gold ring entwined with hair, a small packet of her husband's and children's hair, a little register on which she taught the prince arithmetic, a small notebook,* and miniature portraits of the princess de Lamballe and two childhood friends: the princesses of Hesse and of Mecklenburg.[5] These items were all she had left of those she loved in the world. Only a handkerchief and a small bottle of smelling salts or rose water remained on her person.[6]

After the officers sealed up the small collection of trinkets, Marie Antoinette kissed her daughter. "I beg you to be brave," she said, "to care for your aunt, and to obey her as a second mother."

---

*The historian Joseph Durieux claimed that within the small "green-beaded" notebook was found an address: "Mme Sallantin, chez Mme Lapassade, rue de Grenelle Saint-Germain, no 14." Madame Sallatin had been in charge of all the queen's affairs for a long time, providing her with toiletries while she was incarcerated in the Temple and earlier when the royal family was under house arrest at the Tuileries.

The young princess was so distraught with grief that she stood frozen, unable to utter a single word.

The queen threw herself into Élisabeth's arms. "And you, my sister," she said, "I leave in you another mother to my poor children. Love them as you have loved us, even in this dungeon, and even unto death."

Élisabeth whispered into the queen's ear. No one heard what she said, but given the pious woman's nature, she surely intended her words to comfort the queen in her grief.

When the queen departed, as if her strength might fail her, she never turned back to see her daughter for the very last time. Nor did she cry—her tears were perhaps all dried up. Only an inscription on the prison wall remained as a testament of her love—the lines marking the height of her two children with the inscription "27 March 1793, four feet ten inches and three feet two inches."[7]

As the queen passed the guard's quarters, the infamous Tison, a prison servant and revolutionary spy who had been insolent to the royal family ever since their arrival at the Temple, blew pipe smoke in her face.[8]

The queen passed down to the foot of the tower stairs, where she waited while municipal guards made out a procès-verbal, a detailed account of her

Separation of Marie Antoinette from her family
(Bibliothèque Nationale Française)

discharge from the Temple. There she stood motionless with a small bundle at her feet.* The queen, who now had lost everything dear to her, had also lost any sign of the beauty with which she once graced the galleries of the magnificent Palace of Versailles.

Once the paperwork was complete, one of the guards led the queen away, but on leaving, the queen struck her head on the doorsill.[9] Either she forgot to lower her head, or one of the guards "dragged" her through the door.

"Did you hurt yourself?" asked the guard.

It was likely not an accident because a Temple guard would never have asked such a question unless he had felt some remorse.

"No, nothing can hurt me now," she said without touching her forehead.[10] Perhaps the separation from her family had been excruciating enough.

The commissioners and soldiers quickly surrounded the queen and escorted her across the Temple courtyard to the prison gate, where a coach awaited her. She walked through the great gate and entered the coach with the municipal officer Jean-Baptiste Michonis, his colleague, and two gendarmes.

How little did Michonis's colleagues know him! He was not only a prison inspector and chief of police but also a secret royalist supporter who had already once been involved with a failed plot to rescue the royal family from the Temple.

The coach was accompanied by some forty gendarmes with sabers in hand, pistols charged, and orders to disperse any crowd that might interfere with the coach's passage to the Conciergerie. A few lights glimmered dimly from the street lamps as the queen's coach traversed the sleeping city "at a gallop" along the rues du Temple, de la Tixeranderie† and Coutellerie, and Planche-Mibray before crossing the Notre Dame bridge over the Seine River.[11]

Once on the Île de la Cité, the historic island in the middle of the Seine, the coach turned onto the rue de la Lanterne, then passed through the rue de la Vieille-Draperie to reach the courtyard of the Law Courts that neighbored the Conciergerie.[12] When the queen stepped down from the coach, she was swiftly escorted through an archway to the prison gate.

---

*This bundle must have at least contained a gold ring, a watch, a necklace, a medallion, and several *cachets* in gold, one of which was titled "Amour et la Fidélité." These would all be confiscated from the queen on September 8.

†This street has since been destroyed for the extension of the present rue de Rivoli.

The turnkey Louis Larivière was on nominal guard duty at the front entrance, but he was asleep in a big leather chair. He heard a sudden knock—made not by the door knocker but by the blows of a rifle butt. He opened the door promptly to find a woman in a black dress and bonnet surrounded by guards and officers. Even though the entrance was barely lit by the hall torches, he recognized the widow of Louis XVI, having served her majesty as a patisserie chef at the Palace of Versailles years earlier.[13]

At three o'clock in the morning, the maid Rosalie Lamorlière, who was asleep upstairs, was suddenly awakened by the warden's wife, Marie Barassaint Richard.* "Quick, quick, rouse yourself!" she said. "Take this torch! They are here!"

Earlier that day Madame Richard had been informed of the unexpected arrival of the queen. "Tonight my husband and I shall not go to bed," she had told Rosalie, "and you must sleep on a chair. The queen is going to be transferred here from the Temple."

The warden, Toussaint Richard, complained of not having been informed of the unexpected arrival in time to have a room prepared for the royal prisoner, but one of his assistants remarked, "The most infected dungeon with a few trusses of straw for a bed is all that is necessary."[14]

Although Richard and his wife were known to treat their prisoners with respect and consideration, there are conflicting accounts about the queen's first night at the Conciergerie. According to one, she was confined to the Council Chamber.[15] Another reported her temporarily lodged in Richard's more comfortable chambers for several days until the Council Chamber near the prison chapel could be prepared.[16] The latter account appears more likely because the Council Chamber was at that time occupied by another prisoner, the highly decorated General Adam Philippe Custine.†

However, the queen could only have been lodged in Richard's chambers for the first night of her imprisonment in the Conciergerie. Although instructed by prosecutor Antoine Quentin Fouquier-Tinville to lock her up in a cell like any other common prisoner, Warden Richard moved General

---

*Some historians used the name Magdeleine Rosay.

†General Custine was executed at the place de la Révolution several weeks later on August 28.

Custine out of the Council Chamber and moved the queen into the general's cell the following morning.

It is unclear why Richard would risk infuriating the venomous prosecutor. On the one hand, Richard was known to be merciful and wanted to keep the queen separated from the prison population; on the other hand, it was rumored that one of the municipal officers had requested that the queen be moved to a more secluded area. This officer was more than likely Michonis, the queen's secret ally.

Keeping close surveillance over the prison, Fouquier-Tinville soon discovered that his orders had not been followed. When he angrily inquired why the queen had not been locked up in a common cell, Richard explained that the Council Chamber was the only space available at the time.[17] Fouquier-Tinville would have known that the prison was frightfully overcrowded. In fact, it was so teeming that the air was almost unbreathable: "So tainted it was with the horrible emanations that come from the miserable crowds of prisoners huddled together."[18]

Prisoners seldom had to wait longer than two or three days in the terrifying prison before their rendezvous with the guillotine. Cells had to be quickly emptied in order to fill them up again with the large numbers of new convicts arrested daily. These were turbulent times.[19]

The Conciergerie consisted of a series of damp and dark subterranean dungeons, a stark contrast with the magnificent Palace of Justice above. It was almost daybreak that first morning when Marie Antoinette was led to a guardroom lit by a sepulchral lamp and crowded with jailers. The stench of smoke and liquor filled the air. The jailers drank and smoked night and day, creating a noxious smog that almost smothered the prison's visitors.

The queen was then hurried down the slippery corridors before reaching the iron door of the Council Chamber, which had been hastily furnished after General Custine's transfer to another cell. Perhaps better situated for the queen than other cells of the prison, it was still a far cry from some of the more habitable chambers of the medieval Temple prison. The Council Chamber (*Salle de Conseil*) had windows at ground level, and its floor was below the level of the nearby Seine River, creating a musty, damp environment. Muddy slime covered the floor, and little streams of water trickled down the moldy stone walls.[20]

It appeared that the "most pestilential of all prisons had been purposely selected for the queen."[21] According to General Custine's daughter-in-law, who visited him on the night before his execution, "his old cell was given to Marie Antoinette, one of the worst of the prison."[22] But according to the journalist Philippe Coittant, the entire prison could only be described as horrendously frightening. It was filled with "moans, rags, an unbearable stench, a foul air, and drunken jailers speaking coarsely, carrying large rings of keys, and being followed by vicious dogs to help spread terror throughout."[23]

The noise must also have been unbearable. The historian Alphonse de Lamartine wrote that the splashing of the Seine River underneath the bridges, the continuous noise of the carriages on the quay, and the footsteps of the crowds flocking to the halls of justice during the hours of the tribunals created a bellowing noise that "rolled like distant thunder" and perpetually "shook these vaults."

"The Conciergerie! What an abyss!" reported a frequent visitor.[24] And, indeed, it was a living tomb where the silence of night could be petrifyingly interrupted:

From hour to hour the chimes slowly count out the long hours of suffering; the watch dogs respond with long, drawn-out howls; the jailers charged with the different death warrants take them from cell to cell until far into the night, waking every prisoner with their menacing and insulting voices.[25]

The jailers distributed sixty to eighty death sentences every night and day. The six hundred prisoners were thus kept in a state of perpetual alarm, believing that their last hour was upon them.

The Conciergerie's six guard dogs were perhaps the best jailers of all; they were never intoxicated; nor were they seemingly susceptible to bribes. However, one dog, Ravage, known for his height, intelligence, and ferocity, was on duty every night—until several prisoners duped him; they escaped one night by digging a hole through their dungeon wall.

The following morning a note was found tied to Ravage's tail along with an assignat, revolutionary paper money. The note read, "One can bribe Ravage with one hundred sous and a portion of leg of lamb." The butt of the prisoner's jokes, the humiliated canine was soon relieved of his duties in the Conciergerie.[26]

A number of gendarmes met the queen when she arrived downstairs at her new cell. They had gathered at the door with members of the Revolutionary Tribunal who were waiting in the squalid cell to catch a glimpse of their new prisoner. Lacking any candles, they lit the lamp in the neighboring hallway; the heavily barred window gave but scant light at the break of day. During the ceremony* of the prisoners' registration, the queen was referred to as the "widow Capet" and simply registered as "Prisoner No. 280."

When the official visitors departed, only Madame Richard and Rosalie remained in the cell with the queen.[27] The fleurs de lys, the royal symbol of French heraldry, sparsely decorated the paper on one of the walls—though it was peeling and faded from the humidity and the moisture dripping down the wall. Whenever the Seine River rose just a little, "dampness ruled everywhere" in the prison.[28]

Door of the queen's cell at the Conciergerie

---

*There are conflicting accounts as to the time and place of the queen's registration. While other accounts record the queen as being registered upon first entering the prison in the *greffe*, the registrar's office, Rosalie reported that the queen was registered in her cell the following morning.

The queen's cell was furnished with an uncomfortable folding cot "of which the bands were mended by knotted rope, and which had already been rejected by a guard on duty as being too bumpy."[29] The straw of the mattress was decayed and covered with gray sheets and a woolen blanket riddled with holes. Madame Richard had also added a small table and two straw chairs; a wooden box of powder and a tin pot of pomade* on the table completed the furnishings.

It was extremely humid on the queen's first morning in her cell, and the maid Rosalie noticed that she wiped drops of perspiration from her face several times with her handkerchief. At first the queen stared blankly and silently at the stark room. She then earnestly looked at Madame Richard and Rosalie—as if trying to guess what she should expect from them.[30] When she noticed a nail on the wall, she began to remove the watch from her waist. Rosalie quickly ran to her room to fetch a small stool, and when she returned, the queen stepped on it to fasten her watch on the nail. When the queen began to undress for bed, Rosalie timidly approached her to assist.

"I am grateful, my child," replied the queen, "but since I now have no one, I will serve myself." Her manner, according to Rosalie, was "simple and kind."[31]

This was a remarkable change; the former queen of France, who had for most of her life relied on others, now almost proudly refused any help.

As daylight increased, the queen lay down on her meager bed. Although there was a rickety screen in the corner, there were no curtains for privacy. Madame Richard and Rosalie took their candles and left the queen alone after furnishing her with a pillow.

Marie Antoinette did not come to the Conciergerie alone; she had kept a small dog by the name of Thisbé in the Temple, a loyal companion who followed her everywhere.† When the queen was transferred to the Conciergerie, Thisbé was not permitted to travel with her in the carriage, but the dog was not deterred; it chased the carriage all the way to the Conciergerie. At the main gate, the little dog tried to slip into the prison between its mistress's feet, but the guard stopped it with a quick kick.[32]

---

*Wax made from bear fat or lard used to style hair.

†One account referred to the dog as a "carlin," or a pug named after a French actor who played Harlequin, because of the resemblance of the dog's face to the black mask of the Harlequin; other accounts referred to the dog as a spaniel.

Thisbé waited faithfully for the queen at the guard station outside the gates, and whenever it howled piteously, the gendarmes would poke at it with the butts of their bayonets. Despite the mistreatment, the dog never left the spot where it last saw its mistress—except when hunger forced it to. Simply known as the "queen's dog" in the neighborhood, Thisbé would visit houses near the prison to beg for scraps of food and then return to the prison gates by sunset.

The sole purpose of transporting the Austrian-born Marie Antoinette from the Temple to the Conciergerie was to make the world believe that the prisoner would shortly be tried. Moreover, every effort was made to spread the rumor that her execution was imminent in the hope that France's allies would be motivated to negotiate to save her from the scaffold and thus end the conflict with Austria. She was no ordinary prisoner; she was thought to have some value as a political hostage in the negotiations with France's enemy. However, the radical Jacques René Hébert promised the Revolutionary Tribunal her head, saying he would "cut it off" himself if the Committee for Public Safety delayed giving it to him.[33] But for the time being, no one dared bring the queen before the Tribunal.

Furthermore, in no way did the decree summoning Marie Antoinette to the Conciergerie determine the queen's fate. The revolutionary politicians had been prompted by "fury or fear," failing to specify when she would be called before the Tribunal. A month later, it was still thought that she might be a useful hostage to exchange for Austria's ending the war. Negotiations were already underway between Brussels and Vienna, and the French hoped that "the head of the unhappy queen might command a high price."

After Marie Antoinette spent the first night in Richard's chambers, it became immediately apparent that she needed to be moved to the interior of the prison—the prison's jailers were irritated, anxiously awaiting their turn to guard the late tyrant's wife.[34] She was therefore relocated to the Council Chamber, so called because under the former monarchy the magistrates of the royal courts had always held sessions there to hear prisoners' complaints.[35]

For the next forty days, from August 3 until her transfer to a more secure cell on September 13, the former queen of France would be confined to the Council Chamber—with no indication of the horrors yet in store for her.

À SAVOIR . . .

The Queen of France at the Conciergerie

Poem by Antoine de Rivarol[36]

Widow and mother in the midst of my sad years,
Raising my obscure eyes up to divinity,
Because of their irons my hands are chained,
I die in captivity.
I'm dying, and in this place where horror surrounds me,
Everything is the past to me, time only remains.
It will see my hair, on a forehead without crown,
Turn white in captivity.
Give me back my two children, oh people without mercy!
The fate of their mother they have not inherited.
I forgive you all when their childhood at times
Consoles my captivity.
But all is deaf to me; the world has abandoned me.
In the back of a dungeon, inhabited by crime,
The daughter of Caesars falls from a throne,
And perishes in captivity.
I only see next to me an inhumane guard,
And in every look a mediated plan.
Beyond these walls, a distant pity
For my sad captivity.
Sometimes in sleep if my pain succumbs,
Heaven! What day is offered to me! What horrible clarity!
What ghost walks and, lifting from his grave,
Disturbs my captivity!
That's my husband! It is him! I hear his plaintive voice:
"Where do you come from, dear wife, to this hated place?"
But my answers are in vain, and his fleeting shadow
Leaves me to my captivity.

2

THE QUEEN'S
DUNGEON CELL

"If Marie Antoinette's qualities were her own, then her short-comings were due to her entourage and her times."

—Maxime de la Rocheterie,[1] *Ten Years of a Queen's Life*

Paris
August 1793

At about six o'clock in the morning, Warden Richard took his turnkey Louis Larivière aside. "Go and find your mother," he said. "Tell her that I've decided to place her with the queen for a short period of time. Although old, she is still healthy, and the administrators have accepted my recommendation. I hope she won't disappoint me by refusing."[2]

Larivière scurried off to give his mother the message. Madame Jeanne Larivière, known better as Mère Larivière, was terrified when she heard that the queen of France had been threatened with a court trial, but she did not hesitate for a moment to accept the noble charge.

Later in the morning Marie Antoinette awoke in the Council Chamber to the sight of two new beds being delivered: one was destined for the chambermaid and the other for the gendarmes who would never lose sight of their prisoner—even when she attended to the most "natural necessities of life."[3] The two new guards, François Dufresne and Jean Gilbert, would keep watch over the queen for most of the next month. According to Rosalie, Gilbert was considerably more discourteous to the queen than his comrade Dufresne.[4]

Mère Larivière had arrived just before the two guards. In her eighties, she had previously served as a maid in the Palace of Justice before her son became one of the turnkeys of the Conciergerie. In fact, the Larivière family lived in an apartment on the first floor of the prison overlooking the window of Marie Antoinette's cell that faced the women's prison yard.

Mère Larivière then had a few moments to reminisce with the queen; she had also served as concierge for the admiral of France, the duke of Penthièvre, when Marie Antoinette held court at Versailles. The duke of Penthièvre was Louis XVI's cousin, and his daughter-in-law was the princess de Lamballe, Marie Antoinette's beloved friend.[5]

Marie Antoinette and Mère Larivière would also have most likely crossed paths because Madame Larivière's son, Louis, had served in the royal household. Mère Larivière reminded the queen that Louis had served as one of the pastry chefs at Versailles. She then added that ever since the royal family had been removed from Versailles in 1789, her son had been "reduced to serve as a jailer" in the Conciergerie to earn a living.[6]

The following day Mère Larivière instructed her son to go out and buy half a yard of cheesecloth; she needed to patch the queen's black mourning dress because it was ripped under both arms and threadbare in spots. She also told him to find thread and needles and to bring them as quickly as possible. When Louis Larivière returned, he introduced himself to the queen before giving his mother the items. He was not sure if the queen still recognized him, but she thanked him with a "graceful movement of her head."[7]

On the queen's fourth or fifth day* in the Conciergerie, prison administrators François Heron and Jean-Baptiste-André Amar entered her cell and took her watch, a keepsake that she had brought with her from Austria when she first arrived in France as dauphine.

"This watch," said the queen, "was not purchased with French money; my mother gave it me the day I quitted her."

"Nonsense!" said Heron, a notorious agent of the Committee of Public Safety. "A gold watch is quite useless in a prison. The republic will return it to you when your business is settled."

---

*This was on the seventh day according to General Jean Andoche Junot.

Heron's colleague, Amar, forcefully tore two gold rings—one of which was her wedding ring—and a diamond ring from the queen's fingers. No doubt they feared the expensive jewelry could be used to bribe the warden or any of the turnkeys of the prison.[8]

Madame Richard later told Rosalie that the queen cried when she gave up the gold watch and rings. The officials did not know, however, that she was wearing an oval medallion hidden around her neck at the time. This medallion contained a lock of her young son's curls with his portrait, folded up in a small, canary-yellow kid glove that the child once wore.[9]

The prison administrators soon told Mère Larivière that her job was too strenuous for her age and that she would need to be replaced. The administrators were more likely concerned about Madame Larivière's compassion for the queen. She not only patched Marie Antoinette's ragged, tattered black dress but also kept busy darning her socks, all the while chatting and reminiscing with the queen about Versailles. The administrators needed to hire a woman who not only felt no sympathy for the queen but also could diligently spy on her.

And they found their accomplice in Madame Marie Harel, a thirty-six-year-old woman who resembled a fishwife more than a chambermaid and whose husband was serving as an investigator for the secret police.[10] Also referred to as the "woman Harel," she was quickly assigned to care for the queen, but Marie Antoinette immediately complained about the woman's crude insolence. In fact, the queen distrusted her completely and hardly ever spoke to her.[11]

It was not uncommon to employ spies such as Madame Harel in the prison. A convict named Barassin, a highway robber and assassin serving a fourteen-year sentence, was allowed to roam about the Conciergerie at will on the condition that he spied on both the prisoners and the jailers. Recognizing how singularly adapted Barassin was to all "liberal" employment, Warden Richard soon appointed him to the lowest and most loathsome work of the prison, emptying the chamber pots. And Barassin occasionally visited the queen's cell to fulfill this function.[12]

The French journalist Claude-François Beaulieu, imprisoned in the Conciergerie for his royalist views, said he had never known anyone more ferocious than Barassin or heard a more dreadful voice.[13] "If we were both at liberty and if I met you in the woods," Barassin told Beaulieu, "I would certainly rob and, if necessary, murder you.

"But here I dare not rob you," he continued, "and I would even protect you from a thief. If I were to rob you, the jailers would know who did it, and I would be put in irons and locked up in a dungeon."

Knowing that Barassin had discharged certain duties in Marie Antoinette's cell, Beaulieu asked how Marie Antoinette was being treated during her stay in the Conciergerie.[14] Barassin told him that the queen was supervised day and night by the guards on duty with only a small screen to separate them from her.

"And what does the queen do in her sad chamber?" asked Beaulieu.

"The Capet? Oh, she is sheepish enough," he said. "She mends her stockings always full of holes."*

"Upon what does she sleep?" asked Beaulieu.

"Upon a prison cot like your own," he responded.

"How is she dressed?"

"She wears a black dress which is badly torn; she looks like a magpie."[15]

Barassin was more than likely telling the truth about the dress. When the queen was transported from the Temple to the Conciergerie, she had no clothing with her but the black dress and widow's cap that she wore that evening, the same ragged dress that Mère Larivière spent time patching and mending. In fact, the queen implored Madame Richard for a fresh supply of clothing, but so stern were her orders that the apprehensive concierge did not dare grant the queen's wishes.[16]

The linen that the queen was not allowed to bring with her to the Conciergerie was kept under seal at the Temple; however, the municipal guards of the Temple eventually sent a white robe, two pairs of lisle-thread† stockings, one pair of understockings, and an unfinished stocking that the queen had begun for her son before being sent to the Conciergerie. When the queen opened the package and saw how neatly and carefully it was packed,

---

*The queen's stockings may have been full of holes, but it is doubtful that she mended them. She was not allowed to have any needles.

†A fine, extra-strong cotton thread used for hosiery and stockings.

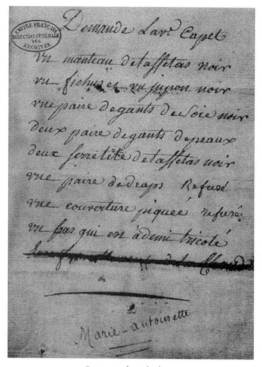

Request for clothing

she said she recognized the work, crying, "By the care taken of these things I recognize the hand of my poor sister Élisabeth."[17]

The queen asked Madame Richard to have her black widow's cap made into two smaller ones called *bonnets nigligis*. "Madame," said the queen, "would you be so good as to entrust this bonnet to your seamstress?"[18]

Madame Richard complied, returning with the two new hairpieces decorated with fine linen and brass. The queen then turned to Rosalie, saying, "I can no longer have anything" and gave Rosalie the hairpieces. Rosalie would preserve these keepsakes until the end of her days.[19]

A week later, Jean-Baptiste Michonis wrote a note to the officers on duty at the Temple asking for some additional clothing: "Citizen Colleagues, Marie Antoinette has charged me to send her four chemises and a pair of slippers, of which she is in pressing need."[20]

The officers complied, but the four gowns requested were soon reduced to three, and the queen only received one at a time every ten days or so. The queen now had two gowns, a black one and a white one, which she wore two days at a time, but they both quickly rotted and needed continuous mending due to the dampness of her dungeon cell.[21] When Marie Antoinette reigned at Versailles, she enjoyed needlework and would have been happy to occupy herself mending her clothes in the Conciergerie, but she was not allowed to have any needles; the officials feared she might use them to take her life. After all, the queen was more valuable alive while negotiations with Austria proceeded.

To keep busy, the queen would pull long pieces of thread from a tapestry that hung on the wall next to her bed and make a lace that Rosalie called a *lacet tres-uni*. The queen sought every opportunity to bequeath her children and friends some token of remembrance. Using the long pieces of thread and converting two toothpicks into tapestry needles, she created a small garter that was later given to her daughter Marie-Thérèse.[22]

The queen also had a passion for flowers, and she was grateful for the bouquets that Madame Richard and Rosalie would occasionally leave on her little oak table, but it is unlikely they were fragrant enough to matter. On one occasion Barassin removed the chamber pot from the queen's cell, and the queen begged Rosalie to please "burn some juniper in order to disinfect the air."[23]

Madame Richard had placed one of the straw chairs in the bay of the window where the queen used to pass her time watching the women prisoners or listening for any news. Some women confined in this courtyard often showed sympathy for their fellow prisoner; they would relate news to her by intentionally speaking loudly near her window.

Many in the Conciergerie, prisoners and guards alike, did not wish to see their former queen treated with indignities she did not deserve. One day an officer of the gendarmerie who was on duty in the prison took one of the queen's shoes and, using his sword as a handle, scraped the mud from the damp floor off the sole, as Rosalie used to do with her own knife. Some of the women in the courtyard begged that they might have the shoe for a moment, and "in the ardor of their loyalty the poor wretches covered it with kisses."[24]

For the first forty days of the queen's captivity in the Council Chamber, Rosalie's functions were confined to preparing the queen's breakfast at nine o'clock and her dinner at two or half past two, but she only visited the queen with Warden Richard or his wife present. At mealtime, Madame Richard would place the dishes on the table, and Rosalie, out of respect or nervousness, would remain at the door. When the queen first observed this, she said, "Come near, Rosalie. Don't be afraid."[25]

One day Madame Richard brought her youngest child, Fanfan, with her into the queen's cell. He was a charming young lad with fair hair and blue eyes. When the queen saw him, she trembled with emotion and, taking him into her arms, covered him with kisses. She then burst into tears and spoke of her own son, about the same age, who was still imprisoned in the Temple, saying she thought of him constantly day and night. The incident made her ill, and she had to lie down on her bed. When Madame Richard and Rosalie left the room, Madame Richard confided to Rosalie that she would take care "never to bring her son into the dungeon again."[26]

Sometimes Marie Antoinette, overwhelmed with boredom, would approach the two soldiers and watch them play cards, but only when Warden Richard or his wife was present. Otherwise, she was forced to do nothing in her prison but pray, meditate, or read the few books that some humane guard or former servants in the Temple, such as the Messieurs François Hüe or Galart de Montjoye, procured for her. She read *Un voyage à Venise*, among others, and she confessed to especially liking books of "the most frightful adventures."[27] Reading was a common pastime for the queen, as documented in a tally of her expenses in the Conciergerie, which included fees for book rentals.[28]

The French press wasted no time in ridiculing Marie Antoinette about her new routine in the Conciergerie:

> Antoinette rises at seven o'clock in the morning and retires at ten o'clock in the evening. She addresses her two guards as "'messieurs" and her chambermaid as "madame." The officers and administrators who approach her address the queen as "madame." She has a big appetite: in the morning chocolate and a small roll and at dinner soup and a large quantity of meat such as chicken, veal cutlets, and mutton. [29]

MARIE ANTOINETTE'S DARKEST DAYS

The press was certainly exaggerating. A large appetite was highly un-likely—the queen had been ill and was prone to uterine hemorrhaging from time to time.

The press continued, "She only drinks water, just like her mother who never drank wine." And it is true, like her mother, Marie Antoinette never drank wine. She could also not tolerate the water of the Seine. This was understandable; the river was the ultimate destination of the trash and sewage of three million Parisians. Even dead bodies were often thrown into the river.[30]

The only water that did not make Marie Antoinette ill was the bottled water from natural springs, such as those at Ville d'Avray, which she was per-mitted to have at the Temple. Her sister-in-law Élisabeth apparently begged the municipal guards to supply the queen with the water at the Conciergerie, and the next day the police administrators consented.[31]

The water from Ville d'Avray was the queen's only beverage for a long time. After Rosalie once removed the half-empty cup and left the queen's cell, she met a prisoner, a Creole by the name of Saint-Léger, returning to the men's courtyard.

"Did the queen drink water from that cup?" he asked. When Rosalie nodded in the affirmative, he immediately took the water and drank it with "respect and elation."[32] This "touching communion" with the queen was a sign that some male prisoners were also sympathetic to the queen's plight. This was quite a change from her final days in the Temple, where the guards' insults had become "rougher, wilder, and on the verge of reaching the ex-treme limits of brutality."[33]

The press, however, was less sympathetic. One journalist wrote, "She has stopped reading about the English revolutions and currently reads about the young Anacharsis."* He was certainly referring to the beheading of the Eng-lish king Charles I in the previous century, a subject about which the queen surely did not want to be reminded.[34]

"She occupies herself with her own toilette with the coquetry that a woman never abandons even when she takes her last breath," the journal-

---

*Perhaps the article is comparing Marie Antoinette to the Scythian philosopher who, also considered an outsider, traveled to Greece and became known as an outspoken barbarian.

ist continued. But this was also not true. The queen no longer had the milliner Rose Bertin or her hairdresser Léonard Autié flitting about her in the boudoir. Her frail figure was now draped in a black woolen dress that was falling apart. Her hair was now uncovered and sparsely sprinkled with powder. The sleepless nights and the long days had by now made powder no longer necessary. Her once celebrated hair, the envy of all France, was turning gray.

Finally, the press gleefully described the queen's loneliness in the Conciergerie: "Her chamber faces the courtyard of the women's prison, but they pay no attention at all to their neighbor, the ex-queen." This, as well, was wishful thinking on the press's part. The queen's chamber did face the Cour de Femmes, the women's prison yard, but the women never for a moment ignored "Her Majesty."

As of August 25, the National Convention still had not opened its case against the queen, despite Antoine Fouquier-Tinville's persistent demands for documents that were needed to begin the hearings. Apparently the delegates did not have a dossier sufficiently prepared to establish the queen's guilt. The delay gave the queen's supporters a vague sense of hope—or at least time to turn the tide of public opinion in her favor.[35] One supporter, Madame Germaine de Staël, published an anonymous brochure to do just that:

> Oh, you women of all countries, of all classes of society, listen to me with the emotion that I feel! The fate of Marie Antoinette contains everything that can touch your heart. If you were ever happy, she has been happy; if you have suffered, for a year, all the sorrows of life have torn her heart for even a longer time; if you were loving, if you were mothers, she has loved with all the might of her soul and she still loves with all her being, as much as anything that we might hold dear.[36]

À SAVOIR . . .

The Queen's Final Portrait

Portraits of Marie Antoinette by Alexandre Kucharski (left) and Jean-Louis Prieur (right)
(Bibliothèque Nationale Française)

During the time that Marie Antoinette was incarcerated, one of her famous painters, Alexandre Kucharski, stole into either the Temple or the Conciergerie to see her.[37] He later painted the queen's last portrait from memory; in it she wears her black mourning gown, a cap, and a white kerchief.[38] Her eyes lack luster, her hair is white at the temples, and her face is sunken in, all depicting the queen's illness and suffering at the time.

Kucharski's portrait should not be confused with that of the little-known artist Jean-Louis Prieur, whose work was based on Kucharski's and unveiled much later, during the restoration of the Bourbons. Considered inferior to Kucharski's, it is still a powerful depiction of the queen's fortitude.

During the days before the Queen's death, a little-known artist, Prieur, engraved without talent the Queen in the Conciergerie; misfortune, vigils and tears have altered her face; the widow's veil covers the thin hair that resisted so much anguish and misery; any attachment to life has disappeared from the once smiling and glowing face; the Queen awaits death with firmness and without fear; everything she loved in the world was taken from her; her sacrifice made, she is ready to die. As poor as this image is, it is powerfully interesting, because we feel that its author was naively honest.[39]

3

THE HORRORS OF
THE CONCIERGERIE

*"The whole prison, from crowdedness, dirt, want of air, and
other incommodities, was so unwholesome that the confined fell
ill and died in such quantities as to exceed credibility."*

—John Adolphus,[1] *Monthly Review*, 1800

Paris
August 1793

Prosecutor Antoine Quentin Fouquier-Tinville kept the Conciergerie full
with political prisoners of every age, sex, and rank, all mingling with
the most treacherous criminals. To separate the two groups, prisoners were
soon classified as either *pailleux*, those who slept on straw-covered floors
and were nightly tormented by rats and vermin, or *pistoliers*, those with the
means to pay for a bed. Every cell contained as many beds as possible, and
prisoners only paid for half of one, sharing the "miserable mattress with
some companion in misfortune."[2]

Prisoners who could afford a bed paid twenty-seven livres and twelve
sous, or about $110, for the first month (about eighteen sous per day) and
then twenty-two livres and ten sous for the following months.[3] This would
have been relatively expensive considering that the average worker might
have only earned fifteen sous (about $3) per day, and the cost of a single loaf
of bread had risen to almost eight sous (about $1.50) by this time.[4]

Daylight and fresh air barely penetrated the dungeons assigned to the poorer *pailleux* prisoners, causing the straw infested with worms to quickly rot. Chamber pots added such an infectious stench that people feared being poisoned whenever the dungeon doors were opened.[5]

These prisoners were removed daily from their cells at around nine o'clock in the morning until an hour before sunset. Because their cells were locked, they were forced to languish in a prison yard or cram, if it rained, into the urine-reeking galleries surrounding the yard.

Finding one's way around the Conciergerie's cells and prison yards was no easy task. Most eighteenth-century diagrams of the thick-walled, archaic fortress were based on a north-south axis with an array of long, jagged, dark corridors; however, the placement of certain cells differed among the various floor plans. Using these plans and consulting the memoirs of Rosalie Lamorlière, Claude-François Beaulieu, and Jean-Baptiste Michonis, I have constructed a more accurate floor plan of the labyrinthine prison.

1. Small courtyard just steps below the palace courtyard (Cour du Mai)
2. Front entrance where one entered and departed through two *guichets* (g)
3. The warden's front office (*avant-greffe*), where Toussaint Richard's desk was located
4. Registrar's office (*greffe*), where the arrival, cell, and departure of prisoners were recorded
5. A room where convicted prisoners awaited the arrival of the executioner and, occasionally, where their "toilette"* was prepared
6. A dark corridor leading to the turnkeys' lodging (7) and Marie Antoinette's first cell (9)
7. Turnkeys' lodging or, occasionally, an area for the prisoners' toilette
8. Continuation of the corridor leading to areas where turnkeys were lodged (11 and 12)
9. Marie Antoinette's first cell, also known as the Council Chamber (*Salle de Conseil*), which overlooked the women's courtyard through a narrow window

---

*The toilette, in the language of the guillotine, was the act of arranging the shirt collar, cutting the hair close to the neck, and other preparations to facilitate the swift operation of the guillotine's blade.

Conciergerie floor plan in 1793

10. Beginning of the long prisoners' corridor with a series of *guichets*, each manned by a turnkey

11. Area for turnkeys' lodging or for preparing the toilette

12. Same as (11)

13. The women's prison yard (*préau des femmes*) with a fountain where inmates washed their clothes and a stone table where they took their meals (both still exist today)

14. The Side of Twelve (*Côté des Douze*), an interesting triangular court-yard separated from the women's prison yard by a grating whose bars were separated with sufficient space to allow for "amorous" encounters

15. An area where the gendarmes kept watch over the queen from behind a small screen when Marie Antoinette was moved to her new cell (16) after the Carnation Plot

16. The queen's second cell from September 13 until October 16

17. A waiting room leading to the men's prison yard (*préau des hommes*) to the north or to the Girondins' Chapel (19) to the south

18. The men's prison yard

19. The Girondins' Chapel, where prisoners often spent their last night

20. Infirmary with adjoining spiral stairwell leading up to the Revolutionary Tribunal

21. Stairway leading to the women's *pistoles*, cells for which the inmates paid

22. Guard quarters under the steps of the Palace of Justice

To reach the queen's first cell, the Council Chamber, it was necessary to enter the Conciergerie via an archway on the courtyard Cour du Mai and step down into a smaller courtyard (1) to reach the first of two *guichets* (g).

A *guichet* was a three-foot-tall gate inserted into a larger gate. When entering, it was necessary to raise your feet and duck your head. "If you didn't bump your nose or your knee," one visitor noted, "you ran the risk of cracking your head against the bar of the large gate, which had happened more than once."[6] The area between these two *guichets*, about three feet, was also referred to as the *guichet* (2).

All the *guichets* throughout the prison were guarded by jailers called "turnkeys," but only the "sturdiest and those possessing the keenest eyesight" had the honor of guarding these first two *guichets*, and they would have more than likely waited a long time for the post.[7] A bouquet of flowers hung at the front gate announced a turnkey's promotion to this coveted position, and he would arrive in his best clothes with his hair dressed by a barber for his first day. Wine always flowed freely on that night to celebrate the special occasion.

Louis Larivière guarded the *guichet* on the night that Marie Antoinette was hustled into the prison. When she was moved into the first room, she would have passed the front office, or *avant-greffe* (3), where either Warden Richard or the senior turnkey would have been stationed, perhaps sitting in the armchair at the end of the long table. To secure access to family and friends, visitors paid homage with deep bows to this official, hoping to catch him in a good mood. Prisoners expecting visitors would also spy on the warden to see if he was having one of his better days.

Archway on the Cour du Mai leading to the prison entrance (far right)

Working from this armchair, Richard dispatched his orders for the management of the prison, settled quarrels among the turnkeys and prisoners, and granted strangers visiting rights. For most other tasks, Madame Richard was in charge, and records showed she was a good superintendent: "The wife of Richard controls her establishment in an astounding way," one account noted. "Nobody has a better memory than she, or more presence of mind, or a more exact knowledge of the minutest details."[8]

On the left, after entering Richard's office, a large room called the *greffe* was divided in two; one half (4) was used for registering the arrivals, assigning prisoners their cells, and noting the departures of all inmates. The other half (5) was reserved for the condemned awaiting the executioner. Here death row inmates were stripped of their belongings. The executioner's wages were low, but collecting prisoners' jewelry, snuffboxes, glasses, and watches could be quite lucrative. The prisoner Beugnot described the scene:

> What a spectacle there where these unfortunates awaited their last hour! Mattresses spread on the floor indicated that they had spent the night; they had already suffered a long ordeal that night. Next we saw the remains of the last meal they had taken;* their clothes were thrown here and there, and two candles that they had neglected to extinguish gave the scene a funeral glow. I was horrified by the animated sepulcher when the door opened noisily to gendarmes, jailers, and executioners. I couldn't see any more after this sudden shock; I felt that my blood had just run cold in my heart, and I fell down on a bench, pursued by this machine of death.[9]

The condemned would sit down on a stool here; their hands would be tied behind their back and their collars pulled down or removed; and the executioner would cut their hair close to the nape of the neck. The condemned were then escorted up the steps to the Cour du Mai, where tumbrils carted them off to the scaffold.[10]

From the warden's office (3), visitors would enter an area where turnkeys and jailers might be found sleeping (7); the rooms on the corridor to the right were set aside for women who had just been sentenced to death (11

---

*Prisoners in these cells were given a last meal in the Conciergerie; it was said that the guillotine was their dessert.

Marie Antoinette's first cell

and 12). After their toilette, the executioner would then collect the women's hair to sell later.

On the opposite side of the corridor, to the left, was the Council Chamber where Marie Antoinette was jailed (9). Any drawings of her first cell should have shown the bed to the left of the entrance, offset by a small screen behind which her jailers kept watch. The window opening onto the women's prison yard (13) should also have been located just opposite the entrance.

The lack of sanitation and the dampness due to the Seine River were not the only detriments of the queen's prison cell. The noise would have been close to unbearable—especially when three or four drunken jailers with half a dozen leashed dogs searched for the exact number of prisoners to be carted off to the scaffold:

> Holding in their hands an incorrect list which they are unable to read, they shout a name that nobody recognizes. They swear, storm, threaten; they call again; there are explanations, they are helped; one at last succeeds in understanding whom they meant to name. They make a mistake; then, their rage always on the increase, they order them to go out.[11]

In addition to these dreaded jailers, gendarmes swarmed around the *guichets*, bringing in new prisoners and rushing them to their cells, while a "haggard-eyed, insolent-voiced usher" shouted orders, accentuated with blows from his stick.

Further into the prison, after one crossed the next *guichet* near the women's holding cells, an unusual space enclosed by iron bars would appear (14). This was the Side of Twelve (*Côté des Douze*), where men were held a dozen at a time. From here they could say good-bye to wives or other women through the grating before being escorted to the tumbril. An eyewitness related what often resulted in an amorous encounter:

> Women, whose sensibility is greater than men's, whose courage is more resolute, whose soul is more pitiful, more inclined to help, to share misfortune, women are almost the only beings who ventured to penetrate there, and, it must be admitted, it was they especially whom one liked to receive there. There then fell an instant's silence, everyone looked at each other in fear, then there would be an affectionate kissing and embracing, and matters took imperceptibly their ordinary course.[12]

The mood at this meeting place ranged from cheeriness, as if everything were rose-colored, or perhaps false optimism to tender affection and tears. These moments of warmth and understanding surely helped to soften the prisoners' despair.

The women's cells adjacent to the prison yard were similarly divided into *pistoliers* and *pailleux*. Those who paid the *pistole*, or half the value of a louis d'or, occupied the second floor, but the *pailleuses* were kept in cells on the dark, damp ground floor that were as unhealthy as they were dirty.[13]

Just outside was an entirely different world. Fine shops filled with perfumes and elegant fashions, manned by courteous shopkeepers, lined the streets near the prison, and there were libraries laden with books on the humanities and Enlightenment ideals.* But no further away than the thick-

---

*These shops surrounded the Palace of Justice and were leased to booksellers, public writers, stationers, and, in particular, boot makers. In 1798 the merchants were driven out, and the demolition of the shops began. However, according to the *Journal de Paris*, the demolition was not complete until 1808.

ness of a dungeon wall were clanging iron doors, miserable groans, and an insupportable stench.

Marie Antoinette was confined to a more secluded area, away from the general population. Had it not been for the compassion of Warden Richard and perhaps Jean-Baptiste Michonis, she might very well have ended up in one of the towers. Any prisoner ordered to be kept apart from both the *pailleux* and *pistoliers* was normally locked away in one of these dungeons, which for the most part were below the riverbed. The most uncomfortable—-Grand-César, Bon-Bec, Vincent, and Bel-Air—have all long since been walled up.

A prisoner named Beauregard was placed in one of these fearsome grottos* with straw bedding, where rats would gnaw on his culottes with "no respect for his behind." Like many other prisoners with holes in their pants, Beauregard also had to cover his face all night with his hands to protect his nose and ears.[14]

Whenever food became scarce in Paris, even at the most lavish tables of the wealthy, the prisoners still received their meals. But the revolutionary government soon grew tired of supplying food to the imprisoned enemies of the republic. It was decided that all meals should be taken communally for the price of two francs per day per person and that the wealthy and the aristocratic inmates should pay for those who could not. "What was sufficiently amusing," wrote an eyewitness, "was that these gentlemen estimated their respective fortune in the prison by the number of sans-culottes they had to feed."† Formerly, they had estimated their fortune by the number of horses, dogs, lackeys, and mistresses they kept.[15]

Despite the poor nourishment, the *pailleux* and *pistoliers* were much better off than those kept in the unsanitary and indescribably foul prison infirmary (20). The dungeon was about twenty-five feet wide and one hundred feet long, closed at each end by iron gratings, and covered by a

---

*These dungeon cells were often referred to as La Souricière, or the mousetrap. The Conciergerie took its name from the house of the concierge belonging to the king's residence in the Middle Ages. Here, below the level of the Seine, a prison called La Souricière was built, so named for the rats, which had a reputation for eating prisoners alive.

†Louis-Sébastien Mercier (1740–1814) was a French writer and a member of the convention who had voted against the death penalty for Louis XVI. He was imprisoned during the Terror.

---

high vaulted ceiling. The smoke of the coal stove and the lamps gave this room a somber hue; light only entered through two very narrow windows in the center of the ceiling. Forty to fifty trundle beds were scattered across the cell floor, and poor wretches suffering from various illnesses could be found lying two and three to a bed. It was impossible to purify the air in the infirmary; more distressingly, "nobody dreamt either of changing the bed-straw or cleaning the sheets."[16]

Royalist spy and street singer Louis Ange Pitou described his day in the infirmary:

> A cadaverous, infected smell on entering; one had his face covered with boils and ulcers, another had black lips as puffy as coal, and two or three others were dying in the same bed. A dirty rascal named Pierre, sentenced to ten years in irons, was our attendant after the death of the Queen, to whom he had once served as a valet. He made his fortune in the midst of putrefaction, because most of the patients were unconscious and easily robbed.[17]

In addition to these unsanitary conditions, the infirmary also had a lack of competent medical care. François Thierry, the infirmary physician, was considered a savage and barbarous man: "Never did a comforting word come from him; never did he show a sign of interest in suffering and tortured humanity." In fact, the invalids had to wait five or six days after a dozen requests for the smallest dose of medicine.[18]

Prison physicians only visited the infirmary for appearance's sake, and a daily visit usually only lasted about twenty minutes, which gave little more than half a minute to each inmate. To save even more time physicians soon adopted a common poultice, which was called "a saddle to fit all horses."[19] This poultice was prescribed for everything, and it was all that was ever administered.

One day Dr. Thierry approached a bed to feel a patient's pulse. "Ah!" he said. "He's much better today than he was yesterday."[20]

"True, citizen doctor," said the attendant. "He's much better, but he's not the same person. Yesterday's patient died, and this one has taken his place."

"Oh! That makes a difference, to be sure," said Thierry. "But never mind; give him the poultice anyway."

Eighteenth-century depiction of the Conciergerie

Whenever a patient died, his body and head were covered with part of the bed covering he shared with his neighbor, who would shiver with cold while waiting for the corpse to be removed. This would not happen immediately due to the expense of transporting a single body; in fact, there would always be a delay until at least three or four bodies could be carried away.[21]

Dr. Thierry had been one of Marie Antoinette's physicians in the Temple prison, where he had once prepared a special "refreshing broth" and "calming potion" for her.[22] The ingredients for theses remedies were authorized by the Commune and prepared by the pharmacist Robert:

> Calming potion composed of lime water, orange blossom syrup, capillary and liqueur Hofmann in a flask (3 livres); and refreshing broth with lean veal, chicken meat and various plants repeated every day (50 livres).[23]

In the Conciergerie, however, Thierry was confined to treating patients in the infirmary, where he was assisted by his "ignorant" colleague, Bernard Naury. Both of these incompetents were monitored by Dr. Joseph Souberbielle, the head physician of prisons.[24]

The queen's secret supporter, Michonis, was troubled when he heard news from the gendarmes about the queen's meals. They told him that she was not eating well, and they brought him a very bony and almost spoiled chicken, saying, "Here's some chicken that Madame did not eat which was served to her four days ago."[25] This story conflicts somewhat with Rosalie's account of the queen's eating habits in the Conciergerie: "Her Majesty ate with enough appetite. She cut her poultry in two, that is to say, to serve her two days. She separated the bones with incredible ease and care. She left few vegetables on her plate."[26]

There were few inconsistencies, however, about Marie Antoinette's illness. Rosalie reported that grief, bad air, and the lack of exercise affected the queen's health. She had fevers and suffered from frequent hemorrhaging. When the queen secretly asked Rosalie for towels for the bleeding, the maid would cut up her own chemises and discretely put the scraps of cloth under the queen's pillow.

Confirming the queen's illness, Michonis petitioned the government to send for Dr. Souberbielle, who was quickly employed to care for the queen and ordered to keep the government informed of her condition. If Souberbielle had ever known the queen, he might not have recognized her now. She was thinner, graying, and suffering from a number of maladies: stomach cramps, fainting spells, and anemia from hemorrhaging due to uterine cancer or perhaps a fibroid.[27] She was also extremely pale and had difficulty breathing, and her legs were painfully swollen.

Although an ardent revolutionary, Souberbielle did take pity on the queen. He had a special chicken broth prepared for her by the pharmacist Jacques Antoine Lacour, who lived near the Conciergerie. The broth was made every morning and delivered to the prison warden's office at exactly nine o'clock by Lacour's son.[28]

No recipe has been found for Souberbielle's potion, but according to the *New Dictionary of Medicine and Surgery* in 1792,

> Everyone knows that chicken is one of the best remedies one can use, and everyone knows that it is the most familiar to the weak and invalids. The broth was called "eau de poulet" and was commonly known to be good for fevers, inflammation, kidney stones, cholera and the colic.[29]

Dr. Souberbielle was ordered not only to care for the ailing queen in the Conciergerie but also to serve on the jury at her trial, an ironic and absurd example of aspects of the Reign of Terror, a violent period when justice was swiftly meted out by guillotine.

Despite the horrific conditions of the ancient prison where death by the "national razor" was the order of the day, many of the condemned actually joked and broke out in song. The chorus of one of the favorite ditties was

When at the guillotine off my head goes,
I shan't be more troubled to blow my nose.[30]

After the journalist Jean-Marie Girey-Dupré was imprisoned in the Conciergerie, his friend wrote, "Nothing was more noble and proud than this heroic young man, waiting for his trial that ended with a death sentence. He went not to death, he stole it. He pulled down the collar of his shirt and so appeared at his hearing, saying, 'Here I am—I am quite ready.'"

The twenty-four-year-old Girey-Dupré was sentenced to death, and he sang the song that he had written the night before all along the route to the scaffold:

For us, what a brilliant triumph!
Holy martyrs of freedom,
Immortality awaits us.
Worthy of a destiny so bright,
Walk to the scaffold without fear,
Immortality awaits us.
Dying for our country,
This is the best way, the most enviable!

When Girey-Dupré reached the scaffold, only the blade of the executioner could silence his chorus.[31]

Marie Antoinette was trapped in the midst of all this hysteria. She heard the drunken jailers clamoring throughout the night; she heard the sobs and the weeping of wives from the gate of the Side of Twelve; and she heard the hair-raising howls of the ferocious guard dogs. Her consolation, if any, would only be the compassion of a few kindhearted souls.

À SAVOIR . . .

The Game "Guillotine"

The prisoners of the Conciergerie passed their short time there reading, conversing, making love through the gates, smoking, playing practical jokes on one another, drinking wine and champagne, and gambling at a variety of games, such as one they called "Guillotine."

To begin the game, players first created a sham Revolutionary Tribunal, with its two sections of liberty and equality. Those who had already appeared before the court and not yet been sent to the scaffold melodramatically imitated prosecutor Fouquier-Tinville. Other prisoners then played the role of court officers. The accused was always condemned to death, and the officers would lay him on the back of a turned-up chair to which they gave a slight tilt. The victim then had to fall convincingly with grace "under the penalty of recommencing the ceremony."[32]

4

KINDHEARTED SOULS

"About three o'clock in the morning, I was asleep in an armchair. Madame Richard, pulling me by the arm, woke me hastily and said these words: 'Rosalie, let's go, let's go; take this torch. They've arrived.'"

—Rosalie Lamorlière,[1] *Monthly Review*, 1800

Paris
August 1793

Rosalie Lamorlière, Madame Richard's twenty-year-old domestic, first served the queen in the Conciergerie alongside Mère Larivière and, after Mère Larivière's dismissal, with Madame Harel. Rosalie left a remarkable account in her memoirs of her time in the prison, though any histories of Marie Antoinette written in the nineteenth century should be carefully reevaluated. During the restoration of the Bourbon monarchy in 1815, many royalist writers were led by their sympathies to exaggerate the anguish of the "victim" and the perfidy of the "villains" during the queen's incarceration.[2]

Because Rosalie was illiterate, she could not have written her memoirs herself; they were penned by the royalist Lafont d'Aussonne, a biographer prone to exaggeration and criticized by his contemporaries for confusing his imagination with reality.[3] However, if Lafont d'Aussonne omitted some details or even enhanced Rosalie's memoirs, Rosalie later certified that the fundamental part of his report was authentic.[4] The historian Émile Campardon also concurred, finding it "absolutely truthful in the most important aspects."[5] Biographer Léon de la Sicotière admitted that Lafont d'Aussonne was "crazy" (*fou*) but maintained that his documentation was still "precious."[6]

Lafont d'Aussonne had made the acquaintance of two ladies, the Mesdames Boze, who spoke to him fondly of a sweet girl. She was Madame Richard's cook in the Conciergerie who prepared the queen's meals and delivered them to her cell twice a day.* When Lafont d'Aussonne interviewed Rosalie in Paris, he found her story in line with what the Mesdames Boze had told him two years earlier.[7]

Rosalie had previously served as a domestic for Madame Beaulieu, mother of the famous actor Jean-François-Bremont Beaulieu of the Théâtre du Cité. When Louis XVI was condemned to die on the scaffold, Madame Beaulieu, already crippled and suffering, grieved greatly for the king. She died shortly thereafter, but not before recommending Rosalie to Madame Richard at the Conciergerie.† Rosalie was "extremely reluctant" to take the position in the prison, but Monsieur Beaulieu, who also worked as a lawyer defending many unfortunate prisoners of the Revolutionary Tribunal, persuaded her to accept the position. He told her that the Richards were a "most honest and accommodating" couple. He added that his theater was only a few steps away, and he promised to visit her as often as possible.[8]

Rosalie gradually became attached to the Richards because they "did not disapprove of her compassion for the poor prisoners." Although her new mistress, Madame Richard, was not as well educated as Madame Beaulieu, Rosalie found her just as kind. Madame Richard had also worked in a toiletry shop and had a great taste for cleanliness in her household, which pleased Rosalie.[9]

During the Reign of Terror, it was quite a task to manage a prison the size of the Conciergerie, but Rosalie never saw Madame Richard become distraught; the superintendent was concise and efficient, responding to

---

*Joseph Boze, son and nephew of the Mesdames Boze, had painted portraits of Queen Marie Antoinette.

†Lafont d'Aussonne erred with respect to Madame Beaulieu's death. She died much earlier.

everyone with few words and always giving clear orders. Sleeping only for short periods and being informed promptly of all goings-on, Madame Richard never missed anything inside or outside the prison.

When Madame Richard noticed that Marie Antoinette's bonnet could no longer be mended, she knew it would be risky to request or supply a new one for the queen. Nevertheless, she took the chance, and government officials acquiesced; the queen received two new bonnets that cost seven livres each, some ribbons and silk for skirts, shoes, and special water for her teeth. Noticing that the queen did not have a drawer to protect her clothing from dust and the jailers' smoke, Rosalie presented the queen with a box, which she accepted with a smile.[10]

The government must have noticed the cost of the new bonnets. On September 26, it ordered the police to search through all the queen's belongings left in the Temple for any clothing that might be necessary and to send it along to the Conciergerie. The decree dryly added, "It is expected that this will result in savings."[11]

Marie Antoinette had been known for the daring in style and fashion she brought to eighteenth-century France, but in the Conciergerie she asked for very little. When she requested a small mirror to coif her hair, she was not aware that mirrors were prohibited in the prison. Madame Richard feared angering the officials with such a trivial request but authorized Rosalie to find a mirror for the queen. Rosalie had a small one with a red frame and Chinese decorations that had only cost her twenty-five sous. She blushed to loan the queen such a simple mirror, but the queen gratefully accepted it and used it each day.[12]

Marie Antoinette kept her hair coiffed as simply as possible once she was in the Conciergerie. After sprinkling it with some fragrant powder, she would pull her hair back, leaving some on her forehead. Although not fond of Mère Larivière's replacement, Madame Harel, the queen allowed the cranky woman to tie the ends of her hair with a long piece of white ribbon, securing it with a forceful tug. Madame Harel then gave the two ends of the ribbon to the queen, who crossed the ribbon herself on the top of her head, giving her coiffure the look of a loose bun.[13]

The change must have been quite drastic for a woman accustomed to being treated as the divine queen of Versailles with hundreds of servants at her command. Rosalie and Madame Richard, conscious of the queen's much reduced circumstances and despite their own dangerous predicament, tried to remain as attentive to the queen's desires as possible. But the queen's tastes had simplified greatly. When they asked what type of foods she preferred, the queen answered, "Whatever would be good for your family will be good for me."[14]

The two women would often run to the market to purchase the best fruit and produce for Marie Antoinette, and even in the marketplace there were those who had not forgotten their queen. When Madame Richard was shopping for melon one morning for the queen's meal, she excitedly asked the lady at the produce stand which was the best.

"I guess from the expression on your face that the melon you want is for our unfortunate queen," the lady said. "Here, take the most beautiful."[15]

Madame Richard took the melon and reached for a coin in her pocket.

"Keep your money," said the woman. "And tell the queen that there are many among us who tremble."

Madame Richard, frightened by the woman's indiscretion, quickly walked away. She prepared the melon for the queen and told her of the woman's kindness at the market. Perhaps Marie Antoinette was consoled to know that she was not hated by all the French; some hearts still were not filled with revenge.

However, public opinion against the queen was strong at this time and had manifested itself in many forms. One was "La Carmagnole," a refrain as popular as "La Marseillaise,"[16] sung while dancing around the "liberty tree."*

Madame Veto has promised to cut every throat in Paris,
But she failed, thanks to our cannons.
Refrain:
Let us dance the Carmagnole.
Long live the sound; long live the sound.
Let us dance the Carmagnole.
Long live the sound of the cannons.
Monsieur Veto had promised to be loyal to his country,

---

*Poplar trees (*arbres de liberté*) were planted to celebrate the new republic during the Revolution.

But he failed, let's not show any mercy.
Refrain.
Antoinette had decided to throw us on our asses,
But the plan was foiled, and her nose was broken.
Refrain

The song referred to Marie Antoinette as "Madame Veto" because she was blamed whenever the king made use of the unpopular veto; after all, they claimed she was "his adviser."

Rosalie and the Richards were not the only compassionate souls working in the Conciergerie. Since the queen's incarceration, she had been under surveillance by two gendarmes night and day. On one occasion when François Dufresne and Jean Gilbert were not on duty behind their screen, another gendarme kept watch, smoking his pipe and loudly playing card games all night. The next morning he realized from the look on the queen's face that she had not slept well. When he asked how she was, she said, "Not well, the tobacco smoke bothered me."[17]

The queen of France in her last prison cell
(Bibliothèque Nationale Française)

"I am guilty," he said to his fellow gendarme, "for not having thought about it and for only adding to her suffering." He tossed his pipe away.

There was a time when jailers of the Conciergerie had absolute power over their prisoners, taxing them for food and other necessities. In the fifteenth and sixteenth centuries, prisoners would not be released until they had paid these debts. Moreover, they were denied the services of a priest.[18] Although Marie Antoinette was now permitted to receive a priest, she would only be allowed one who had taken the oath to the republic in 1790. But she refused.

The clergy had been a privileged class before the outbreak of the Revolution, but afterward all church property was transferred to the state, and all ecclesiastics were forced to take an oath to the republic. Priests who refused were forced into exile; any dissenters or "nonsworn" clergy who celebrated Mass were punished for disturbing the public order. Subsequently, the so-called nonsworn clergy secretly held services in private houses and chapels. If caught, priests were imprisoned or even murdered in the streets.[19]

Drawings and paintings of the queen in her prison cell often showed a crucifix. It either hung on the wall or sat on her small table, but it was not in her cell when she first arrived. According to her biographer G. Lenotre, an unknown source had handed this crucifix to the queen through the grating of her window.[20]

Nonsworn clergy and their supporters outside the prison were also concerned about the queen's well-being. When Madame Antoinette-Marie Adélaïde de Quélen, mother of the future archbishop of Paris, learned that the queen was wearing a tattered black dress mended with white thread to keep it from falling apart, she offered to supply the queen with a better gown.[21] But the queen refused, fearing that to accept would raise suspicion and, more importantly, endanger the kind woman's life.

Madame de Quélen was an acquaintance of another religious woman, Mademoiselle Fouché, who often visited inmates in the prisons of Paris, including the Conciergerie. Her good works were encouraged by the nonsworn Abbé Magnin, who entered prisons under the name of Monsieur Charles to secretly provide prisoners with some consolation. In fact, Mademoiselle Fouché, despite the danger, hid the abbé in her home, referring to him as her domestic servant to avoid suspicion.[22]

When the revolutionary officials got wind of the fact that Mademoiselle Fouché was possibly hiding a priest, they gave orders to search the house. Mademoiselle Fouché learned of the approaching inspection but never lost her nerve. Unable to smuggle the abbé out of the house in time, she told him to pretend that he was a member of the household staff.[23]

The revolutionary *mouchards* (from the word for "fly") showed up as expected and questioned the family and servants, finding nothing out of the ordinary. While the detectives were searching the house from cellar to attic, however, Abbé Magnin accidentally "made an imprudent remark that might kindle suspicion in the minds of the officials." Mademoiselle Fouché slapped the abbé on the cheek, telling the "valet" to mind his own business. The ruse was successful, and the officers thanked the mademoiselle for her help. They went quickly on their way, satisfied that they had found nothing suspicious.[24]

Mademoiselle Fouché knew many of the jailers of the Conciergerie and yearned to penetrate the prison even further to reach the queen's cell. Meeting Warden Richard when leaving the building one day, she asked him softly, "Would it be possible to see the queen?"

"That's impossible," said Richard.

But from the sound of his voice, Mademoiselle Fouché was not discouraged. She knew that other visitors with official escorts had been allowed to see the queen, so she offered the warden a few gold coins.

And that did the trick.

"Listen to me well," Richard said. "Four gendarmes are employed in the custody of the prisoner; two are devils and two others are good lads who keep watch at night. Come at half past midnight and we'll see."

It is not known if Dufresne and Gilbert were the "two devils," but Richard's remark confirmed that more than two jailers guarded the queen.[25]

Mademoiselle Fouché was ecstatic, hurrying off to tell Abbé Magnin.[26] They both arrived at the prison on time that night "despite the danger of death on mere suspicion." Warden Richard kept his word, but only Mademoiselle Fouché was permitted to enter the queen's cell.[27]

The queen rose to her feet in the dank dungeon furnished only with a bed and small table. The room was divided by the small screen from behind which two guards kept close watch. Mademoiselle Fouché was struck by the majestic air the queen conveyed, even though her hair was greying, her cheeks were hollow, and her complexion was pale.

The queen remained silent, curiously gazing at the visitor who had arrived at such an unusual time so late in the evening. According to her nephew, Mademoiselle Fouché was received with "an icy coldness."* When she asked the queen to taste some food that she had brought with her, she got no response. Mademoiselle Fouché ate a piece of the bread with jam to give the impression that her intentions were not sinister, but her efforts were in vain. She needed to adopt more persuasive measures.[28]

"Madame," she said to the queen, "the state of public opinion is such that it is impossible for you to any longer entertain the least hope. Religion alone can give you its final consolation, and it is in order to procure this for you that I have dared to come to you.[29]

"If you accept my suggestion," she continued, "I am confident of being able to put you in touch with a nonsworn Catholic priest. If Your Majesty will deign to answer me, I will neglect nothing in my efforts to serve you."

The effect was immediate and profound. The queen threw herself into Mademoiselle Fouché's arms and embraced her tenderly. Reassured that the priest would be nonsworn, she soon agreed that the Abbé Magnin would be introduced on the next visit. Mademoiselle Fouché also arranged that, if not pleased with the priest, the queen need only make a sign, and he would quickly retire.[30]

On the next visit, the queen tearfully welcomed the Abbé Magnin, and they spoke for an hour and a half. It was agreed that the abbé would accompany Mademoiselle Fouché whenever she visited the queen. Warden Richard permitted the couple to visit the royal prisoner but only when the less devilish jailers were on duty.

The queen confessed several times. According to some sources, approximately two weeks after the Abbé Magnin first visited the queen, she also received communion.

As the nights became colder in the queen's damp cell, Mademoiselle Fouché was well aware that the queen was in need of warmer clothing. She asked the sisters of the charity of Saint-Roch to provide some thicker socks, which

---

*The newspaper *Le monde* (23 July 1864) published a letter from Mademoiselle Fouché's nephew, R. P. Fouché, outlining his aunt's first visit with the queen.

the queen gladly accepted.* Mademoiselle Fouché also sent the queen some rye bread (*farine de seigle*) on learning that she was fond of it.[31]

The queen was grateful for the care of Mademoiselle Fouché and the abbé, but she was aware of the risks they were taking. When the couple generously offered to secure a pen, ink, and paper for the queen, she refused: "If one word from me is discovered, you will undoubtedly perish." This was not an unusual precaution. Her concern for the safety of others during this Reign of Terror was a common theme throughout her stay at the Conciergerie.

Little conversation was recorded between the queen and Warden Richard, but Monseigneur Louis Sifrein de Salamon, a papal envoy in Paris during the Terror, wrote in his memoirs that the warden checked in on the queen quite often, always asking if she needed anything. In turn, the queen never failed to express her thanks, even asking him once if he had ever been a valet.[32]

"Oh! Not at all, madame," replied the warden. "I was almost born in prison."

"The reason why I ask is because everything you give me to eat is so excellent."

"Well, madame," he said, "it's because I often go to the market myself and endeavor to get the best I can."[†]

"Oh!" she said. "How kind you are, Monsieur Richard!"[33]

The compassionate care of Warden and Madame Richard toward the queen was well known to those who had contacts in the prison. Madame Simon-Vouet, a nineteenth-century biographer of the queen, befriended a woman whose husband was in prison at the same time. The woman remarked about the humane way in which the warden and his wife treated the queen, as they did all the prisoners in their care. She added that the queen was especially attracted to the young cook, Rosalie, whom the Richards had assigned to her cell.[34]

Madame Simon-Vouet also interviewed Rosalie after she had left the Conciergerie. The maid gave her a vivid picture of the queen's character.

---

*Fragments of these socks helped identify the remains of Marie Antoinette in the common grave at the Madeleine cemetery two decades later.

†The warden did occasionally shop for the queen's meals. He often looked for duck, the queen's favorite dish.

"Queen Marie Antoinette was described to the people as a violent, vindictive woman," Madame Simon-Vouet said to Rosalie. "Did you observe any signs of the character that was attributed to her, during the cruel treatment to which she was subjected in the Conciergerie?"

"I never heard her complain either of her fate or of her enemies, and the calmness of her words was always consistent with that of her appearance," said Rosalie. "There was, however, in this calmness of deportment something so deeply impressive that, whenever we entered her room, we stood awe-struck at the door, and dared not approach her till she begged us to do so in her gentle voice and gracious manner."

"Did she speak of Louis XVI's death, and did she seem to fear the same fate?"

"She said she was fortunate," replied Rosalie, "but I had reason to think she imagined that she and her children would be sent to Austria."

"This persistent calmness of which you speak—did it not arise from a sort of moral collapse or insensibility, the effect of her sufferings and long imprisonment?"

"She was extremely sensitive, and never failed to notice our most insignificant attentions," said Rosalie. "She carried, concealed beneath her stays,* a portrait of the young King and a curl of his hair, wrapped up in a little yellow kid glove that the child had worn; and I noticed that she often hid herself behind her wretched bed to kiss these things and weep over them. . . . [S]he wept continually at the thought of her deserted children."

"Is it true, as certain authors of repute have declared in writing," asked Madame Simon-Vouet, "that the queen washed and mended her own linen in the Conciergerie?"

"She would have thanked heaven if such a favor had been granted her," said Rosalie. "But she was condemned to the most complete inactivity, and though she never complained I saw that she suffered a great deal from this state of idleness."

Madame Simon-Vouet's interview confirmed the queen's calm demeanor in the Conciergerie as well as her need to keep busy reading, praying, or watching the jailers play piquet, a card game popular since the sixteenth century.

---

*Stays, popular in the eighteenth century, were undergarments stiffened with whalebone.

But was the queen truly calm? The interview revealed that the queen also fidgeted with her diamond rings before they were taken away from her.

"As she sat dreaming," Rosalie said, "she would take them off and put them on again, and slip them from one hand to the other several times in a minute." This was an important observation because such behavior could have been a sign of worry or anxiety.

On the other hand, Simon-Vouet's interview with Rosalie introduced a new aspect of the queen's demeanor: hope. The queen believed she and her children would be released from prison and sent to her homeland. But this would only be possible if negotiations between the governments of France and Austria were successful in stopping the advance of Austrian troops in exchange for the royal hostages—or if the queen and her children escaped from prison.

And one man in particular would have been exceptionally interested in helping the queen and her family escape: Count Hans Axel von Fersen of Sweden.

This dashing young nobleman's (romantic?) friendship with the ill-fated queen led him to put his life in danger on more than one occasion to rescue Marie Antoinette and her family. Fersen's diary related his anguished concern for his friend's well-being. Before the queen's transfer to the Conciergerie, Fersen noted on July 10, 1793, that public opinion was thought to be changing in favor of the queen in the Temple:[35]

A woman just from Paris says they are beginning to feel better towards the royal family. The queen walks in the garden, and the people applaud when they see her; they even cry out, "Vive le dauphin!"

But two days later, on July 12, he commented on the fickleness of the French people and how unstable the queen's situation had become:

Bad news from Paris. The dauphin is separated from the queen by the [word omitted] and put in another room in the Temple; this seems to me very bad; what awful suffering for the queen; unhappy princess!

A week after the queen's incarceration in the Conciergerie on August 11, Fersen reported that he had received news of her transfer from the Temple.

He noted that he also talked with his supporters in Paris about a plan to save the queen, agreeing that it would be best to "push forward at once with a strong body of cavalry." There were no troops guarding the city at that time, but a visit with the Austrian ambassador, Florimond Claude, comte de Mercy Argenteau, quickly dampened Fersen's hopes. Mercy flatly told him that an invasion to save the queen "would be impossible."[36]

On August 14, Fersen mentioned that newspapers confirmed the queen's incarceration in the Conciergerie. There was also news that the convention had proposed that the queen write to the emperor of Austria to withdraw his troops, and "on that being done she and her family would be set at liberty." Marie Antoinette had answered that the very same promise, made to the late king relating to the Prussian troops, had not saved his life. Moreover, "she could not negotiate with assassins." This entire story seemed unlikely to Fersen, and he was correct.

Despite Mercy's news and the ever-growing danger that Fersen faced for his past relationship with the royal family, the queen's admirer never gave up.

À SAVOIR . . .

Rosalie Lamorlière

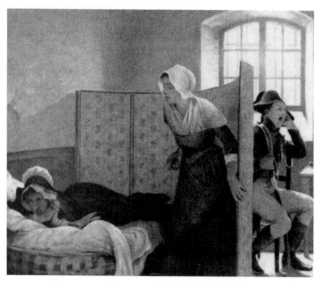

Rosalie attending to the queen

Robert-Fleury produced a very pathetic historical picture of Marie Antoinette crouching on her cot with her "face grey with sorrow." The soldier on guard was yawning behind the screen while Rosalie attended to the queen. This is the only known depiction of the queen's servant in the Conciergerie.[37]

Many objected that this depiction of Marie Antoinette was too daring and resolute; the queen would never have given way in such a fateful manner. Was the artist's work perhaps a slur on the Revolution or a ploy to rouse royal sympathies?

"The picture is both true and tragic," wrote a critic. "There is a difference between holding a brave front before your foes and wrestling with the terror in secret."[38]

RESCUE THE QUEEN!

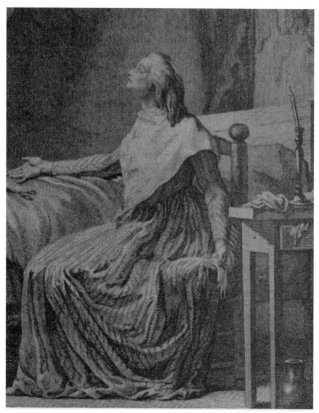

Allegorical depiction of Marie Antoinette in the Conciergerie

5

ROYALIST SUPPORTERS

"It will be a disgrace to the Austrian Government if history shall someday record that there was within forty leagues of Paris a considerable and victorious Austrian army, and that no attempt was made to save the august daughter of Maria Theresa from the scaffold."

—Prince Auguste Marie Raymond d'Arenberg,
comte de la Marck,[1] letter to Ambassador
Florimond Claude, comte de Mercy Argenteau

Paris
June 1793

The Swedish Count Fersen was not the only one who longed to liberate Marie Antoinette from her medieval dungeon. Before her transfer to the Conciergerie, plots had even been hatched to help the queen escape from the Temple prison.

The first scheme was financed by François Jarjayes, a widowed general who had married one of Queen Marie Antoinette's ladies-in-waiting.* Jarjayes was also a trusted ally of Louis XVI and had served the king on several secret missions, including the flight to Varennes, where the royal family had been arrested before reaching the border two years earlier. After the king was

---

*François Augustin Reynier de Jarjaye's new wife was previously married to the queen's harpist.

executed, Jarjayes received a strange visit in February 1793 from François Adrien Toulan, a fervent supporter of the Revolution.[2]

Toulan, a music shopkeeper turned revolutionary, took part in the storming of the Bastille and the march on Versailles at the eruption of the Revolution in 1789. Toulan's devotion to republican principles resulted in his being nominated a member of the Commune and sent to serve in the Temple as a prison commissioner in December 1792. But after spending two days in the company of the royal prisoners, performing duties that brought him into constant contact with the imprisoned queen, Toulan became one of Marie Antoinette's most devoted supporters.[3]

Toulan was also clever enough to conceal his royalist sympathies by assuming the mask of a fervent revolutionary. He was often heard cursing the royals in the Commune and being insolent in their presence.[4] Toulan's transformation from brash revolutionary to caring supporter of the royal family was remarkable. Even more remarkable was how Toulan managed to fool his colleagues, all the while serving the queen to such an extent that she referred to him as *le fidèle*, the faithful one.[5]

In one dangerous maneuver, Toulan conveyed the late Louis XVI's seal and ring to the queen. Before his execution, the king had given his servant Cléry the royal seal, a small packet of locks of hair, and his wedding ring. He knew he would never see his family again.[6]

"After my death, you will give this seal to my son—this ring to the queen," the king said to Cléry as he handed him the articles.[7] "This small parcel contains locks of hair of all my family that you will give her.

"Say to the queen, my dear children, and my sister," he continued, "that I had promised to see them this morning, but that I desired to spare them the agony of such a bitter separation twice over. How much it has cost me to depart without receiving their last embraces!"[8]

Cléry remained at the Temple more than a month after the king's death before he himself was imprisoned.[*] Before Cléry left the Temple, the officials at the Commune confiscated the king's valuables from him and locked them under seal in a room on the ground floor of the Temple.[9]

---

*Cléry was sent to La Force prison but later released; he went into exile in Austria until his death in 1809.

*King Louis XVI's farewell to his family in the Temple
with Jean-Baptiste Cléry in the background*

When Toulan found the personal souvenirs in the Temple, he reported his discovery to the queen, and she was determined to recover what was stolen from her and rightfully belonged to her. Risking his life, Toulan tricked his colleagues: he broke the seals, untied the parcel, removed the articles, and smuggled them to the queen.[10] If caught, Toulan would surely have been sent to the scaffold for this crime; however, since all kinds of people came to the Temple every day, the crime was simply considered an act of common thievery and soon forgotten.

During these chaotic weeks, Marie Antoinette was uncertain about her future. She decided to convey the precious souvenirs to General Jarjayes, a supporter who had shown his loyalty with nothing but "blind devotion."[11] Toulan, as usual, would be the middleman.

"From the turn events are taking," the queen said to Toulan, "I may expect at any moment to be prevented from communicating with anyone. Here are the ring, the seal, and the packet of hair for the recovery of which I am indebted to you."[12]

The queen then asked Toulan to leave the souvenirs in General Jarjayes's hands and to direct the general to forward them on to monsieur the count of Provence* and the count of Artois, the king's brothers in exile. She also sent a note to Jarjayes that began, "T . . . will bring you things."

The rest of the letter gave instructions that Toulan would explain later in more detail. The seal and the locks of hair were intended for monsieur and the wedding ring for the count of Artois. The gifts recognized that the princes of the blood were next in line to the throne after her son, Louis Charles, and represented "a flattering mark of attention to them."[13]

When Toulan unexpectedly called upon him on February 2, Jarjayes was at first suspicious. He feared it might be too dangerous to receive the stranger, but after hearing Toulan had come directly from the Temple, he accepted the guest. The queen's message reassured him even further:

> You may rely upon the man who is seeking you on my behalf. I know his feelings, which have been constant for five months. Do not place any great confidence in the man's [Tison's] wife who is shut up with us. I trust neither her nor her husband.[14]

Jarjayes was well acquainted with the queen's handwriting and felt an unspeakable emotion at seeing her words. The queen went on to inform Jarjayes that the Tisons, the Temple caretakers, were nothing more than spies and he should not trust them.

Jarjayes welcomed Toulan, not hesitating to ask if he had any plans to liberate the royal family from the Temple.[15] And Toulan certainly did. Jarjayes would procure men's clothes for Marie Antoinette and Madame Élisabeth. Toulan's comrade, ardent royalist Jacques François Lepître, would provide tricolored scarves for the disguised ladies to wear around their waists. He would also provide passes, allowing the family to leave at nightfall when the Temple guards on duty would simply take them for inspectors returning from their rounds.†

Taking the children out of the Temple, especially the young heir to the throne, presented greater difficulties. But another friend of Toulan's,

---

*Monsieur is the title used to address the eldest living brother of the king.

†Jacques François Lepître worked in the department that issued prison passes and passports.

Jacques, was to have lamps and lanterns for them; it was his business to clean the prison lamps every morning and light them every evening. He was always punctual, never spoke to anyone, and sometimes brought his two children with him, who were, fortunately, about the same age and size as Louis Charles and Marie-Thérèse.[16]

Jacques would provide ill-fitting and shabby clothes for the royal children, allowing them to resemble his own. Lepître would also provide passports for the entire family, and once clear of the Temple, the royal prisoners would take the road to Normandy in three cabriolets, less likely to attract attention than one large carriage.*

The escape was well planned. The prison guard was always relieved at seven o'clock, and the fresh detachment of soldiers could not possibly know if Jacques and his accomplices had been there or not. Another of Toulan's friends, Ricard, would disguise himself as the lamp cleaner and show his pass at the gate when he arrived to finish the work begun by his children. Toulan would reprimand him for not being punctual, and as soon as his work was done, the royal children, disguised as his own children cleaning lamps, would then leave the prison holding his hand. Finally, Jarjayes would be waiting with the carriages outside the prison gate.

Because supper was never served after nine o'clock, the family would have time to leave Paris before being missed in their chambers. The escape was planned for March 8, and Toulan noted that "all the precautions taken seemed to promise success." In the meantime, however, Austrian troops had started a campaign to the French capital, causing the government to keep more vigilant watch over the royal prisoners and to restrict the granting of passports. Consequently, not all members of the family could be rescued, and the original plan had to be postponed.[17]

Because the queen's life was most in danger, Toulan convinced her—with much effort—to go through with the arrangements but to leave her children and her sister-in-law behind. The queen agreed, but the evening before the flight, she paced frantically back and forth in her chambers until she finally cried out to Élisabeth, "No, it is impossible! It is impossible!"

---

*Remembering the unsuccessful flight to the border two years earlier in a large, ostentatious carriage, the queen this time had insisted on the use of smaller and more discrete carriages.

"You will be angry with me," the queen told Toulan the following day, "but I have been thinking it over. We are, indeed, encompassed with dangers here, but it is better to die than to act against one's conscience.[18]

"And I should die unhappy," she continued, "if I could not express to you my attachment."

"And I, Madame," said Toulan, "should die unhappy if I could not assure you of my devotion."[19]

After thanking Toulan for his unconditional loyalty, the queen sent the "faithful one" to Jarjayes with the following message:

> We have dreamed a lovely dream—that is all! But we have gained much, in that we have a fresh proof of your affection for us. My confidence in you is unbounded. You will always find me strong and courageous. But the interests of my son are my only guide. And great as would have been my happiness to leave these walls, I cannot consent to a separation from him. I recognize your devotion in all that you expressed yesterday, and you must feel assured that I grasp the truth of every argument you can put forward. But nothing could give me pleasure in the absence of my children, and it is this which prevents my feeling any regret.[20]

The government's tightened security in response to the Austrian invasion made any further royalist plots more difficult. Marie Antoinette and her family were subjected to new restrictive measures; their chambers were now searched three times a day. But the government's clampdown did nothing to stop royal supporters from devising new plans to save their queen.[21]

Two months after Toulan's attempt, someone else devised a plan for the rescue of the royal family. Toulan and Lepître had been removed from the list of commissioners at the Temple; they were denounced by the Tisons for having too many "quiet" conversations with the royal prisoners—though their plot to free the family was never discovered.[22] Nevertheless, Marie Antoinette still had a friend and supporter among the other commissioners of the Temple, Jean-Baptiste Michonis.

Michonis realized that the queen's life was becoming less and less valuable to the revolutionary government. He sought out Baron Jean Pierre de Batz, a zealous royalist who was still on the run from the authorities for an earlier plot to save the late king. While hiding in the house of grocer and

National Guard captain Joseph-Victor Cortey, de Batz had Michonis appoint Cortey as one of the commanders of the guard of the Temple. With Michonis and Cortey now at his disposal, de Batz set about executing a simple but daring plan.[23]

The wealthy baron's family was traditionally bound by ancient ties of hereditary friendship to King Henry IV, Louis XVI's ancestor. Ever since the first troubles of the Revolution, de Batz had shown King Louis XVI nothing but the most unwavering devotion. On January 21, he had planned a scheme to rescue the king on his way to the scaffold. But it was never implemented, partly due to the wariness of his own men and partly from the reluctance of Louis himself to approve a mission that might have ended in civil war and shed the blood of his subjects.[24]

Since the king's death, de Batz had devoted his attention and the vast resources at his disposal to helping the queen escape the Temple and cross the French border to safety. With Michonis's help, the plans were quickly devised.

De Batz would first have Cortey enroll him in the company of guards at the Temple under an assumed name, Citizen Forget. Cortey would also include some thirty other men in his section, all enlisted by de Batz and more than likely generously bought with gold coins.[25] To prepare the royal family, Michonis would be on duty at the Temple on the evening of the escape.

The plan was for Cortey to organize some of his guards on the tower stairway from midnight to two o'clock in the morning, with the remainder, including de Batz, patrolling the prison grounds at the same time. Michonis would take care of the night service for the queen and her family in their chambers.

At midnight de Batz would take command of his patrol and lead it up the stairs to the queen's chambers. Michonis, inside the chambers, would alert the queen and the two princesses dressed in National Guard uniforms with hoods over their heads. The women, taking a gun to carry by their sides, would join de Batz's patrol. The young prince would be discreetly encircled by the patrol, hidden all the while from sight.

With all the sentinels now accomplices of de Batz, the entire patrol could then descend the tower stairs. At the bottom, Cortey, who as station commander would have the sole power to open the front gate at night, would wait for the patrol and then order it outside to inspect the Temple and its surroundings. The carriages waiting outside the gate would then transport de Batz and the royal family as far from Paris as possible.

The evening of the rescue arrived. The plan was set into motion, and the queen's supporters were all confident that the escape would be successful. At eleven o'clock in the evening, Michonis was already in the queen's apartment. Suddenly there was a knock at the main entrance of the Temple; it was Antoine Simon, the cobbler turned jailer. An unknown gendarme had given Simon an anonymous note that he found at the Temple gate. It read, "Michonis will betray tonight. Be vigilant!"

After receiving the note, Simon had immediately notified the authorities at the Hôtel de Ville and obtained permission to replace Michonis and relieve him of his duties. Arriving at the Temple, Simon said to Cortey, "If I didn't see you here, I would surely have been very worried."[26]

De Batz was not sure if the authorities had discovered his plan to free the queen, but he was certain of the need to cancel it. He even thought of killing Simon, then and there, and taking the royal family by force, but his men had not yet taken their positions on the tower stairs. Any such action would have simply been impossible.

Simon hastened up the stairs to the queen's chambers and presented Michonis with the decree ordering him to hand over his powers. When told that he must immediately report to the Commune, Michonis quickly obeyed, taking his leave with "imperturbable composure" to keep from raising eyebrows.[27]

Cortey remained calm and collected. Realizing that there was no hope, he was clever enough to save one of the conspirators. He quickly pretended that he heard a suspicious noise in the street and ordered de Batz's patrol outside the gates to investigate, allowing the baron to escape.

When Michonis arrived at the Commune, he replied to the authorities' questions with such poise and good humor that he was no longer suspected of any misconduct. In fact, when it was announced in the Temple the next day that the prisoners' chambers had been searched for nothing, Simon became the object of ridicule for causing such a commotion. The note was treated as nothing but the work of a prankster.

If Simon had not received the anonymous note, the royal family could very possibly have escaped from the Temple prison that evening.[28] But after this failure, every project of escape was abandoned. And a few weeks later the queen was perhaps happy that she had once refused to flee without her son. The young king became very ill, and for several days his life was in the balance, but the leaders of the Revolution cruelly refused to allow the child to see Dr. Joseph Louis Brunier, the family's physician who had cared for him since his infancy.

Liberté, égalité, fraternité. The young king was not to be treated any differently than any other prisoner. "It would be a breach of the principles of equality," said an official, "if any prisoner were permitted to consult any but the prison doctor."[29]

Fortunately, Dr. François Thierry, the Temple physician, was "on this occasion" a sensible man; he took it upon himself to consult with Dr. Brunier, and consequently the young king soon recovered. A few weeks later, however, the queen might have doubted whether her son's recovery was a blessing. At ten o'clock on July 3, while the little king slept calmly, six commissioners violently threw the door of the royal chamber open and carried him off.

With the child now kept in solitary confinement under Simon's watch, it was increasingly questionable if there would be any opportunity, or perhaps any reason, to free the queen from the Temple. But there would be other plots, including one by a pretty young actress of the English theater who had always "admired Marie Antoinette passionately."[30]

Miss Charlotte Walpole made her stage debut in Drury Lane in London in 1777 and was soon wooed by the wealthy Sir Edward Atkyns. When the couple married and moved to Versailles in 1779, the twenty-one-year-old Lady Atkyns was presented at Queen Marie Antoinette's court by the duchesse de Polignac, the queen's favorite. The English couple remained in France until 1790, returning to London during the turbulent events of the Revolution.[31]

After the king's execution on January 21, 1793, Lady Atkyns conceived of a plan to bribe her way into the Temple prison, where she would exchange garments with the queen and take her majesty's place as the prisoner. She felt that security would surely be less stringent with the king no longer in the Temple. With the plan set into motion, Lady Atkyns returned to Paris and succeeded in gaining access to the prison by paying off a guard with a large sum of money for an hour's time.

However, Lady Atkyns was unable to persuade Marie Antoinette to leave her children behind. She did succeed in making it possible to correspond secretly with the queen by giving her two bottles of invisible ink and providing several agents, who had agreed to help, with additional bottles. Lady Atkyns then safely returned to England, but not before putting her fortune at the disposal of faithful royalists.[32]

Marie Antoinette sacrificed her freedom to remain with her children despite the protests of her devoted friends and her sister-in-law Élisabeth, who promised to care for the children like a second mother. All begged her to save her own life, but she refused; she would not flee as long as her children were at the mercy of the revolutionaries. Though her maternal instincts were no doubt involved, perhaps her refusal reflected political considerations as well. What power would the queen ever have as long as her son, the rightful heir to the throne, was still in the custody of the revolutionaries? To secure any power during the minority of her son, the queen would still have to regain the throne for him. She needed him by her side.

Lady Atkyns's rationale for saving the queen did not appear to be political at all; rather, she was a warmhearted, emotional woman with a taste for romantic adventure. It is questionable whether Lady Atkyns visited the queen again in the Temple. A closer look at the brave actress's correspondence at the time suggests that, more than likely, she made a second visit after the queen's transfer to the Conciergerie.[33]

In either case, the story remains the same. Marie Antoinette again refused to flee without her children. She also seemed concerned about endangering the young actress's life, though she did recommend that Lady Atkyns try to save Louis Charles from the Temple tower. Consequently, Lady Atkyns swore to do all in her power to save the young king after she returned to England. She took active steps to carry out her promise, but perhaps she acted with "more ardor and devotion than method." She did not succeed.

The French government had other worries at this time. After the fall of the French town of Quesnoy on September 11, the Austrians and their allies decided to attack the French fortress at Maubeuge. With the cities of Condé, Valenciennes, and Quesnoy already in enemy hands, the fall of Maubeuge would have opened up a wide gap in the fortified French frontier, providing a clear invasion route for an attack on Paris.

The possibility of troops outside the gates of Paris prompted the following note from a general of the Austrian army, Prince Auguste Marie Raymond d'Arenberg, comte de la Marck, to Austrian ambassador Mercy Argenteau:

> It will be a disgrace to the Austrian Government if history shall someday record that there was within forty leagues of Paris a considerable and victorious Austrian army, and that no attempt was made to save the august daughter of Maria Theresa from the scaffold. [34]

Though all plans thus far had failed, de Batz was not discouraged; he was certainly not going to give up.[35] He remained relentless in his attachment to the Bourbon cause and especially the rescue of the queen. Although convicted as the leader of "Cortey's Band," the baron was clever enough to evade the revolutionaries by moving from place to place. He miraculously escaped the guillotine's blade.

Strangely enough, while still in hiding, de Batz would mastermind another incredible plot to rescue the queen from the Conciergerie. This time, however, the repercussions would be considerably more dangerous.

À SAVOIR . . .

The Queen's Expenses in the Conciergerie

(Mémoires des dépenses de la veuve Capet à la Conciergerie)

The Commune documented Marie Antoinette's expenses paid by the government while she was in the Conciergerie. They give an idea of the queen's meals there, whether she ate them or not. There is no mention of breakfast, but Rosalie often provided the queen a cup of chocolate and a roll in the mornings.[36]

For lunch (*déjeuner*) the government gave her coffee, and for dinner she received soup, a plate of boiled vegetables, chicken, and dessert. On some days she was allowed duck and pâté; in fact, Warden Richard often shopped for the duck, knowing that it was one of the queen's favorite dishes.

Seventy-four days of food, coffee for lunch, for dinner, soup, broth, a vegetable dish, chicken and dessert; other days, duck and pâté for such seventy-four days, at 15 pounds each day makes 1,110 livres. Forty-one days of food for the woman who was with said Capet for 3 livres every day makes 123 livres. Two mattresses, one hair, the other wool, a folding bed, a bolster, a cover, a cane chair, all together and rent according to the receipts, 54 livres. A bidet trimmed in red basane, all new, to serve said widow Capet, 60 livres. To rent books, 16 livres. For two bonnets, 7 pounds each, 14 livres. Ribbon and silk lining of a skirt, 3 livres 16 sous. Ribbon for her shoes and her hair, 18 livres 5 sous. A bottle of water for her teeth, 3 livres 12 sous. For laundry, 22 livres. Total 1,407 livres, 6 sous.

6

THE CARNATION PLOT

"Nobody presented me with a carnation. No paper that I saw fell on the ground; something may have fallen, but I did not see it. I think not because the woman who is with me would have been able to see it, and she said nothing to me about it."

—Marie Antoinette, testimony to the
Committee of General Security

Paris
August 1793

Marie Antoinette loved flowers and was grateful to Madame Richard and Rosalie for the bouquets she found on her small oak table. But the queen soon found such gifts were forbidden in her cell after Warden Richard, his wife, and the two jailers on duty were removed from the Conciergerie. The queen's secret friend, Jean-Baptiste Michonis, was ultimately responsible for these changes—all the result of an affair known as the "Carnation Plot."*

There was nothing unusual on August 28, when Michonis, the superintendent of prisons, entered the Conciergerie. He passed through Warden

---

*The details of this plot, the *affaire de l'oeillet*, have been recounted differently in the testimonies of Marie Antoinette, the guards Dufresne and Gilbert, Madame Harel, Michonis, and the chevalier de Rougeville (in order of credibility, with the queen's second testimony considered the most credible).

Toussaint Richard's office to greet Madame Richard and continued to Marie Antoinette's cell, where each day he brought the queen news about her children from the Temple.[1]

Nor was there anything unusual about Michonis's not being alone; he had frequently escorted strangers into the Conciergerie and even into the queen's cell. On this evening, a man with brown hair and brown eyes, of average height and in his mid-thirties, accompanied him. Neither Madame Marie Harel nor the guards on duty—François Dufresne and Jean Gilbert—noted anything peculiar about the visitor. But the queen changed color and became agitated when she recognized him. The man was the chevalier de Rougeville, a noble she had last seen at the siege of the Tuileries a year earlier when the royal family was transferred to the National Assembly for safety.* The Tuileries, the palace where the family had been under house arrest for past two years, was stormed by an angry mob that massacred the king's Swiss Guard.[2]

Alexandre Dominique Joseph Gonzze de Rougeville, also known as a chevalier de Saint-Louis, was a former officer of the National Guard. He was an ardent counterrevolutionary who had formulated a plan to free the queen when she was first incarcerated in the Conciergerie. His men would reach her through the backyard of the chapel after seizing the posts at the main gate with phony patrols. A band of royalists in National Guard uniforms would counter any resistance and then throw the queen in a carriage, transporting her safely to the Château de Livry on the road from Paris to Meaux. From there she would be taken to Germany.[3]

Rougeville was not easily forgotten.† His face was heavily scarred by smallpox, and he ordinarily wore a gray suit in a shade sometimes called the "mud of Paris." The chevalier was also a wealthy man, allowing him to devote his time and money to such a bold plan to rescue Marie Antoinette, as well as to a life of intrigue and debauchery.[4]

Rougeville's enthusiasm for protecting his queen had intensified two weeks earlier on August 15, when he dined at the home of Pierre Fontaine,

---

*Six hundred of the nine hundred Swiss Guards were killed during this siege on August 10, 1792.

†Actually, Rougeville was neither a chevalier nor a noble; even the name Rougeville was usurped.

a forty-two-year-old lumber merchant in the Marais. Among Fontaine's guests was Madame Sophie Lebon Dutilleul, a twenty-three-year-old American widow with whom Rougeville lodged in the village of Vaugirard.* It is unknown how Rougeville convinced Madame Dutilleul to bring him along to Fontaine's soirée; it is even more of a mystery how he linked Fontaine with Michonis.[5]

Perhaps Rougeville was acquainted with Baron Jean Pierre de Batz or was aware of Michonis's attachment to Marie Antoinette. At the party, however, Michonis was only introduced as the superintendent of prisons and the administrator who had escorted the queen from the Temple to the Conciergerie. Michonis proudly spoke about his duties as the director of prisons, how exhausting his work was, and finally about the widow Capet.[6]

"What does she do?" asked one of the guests. "What does she say?"

"She must be very sad," said another guest.

Rougeville trembled as he listened to Michonis. In an indifferent tone, to mask his emotions, he said, "Well, she surely must have changed."

"No, I assure you," said Michonis. "She is quite well although her hair has turned white. You do not know her?"

"No," said Rougeville, detached, not wanting to raise any eyebrows.

"If you would like to see her, I can arrange it," said Michonis.

"It is tempting," said Rougeville, "but I would not want to compromise you."

"Compromise me? Am I not the superintendent?" said Michonis. "Just give me the word, and I will take you with me to visit the Conciergerie."

"Thank you, Citizen Michonis," said Rougeville. "I will think about it."

A different account places this first meeting between Michonis and Rougeville two weeks later, on August 28, and holds that Michonis escorted Rougeville to the Conciergerie on the very same evening. August 15 seems more likely, however, as the two-week interval would have given Rougeville sufficient time to become acquainted with Michonis and perhaps to prepare for the queen's rescue on August 28.

Rougeville invited Fontaine to his home in Vaugirard for dinner in the company of two pretty young seamstresses, Laurence Desguillot and Ad-

*The village of Vaugirard has since been incorporated into the fifteenth arrondisement of Paris.

elaide Provot. Fontaine must have shared Rougeville's libertinism, or *plaisirs facils*, because the two became fast friends, enjoying more than one dinner party. In fact, Michonis joined the two libertines almost every evening for dinner; he was also clearly taken by Madame Dutilleul's charms.[7]

During dinner at Fontaine's on August 28, the conversation returned to Marie Antoinette. Rougeville slyly and tactfully toasted Michonis's role as prison administrator, which soon had Michonis renewing his offer to take him to the Conciergerie to see the queen.

Knowing that Michonis would most likely again insist on accompanying him, Rougeville politely declined. He claimed that he cared little for the visit, that he had little time, and that politics did not interest him at all. When Michonis insisted, Rougeville gave in, asking if they could go the very same evening. Michonis agreed.[8]

Rougeville returned to Pierre Fontaine's later that evening with a bouquet of carnations that he had picked in Madame Dutilleul's garden for the special occasion. He saved two carnations for the queen and pinned them to his coat lapel, but not before inserting a note between the petals of one of them.[*]

In the evening of Wednesday, August 28, Michonis entered Marie Antoinette's cell with Rougeville by his side.[†] The guard Gilbert reported that the queen was sitting in front of her table, while he, the guard Dufresne, and Madame Harel were behind the screen that separated them from the queen.

The queen was dressed in a black caraco;[‡] her hair had been cut shorter in the back and off her forehead. She was so weak that she could hardly stand up.[9]

"Ah, it is you, Monsieur Michonis," she said.

According to Dufresne, Michonis asked the queen, as was customary, if she needed anything, and the queen asked for news of her children. But when she recognized Rougeville, she was immediately taken aback, became flushed, and could not hold back her tears. The guards did not find this reaction unusual; the queen always became upset whenever she heard news about her children.

---

[*]Gilbert reported that there was only one carnation.

[†]Michonis, when questioned the following week, said the visit took place on Thursday or Friday, August 29 or 30, but he was mistaken. The correct date was Wednesday, August 28.

[‡]A caraco was a thigh-length jacket opened in the front with tight, three-quarter or long sleeves.

The queen did not notice that Rougeville had dropped a carnation in front of her next to a small wood stove. When Rougeville observed that she had not seen it, he gestured for the queen to pick it up. She hesitated for a moment, or perhaps, bewildered by the sight of an old friend, she did not understand his signal.

There are contrasting versions of this event. According to one, Michonis and Rougeville left the cell, but the queen asked Gilbert to recall Michonis; she had a complaint about her meals.* Another version states that one of the gendarmes picked up the carnation and noticed that it contained a hidden message. Even more bizarrely, according to Jean-Baptiste Cléry's journal, Madame Richard, attentive to all the movements of the queen and Rougeville, had seen the carnation fall to the ground. When she stooped down to pick it up, Rougeville rushed in at the same time, grabbed the note, and swallowed it.[10]

The most credible accounts, however, hold that after Michonis and Rougeville departed, the queen bent over, picked up the carnation, and then moved a bit behind the screen that separated her from the guards' area in order to read the hidden note. Dufresne, however, recalled that Michonis and Rougeville had not departed but had even followed her. And according to Rougeville's melodramatic account, Marie Antoinette even took his hand while they were behind the screen. "Unfortunate one, your boldness makes me shudder," she supposedly said. "Don't you know the danger of becoming involved in this fretful situation?"[11]

"Don't worry about me," he said. "One of you hairs is more precious to me than my life. I have money, men, and officials—all the secure means to get you out of this sinister place. But I need your help."

"Leave," she said. "I am too weak and exhausted; how could I be of any help to you?"

"A few more days and nature will spare the wicked the last of crimes," said Rougeville. "Do you have the heart to continue?"

"I do, but it is deeply affected," she said.

Fearing that they might attract the guards' attention, Michonis signaled Rougeville that it was time to leave.

---

*This is a very possible scenario because the queen will testify that she saw Rougeville twice that day.

"So I bid you an eternal farewell?" the queen said to Michonis. She might have learned that he had not been reelected as superintendent of prisons.

"No," he said. "Even if I am no longer superintendent, I am still a municipal officer and I will have the right to come and visit you whenever you wish."

After the two men left the queen's cell, neither the guards nor Madame Harel saw the carnation or Rougeville's signal for the queen to pick it up. Nor had they heard the conversation between Rougeville and the queen behind the partition.

As soon as Michonis and Rougeville left, Marie Antoinette took the opportunity—Madame Harel and Gilbert were playing cards—to read the note. Afterward, she tore it up into tiny pieces. Consequently, there are three different versions of what the note contained.

Marie Antoinette testified that the message revealed the following "vague" phrases: "What will you do? What do you plan to do? I've been in prison, but I was saved by a miracle.* I will come Friday." There was also an offer of money.[12]

According to Gilbert's testimony, the message was quite different: "My protector, I will never forget you, I will always seek a way to show you my zeal. If you need three hundred pounds, I am ready to offer them to you."

Finally, Rougeville reported years later that the message read, "I have always remained faithful to you; I've just collected the remainder of my fortune and the rest of my wits to maintain my courage to iron out any difficulties and obstacles that could hinder your escape now, but help me."[13] Such a long message was improbable, and the rest of Rougeville's story about his efforts to save the queen and her children was perhaps more fantasy (or wish fulfillment) than truth.

Marie Antoinette had testified that the message included the phrase "I will come Friday." This was corroborated by Rougeville's story; he recalled that he had indeed returned on Friday, August 30.

After reading the message, Marie Antoinette wanted to respond to Rougeville, but she did not have any means to write. Taking a pin, she pricked holes in a piece of paper to fashion words. At the same time, Madame Harel

---

*A miracle? It was true that Rougeville had been imprisoned from August 16 to 28, 1792, but he was "saved" by bribing the guard with silver (G. Lenotre).

Hallway of Marie Antoinette's cell
(Chambre de Conseil)

finished playing cards with the guards and went to fetch some water. While she was away, the queen made a disastrous mistake.

The queen approached Gilbert, saying, "See how I am trembling? I've just seen a chevalier de Saint-Louis who passed me a note in a carnation that he dropped on the floor in front of me and told me to pick up.[14]

"And I've just responded to him by pricking this paper with a pin," she continued. "You see, I don't need anything with which to write."

It was unusual that the queen confided in Gilbert about her visit from Rougeville. It was even more unusual that the queen would ask Gilbert to forward her note to the chevalier. Had Gilbert been so kind to the queen that she thought she could trust him? He did bring her a bouquet of flowers on one occasion, but why did the queen not wait to give the note to someone more loyal, such as Madame Richard? Knowing the punishment for aiding the royals, the queen would never have wanted to implicate anyone, especially the compassionate wife of the warden.

Perhaps Marie Antoinette chose Gilbert to deliver the note because, in the event of an attempt to escape, he would be the guard most likely to accept a bribe of gold coins. Or, better yet, Gilbert may already have been involved in the conspiracy to rescue the queen.

As soon as Madame Harel returned, Gilbert took the queen's note and left his post to find Madame Richard. He gave her the note and told her about what had just transpired. He also asked her to speak to Michonis about the incident. When he returned to his post, Marie Antoinette asked him to return the note, but he did not have it any longer; Madame Richard had put it in her vest pocket with her other papers.[15]

When Michonis returned to the Conciergerie the next day, Madame Richard gave him the pinpricked note. Realizing that Rougeville's communication with the queen had been discovered and that he might be considered one of Rougeville's accomplices, Michonis told Madame Richard to keep quiet about the affair.

"It's not a matter of any importance," he said. "It's not necessary to deal with it any longer."

Michonis promised not to escort any more visitors to the prison to avoid such problems in the future. Knowing that Madame Richard was wholeheartedly devoted to the queen, he was certain that she would remain silent about the note, but he was not as confident about Gilbert—and rightly so.

Gilbert must have had second thoughts about his own safety because he decided to report the incident to Louis-Claude Adenet, an officer in his company, who would alert Colonel Jacques-Marie Botot-Dumesnil. The colonel, deeming the incident of little importance, did nothing. Adenet then spoke to Jean-Maurice-François Lebrasse, the Conciergerie's post commander, and to François Chabot, a National Convention deputy.*

After no response from Chabot, Lebrasse and Adenet advised Gilbert to reveal the negligence to the Tribunal. He complied on Saturday, August 31,

---

*Chabot was perhaps the wrong party to contact; he had been negotiating with an aristocrat, the marquise de Janson, who had offered him a million pounds to rescue the queen. The offer was tempting, but seeing there was another attempt to save her, he thought it prudent to take advantage of it without compromising himself. He never reported the incident to the Tribunal.

three days after Rougeville's visit. The Committee of General Security was in session on Tuesday, September 3, when Gilbert's letter was finally presented to the delegates.[16]

My Colonel, in such a delicate post, I would be absolutely remiss in my duty not to reveal the risks to you that may arise by suspicious people who enter the Capet woman's cell. Finally, to bring the matter up and not comprise myself, my friend or the entire company, here is the exact truth with all my soul and conscience.

When Citizen Michonis came here the day before yesterday, he came with an individual, whose appearance startled the woman Capet, who told me to be a heretofore chevalier of St. Louis, but it was discovered that she was shaking, and she was very surprised how he could reach her. She even said that he made her take a carnation on the same day in which there was a note, and that he would return the following Friday.

In addition, while her maid was playing a game of cards with me, the woman Capet used this opportunity to write a message with a pin which she handed me purposely to convey someone. But, not wishing to have nothing to reproach myself about the post and the duties that I have to fulfill, I immediately went to the concierge, the woman to whom I handed the note and made the exact same report that I have the honor to present to you. (Signed) Gilbert[17]

Marie Antoinette's note, written with pin pricks, was indeed given to Madame Richard, who said it was not legible. It was long thought to contain the following words: "I advise you not to come here again, nothing escapes my guards. You will only hasten my end; endeavor rather to have me reclaimed from outside."[18]

More precisely, the note was about four inches long and one inch wide; it contained three lines pricked with a pin or needle, but these lines formed neither figures nor letters, only "windings of different lengths." Only later did paleographer Adam Pilinski decipher the note.[19]

The committee considered the incident sufficiently serious to investigate immediately. Two committee members, citizens Jean-Baptiste-André Amar and Joseph Marie Sévestre, were sent to the Conciergerie that same day. They were joined by Citizens Bax, Aigron, and Caillieux; Michonis was

*"I am kept in sight. I cannot talk
to anyone. I trust you. I will come."*
(Deciphered by Adam Pilinski, 1876)

also ordered to appear and to bring Marie Antoinette. At four o'clock in the afternoon, the interrogation of the queen began, with Amar taking the lead.[20]

Deputy: Are you called the widow Capet?

Queen: Yes.

Deputy: Don't you ever see anyone in the cell where you are detained?

Queen: No, only those who are placed next to me and those administrators who come with other persons whom I do not know.

Deputy: Didn't you see a former chevalier of Saint-Louis a couple of days ago?

Queen: It is possible that I have recognized a familiar face; there are so many who come.

Deputy: You do not know any of the names of those who came with the administrators?

Queen: I don't remember the names of any of them.

Deputy: Among those who entered your cell, did you recognize anyone in particular?

Queen: No.

Deputy: Wasn't there anyone who you saw whom you recognized?

Queen: I don't remember.

Deputy: Didn't this same man present you with a carnation?

Queen: There were some in my chamber.

Deputy: Was there not a note given to you by someone?

Queen: How could I receive one with the people who are in my room, and while the woman who is with me does not leave the window?

Deputy: Is it not possible that when you were presented with a carnation that there was something inside it and that, while you were accepting it, a paper may have fallen out, which you may have picked up?

Queen: Nobody presented me with a carnation. No paper that I saw fell on the ground; something may have fallen, but I did not see it. I think not because the woman who is with me would have been able to see it, and she said nothing to me about it.

Deputy: Have you written nothing in the past few days?

Queen: I don't even have the means to write.

Deputy: Could you have used some instrument or some means for transcribing your ideas?

Queen: Not being alone, even for a moment, I could not do it.

Deputy: There was one day a former chevalier of Saint-Louis who entered your cell; you trembled when you saw him. We ask you to answer if you knew him.

Queen: It is possible that I saw familiar faces, as I've said before, and in the nervous state that I find myself, I tremble no matter what day, or for whom, or for what.

Deputy: Did you not declare that this same chevalier of Saint-Louis who presented you with a carnation should return on a Friday?

Queen: I said at the beginning that no one had presented me anything. If I had believed that someone would return, I would not have said it.

Deputy: Did you not take advantage of the time that your maid was playing a game of cards to write with a pin to the same individual who presented you with a carnation in which there must have been a note.

Queen: I just said, and I repeat, that I have not written in any way. If I wanted to do something and hide it, I would not be able to because I am always in sight of the persons who are with me, even during a game of cards. To respond to this individual, it would have been necessary to know him and to have received something from him. And the persons with me, I wouldn't ask them to take part in a scheme because I believe they would only fulfill their duties not to take part in it.

Deputy Amar's questioning then quickly changed direction. Finding that he could not get any more information from the queen about the Carnation Plot, he began to interrogate her about other matters, such as her knowledge of current events outside the prison, her children, and her family. The questions were at times demeaning, but the queen did her best to answer them with dignity.[21]

Deputy: In your situation, wouldn't it be natural to take advantage of every means available to you to escape and to convey your ideas to those in whom you trust?

Wouldn't it therefore be surprising that this chevalier of Saint-Louis was a person who could help you and yet someone to whom you would have no interest in talking?

Queen: If I were alone I would not hesitate to try all means to reunite with my family, but having three people in my room, though I did not know them before coming here, I would never compromise them for anything.

Deputy: Have you any knowledge of current events and the situation of political affairs?

Queen: You must know that at the Temple we knew nothing, and I do not know any more here.

Deputy: You knew without a doubt about the Custine affair.* Did you know anything about his plans?

Queen: I knew that he was in the same prison as me, but I know neither the reason nor the cause.

Deputy: Haven't you received any information in an indirect way about what is happening with your family?

Queen: Not at all. I know that my children are doing well. That's all I've ever known.

Deputy: From whom have you had news about your children?

Queen: From the administrators who told me.

Deputy: Haven't you learned about the advances we've made, in particular, on the Austrians?

Queen: I had often heard the town criers at the Temple cry out, "Great victory!" sometimes for one side, sometimes for the other. I never knew anything more.

Deputy: Hasn't there been any opportunity to inform your family about your situation and take advantage of your friends' help?

Queen: Never, the position in which we found ourselves in the last year at the Temple rendered it impossible.

Deputy: Isn't it true that you have kept contact with the outside by hidden means?

Queen: No, it would have taken power.

Deputy: You are interested in the success of the enemies' armies?

Queen: I am interested in the success of those of my son's nation; when you're a mother, it is the first relationship.

---

*General Adam Philippe Custine was convicted of negligence, for losing Condé, Valenciennes, and the city of Mainz, which he had abandoned when occupation became unsustainable.

Deputy: What is your son's nation?

Queen: Can you doubt it? Isn't he French?

Marie Antoinette's last response rang sarcastic, and as the questioning became more personal with respect to her son, she became increasing annoyed, occasionally answering the deputies' questions with her own. The queen was constantly on her guard and unwilling to compromise anyone; she told the truth as long as those devoted to her were in no danger of losing their heads.

Deputy: Your son is now only a commoner, so you've therefore renounced all the privileges the vain title of "king" gives him?

Queen: There is nothing more beautiful, including us, than the welfare of France.

Deputy: So you are glad that there is neither king nor kingdom?

Queen: That France is great and happy is all that is needed.

Deputy: So you must wish that people are no longer oppressed and that your family who enjoy an arbitrary authority must suffer the fate suffered by the oppressors of France?

Queen: I will answer for my son; for me, I am not responsible for others.

Deputy: So you have never shared the views of your husband?

Queen: I have always fulfilled my duties.

Deputy: You cannot, however, hide the fact that at court there existed men whose interests were the opposite of those of the people?

Queen: I have fulfilled my duties in all that I did, in those times just as in the present.

Deputy: How do your duties correspond with the flight you had premeditated and executed to Varennes?

Queen: If you had let us finish our journey and we had been able to do what we had planned, justice would have prevailed.

Deputy: What then was your purpose in leaving the center of France?

Queen: To give us a bit of freedom that we had not had since October 1789, but never to leave France.

Deputy: Why did you promise the people on your return from Versailles to stay attached to Paris and that it would please you to live among the people of Paris?

Queen: It was to live freely in Paris that we returned.

Deputy: What did the flight have to do with the question that you posed to the municipality the day before your flight? You asked, "Does one still ask if we want to leave Paris?"

Queen: It is not of the municipality of Paris that I asked this question. It was of Lafayette's assistant,* who tracked people who were leaving.[22]

Deputy: How, having prepared everything for your flight on the 21st, could you respond to those who had invited you to attend the ceremony of Fête Dieu that you said you would attend?

Queen: I do not remember having personally given this answer. I had to follow my husband and my children; I had nothing to say. I am keen knowing that I did not make an inquiry to anyone about our flight. We have always set an example of respect for the authorities.

Deputy: Having confessed that you only want prosperity and greatness for the French nation, how have you also been able to demonstrate such a strong desire to use all means to reunite with your family at war with the French nation?

Queen: My family is my children; I can only be good with them, and without them nowhere.

Deputy: So you regard those who make war on France as enemies?

Queen: I regard all those who could harm my children as my enemies.

Deputy: What is the nature of the harm that can be done to your children?

Queen: Every kind of any harm.

Deputy: According to your ideas in connection with your son, you do not consider the abolition of royalty a crime. How do you respond?

Queen: If France is to be happy with a king, I want it to be my son. If it must be without a king, I will share my happiness with it.

Deputy: France being made a republic by the wishes of 25 million men from all segments of society, you therefore declare that you and your son wish to exist as mere commoners in the republic and wish that all enemies who attack it are expelled from its territory?

Queen: I have no answer other than that for the previous question.

---

*This assistant was Monsieur Gouvian, Lafayette's aide-de-camp.

After the queen was escorted back to her cell, new witnesses were then called to testify: Michonis, the maid Marie Harel, the gendarme Gilbert and his comrade Dufresne (who would confirm Gilbert's story to a certain extent), and Madame Richard, among others. The main purpose was to discover the identity of the man who had dropped the carnation on the floor and where he had gone. Madame Harel was questioned first.

Deputy: What is your name?

Harel: Marie Harel, the maid.

Deputy: Did you not see a former chevalier of Saint-Louis come here?

Harel: I did not see anyone.

Deputy: Aren't you acquainted with Citizen Michonis?

Harel: Yes, I know him.

Deputy: Do you remember on which day he came here?

Harel: No.

Deputy: Didn't Citizen Michonis come here a few days ago, accompanied by someone?

Harel: Yes, he came with a young man whom I do not know.

Deputy: Did he speak to the widow Capet?

Harel: He stood beside the gendarme, and he didn't breathe a word.

Deputy: Did the individual who was with Michonis speak to the Capet woman?

Harel: No, she dreads all those who come here, and I did not notice the person in question speak.

Deputy: How was this young man dressed?

Harel: I cannot say how.

Deputy: Did you not notice on the same day that this young man gave a carnation to the Capet woman?

Harel: I did not see that.

Deputy: Doesn't she receive flowers?

Harel: Yes.

Deputy: Who brings them to her?

MARIE ANTOINETTE'S DARKEST DAYS

Harel: It is the gendarmes' duty.

Deputy: Did she ever ask for flowers?

Harel: No.

Deputy: Among the flowers that were presented, were there any carnations?

Harel: Most were carnations, but there were also some tuberose and dame's rocket.

Deputy: After the young man left with Michonis, did the widow Capet say anything?

Harel: No, the gendarmes asked me if he was Michonis's son, and I said that I didn't know.

Deputy: While this individual and Michonis were in the cell, were you not busy playing some cards?

Harel: No.

Deputy: Have you ever played cards with any guards?

Harel: Yes, twice with the guards in the widow Capet's chambers.

Deputy: With which gendarmes have you played?

Harel: With Gilbert.

Deputy: While playing cards, you didn't notice any signal or any communication between Michonis and the individual who accompanied him to see the widow Capet?

Harel: Not on that day, because when Michonis and the individual about whom you are talking came, I was not playing cards. I was working.

Deputy: While you were playing cards, didn't someone enter?

Harel: The citizens Jobert and Michonis entered.

Deputy: Since you've been with the widow Capet, you've not left the premises?

Harel: No.

Deputy: Since you've been with the widow Capet, has she not talked about her situation?

Harel: She told me about her children and that she was mortified at the Temple.

Deputy: Have you ever noticed the use of a pin or other instrument with which to write?

Harel: No, never.

Deputy: Do you know any of the people presented to the Capet woman?

Harel: No.

Deputy: You don't know anyone?

Harel: I know only the administrators and secretaries.

Deputy: Does anyone ever come other than the administrators and secretaries?

Harel: Yes, once or twice; but I do not know these people, and I cannot say who they are.

The deputies must have been frustrated by Madame Harel's testimony because she did not know the name of the man who accompanied Michonis that day. After all, Harel had been brought into the Conciergerie to replace Mère Larivière and spy on the queen. Moreover, Gilbert had testified that Madame Harel was playing cards with him when Michonis escorted a chevalier of Saint-Louis to see the queen, but Madame Harel said she was not playing cards at the time—either Madame Harel or Gilbert was lying. Hoping to make sense of the previous testimonies, the deputies then called Michonis to be interrogated.

Thus far the committee deputies faced a maze of contradictions. Even the queen's testimony conflicted with Gilbert's accusation. It was obvious that the queen was also lying, but she did not know that the deputies would soon realize it.

Marie Antoinette in her cell

It is unclear why Gilbert ever denounced Marie Antoinette in the first place. Did he fear that the queen would betray herself? If so, was he perhaps trying to prove his innocence by implicating her? Had Gilbert possibly been bribed? Or did he fear being implicated if he was not the first to come forward? After all, he did wait three days before reporting the incident to the committee. All the knots and loops make the truth hard to determine.

À SAVOIR . . .

Le chevalier de maison-rouge

Le chevalier de maison-rouge, translated as "the knight of the red house," was a novel written by Père Alexander Dumas in 1845; it was based on Alexandre Dominique Joseph Gonzze de Rougeville's attempt to communicate with Marie Antoinette by hiding a secret message in a carnation's petals.[23] It was to be titled *Le marquis de Rougeville* until Dumas received a letter from Rougeville's son:

> Monsieur, my father's mark in the Revolution was so brief, and also so mysterious, that it is not without anxiety, being aware of your republican principles, that I see his name at the head of your forthcoming novel. I would venture to ask with what incidents you have accompanied the bare facts which attach to his name, although I am well aware of the respect you profess for fallen greatness. [Signed] Marquis de Rougeville.[24]

Dumas immediately replied that he had not been aware of any descendant of the late chevalier, and although the story was favorable, he would change the title from *Le marquis de Rougeville* to *Le chevalier de maison-rouge*.[25] Dumas then received a second letter:

> Monsieur, call your story what you will. I am the last of my family, and in another hour I shall have blown out my brains. [Signed] Marquis de Rougeville.

Upon receipt of this letter Dumas sent his secretary to Rougeville's residence on the petite rue Madame. Rougeville's son had in fact shot himself in the head and was not responsive, but he was still alive, and doctors hoped to save him. Dumas asked his secretary to return every day for news. On the second day the secretary reported improvement in Rougeville's improvement, but on the third day he reported that the marquis had died that morning.

Dumas, still feeling bound to honor his word to Rougeville's son, kept his promise and the work was titled *Le chevalier de maison-rouge*.[26]

7

THE QUEEN'S
NEW CELL

"Every day and at every moment new spies came to trouble her resigned silence and her fervent prayers; architects, brutes in red caps, ferocious and threatening wretches with their caps on their heads forced their way into her new cell, examining the bars, gratings, bolts, doors, the walls, and even the stones of the pavement."

—Jules Janin, "The Queen's Gray Hair"[1]

Paris
September 1793

Months earlier Jean-Baptiste Michonis had put his life on the line to help Marie Antoinette and her family escape from the Temple prison. Now he faced the deputies from the Committee of General Security, who had the authority to refer suspects to the Revolutionary Tribunal—one fateful step from the guillotine—and this time he found it difficult to conceal his crime in the Conciergerie.[2]

Deputy: What is your name?

Michonis: Jean-Baptiste Michonis.

Deputy: What is your status?

Michonis: Café owner, rue du Puits.*

Deputy: Do you come here to see the Capet woman?

Michonis: Every day or almost every night.

Deputy: What are the functions that bring you here?

Michonis: Police administrator responsible for certain prisons of Paris.

Deputy: Didn't you come here a few days ago with a chevalier of Saint-Louis?

Michonis: I don't know, but I often came with people whom, being curious, I would not have refused to accompany me.

Deputy: Among these individuals you brought here, did any appear to have any other interest than curiosity?

Michonis: I assure you that I only knew those who came here out of curiosity.

Deputy: Didn't these individuals ever talk to the widow Capet?

Michonis: No, not to my knowledge.

Deputy: Did some of these individuals ever cause the Capet woman to become emotional?

Michonis: I never noticed.

Deputy: Did the Capet woman pay any attention to any of the many people who came here?

Michonis: I never noticed.

Deputy: Did you know all those who desired to accompany you to visit the Capet woman?

Michonis: Yes, I know them all; I'll try to name them.

Michonis recalled the following people: a schoolmaster by the name of Giroud, a café owner from the faubourg Saint-Denis, a clerk who lived in the rue de la Juiverie, another clerk, a painter (Kucharski?), and several others whose names he did not remember. He added that he brought all those who had an interest, because they knew that he was responsible for the prisons. But he was adamant that he did not know everyone.[3]

---

* Michonis was called a "limonadier." He not only prepared lemonade but would have been known as a "Maître de Café," offering coffee, chocolate, and perhaps distilled liqueurs in his café.

Deputy: How many did you introduce at a time?

Michonis: I have never taken more than one at a time, and always in the presence of the warden and his wife.

Deputy: How long have you been coming here to see the widow Capet?

Michonis: Ever since she left the Temple.

Deputy: Were you not accompanied by an individual, the unknown one, on the time before last that you visited?

Michonis: Yes, he was unknown to me.

Deputy: Can you describe this individual?

Michonis: He had a gray coat and a pockmarked face. He was thirty to forty years old and about five feet, one or two inches tall.

Deputy: Where did you meet this individual?

Michonis: At the home of Citizen Fontaine, rue de l'Oseille in the Marais.

Deputy: This individual was very interested in coming with you to see the Capet woman?

Michonis: Yes, he said it would be an infinite pleasure to see her.

Deputy: What is his status?

Michonis: He lives off his property.

Deputy: Do you know his name?

Michonis: No, but I will find out for you.

Deputy: On what particular day did he come with you to see the widow Capet?

Michonis: Last Thursday or Friday.*

Deputy: Do you remember when he asked to accompany you at the home of Citizen Fontaine?

Michonis: It was about a fortnight ago.

Deputy: Did he ask you this out loud?

Michonis: Yes, in the presence of everyone. There were even three members of the convention whose names I know.

---

*Was Michonis being sly? Rougeville accompanied him on Wednesday, not Thursday or Friday.

The deputies of the committee must have been astounded by Michonis's denial of knowing Rougeville or his name, and it seemed beyond curious that Michonis would let Rougeville, someone he did not know at all, visit the queen. They must have been even more astounded that an honorable chief of police and prison administrator sat in front of them, implicated in a scheme to rescue Marie Antoinette, an enemy of the republic.

The gendarmes were then sent to fetch Pierre Fontaine. In the meantime, the deputies questioned Jean Gilbert, whose letter had prompted the investigation.[4] The deputies must have shuddered that such activities were ever possible in their fortress of a prison.

Deputy: What is your name, and what is your profession?

Gilbert: Gilbert, national gendarme of the courts.

Deputy: Is it you who wrote your lieutenant colonel (of the gendarmerie) Botot-Dumesnil to denounce a citizen's special interview with Louis Capet's widow, to whom he had given a carnation in which was found a note?

Gilbert: Yes.

Deputy: Recite the particular circumstances of this to us, such as you know them.

Gilbert: Citizen Michonis came with an individual a few days ago; it was his second to last visit to the widow Capet. Citizen Michonis gave her news of her family, and during this time, the individual approached the maid who was in front of the widow Capet, signaling to the widow that he had dropped a carnation. The widow Capet did not seem to understand the signal, so he approached her and said in a low voice to pick up the carnation he had dropped next to the stove, behind the maid. She picked it up soon thereafter. I declare that the widow Capet herself confessed to me what I have to report, as I had not seen the signal or heard the individual's words. After Michonis and this individual had left, the widow Capet told me, "See how I am trembling. This party you just saw is a former chevalier of Saint-Louis, employed in the army, to whom I am indebted for not abandoning me. You couldn't imagine the manner in which he gave me a note. He made a signal with his eyes and, as I did not understand what he meant, he approached me and said in a very low voice, 'Pick up the carnation that fell on the ground, which contains my most ardent wishes; I will come Friday.' After he spoke, I bent down, and I picked up the carnation in which I found the note containing the sincerest wish of the individual."

Gilbert added that he had indeed seen the queen bend over but did not know the reason was to pick up a flower. He saw nothing except that she was upset, her complexion changed color, and she was trembling. A moment later, when Michonis and the individual who had come with him took their leave, the queen gave Michonis her "eternal adieu."

But Michonis explained to the queen that even though he might no longer be a chief of police, he would still be a municipal officer and had the right to return and visit as often as the queen wished.[5]

Gilbert also noted that after Michonis left with the visitor, the queen showed him a note with two or three lines of writing that she had pricked with a needle. "See, I don't need a pen in order to write," she said.

The queen told Gilbert that her note was intended for the one who had given her a message inserted in the petals of the carnation and who would return on Friday. Gilbert continued his deposition with additional information about the pinpricked note:

Gilbert: The maid, who was out some time to fetch water, returned just as the widow Capet finished speaking. I took the note that she had pricked with a pin, put it in my jacket, and left on the spot to find the warden's wife. I told her that I had something to confide in her. Pulling her aside, I handed her the pinpricked note, telling her what had happened, as I just said, and telling her not to lose this note. She immediately put it in her pocket. I later recommended that she inform Citizen Michonis, and she said she had already informed him. He told her to forget about it and that he would no longer bring anyone with him to the prison to avoid such problems in the future. The day after I surrendered the note to the warden's wife, the widow Capet continued, as she had done the day before, to request that the note be returned. I replied that it had fallen into the hands of the warden's wife, and she had put it into her pocket with several other papers in order to avoid any persecution.

Deputy: Have municipal police administrators or officers brought many people with them into the widow Capet's cell whenever they came?

Gilbert: Many came at different times with one, two, and sometimes three whom I presumed to be public functionaries.

Before Gilbert was asked to sign his deposition, a deputy asked him if Marie Antoinette had told him what the note from the chevalier contained.

Gilbert replied that she had told him and François Dufresne that the note said, "My protector, I will never forget you. I will always try to show you the mark of my zeal. If you need three hundred pounds, I am willing to offer it to you."[6]

The deputies ordered that Marie Antoinette, Madame Harel, and Michonis be placed in individual cells next to each other, but without any possibility of communication between them. Pierre Fontaine had just arrived at the Conciergerie and was brought in front of the committee.

Deputy: What is your name?

Fontaine: Pierre Fontaine, resident of rue de l'Oseille in the Marais.

Deputy: About fifteen days ago did you not have ten to twelve people dining with you, among them being Citizen Michonis?

Fontaine: Yes.

Deputy: Were you acquainted with all the individuals dining with you, especially a former chevalier of Saint-Louis?

Fontaine: I've known an individual who was brought by a woman named Dutilleul; he dined with me two or three times and said his name was Rougeville, living with her in the village of Vaugirard.

Deputy: Do you have any relationship with this individual?

Fontaine: No.

Deputy: How many times did you dine together?

Fontaine: I dined with him three times. The last time was last Sunday with two women, a merchant living near the St. Denis gate, and one whose name I do not know from the rue Philippeaux.

Deputy: Did you talk about news of the Revolution?

Fontaine: We talked interchangeably.

Deputy: Do you know in which company Rougeville is appointed and in what capacity?

Fontaine: I don't know anything.

Deputy: How did you know he was a chevalier of Saint-Louis?

Fontaine: From the citizeness Dutilleul.

Deputy: The house where Rougeville resides with Citizeness Dutilleul, is it only occupied by them?

Fontaine: Yes, they occupy the entire house and garden.

Deputy: Are there any servants in the house?

Fontaine: I only saw a woman servant and another old servant in the garden.

Deputy: Has it been a long time since Citizen Michonis and the individual Rougeville dined with you?

Fontaine: They dined there today.

Deputy: Do you know if that individual is currently in Paris?

Fontaine: I presume that he will remain in Paris tonight. According to the Dutilleul woman, they had business in Paris, and they would both stay here.

The importance of the interrogation with Fontaine was the discovery of Rougeville's name and that he was still in Paris. Moreover, they discovered that the chevalier had dined with Michonis and Fontaine on the very same day they interrogated Michonis. The deputies must have found it strange that Michonis had dined with the chevalier on the same day he denied even knowing him.

The widow Sophie Lebon Dutilleul, with whom Rougeville lodged, testified the next day that she had known Rougeville for eight months, during which he had only spoken about Marie Antoinette "with indifference." He had never mentioned visiting the Conciergerie or any plan to rescue the queen.[7] Dutilleul also stated that she had only seen Michonis and the chevalier de Rougeville dine together twice: once at Fontaine's home and the second time at her own. She remembered that the chevalier had once said, "Marie Antoinette must be much changed, and I suppose complains [*chafes*] a great deal." Michonis then replied, "No! She is tolerably cheerful. She's hardly changed at all, but her hair is almost white."[8]

The gendarmes who fetched Fontaine informed the deputies that he had made some curious remarks when he was brought to the Conciergerie. The deputies found it necessary to recall him for a second interview.[9]

Deputy: When you were called to appear here, how could you have suspected the reason why you were being called here? You said, "Ah, I know what this is about!"

Fontaine: Because you spoke about a chevalier of Saint-Louis, and that put me on track.

Deputy: Do you have some knowledge that Rougeville had relations with the widow Capet?

Fontaine: None at all.

Deputy: When coming here accompanied by a policeman, you said, "I know what it is about; it concerns the widow Capet, but I have nothing to say." Why did you say that?

Fontaine: Because nothing has been talked about but the widow Capet's testimony to the committee.

Deputy: What is the description of the man named Rougeville?

Fontaine: He's a small man, about five feet and pockmarked, with a little hair on the top of his head, wearing dangling earrings, a striped gray suit, brown hair, pale, clear complexion, and a face that is a little round.

After reviewing the interrogations thus far, the deputies decreed that Madame Dutilleul and Rougeville be arrested. Rougeville was to be held in solitary confinement until a thorough search could be made of both his papers and Dutilleul's. Fontaine was swiftly incarcerated in the Conciergerie with no possible communication with the outside world. This would prevent him from tipping Rougeville and Dutilleul off about their impending arrests.[10]

The next deposition was that of Gilbert's colleague, François Dufresne, who also guarded the queen's chambers.[11]

Deputy: Are you aware of a visit a few days ago to the widow Capet by Citizen Michonis who was accompanied by another man?

Dufresne: Yes.

Deputy: Could you tell us the particular circumstances of this interview and what has been said about it by Louis's widow?

Dufresne: Citizen Michonis came with an individual who was unknown to me. They both approached the table where she was sitting. She asked Michonis for news about her children, and he replied that they were well. Then I noticed a change in the expression on her face. Tears swelled up in her eyes, and her face turned red before she withdrew a little in front of the screen. She spoke to Michonis as the other individual stood behind Michonis, but I could not distinctly hear what they said. After this conversation, Michonis retired with the individual. My comrade reported to me that the widow Capet had made a confession relating to the interview with the individual whom Michonis had introduced in her cell. I have proof myself, because I've heard the same story that she had told my comrade; namely, that this person was a chevalier de Saint-Louis who had dropped the carnation in which was found a message, but she would not have noticed it if he had not made a signal to pick it up. She responded by pricking a piece of paper with a needle to form letters. My companion told me in front of the widow Capet that he had put the paper in his pocket as soon as the maid returned and, when she left, the woman caretaker (Madame Richard) put her hands in his pockets and took his papers, including the said note. In this manner he was letting the widow Capet know that she should not ask for the piece of paper, that it was in the hands of the warden's wife. I would add that the evening after being interviewed, she said in front of my comrade and me that she feared that we had noticed this individual and, shedding tears, she asked us not to repeat what she had said in this regard to us.

Next to be examined was the warden's wife, Madame Richard.

Deputy: What is your name?

Madame Richard: Marie Barassaint Richard, caretaker.*

Deputy: Do you have any relationship with the widow of Louis Capet?

Madame Richard: No.

Deputy: Do you know the means that one uses to talk to her?

Madame Richard: I don't know of any.

Deputy: Do you not know the individual who was seen with Citizen Michonis?

Madame Richard: I didn't notice anyone.

Deputy: Did you not receive a piece of paper that was given to you by a gendarme that had been pricked with a pin and had just come from the widow Capet?

Madame Richard: Gilbert, one of the gendarmes in the custody of the widow Capet, handed me a piece of paper and advised me to give it to Citizen Michonis, warning me that people here could compromise me. I then handed the paper to the citizen Michonis, who came here on the same day and almost at the same time.

---

*Some historians have used the name Magdeleine Rosay.

The deputies now had to recall Michonis, having evidence that he might have the infamous pinpricked note in his possession. Moreover, they were likely dissatisfied with his first testimony and frustrated by his inability to name the mysterious chevalier.[12]

Deputy: Do you have knowledge of the note that was given to the concierge by Gilbert?

Michonis: Here is the note that Citizen Richard gave to me.

Deputy: (Taking the note from Michonis) Do you know from whom this note comes?

Michonis: I have the honor to inform you that Madame Richard gave it to me. That is all I know.

Deputy: On what day did you receive the note?

Michonis: The next day or the second day after I entered with the individual about whom I spoke in my previous interrogation.*

Deputy: You've stated that you have never come here with more than one person at a time; however, it has now been established that you have introduced two or three persons at times.

Michonis: That could be.

Deputy: You've stated that you did not know the individual whom you introduced into the widow Capet's chambers. It is known that you were frequently found with him and that even today you have dined together at Fontaine's home!

Michonis: I was at Fontaine's home at three o'clock, and I found the individual sitting at the table.

Deputy: How is it possible that you didn't know his name when you have seen him several times?

Michonis: I swear to you that I did not know him.

Deputy: Didn't you have certain relations with him or some conversations during the time that you saw him at Fontaine's home!

Michonis: I have never had a conversation or a shared a secret with him because I do not know him. And we were only seen in public in front of all who were there.†

---

*Madame Richard testified that she gave him the note on the same day.
†This statement conflicts with Madame Dutilleul's prior testimony that Michonis had spoken with Rougeville.

Deputy: In the conversations of this individual were you ever suspicious that he was a counterrevolutionary or an uncivil man?

Michonis: I never heard anything; he only talked about things in general. If he had said something contrary to the revolution, I wouldn't have tolerated it.

Deputy: How, not knowing the character of this man, could you have been so foolish to bring him so unconcernedly where only public officials are permitted to keep special watch over the widow of Louis Capet!

Michonis: I did the same thing for him as I did for others, and knowing that surveillance was strongly in place for the widow Capet, I never had any second thoughts.

Deputy: You just said that you had reproached this citizen for having compromised you. How then, and in what manner, did you know that you were compromised?

Michonis: Because Madame Richard told me that it was a chevalier and that someone had given her the note that she had put in my hands.

Deputy: Knowing that this individual had compromised you, and you, a public official, being found with him, how were you not informed of the name of someone you learned to be a chevalier?

Michonis: Because I did not think it a matter of importance and thought that there was nothing more to the matter; I didn't follow up on the matter because it didn't seem to merit it.

Deputy: We discovered that when Citizen Richard gave you the note from the widow Capet, you told her that she should forget about it and there was no reason to speak of it. Avow that this is true.

Michonis: I did tell her what you have just said because in effect I did not attach any importance to it.

Deputy: When Citizeness Richard gave you the note that she was asked to give you, didn't she tell you that the note came from the Capet woman and that it was destined for the chevalier in question?

Michonis: She did not tell me that it was destined for this chevalier.

Deputy: Wasn't it your duty, knowing that the note came from the Capet woman and that it was written with pin pricks, to discover for whom it was intended and what it contained? And wasn't it probable, because there was a complaint about the introduction of this individual when you received the note, that you should have been suspicious that it could have been him to whom it was addressed? That it was an affair to be investigated for the public interest! Being found with this individual, why did you not follow up on such a serious matter as expected of a public official?

Michonis: I reiterate that I attached little importance to the event, and I thought it was no longer important.

Deputy: You have stated that Madame Richard warned you that the man you brought with you to see the widow of Louis Capet was a chevalier. You realized the danger of admitting him and you have even reproached him today; therefore, you must have known that such a man would be dubious. You must have been blind or indifferent about your duties in order not to have arrested this man immediately after receiving the note from Madame Richard!

Michonis: I tell you that I regarded the event as being finished and not needing to be followed up on further. It is so true, that I found myself with him today without knowing him and, since it is true, I therefore did not give him the note.

Deputy: When we asked if you had asked the individual if it was he for whom the note was intended, you responded in the negative. However, you just told us that you reproached him because this note could have been intended for him.

Michonis: I have complained to this individual for putting me in the most embarrassing situation and that it was enough to assume that the note that was given to me could have possibly been destined for him.

Deputy: How did the individual respond to your reproaches?

Michonis: He told me that he was angry and that he didn't see it in that respect.

Deputy: Do you know where this man lives?

Michonis: Yes, citizen. He lodges in Vaugirard with Citizeness Dutilleul.

Deputy: Do you know his name?

Michonis: No, I do not know it, and I never did.

D: As you have dined many times with him at Citizen Fontaine's home, we are aware that you know each other. Because you know the name and address of the woman with whom he lodges, it is surprising that you wouldn't know his name as well and that, in all probability, that you wouldn't know each other!

Michonis: I tell you I don't know him.

Deputy: So you didn't hear his name pronounced at Citizen Fontaine's home? And despite the interest you must have in knowing him, since this man has compromised you, why haven't you since tried to discover his name?

Michonis: I give you the same answer that I gave you before. I didn't believe it was important for me to know it because I didn't find the affair to be of any importance.

The deputies found Michonis's testimony farfetched—he surely had to know the chevalier's name. They immediately had him arrested, and he was sent to the Abbaye prison, where he would remain until May 1794.* While there, he wrote the minister of justice, asking to be brought to the Tribunal for trial as soon as possible. He also wrote his superiors thanking them for not filling his post with another deputy until he was found guilty of a crime.[13] This was perhaps an indication that Michonis believed he would soon be set free.

Rougeville, however, could not be found. Madame Dutilleul reported that he had packed two shirts and some socks on September 3, the day he had lunch with Michonis at Fontaine's home. After the meal, Rougeville left, and she never saw or heard from him again. Rougeville had hastily fled Paris to avoid prosecution; he was well on his way to safety in Belgium.[14]

After Michonis's second interrogation, the deputies now had the pin-pricked note in their possession but were unable to decipher it. They therefore recalled Madame Richard.

When shown the illegible pinpricked note, she confirmed that it was the same note that she had given Michonis. The note she was shown, however, had additional pinpricks to scramble the original message. Therefore, if she was telling the truth that this was the exact same note, then she would have had to be the one who scrambled the message before giving the note to Michonis. Gilbert would not have had time to alter it.

The question would then arise as to whether Madame Richard could have been so loyal to the queen as to undertake such a cover-up. If she did not mean it was literally the exact same note, then Michonis must have scrambled the message.[15]

The interrogators had no other option but to recall Marie Antoinette for another round of questioning. It was obvious that the queen had lied in her first interview, and the deputies now had the evidence to confront her.[16]

---

*The Abbaye prison was demolished in 1854 for the construction of the boulevard Saint-Germain.

Deputy: From the testimony and the exhibits which are in our hands, we know your earlier denial was false.

Queen: Give me proof.

Deputy: You were asked if you had one day seen and recognized the former chevalier of Saint-Louis, and you said no.

Queen: Recalling the day he came, I now know who he was.

Deputy: We asked you if the same man had given you a carnation, and you said no, but the opposite has been learned in others' testimonies.

Queen: The second time that he entered my cell is when I learned that there was a carnation. I hadn't paid enough attention to notice it.

Deputy: You confirm that there was one?

Queen: Yes.

Deputy: You denied having picked up the carnation and taking a note from it.

Queen: I picked it up and took the note from it.

Deputy: What did the note contain?

Queen: Some vague phrases: "What do you want to do, what do you plan to do, I was in prison, I got away by a miracle; I'll come back Friday."

Deputy: Was that the first or the second time that you saw him?

Queen: I only recognized him this one time, and if he had come before, I would not have known him.

Deputy: This note didn't contain anything else or any offer?

Queen: There was an offer of money, but I didn't need it, and I wouldn't accept it from anyone.

Deputy: It appears that you recognized this person. Do you know his name?

Queen: I remember seeing him often, but I don't know his name.

Deputy: On what occasion did you see him?

Queen: I saw him at the Tuileries.

Deputy: Why did he call you his protector in the note he wrote you?

Queen: That was not so.

Deputy: What happened to that note?

Queen: I tore it into a thousand little pieces.

Deputy: Did you respond to his note?

Queen: Respond? No.

Deputy: If you didn't respond, did you at least write? What did you write?

Queen: With pinpricks I tried to write, "I am being watched; I can't talk or write."

Deputy: Do you remember the paper on which you wrote?

Queen: Yes.

Deputy: Is this the note?

Queen: (After looking at it) Yes, it's the same one.*

Deputy: Did this man say a few words to you?

Queen: Some vague words.

Deputy: Do you remember these words?

Queen: At the moment I spoke of sensitivity, he said, "Do you still have heart?" And I replied, "All I will ever need, but it is deeply afflicted."

Deputy: Did this man shed any tears?

Queen: He could have been moved; it could have seemed so.

Deputy: Did the administrator Michonis make you a proposal?

Queen: Never.

Deputy: Why did you exhibit so much interest in seeing him again?

Queen: Because his honesty and humanity for those who are so unfortunate is touching.

Deputy: There seems to have been, however, another motive when he introduced a man into your chamber who offered you his services?

Queen: It is believed that Michonis didn't know this man himself. As to my interest, I showed it at the time of his nomination as municipality official.

At this point the interrogation turned to past events to ascertain whether Michonis had been of service to the queen in the Tuileries or the Temple before transferring her to the Conciergerie. She was adamant that she had never seen him there and had no relationship with him whatsoever. The deputies then questioned the queen about her political prowess

---

*The queen, as well as the deputies, must have known at this point that someone had altered the note with additional pinpricks to make it illegible. Michonis was the likely culprit.

while the king was still on the throne, as if recollecting why the queen was imprisoned in the first place.

Deputy: Were you instructed about political affairs?

Queen: I only knew about what was told to me by the person [the king] to whom I was uniquely attached.

Deputy: Did he impart his projects to you?

Queen: He told me what his confidence in me prompted him to tell.

Deputy: Did you approve of those projects?

Queen: Anything that could bring tranquility to all was his wish and mine.

Deputy: If those are your sentiments, why didn't you punish those in the Tuileries who insulted the republican troops by singing, "Ensure the salvation of the Empire"?

Queen: I don't know these details. I enjoyed his confidence, I strongly shared his sorrows, but I didn't ask for any punishment.

Deputy: How can it be that, if the happiness of the people was the sole object of your wishes, the people were so unhappy, so constantly annoyed, and bullied by the treachery of the throne?

Queen: There has been a lot of betrayal, and I am not able to know all or tell all; what I know is that his heart only wanted happiness.

It was surprising that the deputies continued on without objection to Marie Antoinette's vague and ambiguous responses about the Carnation Plot. It was even more surprising that the deputies did not question her about the details of Gilbert's letter and Dufresne's confirmation of them. More specifically, they did not question her about showing Gilbert the pinpricked note or about asking him to convey the letter to the carnation-bearing visitor who had accompanied Michonis.

Perhaps the deputies did not believe Gilbert's story. The queen surely would not have been foolish enough to ask the prison guard to convey such a message—at least not without a bribe or reward. Or perhaps the deputies believed Gilbert's story but knew that Marie Antoinette would never be forthcoming about it.

Once the interview and answers were transcribed, the deputies attached the infamous pinpricked note to the transcription with a pin. Because it was impossible to read the note, the deputies believed that additional holes had been added to scramble the message. The note had changed hands from the queen, to Gilbert, to Madame Richard, and finally to Michonis; it was most likely altered by Michonis, who realized he had the most to lose.[17]

In all, the deputies were most likely fed up with the all the lies, ambiguities, and contradictions of the depositions. It had been a long night, and the Committee of General Security had discovered nothing of importance after fifteen hours of interrogations. Indeed, they had failed to uncover an intricate plan to rescue the queen set in action the night before and were none the wiser that Warden Richard and his wife had been bribed and that Gilbert and Dufresne had been paid fifty gold louis to keep quiet.[18]

According to the conspirators' plan, Michonis would enter the Conciergerie with orders to return Marie Antoinette to the Temple prison. To protect the warden and his wife, a false entry for the queen's discharge would have been entered in the registrar's book. Once Michonis escorted the queen outside the prison, Rougeville would then escort her to the border.

En route to the border, the queen was to find safe haven with Madame Jarjayes at Livry. This could only mean that Baron Jean Pierre de Batz was perhaps the mastermind behind the escape or one of the conspirators in the plot. At the very least de Batz was aware of the attempt to free the queen and had the wherewithal to fund it.

On Friday, August 30, the plan was put into motion. Michonis and Rougeville returned to the Conciergerie to inform the queen of the details of the escape for the following Tuesday, September 2, at ten o'clock. Warden Richard, his wife, and Madame Harel were also informed. Rougeville left four hundred gold louis and ten thousand pounds in revolutionary assignats to bribe the prison guards. The queen was weak from bouts of hemorrhaging, but she promised to comply with her conspirators' plans.*

The queen was ready when Michonis arrived on Tuesday evening at ten o'clock. She left her cell, crossed the adjoining room where the guards kept watch, and entered Richard's office before passing through two *guichets* into the small courtyard. Just before she went through an iron gate into the Cour du Mai, either Gilbert or Dufresne stopped her.

---

*Axel Fersen reported in his memoirs that Rougeville confirmed the queen's bleeding spells at this time.

Although bribed earlier, whichever guard it was must have changed his mind and refused to let the queen leave the premises. Despite Michonis's pleas, the guard threatened to call for assistance if Michonis pressed the matter any further.

It is unknown whether the guard lost his nerve at the last minute, demanded more money, or had simply planned all the while to pocket the bribe without helping the queen escape. Whatever the reason, the attempt to free Marie Antoinette had failed, and she was escorted back to her cell.

It is more likely that Gilbert, rather than Dufresne, had stopped the queen.* The following day, Gilbert submitted his letter denouncing the queen and Michonis. He also revealed the existence of the mysterious note hidden in the carnation's petals. By the time the deputies held their first interrogation at four o'clock in the afternoon, Rougeville had long since disappeared. Warden Richard and his wife were immediately relieved of their duties and imprisoned.

Mademoiselle Fouché, the pious woman who had gained the confidence of the queen, confirmed the Richards' arrest. Mademoiselle Fouché visited the Conciergerie the same day as the interrogations and, finding that much had changed from her previous visit, hurried to La Force prison to speak with its warden, Monsieur Antoine Bault, and his wife. There she learned about the Carnation Plot and that Michonis and the Richards had been arrested.

Rougeville later related his failed attempt to Count Hans Axel von Fersen, and although Fersen believed Rougeville to be "slightly crazy" and "full of himself," the chevalier's description of the events and their timing seem logical.[19] Also, the memoirs of the queen's daughter do not contradict Rougeville's narrative:

> I learned since her [the queen's] death that they had wanted to save her from the Conciergerie, and that, unfortunately, this charming plan failed. I was assured that the gendarmes who guarded her and the warden's wife were bribed. The attempt to escape failed because she was told to go to the second guard, but she made a mistake and went to the first; others say she was already

---

*Gilbert was known to be a gambler. Was this a ruse to help pay his gambling debts?

out of her room and down the stairs when a jailer objected to her departure, although he had been bribed, and he forced my mother to go back to her cell, which foiled the scheme.[20]

The revolutionaries were in the dark about the actual plot to free the queen, but surely they were shocked by the carnation affair leading up to it: strange visitors had been allowed to enter the queen's cell, the stories of the guards and the maid were aggravatingly contradictory, and the queen had blatantly lied to the deputies in her first interrogation. Therefore, on September 10, municipal officials entered the queen's cell and removed all of her remaining jewels and trinkets and anything else that could be used to bribe someone. The queen's guards and Madame Harel were dismissed, and the guards were replaced with a sentinel at the queen's door. He was instructed to permit no one to enter or to come within ten steps of her window facing the women's prison yard.

This arrangement did not last long. The queen's cell was no longer considered safe, and on September 11 six deputies arrived at the Conciergerie "for the purpose of choosing a place for the detention of the widow Capet other than that in which she was then confined." They examined various rooms of the prison before deciding upon one used by the pharmacist Jacques Antoine Lacour. He was to vacate the chambers and clear it on the same day. This would allow the citizen Jean-François Godard to make the alterations necessary to transform it into a cell "with the least possible delay."[21]

Marie Antoinette was moved to her new cell nearer to the Girondins' Chapel two days later, on the forty-second day of her captivity; it was so humid and damp that her sleeves and hair were soaking wet. And the queen was never left alone; someone was always entering her cell, day and night, to be certain that she was securely locked up. Rosalie told historian Lafont d'Aussonne:

> Every day and at every moment new spies came to trouble her resigned silence and her fervent prayers; architects, brutes in red caps, ferocious and threatening wretches with their caps on their heads, forced their way into her new cell, examining the bars, gratings, bolts, doors, the walls, and even the stones of the pavement.[22]

Marie Antoinette's new cell (16) as of September 11

Rosalie added that she was obliged to provide dinner every day for over a dozen persons who kept watch on everything. Whenever they tried the bars and sounded the walls, they would mutter to themselves, "Is it possible that she can escape here? Could she escape there?"

À SAVOIR . . .

The Controversy

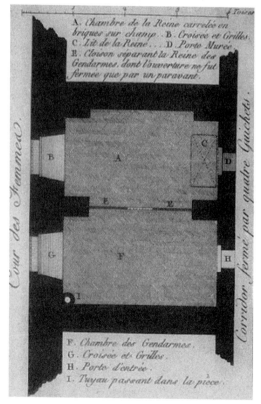

Marie Antoinette's new cell

Marie Antoinette's new cell reconstructed from Lacour's pharmacy (A) was separated from an adjoining chamber (F) by a partition and a screen. Her bed (C) was placed next to a door (D), which had been walled up. The window (B) that opened onto the women's prison yard was closed with a sheet of iron up to the fifth crossbar; the rest was grated with iron bars placed close together. The second window (G) was completely blocked with a sheet of iron. Two additional bolts were attached to the existing door (H), and a second heavier door was added, opening on the inside of the cell and secured with a lock.[23]

It is not known whether the pharmacy was on the ground floor or the first floor. The first floor would have been more secure, but most historians have agreed that the queen's new cell was on the ground floor. If so, this cell would at least have been more secure than the previous one because it was further from the entrance, with more guarded *guichets* through which to pass.[24]

8

TIGHTENED SECURITY

When the queen asked for an English cotton cover for her bed, Warden Bault asked Fouquier-Tinville if he could procure one. "You dare ask?" snapped the prosecutor. "You deserve the guillotine!"

—Jules Janin, "The Queen's Gray Hair"[1]

Paris
September 1793

On September 21, the warden of La Force prison, Monsieur Antoine Bault, became the new warden of the Conciergerie.* It was not a coveted post, and Bault and his wife hesitated before taking on the daunting responsibility. They knew, of course, that Warden Toussaint Richard, his wife, and his eldest son had all just been arrested.† But the Baults were indebted to Marie Antoinette, who had patronized them when she was queen of France. When the new prison administrator, François Dangé, informed the Baults that the brute Antoine Simon from the Temple prison was being considered for the wardenship of the Conciergerie, they quickly solicited and obtained the position. In fact, they looked forward to using the opportunity to console

---

*Bault's name was sometimes written Lebeau and Beau, but Bault was the correct spelling.
†The family was imprisoned and placed in solitary confinement at the Sainte-Pélagie and Madelonnettes prisons.

and soften the captivity of their former mistress, as they had done for the royal prisoners in La Force.[2]

Madame Bault had shared her husband's responsibilities at La Force while raising her children there. When Jean-Baptiste Michonis was superintendent of prisons, he became acquainted with the Baults. Moreover, he had even informed them of his plan to escort the chevalier de Rougeville into the queen's cell, where Rougeville would propose the plot to rescue her. He also told them that Warden Richard was involved in the conspiracy. He may not have known, however, that the Baults had already met Rougeville when they dined on one occasion at the home of Madame Sophie Lebon Dutilleul in Vaugirard.

When Warden Bault made his first appearance before Marie Antoinette in his capacity as warden, she immediately realized that the Richards had been replaced. Bault jingled the keys in his hand, dressed in the carmagnole, the revolutionary style of the day, with his neck shirt open.* He kept his head covered because nobility was no longer recognized by removing one's hat,[3] but the queen still recognized a familiar face.

"Ah, it is you!" the queen said. "I am so happy that it is you who has come here."

Warden Bault was known to be an honest man, and Rosalie said that although at first sight he seemed rough and severe, he was really "not a bad fellow." She continued to prepare the queen's food, but both she and Bault's oldest daughter, Victoire, were forbidden to go outside the walls of the prison for provisions. A sentinel was placed in the women's prison yard in front of the queen's window; it was low enough to allow him to see everything that took place in the new cell.[4]

Bault was warned that he risked his head if the queen was not kept incarcerated according to the newly decreed and more secure conditions. Although Jean Gilbert and François Dufresne had been removed from their posts, Bault was not permitted to approach the prisoner unless accompanied by two gendarmes. The deputies told him that she would receive the same "coarse" food as any other prisoner.[5]

---

*The carmagnole was a short jacket worn by the working-class sans-culottes; the name derives from the peasant costume of the town of Carmagnola in the Piedmont region of Italy.

"I won't hear of it!" said Bault. "This is my prisoner whom I must protect with my head. Someone could poison her.

"It must be me who ensures her food," he continued. "Not even a drop of water will enter here without my permission."

And the deputies agreed with Bault. From that moment forward Madame Bault and her daughter were in charge of planning the queen's meals. When the Baults arrived, they also noticed that the queen was being served impure water in a filthy pitcher. They immediately corrected the situation with spring water from Arcueil.[6]

Madame Bault and Victoire, helped by Rosalie, who had become accustomed to the queen's tastes, attempted to improve their cooking for the queen. An ordinary meal consisted of soup and two dishes, and the vendors at the market provided desserts such as melons and peaches for their pitiful queen. However, the fruits had to be smuggled into the Conciergerie, requiring some precaution. Since the departure of the Richards, the warden could no longer shop for the provisions; food suppliers had to pass through the *guichets* with their goods.

One of the suppliers was Monsieur Lemaire, who lived nearby on the rue Sainte-Anne. After he showed an interest in having a glance at the queen, the gendarmes told him that if he brought them their dinner, it could be arranged the very same evening. When Lemaire returned with their meal, one of the guards asked for some sugar for the peaches, but Lemaire had forgotten it. Out of the blue, the queen said, "Messieurs, here you are," and gave the guards her sugar.[7]

It is doubtful that the queen's kind gesture could sway the gendarmes. As guards of the former queen of France, they were monitored themselves by prison inspectors, police officers, and the ruthless deputies of the Committee of General Security.

Distracted by Victoire's cheerful nature, the guards did give her some leeway to mend the queen's linen, to hem her dress, left tattered by the humidity, and to distribute the scraps to prisoners in the women's yard as mementos. Victoire stayed busy mending socks and slippers and cleaning the queen's chambers every day. She was worked to the point of exhaustion—tears would even fall down her cheeks—but there was a limit to the gendarmes' compassion.

Warden Bault, for example, was observed very closely as well. He was even reprimanded for stretching an old piece of tapestry along the wall to alleviate the humidity in the queen's cell.[8]

"Don't you see?" said Bault. "It's to block the voices so that nothing can be heard from the next room?"

The guise worked. "That's good," said a deputy. "You did well."

To deceive the wretches, Bault later told his wife, he had to "speak their language."

Madame Bault and Rosalie rarely entered the queen's cell, but Victoire entered it quite often to make the bed and serve the queen's meals. On one occasion, when Rosalie happened to serve dinner, the queen removed her cap and asked the maid if she would dress her hair.[*]

Rosalie took the comb and was about to start combing when Warden Bault entered the cell. He rushed forward and pushed Rosalie aside.[9]

"Away, away, I am supposed to do that!" he said.

Astonished by his behavior, the queen stood, gave him an imperious look, and said, "Thank you, I can manage it myself."

She twisted her hair up in a bun and put her cap back on her head. Then she sadly offered Rosalie a piece of white ribbon that was on the table. "Take this ribbon," she said. "Keep it always in remembrance of me."[†]

Rosalie took her leave of the queen, wiping away her tears, but Bault joined her in the corridor and snatched the ribbon from her hands. Did he fear for Rosalie's life, or perhaps his own, over such a small gift from the queen?

"I am very sorry to have vexed that poor lady, but my post is so difficult that a mere nothing is enough to make one tremble," he said.

"I can never forget that poor Richard and his wife are at the bottom of a dungeon," he continued. "In God's name, Rosalie, do not commit any act of imprudence, or I should be a lost man."[10]

Bault's reaction may have hurt Marie Antoinette's feelings, but she must have realized the danger of being her caretaker. The Richard family was already imprisoned and could very well be escorted to the scaffold for their

---

[*]"Vous allez faire mon chignon?"
[†]The same ribbon was recorded in the expense register in the amount of eighteen cents.

compassion. She must also have understood that the warden was doing his best to soften her situation without compromising himself.

Bault had already risked being chastised for worrying about the queen's comfort in a cell with no stove for heat. When the queen asked for an English cotton cover for her bed, Warden Bault asked prosecutor Antoine Quentin Fouquier-Tinville if he could procure one.

"You dare ask?" snapped the prosecutor. "You deserve the guillotine!"[11]

Madame Bault found a way to bypass Fouquier-Tinville's consent. She exchanged the queen's cover with the best wool blanket that she could find by attaching it to the mattress without the prosecutor ever knowing.

"I don't know how I could have been proud for not doing what I did or what I could do for the queen," she said. "She is the model of the most religious resignation and the most heroic constancy. So much kindness, gentleness, and sensitivity along with her courage brought us to tears when we were alone."[12]

Marie Antoinette sometimes said to the Baults, "I will never be happy enough to be able to reward you for what you do for me." And she gave them a pair of gloves and a lock of her hair that appeared to be a keepsake. Bault clenched the gift in his hand, but the watchful gendarmes noticed it; one of them lurched forward, saying, "What did someone just give you?"[13]

Bault had no choice but to open his hand and show the guards what he had received. The guards confiscated the items on the spot and conveyed them to Fouquier-Tinville. If the Baults later understood that the keepsakes were intended for the queen's children in the Temple, they would have surely shared the queen's pain.

The Baults used every occasion to spend time with the queen. Perhaps they were saddened when they watched her forlornly writing on the wall, using one of the pins that held her clothing together to prick words on the wall.*

When Warden Bault combed the queen's hair, she would take advantage of these moments to ask about her children and Élisabeth at the Temple. Bault could sometimes give her news because he had information from

---

*The writing was later whitewashed.

Monsieur François Hüe,* who still had connections in the Temple and never feared visiting the Conciergerie.[14]

The queen would always show her gratitude, but without a gesture or a movement that could betray her.

"I call you good [*bon*] because you are," she whispered with a smile. "And this is better than being beautiful [*beau*]." Bault is pronounced the same as *beau*.[15]

Marie Antoinette feared compromising those who took an interest in her. She had to keep her composure and be careful when talking at all times; the slightest wink or gesture could raise her guardians' eyebrows.

To keep the guards from loitering in the queen's cell, where they passed the time drinking, playing cards, and smoking on the other side of a screen, Warden Bault took the key, leaving the guards outside the exterior door. The noise and swearing were eliminated, and because there was less light for reading a copy of *The Voyages of Captain Cook* that Bault had provided, the queen spent more time in prayer.[16]

As Bault was combing the queen's hair a few days after his arrival, Rosalie was making the queen's bed when she noticed patches of white hair at the queen's temples, though there were none on her forehead or in the rest of her hair. The queen said that the cause of the white hair was the trouble when the mob of Parisians marched to Versailles and attacked the palace on October 5 and 6, 1789. Rosalie's story, if true, would thus refute the oft-told account that the queen's hair turned white overnight during the violence at Versailles.

The previous caretakers, Richard and his family, were not the only supporters of the queen suffering for their loyalty. Jean-Baptiste Michonis was incarcerated for introducing the chevalier of Rougeville into the queen's cell, and rumors were also circulating that Michonis was receiving visits from aristocrats and unsworn priests in his cell. This only fueled the clamor for the queen's head.[17] The police observer Perirère wrote,

A public outcry is spreading about a great conspiracy of Marie Antoinette, where all the people who surround her are accused of having favored her

*Hüe had attended to the royal family in the Temple with Jean-Baptiste Cléry for a short time.

correspondence with the enemies from within and from outside. Michonis, the police director, was responsible for giving her a bouquet that contained a note with approximately these words: "Rest assured; I have money and men ready."

In public and in private, citizens are outraged by this plot, and I think the moment is right to press for the trial of this proud and forever conspiratorial Queen, who continues to put her head in the balance with that of all the French.[18]

Security tightened in the Conciergerie as the public uproar increased. The guards searched through the queen's laundry, and she was only allowed a change of clothing every ten days. At the same time, the queen's health was faltering. She complained of pain in one of her legs, covering it with her cushion to keep it warm.

The queen also suffered from insomnia, anxiety, dizziness, weakness, and frequent bouts of vaginal bleeding. Rosalie attributed the hemorrhaging to the "crushing sorrows, the foul air in her cell, and lack of exercise."[19] These miseries were perhaps every bit as disturbing as the presence of the guards, who violated her modesty as they watched her change clothes. When the queen discretely removed the bloody dressings, Rosalie disposed of them secretly but with great difficulty; the inspections were multiplying at all hours of the day and night. And the noise became unbearable, with the locks continuously clanking and the door of the queen's dungeon screeching as deputies entered and exited.

On October 3, Deputy Jean-Baptiste-André Amar of the Committee of General Security decreed that 129 deputies of the Gironde party be denounced as outlaws, arrested, and brought to trial.* The Girondins had campaigned for the end of the monarchy but came into conflict with the more radical Jacobins. On the same day, a large number of the Girondins were imprisoned in the Conciergerie, the same prison that housed the fallen queen of France. That these Girondins would be tried and most likely face the guillotine before the queen sparked another public contro-

---

*The Gironde party campaigned for the end of the monarchy but later called for more moderate measures, conflicting with the more radical factions and thus leading to their mass conviction and execution.

versy. They argued that the queen was the "guiltiest of all" and "her head should be the first to fall."[20]

The committees, clubs, and cafés of Paris were all calling for a speedy trial of the Agrippina, a reference to the ruthless, domineering, and violent mother of Nero. "I rang my alarm bell to all French ears on the infamous Antoinette," wrote lawyer and politician Armand-Joseph Guffroy in his journal. "Keep Marie Antoinette in prison to make peace, you say drearily, and I say to you, 'Make her jump like a carp with its hands tied behind its back.'"

"We aim to judge the Austrian tigress from twelve until two o'clock in the afternoon," the deputy Louis Marie Prudhomme wrote, "and we demand the offenses to condemn her; if justice is served, she will be hacked up like mincemeat in a pâté."[21]

And the town criers shouted in the Parisian streets, often using profane language:

> All dogs chase their prey. It is just as natural for the royals and their offspring to eat men as the wolves eat sheep.
>
> Since the f**king bitch has reigned, she has dreamed only of murder and carnage. More than a million men have been her victims. The crimes that she has committed aren't any more than rose water compared to those she plans to commit.
>
> Pity could not touch this ogresse!
>
> The Capet woman hasn't been punished. It is finally time that the convention draws the sword of law on this guilty head. Already malice abuses your silence and the rumor spreads that Marie Antoinette has been secretly tried by your court, exonerated, and sent to the Temple—as if it were possible that a woman covered with the blood of the French people could be bleached by a people's court!
>
> The f**king bitch needs to be skinned alive.[22]

The town criers in the provinces were just as vicious and profane as those in the capital in expressing their rage. However, there remained those who were not stirred by the public's cry for revenge. Citizen Le Tomm (Thome?), owner of the magnificent Hôtel de France on the rue de Bourbon-Villeneuve, dared to demand the acquittal of the queen and her exile to Austria. He claimed that such an act would be politically sound, honor humanity, stop the emigration of citizens, and free thousands of soldiers from battle.[23]

It had also been rumored that the emperor of Austria offered twenty thousand French prisoners caught in recent battles to the French republic in exchange for Marie Antoinette. While the government continued to discuss the upcoming trial of the queen, there were those, especially workers and bourgeoisie, who had become disillusioned with the Revolution and dared even to whisper in favor of the exchange. In the privacy of their homes, they pled the queen's case, but they did not have the courage to express their opinions in public, as Le Tomm did. He soon "groaned in the dungeons of the Conciergerie" for having criticized the government too harshly.[24]

Le Tomm had risked his freedom, his life, and his fortune, as well as those of his family, by speaking his mind in his struggle against the will of the revolutionaries. His speech has been preserved:

> Citizens, I will not seek to contradict the speakers before me. Almost all spoke badly about Marie Antoinette, and I want to think they sincerely believed what they said. They repeat what they have heard without inquiring whether there was truth or calumny in all these stories. As for me who, long before the Revolution, lived in Versailles, I declare before God that during this time I only heard this princess spoken of with admiration for her charity and her virtues. Consult the poor in these provinces, and you will be astonished at their stories.
>
> Finally, assume that Marie Antoinette is not faultless; returning her to her family, you are separated from her and freed forever. And remember, please, the great advantage that a similar action gives you. Twenty thousand captive soldiers returned to their families who mourn them, and our representatives themselves see their irons unlocked. This political act and humanity will have, I have no doubt, other benefits: foreign powers will calm down, the wealthy of all countries will return to France, and finally work will resume in this capital, where the grass covers our pavement.[25]

Fouquier-Tinville was far from being swayed by martyrs such as Le Tomm. The more obscene and absurd the denunciations, the happier he was that the day was soon coming when the queen would be convicted. He was ready to help in any way possible to see this end, though he had no luck in searching the infamous iron chest (*armoire de fer*).

The iron chest (Note the serpent, Louis XVI, vomiting into the Phrygian, the symbolic cap of the Revolution.)
(Bibliothèque Nationale Française)

The iron chest was Louis XVI and Marie Antoinette's hiding place for secret documents while they were under house arrest at the Tuileries. Fouquier-Tinville discovered that the queen had most likely burned all compromising documents. This setback prompted the prosecutor to repudiate the decree of October 3 calling for the speedy trial and judgment of the queen.*

Fouquier-Tinville wrote the president of the convention two days later: "I have the honor to inform the convention that the decree issued by it on the 3rd of this month, ordering the revolutionary court to promptly transact, and without interruption, the judgment of the widow Capet, was given to me last night. But until now, no evidence against Marie Antoinette has been

---

*"The National Convention, on the proposal of a member, decrees that the revolutionary court will transact promptly and without interruption the judgment of the widow Capet."

conveyed to me. So, considering the decree of the convention, I am unable to execute it until having all such documents."[26]

While Fouquier-Tinville pushed for the queen's trial, the queen was watched even more closely after Madame Marie Harel and the guards were removed. Rosalie, however, was kept in the service of the queen after the Carnation Plot. After all, the deputies had no reason to be suspicious of her; she never mingled with anyone in the prison. However, even though prohibited from leaving the grounds, she was still watched closely.

Rosalie's father came from the province to visit her soon after the Carnation Plot, but security was very tight. He was able to see his daughter with some difficulty, and she escorted him to her room. Warden Bault chastised Rosalie for this. "It is forbidden to receive and allow any visit," he told her. "My own family does not come here."[27]

The warden turned to her father and said, "Do not be with your daughter more than four or five minutes, sir, and do not come back."

Rosalie did not even have time to offer her father a refreshment. She pointed to a chicken that was roasting on the spit and whispered, "It is for the poor queen that we have here." Her father sighed and departed.

The next day Rosalie accidentally dropped a morning newspaper in the queen's cell. She had put it under her scarf and did not notice it was missing until she was in the warden's office. Worried, she quickly confessed the accident to Bault, who became even more concerned.

"Come quickly," he said, "let's go back to the dungeon. Take this carafe of water, and we will exchange it for the other; I see no way to get us there."

They had to alert the guards, and when they entered the queen's cell, Rosalie found her paper. Fortunately, neither the queen nor the guards had noticed it.

Marie Antoinette had not felt well during the heat spell at the end of August, and now she suffered from the cold and the humidity during the first two weeks of October. She rarely complained to Rosalie, but Rosalie was saddened not to be able to ease the queen's suffering. In the evenings, Rosalie never failed to take the queen's jacket from underneath her pillow, warm it by the fire in her room, and quickly put it back under the queen's blanket.

The queen noticed these small touches of Rosalie's devotion, and she would thank the maid with grateful eyes. Since the queen was never given a lamp, Rosalie prolonged her evening cell duties as long as possible before leaving the queen to her solitude in the obscure light of the lamp in the women's prison yard.

Unbeknownst to Marie Antoinette, there were other schemes to rescue her besides the Carnation Plot. One would not attract any attention until months later, but a barber by the name of Jean-Baptiste Basset and his accomplice, Catherine Fournier, were swiftly arrested in October.

Among the other sixteen accomplices arrested were Fournier's fourteen-year-old son, another barber, Guillaume Lemille, and his wife, and workers and small merchants of a nearby neighborhood. Their plan was to assemble five hundred men, including soldiers who they believed could win over and carry the queen off by force.[28]

"It will not happen as the death of the king," said Madame Fournier. "It is time to act, to meet; if we remain inactive, this poor unfortunate will perish."

Fournier's son could not restrain his joy at the thought of restoring the monarchy. He said that three-quarters of the inhabitants of Paris were waiting for such a riot to rise and save the queen.[29]

However, Basset and Madame Fournier were betrayed by an agent of the police who had wormed himself into their confidence by pretending to be a royalist.

À SAVOIR . . .

Count Fersen Meets Rougeville

Immediately after the Carnation Plot, the chevalier de Rougeville fled from the French authorities and found refuge in Brussels. When Count Hans Axel von Fersen, also in Brussels, was informed of the chevalier's arrival, he visited him for news of Marie Antoinette in the Conciergerie. At first sight, Fersen found the chevalier to be a man "slightly crazy and full of himself for what he had done, giving himself airs of great importance."[30]

Rougeville told Fersen that he knew the rich American widow Madame Dutilleul, and together with an acquaintance named Pierre Fontaine they had devised a scheme to save the queen. After their meeting at Fontaine's home, Michonis invited Rougeville into the prison of which he was the superintendent.

Rougeville told Fersen about the events that took place that evening in the Conciergerie. Rougeville said that he and Michonis left the queen, but she asked the gendarmes to recall them; he then told the queen to be brave and that he would bring her money to bribe the gendarmes.

However, Rougeville's story differed from those of the witnesses brought to testify in front of the Committee of General Security when he told Fersen that he had carried on what appeared to be a very lengthy conversation with Marie Antoinette. Fersen was perhaps right when he said Rougeville was "slightly crazy." Such a long conversation would not have been possible with the guards Gilbert and Dufresne both on watch.[31]

III

THE QUEEN'S ARRAIGNMENT

ACTE D'ACCUSATION.

ANTOINE QUENTIN, FOUQUIER-TINVILLE, Accusateur Public du Tribunal Criminel extraordinaire et révolutionnaire, établi a Paris par *Décret de la Convention Nationale du 10 mars 1793,* l'an deuxième de la République, sans aucun recours au Tribunal de Cassation, en vertu du pouvoir a lui donné par *l'Article deux, d'un autre Décret de la Convention du cinq avril suivant,* portant que l'Accusateur Public dudit Tribunal est autorisé à faire arrêter, poursuivre et juger sur la dénonciation des autorités constituées où des Citoyens ————

EXPOSE que *Suivant* ...

Arraignment of the widow Capet

9

PROSECUTOR
FOUQUIER-TINVILLE

"Marie Antoinette, the widow of Louis Capet, has since her residence in France been the scourge and bloodsucker of the French people."

—Antoine Quentin Fouquier-Tinville,
public prosecutor's indictment

Paris
October 1793

Since April 5, 1793, Antoine Quentin Fouquier-Tinville had enjoyed the right as public prosecutor to arrest and bring to trial individuals suspected of any crime of conspiracy or "national offense" against the republic. He only needed information provided by the authorities, or even private citizens, to serve warrants on the accused and have them imprisoned in the Conciergerie until their hearings.[1]

After indicting anyone who acted "wickedly and intentionally" with a view "to provoke the national dissolution and the re-establishment of royalty," Fouquier-Tinville supported the accusations against the suspects in the trial. If they were found innocent, they were usually released from custody. But if they were found guilty, Fouquier-Tinville then moved that the law be applied, which in most cases meant that they should be sent to the guillotine.

Fouquier-Tinville wasted no time in preparing warrants for the arrest of those involved with the latest plot to snatch the queen from the hands of the revolutionaries. The barber Jean-Baptiste Basset, the hunchbacked woman Catherine Fournier, the Lemille family, and the soldiers who had been bribed were arrested and imprisoned on October 12. The plot failed due to its extensive network of over five hundred accomplices, making it easier for spies to infiltrate the group and then denounce the conspirators who had confided in them.[2] Fouquier-Tinville wrote,

> The accused, having conspired in the month of September against the unity and indivisibility of the republic and the peace and security of the republic, of inciting civil war, of saving the widow Capet from punishment for her crimes, and of provoking the reestablishment of the royalty, have been condemned to death.

According to Tribunal records, the following were guillotined: Jean-Baptiste Basset, twenty-eight years old, hairdresser; Catherine Virgon-Fournier,* forty-eight years old; and Guillaume Lemille, hairdresser, and his wife, Élisabeth Lavigne-Lemille. Catherine Fournier's fourteen-year-old son, Jean Fournier, was considered too young to be guillotined; he was sentenced to twenty years in prison.[3]

There is no indication that Marie Antoinette ever knew of the plight of these fervent supporters. On the one hand, the compassion of common workers, hairdressers, and small merchants who were trying to save her life would have humbled the queen; on the other hand, she would have certainly been devastated to discover that any of her subjects had been escorted to the scaffold for their loyalty.

Fouquier-Tinville was conscientious in drawing up indictments for Basset and his accomplices. The prosecutor always followed the law carefully, never going beyond the rights and powers legally conferred upon him. Although monotonous in style, his indictments were full of exaggeration and ambiguous terminology. And he conducted his investigation of suspects

---

*The name Catherine Fournier is interesting because this was also the maiden name of Léonard Autie's mother; Léonard was the famous hairdresser to Marie Antoinette. Research to date has not found any connection, but Léonard did bring his two brothers and a cousin to Paris to work with him. Catherine may also have been a cousin.

Antoine Quentin Fouquier-Tinville
(1746–1795)

with zeal and without discrimination "whatever the social class to which they belonged, and whatever their position, their origin, or their opinions."[4]

On October 5, Fouquier-Tinville had complained to the president of the National Convention that he did not have the information needed to bring Marie Antoinette to trial or sufficient information to ensure her conviction. The prosecutor's biggest fear was an acquittal for the widow Capet.

The president of the convention notified Fouquier-Tinville that the Committee of Public Safety would address his concerns:[5]

In receipt of your letter of yesterday, we advise you, citizen, that the Committee of Public Safety, on that day, just authorized our colleague, the custodian of the National Archives, to communicate to you all documents concerning the trial of Capet [Louis XVI] and those to be used to instruct that of his widow that may be in his depository.

We invite you to see the citizen Rabaud Pommier, so he can give you information on the documents that you need. On our side, we will write him to make us privy to what he knows on this subject. [Signed] Hérault, Billaud-Varenne, B. Barrère, Robespierre, Saint-Just

In the meantime, Fouquier-Tinville might also have spoken to Jacques René Hébert about the upcoming trial because the mayor of Paris, Jean Pache, and the procurer of the Commune, Pierre Chaumette, accompanied Hébert and several prison commissioners to the Temple on October 6.[*] They intended to question Marie Antoinette's young son, Louis Charles, with the goal

---

[*]Jacques René Hébert was a leader of the Commune of Paris and editor of *Père Duchêsne*, an extreme radical newspaper during the French Revolution; Pierre Gaspard Chaumette was a national agent of the Commune; and Jean Nicholas Pache was the mayor of Paris.

of discovering additional evidence against his mother. Hébert must have brought Pache and Chaumette along to add more solemnity and pomp to the occasion. Hébert and Chaumette were actually responsible for the child's solitary confinement in the Temple.[6]

Most historical works have since refused to describe the interview with the eight-year-old prince, beginning with the role that the officials and the brute Antoine Simon played in preparing their young protégé. But this information is important for understanding how Hébert would provide the decisive accusation, the one he thought would secure a verdict. But how did he arrive at the solution to such a sensitive problem of eliminating an heir to the throne?

Hébert remembered an accident that had happened to the dauphin Louis Charles three months earlier when the child had bruised his right testicle while playing. Although he was under the care of the prison physician, Dr. François Thierry, Thierry's colleague, Dr. Soupé, recommended that Dr. Jean-Baptiste Pipelet care for the prince.[7] This raised a red flag in the committee because Dr. Pipelet had served as the court physician at Versailles. The royal prisoners, now only citizens of the republic, were not allowed any special treatment, but the queen insisted, and Dr. Pipelet was permitted to prepare a special bandage for the child, who soon recovered. In any event, due to change of doctors, the bruised testicle became known to Hébert in the committee; he would use the injury to concoct an incredible story.[8]

Furthermore, just before interrogating the young prince, Chaumette had delivered a virulent speech to the General Council against bad morals, obscene books, and corrupting prints. Having set the tone for the upcoming accusations, it was now up to Simon to prepare his pupil—any accusation against Marie Antoinette would have to come directly from the prince's mouth.[9]

Simon was already on task. The evening before Hébert and his deputies arrived at the Temple, Simon had forced Louis Charles to go to bed without dinner. The following morning, Simon made him drink wine and liqueurs to the point of inebriation; he was then able to coerce the child with threats of brutal force to say and sign anything that he desired, including statements regarding the most unthinkable relations with both his mother and his aunt Élisabeth.[10]

The officials arrived at the Temple and went directly to the council room before ascending to Simon's apartment. The former shoemaker had arranged the chairs and a table, where citizen Jean-Jacques Laurent would serve as recorder of the proceedings. Laurent later outlined the young prince's deposition in the following report:

We, the mayor, the attorney trustee, and members of the Paris Commune, appointed by the General Council of the said municipality to collect information on different facts that occurred in the Temple and to receive declarations in this regard, went to the Temple and arrived in the so-called Tower, met with the Temple Council, and went up to the apartment occupied by Louis Charles Capet to hear statements about the words and the events of which he might have knowledge.

He told us that, having been surprised several times in bed by Simon and his wife, who were charged with watching over him by the municipality, committing indecencies on himself harmful to his health, he assured them that he had been instructed in these pernicious habits by his mother and aunt, and several times they were amused to see him repeat these practices before them, and that this often happened when they slept together.

In the manner that the child explained, he let us hear that once his mother brought him near her, it resulted in copulation and that the result was a swelling of his testicles, known to Citizen Simon, for which he still wears a bandage, and that his mother advised him never to mention that this act has been repeated several times since.

He added that five other individuals named Marrow, Leboeuf, Beugnot, Michonis, and Jobert had conversed with more familiarity than other commissioners with his mother. The citizen Simon and his wife say that we have learned the facts from the mouth of the child, that he has repeated them several times, and that he often urged them to put it within our reach to prepare a declaration. [Signed] Louis Charles Capet

A comparison of the young prince's signature with his earlier signatures revealed that he was nervous and under duress when signing this declaration. Pache, Hébert, Chaumette, and Simon then added their signatures to

louis Charle capet

Signature of the abused and inebriated Louis Charles

the document. They would return the following day to speak to the young princess Marie-Thérèse and her aunt Élisabeth to confirm the abuse that the young prince had recited.

It was one o'clock in the afternoon on Tuesday, October 7, when Mayor Pache and Chaumette returned to the Temple.* Hébert was absent, but Jacques-Louis David, the king's former painter and a staunch revolutionary, took his place. The municipal officer Louis Daujon also accompanied the officials. After checking in at the Temple Council, they climbed the stairs to the third floor to order Marie-Thérèse downstairs for questioning. The princess narrated the event in her memoirs: "My aunt only opened when she was fully dressed. Mayor Pache, turning to me, asked me to come downstairs. My aunt wanted to follow me, but he refused. When she fearfully asked if I would be returned, Chaumette replied that she could rely on the word of a good republican."[11]

Marie-Thérèse kissed her trembling aunt and went downstairs. It was the first time that Élisabeth had been separated from her niece in the Temple. Marie-Thérèse was embarrassed; she had never been alone with men before, and she had no idea what they wanted. "I recommended myself to God," she said.

She went down one floor and was brought to her little brother's room. When she saw him for the first time in over a month, she kissed him tenderly. Simon quickly snatched him away from her arms and instructed her to go into the next room. Chaumette then questioned her about activities in the Temple and the "thousand bad things" that her mother and her aunt were accused of doing.[12]

Chaumette: Your name?

Marie-Thérèse: Thérèse

Chaumette: Speak the truth; this concerns neither you nor your parents.

Marie-Thérèse: It doesn't concern my mother?

Chaumette: No, it concerns persons who have not done their duty.

The officials then questioned the princess about the citizens Lepître, Vincent, Bruno, Beugnot, Moelle, Michonis, and Jobert, but she said she did not

*Marie Thérèse incorrectly remembered the date as October 8.

know these gentlemen. The officials also asked Marie-Thérèse whether she knew the Messieurs François Dangé and François Adrien Toulan. It was rumored that Dangé had once told the young prince that he wished the prince would retake King Louis XVI's throne. Toulan was one of the conspirators discharged from the Temple due to Simon's denunciation of his friendly demeanor toward the queen. The princess replied that she never knew either of them. She also denied knowledge of Toulan instructing the town criers to relate important information to the queen from the street outside the Temple.[13]

The officials then had Louis Charles brought into the room. They sat him down in an armchair, and as "he swung his little legs, which did not reach the ground," they called upon him to declare whether he persisted in upholding the truth of the wanton scenes revealed by him the day before. The child repeated the accusation. A very confused Princess Marie-Thérèse obstinately denied it, but her brother intervened. "Yes, it is true," he said.[14]

Marie-Thérèse was horrified by the accusations. She told the officials that she and her brother had been together almost all the time, and she had not seen anything; it was impossible that she could not have seen what her brother reported. Despite her protests, the officials were adamant. Marie-Thérèse then admitted that there were things that she did not understand. And what she understood she found to be "too horrible" to believe.

The questioning then turned to the royal family's flight to Varennes and how they escaped from the Tuileries Palace. The prince and princess answered several questions, but they often contradicted themselves, especially regarding the queen and Élisabeth's communications with Toulan.

Louis Charles said that his sister saw the municipal officers talk with his aunt and his mother but that she had probably since forgotten it. Marie-Thérèse said it was possible that she had forgotten, but she was not sure. Louis Charles then reminded her of the story when they had been locked up in a room in the tower to play with toys, allowing their mother and aunt to talk privately with Toulan. This she remembered well.

She said that her brother was more spirited and more observant than she; her memory may have escaped her. Louis Charles then recalled that even when they came out of the tower, Toulan and Lepître, whom Louis Charles called "lame" (*boiteux*), were still talking to their mother and aunt. Marie-Thérèse said she did not notice this because she was reading a book at the time.[15]

She did recall, however, that she had once overheard Toulan talk about politics with one of his colleagues during dinner. This statement shows that the princess perhaps made a special effort not to compromise anyone and to especially protect Toulan. First, she said she did not know Toulan; now she remembered him.

After three hours, the interrogation finally came to a close. Before being returned upstairs to her aunt, the princess asked to be reunited with her mother.

"I cannot help you," Chaumette said.

"What, sir! You cannot speak to the committee?"

"I have no authority there," he said.

The three interrogators then told the princess she was not to say anything to her aunt, and she was escorted upstairs to her chambers. After she and Élisabeth embraced each other, Élisabeth was immediately ordered downstairs.

The officials first asked Élisabeth if she knew the following men: Dangé, Toulan, Lepître, Brunot, Vincent, Moelle, Leboeuf, Beugnot, Michonis, and Jobert. She said she knew them all by name, as well as all the officers present in the room.

They then asked Élisabeth if she had ever seen Dangé take Louis Charles in his arms, kiss him, and profess his royal support by saying, "I would like to see you in your father's place." The officials were attempting to prove that Dangé desired a return of the monarchy to see Louis Charles crowned as Louis XVII, but Élisabeth replied that she had never noticed it. She also claimed never to have had any discussions with Toulan and that she had never heard him promise to have town criers relate information to the royal prisoners.

The officials then recalled Louis Charles. They asked him to repeat what he had earlier deposed, and it caused a heated discussion between him and his aunt. But the child insisted that he had told the truth. After reading the declaration about the child's masturbation and the accusation of incest with his mother, Élisabeth told the officials that such an infamy was too much beneath her to permit any reply to it; however, she did admit that the child had practiced "that habit" for some time and that he should remember that his mother had scolded him many times for it. When questioned again about this shocking activity in the Temple, Louis Charles still insisted that he was telling the truth.[16]

When Louis Charles was asked if this behavior occurred in the morning or in the evening, he said that he did not know but that it happened quite frequently; he thought it was in the morning. When asked who had taught him this practice, he said it was "both of them together," referring to his mother and aunt.[17]

"Oh, the monster!" Élisabeth cried out.

Élisabeth flatly denied all the boy's accusations. She was then questioned about her role in the flight to Varennes and other minor matters. After the interrogation, the sister of Louis XVI signed the deposition "Élisabeth Capet" and rejoined her niece on the third floor. She left her nephew—whom she and Marie-Thérèse would never see again—with Simon, who likely felt triumphant.

After almost four hours, the interrogation finally came to a close. Daujon said that Louis Charles was visibly giving away; either his excitement was on the decline, or he was getting tired of sitting. More than likely his audacity was weakening in the presence of his aunt Élisabeth.

Daujon also said that he believed the child's replies had been suggested to him.[18] The prince was, after all, as impulsive as any eight-year-old child. It was rumored that, because Simon had forced him by "blows, drink, threats and privations" to give evidence against his mother, the child sank into a "state of melancholy and consumption" and was determined never to speak another word again.[19]

Chaumette left the Temple with his report and conveyed it to Fouquier-Tinville; three days later, Chaumette presented it to the General Council with severe consequences for Temple commissioners named by the young prince. Lepître, Dangé, and Leboeuf, among others, were immediately arrested.

On Saturday evening of October 12, two judges of the Revolutionary Tribunal, a police inspector, and a jailer entered Marie Antoinette's cell. Accustomed to going to bed before dark, she was startled awake and quickly donned her black dress. She followed two gendarmes up the staircase in the Tour Bon Bec and along the gallery to the Grande Chambre of Parliament, where the Revolutionary Tribunal held its proceedings.*

---

*The Tour Bon Bec was so called because here was the torture chamber, and here men found "a good mouth," or a mouth that would not shut up when tortured. In this tower was a staircase leading down to the prison of the Conciergerie.

Seated between the two guards, the queen faced Tribunal president Martial Joseph Armand Herman, prosecutor Fouquier-Tinville, and the clerk Fabricius. It was dark, and the two candles on the table only made the darkness in the chamber more intense.[20] The queen probably could not even discern who the other observers in the gallery were. Was this darkness an omen?

Marie Antoinette must have found being called up to the Grande Chamber at this time of night for her first preliminary examination quite bizarre. The proceedings were called to order at six o'clock, and Herman began by asking Marie Antoinette for her name and age. "Marie-Antoinette-Lorraine of Austria," she replied. "Thirty-eight years old, widow of the king of France." The queen was actually only thirty-seven years old at the time; she would not turn thirty-eight until November 2.[21]

Herman: What was your residence at the time of your arrest?

Queen: We were not arrested. We were removed from the care of the assembly and taken to the Temple.

Herman: You had relations with the king of Bohemia and Hungary before the Revolution, and these were contrary to the interests of France, where you kept your property.

Queen: The king of Bohemia and Hungary was my brother, and I had only a relationship of friendship and not a political one with him. If I had a political relationship, these dealings would only have benefitted France, where I stood by the family into which I had married.

Herman: Not content to squander away the finances of France, the fruit of the people, in a frightful manner for your pleasure and your intrigues, you

Marie Antoinette's brother, Holy Roman Emperor Joseph II

have, together with your minister, passed millions to the emperor* to use against the people who fed you.

Queen: Never. I know that this has often been used against me. I loved my husband too much to squander the money of his country, and my brother did not need money from France. By the same principles that bound me to France, I wouldn't have given it to him either.

Herman: Since the Revolution you have not ceased to operate with foreign and domestic powers against freedom, even when we had the mandate of freedom that the people of France absolutely wanted.

Queen: Since the Revolution I was personally banned all correspondence outside of France, and I never meddled with the domestic powers.

Herman: Did you employ any secret agent to correspond with foreign powers, especially with your brother, and wasn't Delessart the principal agent?

Queen: Never in my life.

Herman: Do you know that this answer does not seem correct to us? There were secret meetings in the night at the Tuileries Palace that you presided over yourself and in which you deliberated the statements to the foreign powers, the constitutional assembly, and the legislative assembly.

Queen: The answer is perfectly correct because there was constant uproar from these assemblies whenever they wanted to deceive the people for amusement. I never experienced the [secret] meetings; they never existed.

Herman: Louis Capet sanctioned to veto the decrees of November 1791 against his brothers, emigrants, and unsworn priests and fanatics. Was it not you who, notwithstanding the strong representation of Duranton, then minister of justice, determined that Louis Capet oppose the vetoes of which the sanctions would have prevented the evils that have since troubled France and obviously shows that you attended these meetings?

Queen: In the month of November, Duranton was not a minister. Moreover, my husband did not need to have someone push him to do what he believed to be his duty. I was never at the council, and it is only there that these kinds of affairs were conducted and decided.

---

*From 1789 until his death in 1790, Joseph II had plans to help Louis XVI and his family escape, but Marie Antoinette would not leave her children behind so that she could take a smaller, faster coach, and Louis did not want to be a king in exile.

Herman: It was you who taught Louis Capet the art of profound dissimulation with which he deceived the good people of France for so long who had no idea that one could bring such a degree of villainy and perfidy?

Queen: Yes, the people have been deceived, and cruelly deceived, but by neither my husband nor me.

Herman: By whom have the people of France been deceived?

Queen: By those who were interested; it was not us.

Herman: Who are those who, in your opinion, had an interest to deceive the people?

Queen: I only know our interest, and that was to enlighten them, and not to deceive them.

Herman: You did not answer the question directly.

Queen: I would respond directly if I knew the names of the people.

Herman: You have been the main instigator of Louis Capet's treason. It is by your advice, and perhaps your persuasion, that he wanted to flee France to put himself at the head of maniacs wanting to tear apart their country.

Queen: My husband had never wanted to flee France. I followed him everywhere; but if he wanted to leave his country, I would have employed every possible means to dissuade him, but it was not his intention.

Herman: What was the purpose of the journey to Varennes?

Queen: To give himself the freedom he could not have here and then reconcile all parties for the happiness and tranquility of France.

Herman: Why were you traveling then under a name borrowed from a Russian baroness?

Queen: Because we could not leave Paris without changing our names.

Herman: Were not Lafayette, Bailly,* and the architect Renard among those who favored his escape?

Queen: The first two people would have been the last he would have used, and the third was under them, but they would never have been used for this purpose.

Herman: Your answer is contradictory to statements made by people who fled with you and which show that Lafayette's coach, when all fugitives descended from the

---

*Marie-Joseph Gilbert du Motier, the marquis de Lafayette, was at the time commander in chief of the National Guard; Jean Sylvain Bailly was mayor of Paris from 1789 to 1791; architect Jean-Augustin Renard was controller of the Tuileries in 1791.

apartment of your woman servant, was visible, and that Lafayette and Bailly watched while Renard led the escape.

Queen: I do not know what arrangements were made by the people who were with me. I know that I saw Lafayette's coach on the place du Carrousel; it passed us on the way, but it was far from stopping. As for Renard, I can assure you that he did not direct the escape. It was I alone who opened the [palace] door and made everyone leave.

Herman: In that case, you opened the doors and made everyone leave. There is no doubt, then, that you directed Louis Capet in his actions and that you determined his escape.

Queen: I don't believe that, by opening a door for everyone, it can generally prove that one is directing one's actions. My husband wanted and believed he had to leave here with his children. I was only used to provide a safe departure.

Herman: You have never ceased for one moment wanting to destroy liberty. You wanted to reign at any price and retake the throne on the cadavers of patriots.

Queen: Whether it was necessary to retake the throne or not, we only desired the happiness of France. If France was happy, we were always content.

The questioning then turned to the Treaty of Pillnitz, calling for the joint support of Leopold of the Holy Roman Empire and King Frederick William II of Prussia for King Louis XVI against the French Revolution.* If Marie Antoinette wanted peace for France, the interrogators wanted to know why she did not use her influence over her imperial brother to break the treaty with William II of Prussia.[22]

She answered that she had no knowledge of the treaty until after it was made and that it was not the foreign powers that declared war or attacked France first. Actually, the Legislative Assembly had asked Louis for a declaration of war against the foreign powers, but he only consented after the unanimous vote of his council.

Marie Antoinette was then asked if she had communicated or conspired with the previous princes of France, the king's brothers, since they left France. She replied that she never had any correspondence outside of

---

*Leopold, Marie Antoinette's brother, was Holy Roman Emperor and king of Hungary from the death of Joseph II in 1790 until 1792. He was succeeded by his son Francis II, who was completely indifferent to his aunt's fate.

France, but it was possible that she wrote one or two "insignificant" letters to the king's brothers.

Herman: You said on October 4, 1789, that you were delighted on the first day of October when the orgy of the Flanders regiment took place. The intoxicated regiment expressed their devotion to the throne and their aversion to the French people, and they trampled on the national *cocarde** to wear the royal white cap.

Queen: I don't remember saying such a thing, but it is possible that I was touched by the animated sentiments of the feast. As for the rest of the question, it was not due to intoxication that the regiment showed its devotion and attachment to those whom it was serving. As for the *cocarde*, if it existed, it could only have been a mistake of those who didn't know.

Herman: What interest do you have in the republic's armies?

Queen: I only want the happiness of France above all.

Herman: Do you think that kings are necessary for the happiness of the people?

Queen: An individual cannot decide such a thing.

Herman: You regret, without a doubt, that your son has lost the throne on which he could rule.

Queen: I would never regret anything for my son if his country was happy.

Herman: What is your opinion of August 10 when the Swiss (Guards), by order of the master of the castle, fired on the people?

Queen: I was not in the château when the firing began. I don't know what happened, but I do know that the order to fire was never given.

The insurrection on August 10 was significant in French history in that it resulted in the fall of the monarchy. Marie Antoinette was telling the truth when she said that Louis XVI had not given any order for his Swiss Guards to fire on the National Guard of the Paris Commune that day. In fact, the king dreaded violence; instead of defending the palace, he fled with his family through the Tuileries gardens to seek shelter in the assembly. The queen did, however, beg the king to stay and fight.

---

*Revolutionary cockades (*cocardes*) were red, white, and blue badges worn on hats. Refusing to wear the cockade could be punished with a week in prison.

When the insurrection was victorious, the delegates of the assembly demanded that the king—now called Citizen Capet—and his family be taken to the Temple prison.

Herman: During your stay in the Temple, weren't you informed of political affairs, and didn't you carry on communications with the enemies of the republic with the help of some municipal officers who served there or some persons that were introduced in your chambers?

Queen: For the fourteen months that I was imprisoned, there was no news or information about political affairs. I didn't have any correspondence, and I couldn't have had any because, since the beginning of October, pens, ink, paper, and pencils were removed. I never addressed any municipal officer, believing that it wouldn't be useful.

Herman: Your response contradicts the declarations of those who lived in the same place.

Queen: There were not many persons living in the Temple. We were the only ones, and those who make such declarations must try to prove them, because they are not true.

Herman: Since you've been in the Conciergerie, weren't different persons introduced in the chambers where you stayed? Didn't one of these persons bring a carnation in which a note was found, and wasn't it you who took the carnation, according to the gestures by the same person?

Queen: Different persons entered my cell with the police administrators, but I didn't know them at all. There was one that I did recognize, and it is true that he dropped a carnation on the ground as I have already deposed once before. But I paid so little attention that without a signal I wouldn't have picked it up. I did pick it up, fearing that someone might be compromised if it were found.

Herman: Didn't you recognize this person when he was at the Tuileries Palace on June 20? And didn't this person stay next to you during this said day?

Queen: Yes.

Herman: Didn't you recognize this same person who could be found at the palace on August 10?

Queen: No.

Herman: Do you know his name?

Queen: No, I don't remember if I knew him.

Herman: It is difficult to believe that you didn't know his name, because this person was flattered that you had rendered him such a great service, and one does not ordinarily render such great services without knowing the person in a particular manner.

Queen: It could be possible that those who have rendered a service forget it or those who have received it remember it. But I have never rendered him any service, and I hardly know him.

Herman: Did you respond to the note found in the carnation?

Queen: I tried to write with a pin, but not to respond to it but rather to persuade the person not to return.

Herman: Do you recognize the response (showing her the pinpricked note)?

Queen: Yes.

Herman: Did you react at the moment when this person was presented to you?

Queen: Not having seen a familiar face in thirteen months, it was rather normal that I would react at that moment, but it was only the idea of the danger that one risked by entering my cell. Afterward I believed he had been employed at some time, and I was reassured.

Herman: What do you mean by the expression "I believed he had been employed at some time, and I was reassured"?

Queen: Many people came with the administrators whom I did not know. I believed he could have been employed some place, so he didn't risk any danger.

Herman: Did the police administrators often bring people to you?

Queen: They were almost always accompanied by one, two, or three people that I did not know.

Herman: What are the names of the administrators who came most often?

Queen: Michonis, Michel, Jobert, and Marino came most often.

Herman: Did these four administrators always bring people whom you did not know?

Queen: I believe so, but I don't remember.

Herman: Do you have anything to add to these different answers? Do you have counsel?

Queen: No, and I am waiting for counsel because I do not know anyone.

Herman: Would you like the Tribunal to provide one or two defenders?

Queen: Yes, I would.

After Herman suggested two counselors, citizens Guillaume Alexandre Tronçon-Ducoudray and Claude François Chauveau-Lagarde, to defend Marie Antoinette, she signed the declaration. Herman, Fouquier-Tinville, and the recorder Fabricius also signed before ordering Marie Antoinette to be escorted back to her cell. From this point forward, the queen would have an additional gendarme keeping watch over her around the clock.

Fouquier-Tinville felt he now had sufficient evidence to bring Marie Antoinette to the Revolutionary Tribunal. His scathing accusation described the queen as, among other things, the ruthlessly murderous and sadistically cruel French queen Frédégonde:

> From an examination made of all the documents transmitted by the Public Prosecutor, it is clear that, like the Messalinas, Brunehaut, Frédégonde and Médicis,* who were formerly described as Queens of France and whose eternally odious names will not be effaced from the annals of history, Marie Antoinette, the widow of Louis Capet, has since her residence in France been the scourge and bloodsucker of the French people; that she had political relations with the man described as the King of Bohemia and of Hungary even before the happy revolution that has given back their sovereignty to the French people; that those relations were contrary to the interests of France.[23]

À SAVOIR . . .

Jacques-Louis David

Before the Revolution, Jacques-Louis David had become an eminent painter in the neoclassical style whose works were in tune with the political climate of the time. During the Revolution, David enthusiastically entered the politi-

---

*Messalina refers to the third wife of the Roman emperor Claudius, a powerful and promiscuous woman who conspired against her husband; Brunehaut (Brunhilda), the wife of King Sigebert, was publicly accused of incest and cruelty; Frédégonde was the queen consort of Chilperic I and known as an assassin; and Médicis refers to Italian Catherine de Medici, regent of France after the death of Henry II and allegedly responsible for the deaths of thousands of Huguenots in Paris.

cal debates and became a representative for Paris in the National Convention in 1792. When the newspapers reported that King Louis XVI's court would not allow the showing of his *The Lictors Bring to Brutus the Bodies of His Sons*, the people were outraged and the court was forced to concede.[24]

This painting depicted the Roman leader Marcus Brutus grieving for his two sons, whom he had ordered killed for conspiring to overthrow the government. David's study for the work shows Brutus sitting alone on the left and brooding, yet knowing what he did was best for his country. Because Brutus was the heroic defender of the republic, even at the cost of his family members, the painting became a symbol of the French republic.[25]

10

THE INDICTMENT, THE JURY, AND THE WITNESSES

"I must tell you, my brother, that I am one of the jurors who will judge the ferocious beast that devoured a large part of the republic—the former queen of France."

—François Trichard, juror of the Revolutionary Tribunal

Paris
October 1793

It was late when Lieutenant Louis-François de Busne escorted Marie Antoinette back to her cell after hours of interrogation.* She had held her composure with dignity throughout the questioning, but once in her cell she could not hold back the tears.[1]

"I boasted that the murderers of my husband would not be prepared for the days of his unfortunate widow," said the queen. She was speaking to a lieutenant who was sympathetic to the royal cause and to his queen, although he appeared to be a die-hard revolutionary.

"I thought that being the sister or aunt of so many sovereigns, the convention would waver about whether to destroy me," she continued. "But you see, sir, there is no obstacle or consideration that will stop them now. I will defend my life in the interest of my daughter and my son, and I also want

---

*Louis-François Busne first served under Louis XV in the Dauphin's Regiment; he also later served under Louis XVI and Napoleon.

to keep it to reward my faithful servants, but only God will decide. I submit with resignation to his will."[2]

Suddenly, in a fit of anxiety, she cried, "Oh, let me die, let me die!"

"Madame," said the bewildered officer, "in the name of God your creator and in the name of your innocent glory, do not call for death; allow me to help you!"

Lafont d'Aussonne reported that the lieutenant then picked up the swooning queen in his arms and carried her to her bed, but this is unlikely. When Rosalie arrived soon afterward to make the queen's bed, she reported that the queen had in fact not gone to bed but was pacing hurriedly around her cell. The scene was so heartbreaking that Rosalie did not dare look at the queen, and the queen continued pacing until the early morning hours.[3]

The next day, on October 13, at two o'clock in the afternoon, a judge, his notary, and two ushers entered Marie Antoinette's cell to read prosecutor Antoine Quentin Fouquier-Tinville's indictment to her.[4] The opening language of the document gave a formal air to the hollow and trumped-up charges:[5]

Antoine Quentin Fouquier-Tinville, Public Prosecutor of the Criminal Revolutionary Tribunal, established in Paris, by a decree of the National Convention of the 4th of March 1793, without any recourse to the Court of Appeals, stating that the Public Prosecutor of the said Tribunal is authorized to arrest, prosecute and judge upon the denunciation of the Constituted Authorities or of the Citizens, states:

That by a decree of the Convention, of the 1st of August last, MARIE ANTOINETTE, widow of Louis CAPET, has been brought before the Revolutionary Tribunal, as accused of conspiring against France; that by another decree of the Convention, of October 3, it has been decreed that the Revolutionary Tribunal should occupy itself without delay, and without interruption, on the trial; that the Public Prosecutor received the papers concerning the widow Capet on the 11th and 12th of October of the present month; that one of the Judges of the Tribunal immediately proceeded to the interrogatories of the widow Capet; that an examination being made of all the pieces transmitted by the Public Prosecutor, it appears that, like Messalinas, Brunehaut, Frédégonde and Médicis, who were formerly qualified with the titles of Queens of France, whose names have forever been odious, and will never be effaced from the pages of history.

Marie Antoinette, widow of Louis Capet, has, since her residence in France, been the scourge and the bloodsucker of the France; that even before the happy Revolution which gave the French people their sovereignty, she had political correspondence with a man called the King of Bohemia and Hungary; that this correspondence was contrary to the interests of France; and not content with acting in concert with the brothers of Louis Capet, and the infamous and execrable Calonne, at that time Minister of the Finance, of having squandered the finances of France (the fruit of the sweat of the people) in a dreadful manner, to satisfy inordinate pleasures, and to pay the agents of her criminal intrigues, it is notorious that she has at different times transmitted millions to the Emperor, which served him, and still supports him to sustain a war against the Republic; and that it is by such excessive plunder that she has at length exhausted the national treasury.

The first part of this indictment set the stage for the antagonists: Marie Antoinette, who had squandered the finances of France to the point of ruin, her husband and his brothers, and her own brother, Emperor Joseph II of Austria, the longtime enemy of France. The protagonists were the republic and the people of France whose sweat had paid for all of the queen's "inordinate pleasures."

The indictment then quickly turned to Fouquier-Tinville's exaggeration of one of these pleasures, the so-called orgy that took place at a banquet welcoming a new Flanders regiment to Versailles on October 1, 1789. Organized by the king's guards, it included a sumptuous dinner for some two hundred troops at the Royal Opéra in the palace. It was rumored that, when the royal family arrived, the guests were inebriated and showed their support by trampling on the revolutionary cockade. The Parisian newspapers sensationalized the banquet and transformed it into an orgy—at a time when many of the king's subjects were going hungry.[6]

That since the Revolution, the widow Capet has not for a moment withheld criminal intelligence and correspondence from foreign Powers, and in the interior of the Republic, by agents devoted to her, whom she subsidized and caused to be paid out of the treasury; that at various epochs she has employed every maneuver that she thought consistent with her treacherous views to bring about a counter-revolution; first, having, under pretext of a necessary reunion between the former guards, and the officers and soldiers of the regiment of Flanders, contrived a feast between these two corps on the first of October 1789, which degenerated into an absolute orgy as she desired, and during the course of which the agents of the widow Capet perfectly seconded her counter-revolutionary projects; brought the greater part of the guests, in the moment of inebriety, to sing songs expressive of their entire devotion to the former throne, and most marked aversion for the people; of having excited them insensibly to wear the white cockade, and to tread the national cockade under foot; and of having authorized, by her presence, all the counter-revolutionary excesses, particularly in encouraging the women who accompanied her, to distribute these white cockades among the guests; and having, on the 4th of the same month testified the most immoderate joy at what passed during these orgies.

The royal family attended the banquet for the Flanders regiment amid the cries of "Long live the king!" (*Vive le roi!*), and the queen would certainly have been touched by the cheers from the loyal troops. However, while it was true that the troops sang "O, Richard," a refrain about Richard the Lionhearted who, like Louis XVI, had been held hostage, it was doubtful that the troops ever trampled on the revolutionary tricolored cockades. The National Guards who organized the event vehemently denied it, and the queen backed them up.[7]

"It is incredible," she said, "that such devoted subjects should trample under foot or wish to change the insignia that their king himself was wearing."

White cockades representing the monarchy were likely seen at the banquet—the army at that time still wore them—but only the king and the National Guards wore the tricolored cockades that evening.[8]

Troops from the National Guard were presented to the queen the day after the banquet to thank her, and she replied that she was "delighted" and "highly pleased with the 1st of October." This comment not only angered the revolutionaries but made the royalists even more brazen in their display of loyalty to the crown.[9]

Secondly, having in concert with Louis Capet distributed publications of a counterrevolutionary nature very plentifully throughout the kingdom, some of which were published by the conspirators on the other side of the Rhine in Coblenz, of having even carried her treachery and dissimulation to such a height, as to have circulated writings in which she herself is described in very unfavorable colors, in order to cloak the imposture; thereby to make Foreign Powers believe that she was extremely ill-treated by Frenchmen, to instigate them to go to war with France.

The indictment's reference to the other side of the Rhine reflected the large number of aristocrats and royalists who had escaped to the town of Coblenz in Germany. Some fifteen hundred of these emigrants gathered there to organize militarily with assistance from the Austrian monarchy. They threatened to invade France to recover their confiscated estates and to rescue the royal family. However, rumors of this growing army agitated the people of France, and Marie Antoinette was accused of having corresponded with these emigrants and having urged her brother in Austria to take up arms against France.[10]

Marie Antoinette did indeed seek help from the foreign powers, but her calls for help may have been misinterpreted. She only sought intervention from the powers to free the king from his house arrest at the Tuileries Palace and to restore his kingly powers, not to wage war against France.[11]

Satirical depiction of Marie Antoinette
(Bibliothèque Nationale Française)

It was also true that Marie Antoinette was "ill-treated" in the French press and elsewhere. An abundant number of provocative and obscene pamphlets were distributed throughout the capital, the provinces of France, and other European capitals. They argued not only that the queen corrupted the morals of her people but that her luxurious habits were the cause of their hunger. She was even said to powder her hair with the precious flour needed for the people's bread.

Cries for bread soon led to demonstrations in the streets and finally to the great march on Versailles on October 5, 1789. Although the French National Guard had been dispatched to protect the royal family, the mob still managed to break into the palace and find the queen.[12] She narrowly escaped by fleeing to the king's secure apartments through secret passageways, but two of her bodyguards were not so lucky; their severed heads were impaled on pikes—a clear statement of the mob's intent.

When the rioters assembled in the palace courtyard and demanded to see the queen, she eventually emerged with her two children. The crowd then demanded she face them alone. For ten agonizing minutes, Marie Antoinette stood on the balcony with her head bowed while the angry throng below screamed and waved their axes and pikes at her. After a moment of silence and, arguably, recognition of the queen's courage, their cries turned to "Long live the queen!" (*Vive la reine!*). The family was then escorted to the Tuileries Palace in Paris.[13]

> That in order to carry on her counterrevolutionary designs with more efficacy, she, by means of agents, caused in Paris, toward the beginning of October 1789, a famine, which occasioned a new insurrection; in consequence of which, an innumerable crowd of citizens of both sexes set out for Versailles on the 5th of the said month; that this fact is proved beyond all contradiction, as the next day there was a plenty of everything, even after the time that the widow Capet arrived with her family in Paris.

Soon after the royal family arrived in Paris, Count Hans Axel von Fersen masterminded an elaborate plan to free the royals from their house arrest at the Tuileries Palace. It aimed to bring the royal family to the town of Montmédy in northeastern France to unite with soldiers gathered there who were loyal to the monarchy. The plans were executed but failed when the family was arrested on the outskirts of Varennes. After the family was returned to Paris, the French people lost all trust in their king. Believing that his majesty was leaving the country to join enemy forces to invade France, they demanded his throne.[14]

> That being scarcely arrived in Paris, the widow Capet, fertile in intrigues of every kind, formed Committees, consisting of all the Counterrevolutionists and intriguers of the Constituent and Legislative Assemblies, which held their meetings in the dead of night; that plots were there formed how to destroy the Rights of Man, and the decrees already passed, which were to form the basis of the new Constitution; that it was at these Committees, or Meetings, that the necessary measures were deliberated to revise those decrees which were favorable to the People; that the flight of Louis Capet, his Widow, and his whole family, was impeded, as they travelled under fictitious names, in the month of June 1791; that the widow Capet confesses in her interrogatory, that it was she who opened and locked the door of the apartment through which the fugitives passed; that independent of the confession of the widow Capet in this respect, it is confirmed by the testimony of Louis Charles Capet, and by his sister, that La Fayette favored all the designs of the widow Capet, in the same manner as Bailly did while he was Mayor of Paris, and that both were present when the fugitives escaped, and favored their flight as much as lay in their power.

The indictment equated the king's council meetings to the queen's orgies, where they plotted against the revolutionaries. This was an exaggeration, but the king was becoming more and more incompetent in matters of state. Consequently, the queen was forced to take charge of the king's council. "The Queen was the only man among the King's advisers," one of the king's ministers remarked.[15]

When Fouquier-Tinville implicated the marquis de Lafayette and Mayor Jean Sylvain Bailly of Paris in his indictment, it raised eyebrows whether Lafayette and Bailly were actually conspiring with the crown. Both men were heroes at the beginning of the Revolution, but Lafayette, as leader of the National Guard, was responsible for the royal family's custody. He was called a traitor by the people when the royal family was able to escape under his watch.

Mayor Bailly lost the confidence of the people after dispersing the National Guard troops at the Champ de Mars massacre.

That the widow Capet after her return from Varennes recommenced her intriguing Coteries, at which she herself presided; and that, aided by her favorite La Fayette, the gates of the Tuileries were kept locked, which deprived the Citizens of the power of passing backwards and forwards in the Courts of the Tuileries; that those only who had cards were permitted to pass. That this order was given out by La Fayette as a measure of punishment to the fugitives; though it served only as a trick to prevent the citizens from knowing of what passed at these midnight orgies, and from discovering the plots against Liberty carried on in this infamous abode. That it was at these meetings that the horrible massacre that took place on the 17th of July 1791 was planned, when so many zealous patriots were killed in the Champ de Mars.

On July 17, 1791, the National Constituent Assembly issued a decree that Louis XVI would remain king under a constitutional monarchy; later that day, leaders of the republicans in France rallied against the decree. When Jacques Pierre Brissot, editor of *Le patriote français*, drew up a petition demanding the removal of the king, a large crowd gathered at the Champ de Mars to sign it. General Lafayette and the National Guard, under Mayor Bailly's orders, were able to disperse the crowd; however, later in the afternoon the crowd returned in even greater numbers.[16]

When Lafayette again tried to disperse the crowd, the angered rioters threw stones at the National Guard in retaliation. After several warning shots, the National Guard opened fire directly on the crowd. The exact numbers of dead and wounded were unknown, but Bailly and Lafayette never regained the stature they once held in the people's eyes, and they were ridiculed in the pamphlet press of the day.[17]

After Louis XVI reluctantly accepted the Constitution of 1791, he angered the revolutionaries by vetoing certain pieces of legislation, especially that requiring the arrest of all priests who did not swear an oath of loyalty to the Civil Constitution. Fouquier-Tinville's indictment blamed the queen not only for this veto but for all of Louis XVI's vetoes.

That the Constitution of 1791 being once accepted, the widow Capet took every means in her power to destroy its energy by means of her maneuvers; that she employed agents in different parts of the Republic to affect this object of annihilating liberty, and to make the French once more to fall beneath the tyrannical yoke under which they had languished for so many years; that for this purpose the widow Capet ordered it to be discussed in these midnight meetings, which were truly called the Austrian Cabinet, how far it might not be possible to counteract the laws passed in the Legislative Assembly; that it was in consequence of the councils and her advice that Louis Capet was persuaded to oppose his veto to the famous and salutary decrees passed in the Legislative Assembly against the former Princes, brothers of Louis Capet; against the Emigrants, and against the horde of refractory and fanatical priests who were spread all through France; a veto which has proved to be one of the principal causes of the evils that France has since experienced.

That it is the widow Capet who caused perverse Ministers to be nominated, and placed her creatures in the armies and public offices, men who were known by the whole nation to be conspirators against liberty; that it was by her maneuvers and those of her agents, as able as they were perfidious, that she got a new guard formed for Louis Capet, composed of ancient officers who had quitted their corps, and had refused to take the constitutional oath; that she gave appointments to refractory priests and strangers; and in short, to all those who were disliked by the nation, and who were worthy of serving in the army of Coblenz, whither many of them fled after their being dismissed.

Marie Antoinette was accused of influencing Louis XVI's choices of ministers. This was indeed true; the king had become too apathetic to rule. When the queen's favorite, Diane de Polignac, urged her to nominate Charles Alexandre de Calonne to be general comptroller of the finances in 1783, the queen yielded, and Calonne soon became one her favorites as well. The country's deep deficit and Calonne's perceived proximity to the queen forced him out of office despite the fact that he had presented a plan for progressive taxes that would have affected the nobles most.[18] Calonne went into exile and became a chief adviser to the émigrés in Coblenz from December 1790 until the fall of the monarchy in August 1792.

Marie Antoinette held his successor, Étienne Charles de Loménie de Brienne, in high esteem. He had been recommended by her former tutor, the abbé de Vermond, and her brother, Emperor Joseph II. Even the king felt that the people thought highly of de Brienne, who had been the archbishop of Toulouse.[19]

"I have always heard Monsieur de Brienne spoken of as a very distinguished man," said the king.

"I shall see him enter the ministry with pleasure," replied the queen.

Quite incapable of assuming the duties of general comptroller of the finances, de Brienne could only attempt to resume Calonne's plans of reform. But the minister's call for subsidies for the king and the public's outrage at the country's debt required calling the Estates-General (États-Généraux). Although Marie Antoinette had instituted economies in the palace households, she regretted that she was unaware of the condition of the treasury.[20]

"If I had known it," she said, "I should never have made so many acquisitions, and I should have been the first to set the example of reform in my household; but how could I form any idea of this distress, since when I asked for thirty thousand francs, they sent me sixty?"[21]

Whether Marie Antoinette was aware of the country's dire financial situation or not, her efforts to cut costs at Versailles came too late. The press also published reports of de Brienne—the queen's handpicked appointee—who was misusing his ministry to enrich himself and his family.

The fiasco culminated in the convocation of the Estates-General in 1789.* However, problems in voting rights brought an end to the assembly. The National Assembly was then created in its place, signaling the outbreak of the Revolution.

That it was the widow Capet, who, in conjunction with a scandalous faction, at that time domineered over the Legislative Assembly, and for some time over the Convention; who declared war against the King of Hungary and Bohemia, her own brother; that it was through her maneuvers and intrigues, at all times pernicious to France, that the French were obliged to make their first retreat from the French territory of Belgium.

That it is the widow Capet who forwarded to the foreign Courts the plans of the campaign, and the attacks which were agreed upon in the Council; so that, by means of this double treason, the enemies of France were always informed beforehand of the movements of the armies of the republic; from whence it follows—that the widow Capet is the authoress of all those reverses of fortune, which the armies of the Republic have experienced at different times.

*This was the first meeting since 1614 of the general assembly representing the three French estates: the clergy, the nobles, and the common people.

Austria and Prussia had been at war with France since 1792, but on February 1, 1793, France declared war on Great Britain and the Dutch Republic, drafting hundreds of thousands of men into the military. When the allied forces launched an attack against the French during the Flanders Campaign, France suffered severe losses and was driven out of Belgium. The indictment was thus accusing Marie Antoinette of having conspired with the enemy and blaming her for this loss.[22]

> That the widow Capet combined and plotted with her perfidious agents the horrible conspiracy which broke out on the day of August 10; which failed only through the courageous and incredible efforts of the patriots; that to this end she seduced into her dwelling of the Tuileries, and even into the subterraneous passages under it, Swiss soldiers, who, at the expiration of a decree then passed, were no longer to belong to the bodyguard of Louis Capet; that she kept them in a state of drunkenness, from the 9th to the 10th in the morning, the day appointed for the execution of this horrible conspiracy.

A year earlier, on August 1, 1792, the people of Paris had learned of the Brunswick Manifesto, which threatened the "city of Paris and all its inhabitants" with extreme vengeance if Louis XVI and his family were ever harmed.[23]

> Their said majesties further declaring, upon their faith and word as emperor and king, that if the palace of the Tuileries is forced or insulted, that if the least violence, the least outrage is done to their majesties the king, the queen, and the royal family, if provision is not immediately made for their security, for their preservation and liberty, they will inflict an exemplary and memorable vengeance, by giving up the city of Paris to military execution and total overthrow, and the rebels guilty of the outrages to the punishment which they shall have merited.*

On that same day the Parisians were informed that Austrian and Prussian armies had crossed the border into France. Paris reeled with fury, and on the morning of August 10, the king and his family were forced to flee the Tuileries Palace and take shelter in the National Assembly building. Just a few

---

*This document was signed at Coblentz on July 25, 1792, by Charles William Ferdinand, Duke of Brunswick-Luneburg.

hundred volunteer soldiers and the king's ceremonial Swiss Guards stood in the way of the advancing horde.[24]

> That the widow Capet, fearing no doubt that this conspiracy might not have the promised effect, went on the evening of August 9, at half after nine, into the room where the Swiss, and others in her interest, were busy making cartridges; that in order to excite them the more, she took up the cartouches and bit them. That the next day, August 10, she pressed and solicited Louis Capet to go to the Tuileries at five in the morning, to review the real Swiss Guards and those who had assumed their uniform; and at his return she presented him with a pistol, saying, "This is the moment to show yourself." On his refusal, she called him a coward.
>
> That notwithstanding the widow Capet denies having given any orders to fire on the people, her conduct on the 9th—her deeds—her deeds in the room of the Swiss guards—the councils she held all the night long—the article of the pistol and her words to Louis Capet; their sudden retreat from the Tuileries, and the firing on the people at that very moment he and she entered the room of the Legislative Assembly; in one word, all these circumstances united, leave no doubt but that in her councils during the night it was resolved that the people must be fired at, and that Louis Capet and Marie Antoinette, the female director of that conspiracy, should themselves give the orders to fire.

The indictment's charge that Marie Antoinette was carrying a pistol and chastised her husband for not firing on the crowds outside the Tuileries windows was partially true. It is doubtful that she carried a weapon, but she did beg the king to call his troops to arms, despite the calls for the family to leave the palace.[25]

"There is not five minutes to lose, Sire," said Pierre Louis Roederer, an official in the Department of Paris.* "There is no safety for Your Majesty but in the National Assembly. The gunners are not willing, they cannot be relied upon, and they will not fire; yet the assault on the palace will begin immediately."[26]

The queen continued to resist leaving the palace.

"Madame," said Roederer, "you expose the lives of the king and your children."

---

*Roederer would be criticized by the royalists and the revolutionaries for his actions for facilitating the end of the monarchy and saving the king's life, respectively.

She was undeterred. "We have muskets," said the queen.

Roederer stepped toward the king. "Time is pressing, Sire. We will not again beseech you, we will not again advise you, but we ask the king's permission to take him away."

The king arose from his chair. "Let us go," he said.

"You answer for the king's life, Monsieur," the queen said sharply to Roederer.

Before leaving the Tuileries, the king gave no orders for his troops to fire upon his people, but in the confusion, this is exactly what the troops did. A bloody massacre of the troops ensued.[27]

The final paragraph of Fouquier-Tinville's indictment was intended only to inflame the French people's hatred of their queen.

> That finally, the widow Capet, in every respect immoral, and a new Agrippina, is so dissolute and so familiar with all crimes, that forgetting her quality of mother, and the limits prescribed by the law of nature, she has not hesitated to prostitute herself with Louis Charles Capet, her son; and according to the confession of the latter, she has committed indecencies with him, the very idea and name of which strikes the soul with horror.

In sum, Fouquier-Tinville's eight-page indictment accused Marie Antoinette of maliciously and intentionally conspiring with the king's brothers, draining the treasury for her own purposes, and aiding the enemies of France, including her own brother. The indictment ends with the horrific and unfounded accusation of incest with her young son.

This claim was the final attack on the queen's immorality. She had been called the Messalina, Brunehaut, Frédégonde, and Médicis of France; now she was Agrippina, one of the most ruthless, violent, and domineering women in Roman history.

> Done in the chamber of the Public Prosecutor, the 1st day of the third decade of the first month of the 2nd year of the French Republic, one and indivisible.

When the judge finished reading her indictment, Marie Antoinette replied with a disdainful silence. He then asked her if she had chosen a defender.

"I do not know one," said the queen.

The judge then officially appointed Citizens Tronçon-Ducoudray and Chauveau-Lagarde, who were known to take on the most sensational cases.

"Not knowing any others and not being able to choose," said the queen, "I will willingly accept them."

The Revolutionary Tribunal upheld Fouquier-Tinville's indictment against Marie Antoinette-Lorraine of Austria, the widow of Louis Capet. The court bailiff ordered that the queen be taken into custody and officially registered in the Conciergerie, where she was already being detained, and that the municipality of Paris be informed of the arrest while the queen awaited trial. The bailiff added, unsurprisingly, that the trial would be open to the public.[28]

THE JUDGES

The five judges appointed by the National Convention to be present at Marie Antoinette's trial were (1) Martial Joseph Armand Herman, president of the Tribunal, who had previously served in the same capacity in the town of Pas-de-Calais; (2) Pierre-André Coffinhal, who practiced medicine before being named vice president of the Tribunal; (3) Gabriel Deliège, an attorney and deputy of the National Assembly; (4) Antoine-Marie Maire, an attorney at the Parliament of Paris and former king's lieutenant in the town of Vermanton; and (5) Joseph-François-Ignace Donzé-Verteuil, former public prosecutor of the Revolutionary Tribunal in the town of Brest.[29]

These judges chose Nicolas-Joseph Pâris, better known as Fabricius, as the recorder for the proceedings of the Tribunal. Fabricius wrote that he had stopped using his surname, Pâris, when his father was arrested for the murder of Michel le Peletier.* The brutal crime made the family name too "odious" to him.[30]

THE JURY

The members of the Tribunal jury were considered either hirelings, furious Jacobins (the most radical and ruthless of the factions), or idiots who were

---

*Le Peletier was a French politician who had voted for Louis XVI's execution. He was stabbed in the chest by Philippe Nicolas Marie de Pâris, a royal guard who allegedly used a saber that he had hidden under his cloak. Pâris supposedly shot himself in the head when caught.

"mortally fearful" of prosecutor Fouquier-Tinville.[31] Whether these characterizations were true or not, the jurors were all quite unique and more than likely predisposed to finding the queen guilty.

The first juror, Marquis Pierre-Antoine d'Antonelle, was a lieutenant in the military who once commanded his own regiment; he abhorred army life and had resigned. Although he came from an aristocratic family, he supported the revolutionary factions. He was later elected mayor of the town of Arles and then deputy in the National Assembly, before being named a juror of the Revolutionary Tribunal of Paris.

The second juror, Léopold Renaudin, was a luthier who built and repaired stringed instruments. He worked in the Royal Academy of Music before being seated in the Paris Commune. Renaudin was practically illiterate, as shown by his poorly written correspondence; his spelling was so atrocious that he hesitated before writing anyone. As a juror of the Tribunal, however, he was forthright with his opinions; he never wanted to acquit anyone.[32]

The third juror, Dr. Joseph Souberbielle, a surgeon of the Hôtel-Dieu, had cared for the queen during her incarceration at the Conciergerie by prescribing chicken broth for her hemorrhaging. Consequently, he wanted to recuse himself but was rebuffed. "If someone had to challenge you," President Herman told him, "it would be the charge that you gave care to the accused, and you must have been moved by the greatness of her misfortune." Dr. Souberbielle had nothing more to say and took his seat in the jury box.[33] One of his colleagues said Souberbielle was a harsh rogue who had the sad responsibility of examining women prisoners who claimed to be pregnant to avoid the scaffold. But Souberbielle was such a revolutionary that he "never or almost never wanted to see the signs [of pregnancy]."[34]

The fourth juror, Claude Besnard, was an auctioneer and an administrator at the Department of Public Works of Paris (Établissements *Publics de Paris*). Besnard had been accused of appropriating considerable sums from his sales of furniture as an auctioneer, but his election as a member of the jury saved him—no bailiff would risk proceeding against a juror of the Tribunal.[35]

The fifth juror, Pierre Nicolas Chrétien, was a lemonade shopkeeper before the Revolution and a member of the revolutionary committee of his precinct.[36] He was also one of Maximilien Robespierre's minions; before the queen was ever brought to trial, Chrétien told others that he was truly convinced of her guilt.

Georges Ganney, the sixth juror, was a wigmaker before and during the Revolution. A colleague said that Ganney was an excellent juror because he was an idiot who could not understand the responses any more than the questions. Accordingly, Ganney called for the death penalty "whenever he had the chance."[37]

François Trichard, the seventh juror, was formerly a soldier in the Bourbon regiment before becoming a fervent revolutionary. In a letter to his brother, he wrote, "I must tell you, my brother, that I am one of the jurors who will judge the ferocious beast that devoured a large part of the republic." One of Trichard's colleagues said, "Trichard was as illiterate and as cruel as Renaudin."

The eighth juror was Charles-Léopold Nicolas, an intimate friend of Robespierre and a member the Jacobin Club. Seated in the Commune, Nicolas was the printer for the Committee of Public Safety. When he took possession of the former royal press and that of the guillotined Louis Pottier de Lille, Nicolas prospered as the primary printer of the new republic.

Before being named to the Tribunal as jurors, Charles-Huant Desbois-seaux, a cobbler, was a member of the Commune; Jean-Baptiste Sambat was a portrait painter; Devèze was a carpenter; and Baron was a hat maker.

Little has been discovered about other jurors who sat in the jury box: Jourdeuil, an usher; Chatelet, a painter; Suard; Thoumain; Gemon; and Fiévé. Interestingly, under the restoration of the Bourbons in 1815, Gemon recanted the story that he had ever been a juror at the trial of Louis XVIII's sister-in-law.

THE WITNESSES

Fouquier-Tinville had written a scathing indictment of the former queen of France, but the document was meaningless without evidence. For example, the indictment accused the queen of supplying France's enemies with its military plans. Though the queen was in fact guilty of this charge, Fouquier-Tinville could not prove it; the queen's correspondence with

France's enemies would not be discovered until two hundred years later. For this reason the witnesses had to be chosen carefully. After all, they had to provide the proof.

The first witness on the prosecutor's list was Laurent Lecointre, a painting merchant who had proclaimed himself "one of the most faithful subjects" of the king and queen until he was elected to the National Assembly at the onset of the Revolution. As early as September 15, 1792, he had proposed that the dauphin and his sister be separated from their parents. At the trial of Louis XVI in January 1793, he had voted for the death of the king.[38]

Lecointre's history was similar to that of other witnesses to give testimony in the upcoming trial. Jean-Baptiste Lapierre, Antoine Roussillon, Jacques René Hébert, Abraham Justin Silly, Pierre-Joseph Terrasson, Pierre Manuel, Jean Sylvain Bailly, Jean-Baptiste Béguin, Reine Millot, Jean-Baptiste Larenette, and Honoré Nicolas Tarré were all fervent revolutionaries.[39]

Fouquier-Tinville's list of witnesses also included those who had been in close proximity to the queen in the Conciergerie: Marie Anne Barassin and her husband Toussaint Richard, Madame Marie Harel, and the guards Guillaume Gilbert and François Dufresne.[40]

As Marie Antoinette sat in her cell, she surely had no idea about the growing number of witnesses being selected to testify against her. She also had no information about the two lawyers who would defend her—except that her accusers had chosen them.

À SAVOIR . . .

Le Tribunal Révolutionnaire

The following articles of the Revolutionary Tribunal prescribed the organization of the court that would hear Marie Antoinette's case, among others:[41]

ARTICLE I: An extraordinary criminal tribunal will be established in Paris to try antirevolutionary acts; attacks against the freedom, equality, unity, and indivisibility of the republic, the internal and external security of the state; and all plots to reinstate royalty or establish any other authority interfering with the freedom, equality, and sovereignty of the people, whether said defendants are civilians, military officials, or private citizens.

ARTICLE II. The tribunal shall consist of a jury and five judges who will lead the investigation and apply the law after the statement of the jurors on the facts.

ARTICLE III. Judges cannot make any judgment if they are fewer than three in number.

ARTICLE VI. The Tribunal will have a public prosecutor and two deputies or substitutes to be appointed by the National Convention in the same manner as the judges.

ARTICLE VII. The National Convention will name twelve citizens from Paris and four surrounding departments to fulfill the functions of jurors and four alternates who will replace the jurors in case of absence of revocation or illness. The jurists shall hold office until the 1st of May each year, and the National Convention will provide for their replacement and training.

ARTICLE XV. The judges of the tribunal will elect a clerk and two bailiffs by a majority of votes; the clerk will have two assistants who will be confirmed by the judges.

11

THE REVOLUTIONARY
TRIBUNAL—DAY ONE

*"Citizen President, I invite you to make known to the accused
that she did not respond to that which Citizen Hébert spoke—
with respect to what took place between her and her son."*

—Unknown juror, Revolutionary Tribunal

Paris
October 14, 1793

After her preliminary interrogation on Saturday, October 12, Marie
Antoinette accepted the counsel of Citizens Chauveau-Lagarde and
Tronçon-Ducoudray for her defense. The court recorder, Fabricius, sent
Ducoudray the following notice dated October 12, but Ducoudray did not
receive it until midnight on October 13:

> Citizen, you are informed that the tribunal has named you the official defender
> of the widow of Louis Capet, and you will be able to communicate with her
> as of tomorrow morning, her trial beginning Monday the 14th of October.[1]

Curiously, Ducoudray had wanted to defend the unpopular King Louis
XVI at his trial earlier in January but was refused by the convention. When
the convention did not publish his request in their journals, he submitted his
complaint to any newspaper that dared to print it:

If Louis had enjoyed a free choice of his counsel, I should not have ventured to propose myself. But when it became certain that [the lawyer] Target had refused, and probable that Tronchet would do so too, it seemed to me frightful that such a prisoner should be deserted by all those whose profession it is to defend the unfortunate. I know my insufficiency, but as one of the oldest members of the bar, I feel it to be my duty, if there be any risk, to be among the first to encounter it.[2]

Since the king's execution, Ducoudray had never indicated any desire to defend the queen. He may have realized the complexity and fruitlessness of the case, as well as the inherent danger in representing the unpopular "Madame Deficit." He perhaps accepted the case for the same ethical reasons he wanted to defend the king. However, he would have only one night to prepare for the trial.

His colleague, Chauveau-Lagarde, was at his country home and did not receive his summons to the trial that would begin that very day until the wee hours of Monday morning. He set out immediately for the Conciergerie and accompanied Ducoudray to the queen's cell at six o'clock in the morning.[*] He said he found the queen dressed in white with "extreme simplicity." His knees trembled and his eyes teared up when the queen kindly received him with such an air of majesty.[3]

In the first of only three short consultations with the queen, Lagarde and Ducoudray took notes for their defense as they read the indictment together with the queen, an indictment that Lagarde called a "work from hell." When the lawyers went upstairs to examine the evidence (*pièces du procès*) against their client, they found the voluminous documents in such confusing disarray that they would need weeks to scrutinize them. They returned to the queen's cell and explained that they needed to petition the court for a delay.[4]

"To whom must the request be addressed?" asked the queen.

"The National Convention," Lagarde said cautiously, knowing that the queen most likely abhorred the institution that had dethroned her husband.

---

*Lagarde's memoirs reported that he was not informed of the trial until October 14, whereas Christophe Montjoie argued that both Lagarde and Ducoudray received the notices at midnight on October 13. George Gower, however, stated that Lagarde was notified on October 15 that the trial would resume at eight o'clock the following morning; this would have been impossible as the trial ended at four o'clock in the morning on October 16.

"No, never!" she said.

But Lagarde insisted on having more time—not only for the queen's benefit but also for that of the late king, her children, and her sister-in-law, who were all named in the indictment. Marie Antoinette had never met these men before and had every reason to be suspicious; after all, they had been appointed by the zealous revolutionary court that aimed to try her and put her to death. Therefore, she may have been reluctant to take their advice, but when Lagarde showed compassion by remembering her family, she agreed to go forward with the request and wrote the following note:

> Citizen President, The Citizens Tronson and Chauveau, whom the Tribunal have given me as defenders, call my attention to the fact that they have only today been told of their mission, and this is so short a time it is impossible for them to examine the charges, or even go through them. I owe it to my children to omit no way of entirely justifying myself of these charges. My defenders ask for a delay of three days. I trust that the Convention will accord this to them.[5]

Interestingly, Marie Antoinette wrote the request in the name of the defenders and not that of the former queen of France. Furthermore, she wrote the note from the perspective of a mother, not a political prisoner. She was being accused of the most atrocious crimes; by requesting the delay for the sake of her children, she was able to reassert her damaged sense of motherhood.

The request was forwarded to Antoine Quentin Fouquier-Tinville, but nothing more was ever heard about it. The prosecutor had simply ignored it.[6]

It was eight o'clock in the morning when Lieutenant Louis-François de Busne and two gendarmes escorted Marie Antoinette out of her cell. The autumn chill permeated the prison as they walked down the hallway and up the stairs to the Salle de Liberté, the Tribunal hall.

A murmur broke out as she entered the crowded assembly in her black robe and bonnet. She walked freely; she was not in chains, and her hands were not bound. The spectators were perhaps more surprised by the former queen of France's drab clothing than by her emaciated figure and pale face. Rosalie said that the queen was taken from her cell before having anything to eat or drink. The judges likely wished to weaken the queen even further for the long trial to follow.

Marie Antoinette stood as the jurors entered the densely crowded room in front of her and sat to her right. The judges took their seats at a table on a platform to the left while the recorder Fabricius sat at his table in front of the jurors. Fouquier-Tinville took a seat at his own desk at the foot of the judges' platform. A cap adorned with feathers covered his long dark hair. The queen's defenders, Lagarde and Ducoudray, entered and sat at a nearby table.

Martial Joseph Armand Herman, president of the Tribunal, stood and opened the session with a short preamble. Although he reminded the court that no signs of condemnation were tolerated, he himself inferred that the queen was one of the "greatest criminals":

> Citizens, you have come to assist in the judgment of a woman whom your eyes have seen upon the Throne and that you see, at this moment, at the bench reserved for the greatest criminals. The Tribunal, always equitable, requests that you be calm and peaceful. The law prohibits any sign of your esteem or condemnation.[7]

Herman then addressed each juror individually to administer the following oath, taking one hour to finish the process.

> You swear, Citizen, and promise to examine with scrupulous attention the charges brought against Marie Antoinette, widow of Louis Capet; to not communicate with anyone until after your declaration; not to listen with hatred, nor evil, nor fear, nor affection; and to decide after hearing the charges and means of defenses and following your conscience and your intimate conviction, with impartiality and the firmness of a free man.[8]

Surprisingly, the queen was now alone with her accusers. Lagarde and Ducoudray were not permitted to offer any advice or to respond to any questions during the testimonies of the witnesses or the examination of the queen. Her defenders would have only three short, closely watched interviews with her lasting a quarter of an hour from Monday morning until late Tuesday night.[9]

When Herman turned to the queen and asked her to state her name, profession, and residence, she said, "Marie-Antoinette-Joséphine-Jeanne de Lorraine, Archduchess of Austria."[10]

"No archduchess here!" interrupted Herman. "The republic doesn't recognize such miseries!"

"Widow of the king Louis XVI and thirty-seven years old," said the queen, ignoring the interruption.

President Herman next instructed Fabricius to read Fouquier-Tinville's indictment against the queen. After the clerk had done so, the president addressed the queen: "This is what you are accused of. Lend an attentive ear; you are now going to hear the charges brought against you."[11]

Herman told Marie Antoinette to take her seat on an ordinary wicker chair. Then he turned to the witnesses who had been summoned, or perhaps bought, by the prosecutor to testify against her. The prosecutor introduced the forty-one witnesses, each of whom held up his hand as the president administered the oath one at a time: "You swear and promise to speak without hate and without fear, and to tell the truth, all the truth, and nothing but the truth?" Then he asked of each his name, residence, and profession and if he was related to, allied with, or a servant or domestic of the defendant.

Herman then called the first witness. Of the forty-one testimonies, only thirteen were actually detrimental to the queen's defense.*

FIRST WITNESS WITH DAMAGING TESTIMONY

The first witness, Laurent Lecointre, was permitted by the court—against all the rules—to read the testimony that he had himself written. More like a memoir than a testimony, his deposition was vague and included little proof against the queen. He said the wife of the former king of France had asked him, as a deputy to the National Convention, to request twelve to fourteen domestics for her while she was under house arrest in the Temple. The convention had ignored the request on the grounds that she should petition the municipality for the servants.[12]

Lecointre then spoke of the festivals and "orgies" that took place at the château of Versailles, causing a dreadful dilapidation of France's finances. What then followed was essentially a brief history of the Revolution from the

---

*These thirteen will be examined in more detail; the remaining twenty-six were either neutral or favorable to the defense.

opening of the Estates-General to the banquet for the Flanders regiment and the march on Versailles.

Lecointre had attended the banquet and testified that the queen appeared there with her husband and that they were "loudly applauded" by the troops. "O Richard! O My King!" had been played and the health of the royal family toasted—a toast to the health of the nation was summarily rejected.

"It was there that the most violent outrages were committed upon the national cockade, which was trodden under foot," he said.

When speaking of the march on Versailles, Lecointre reported that he was at Versailles, but the king was out hunting at the time and "entirely ignorant of what was happening."

Herman (to the queen): Do you have any statements to make about the testimony of this witness?

Queen: I don't have any knowledge about most of the facts about which the witness testified. It is true that I gave two flags to the National Guard of Versailles. It is also true that I made a tour of the tables at the banquet, but that was all.

Herman: You state that you were in the banquet hall. Were you there when the musicians played "O Richard! O My King!"?

Queen: I don't remember.

Herman: Were you there when the toast to the health of the nation was rejected?

Queen: I don't believe so.

Herman: It is notorious that all of France was in an uproar at that time, yet you visited the troops in Versailles to engage them to defend what you call the prerogatives of the throne.

Queen: I have nothing to say.

Herman: Before July 14, 1789, didn't you hold secret meetings at night, assisted by Madame de Polignac, and didn't you deliberate there about the means to remit funds to your brother, the emperor?

Queen: I never attended any secret meeting.

Herman: You don't deny that there were troops at the Champ de Mars; you must have known the cause for their assembly?

Queen: Yes, I knew at the time that they were there, but I did not know the reason why.

Herman: When did you use the immense sums that were given to you by various finance ministers?

Queen: No one ever gave immense sums to me. Any sums given to me were used to pay those employees who were in my household.

Herman: Why were the family Polignac and many others engorged with gold?

Queen: They had positions at the court that procured riches for them.

Jean-Baptiste Lapierre was then called. He had witnessed a number of unfamiliar people coming and going at the Tuileries Palace on June 20, 1791, the evening of the royal family's flight to Montmédy, while he was on duty there. His testimony was short and was neither favorable nor unfavorable to the queen's cause.[13]

Herman turned to question the queen, hoping to incriminate the marquis de Lafayette and Jean Sylvain Bailly, the former mayor of Paris.

Herman: When you left the palace, was it on foot or by coach?

Queen: By foot.

Herman: Was Lafayette or Bailly at the palace when you left?

Queen: I don't believe so.

Herman: What time did you depart?

Queen: At a quarter to midnight.

Herman: You did not see Lafayette or Bailly that day?

Queen: I don't recollect.

SECOND WITNESS WITH DAMAGING TESTIMONY

Antoine Roussillon, the surgeon, was best known for giving Fouquier-Tinville the idea about finding empty and full bottles of wine under the queen's bed. This happened, he said, at the Tuileries Palace on the morning of August 10 when the royal family was forced to leave the palace and take refuge at the National Assembly.[14]

Roussillon: All the facts contained in the Act of Accusation are of such public notoriety that it is unnecessary to spend time on them. If my fullest conviction can be

MARIE ANTOINETTE'S DARKEST DAYS

of any weight, I will not hesitate to affirm that I am fully persuaded that this woman is guilty of the greatest crimes and that she has always conspired against the liberty of the French people. The following is a circumstance that I must relate to you. On August 10, I was present at the siege of the Tuileries Palace. I saw under the bed of Marie Antoinette full and empty bottles from which I concluded that she had herself distributed wine to the Swiss soldiers, that these wretches in their intoxication might assassinate the people.

Herman (to the queen): Have you any observations to make, Marie Antoinette, about the testimony of this witness?

Queen: I left the palace, and I don't know what happened.

Herman: Where did you spend the night of August 9?

Queen: I spent the night with my sister [Élisabeth] in my chambers, and I did not sleep.

Herman: Why didn't you sleep?

Queen: Because at midnight the alarm bells of Paris were sounding, and it was announced that there was going to be an attack.

Herman: Isn't it true that nobles and Swiss officers were assembled in your chambers, and it was there decided to fire on the people?

Queen: No one entered my chambers.

Roussillon also stated that considerable sums were passed on to the emperor. He claimed to have obtained this information from a good citizeness in whom a former favorite of the court of Versailles had confided. He did not reveal her name, but when Fouquier-Tinville discovered her address, he ordered the woman brought to the Tribunal to find out if she had more information.

THIRD WITNESS WITH DAMAGING TESTIMONY

Jacques René Hébert, once a ticket taker at a theater where he robbed his employers, published the revolutionary newspaper *Père Duchêsne*. At the trial he aimed to prove the queen's conspiracy with the discovery of a religious book that she had owned. In its pages was an emblem identified with the counterrevolutionaries: a heart pierced by an arrow with the inscription "Jesus, have mercy upon us" (*Jesu, miserere nobis*).[15]

The testimony about this emblem was less significant than other testimony Hébert would have to offer. Antoine Simon, caretaker of the young Louis Charles, had recently asked Hébert to come to the Temple prison because he had important information. Simon told Hébert that he had surprised the "little Capet" alone—in the commission of very unnatural acts. Simon said he was astonished to see an infant committing such "crimes" at such an early age.

When Simon asked the child who had been his instructors, Louis Charles answered "with all the naiveté and candor of his age" that he had been taught by his mother and his aunt as he slept between them. Moreover, the mother had also molested him. As a result of the damage inflicted upon him, Simon said, the child had to wear a bandage; however, once he was taken away from his mother, his health returned robustly.

Hébert referred to the child's behavior as "criminal enjoyment," a piece of political strategy intent on degrading the child's physical and mental health.* This would allow the mother to rule for the incompetent child if he one day occupied the throne.

In his closing statement, Hébert reminded the court that since the death of Louis Capet, the infant was regarded by his mother and aunt as the king of France while they were incarcerated in the Temple prison. At mealtime he was seated at the end of the table and elevated on a cushion, and the family paid respect and homage to him, calling him "sire." Moreover, they always walked behind him as court etiquette had mandated before the end of the monarchy.

Herman (to the queen): How do you answer these charges from the witness?

Queen: I have no knowledge of these facts to which Hébert refers. I only know that the heart he talks about was given to my son by his sister.

Herman: When the administrators Michonis, Jobert, Marino, and Michel[†] visited you [at the Temple], did they bring any people with them?

---

*The word *jouissance* is here translated as enjoyment. However, Hébert's use of the term could have been deemed outrageous in this context because the word also denoted orgasm or sexual rapture.

†Jean-Baptiste Michonis, Augustin Germain Jobert, Jean-Baptiste Marino, and François Michel were police administrators when the royal family was imprisoned in the Temple.

Queen: Yes, because they never came alone.

Herman: How many people did they bring each time?

Queen: Often three or four.

Herman: Weren't these people administrators themselves?

Queen: I don't know.

When President Herman asked Hébert if he was aware of the manner in which the administrators performed their services, Hébert responded that he was not exactly sure. However, on the occasion of the statement just made by the accused, the Capet family, although locked up in the Temple, was still informed of everything that was going on in the city. Moreover, the accused was acquainted with all municipal officers who came to work every day, as well as with the nature of their different functions and activities.

Herman (to the witness): You saw that?

Hébert: No, I did not see it, but the entire department can confirm it.

Herman (to the queen): Were you not elated with joy when you saw a man enter your chambers at the Conciergerie with Michonis? The individual was wearing a carnation.

Queen: Being confined for thirteen months without seeing a familiar face, I trembled in fear that he might be compromised because of me.

Herman: Had this individual been one of your agents?

Queen: No.

Herman: Wasn't he at the Tuileries Palace on June 20?

Queen: Yes.

Herman: And probably on the night of August 9?

Queen: I do not remember seeing him.

Herman: Didn't you meet with Michonis on behalf of the individual wearing the carnation? What is this individual's name?

Queen: I do not know his name.

Herman: Didn't you tell Michonis you feared he would not be reelected to the new municipality?

Queen: Yes.

Herman: What was the reason for your fears in this regard?

Queen: He was humane toward all prisoners.

Herman: On the same day, you said to him, "This is perhaps the last time I will see you"?

Queen: Yes.

Herman: Why did you tell him that?

Queen: It was for the general interest of the prisoners.

Before President Herman proceeded to the next witness, one juror requested that the president direct Marie Antoinette to answer with respect to one of the crimes with which she was charged but had not responded.[16]

Juror: Citizen President, I ask you to remind the accused that she did not respond to the charge about which Citizen Hébert spoke, the proof of which rested on the declarations of the young Capet.

The president of the Tribunal went red in the face. He had refrained from any questioning about Hébert's absurd charges of incest against the queen. Rather than addressing the specific indictment, he simply motioned for the queen to respond to the juror's request to speak about the charge.*

Queen: If I did not respond, it is because nature refuses to respond to such an allegation made against a mother.

For the first time in the Tribunal, Marie Antoinette displayed emotion. Her voice trembled at first; recovering herself, she then stood up and turned toward the women who thronged the hall.

Queen: I appeal to the hearts of all mothers who are present in this room.

The tone in her voice—so rich with emotion—made the liveliest impression on the audience. The fishwives and the women from the market stopped their knitting and remained silent; for a moment it was as if they too

---

*When Robespierre heard about the abominable accusation, he exploded, "That imbecile Hébert! He's allowed Marie Antoinette—and at the very last minute—to triumph publicly!"

were being attacked. The other spectators and even the judges all looked at Hébert with frowns and disgust on their faces.[17]

Perhaps remaining secluded in her cell for the past weeks, unaware of the most outrageous charges being formulated against her, had been to Marie Antoinette's advantage. For most of her reign as queen of France, her honor had been attacked; she was an adulteress, a thief, and a traitor. But this was beyond the pale: surely the contrived testimony from her son Louis Charles, accusing her of incest, had shocked her.

President Herman was silent as Hébert left the jury box. He then called Abraham Silly to the box to testify about the night of June 20, when the royal family escaped from the Tuileries. Silly was working there that night and testified that the queen came to him about six o'clock in the evening and wanted to take a walk with her son. After that he saw Lafayette come and go five or six times during the evening to see his assistant, Monsieur

Marie Antoinette appeals to the mothers in the audience

Jean-Baptiste Gouvion, who had been ordered to lock all the doors of the palace—except those on the courtyard belonging to the royal family.[18]

Silly claimed that upon entering the royal apartments the next morning, he saw Gouvion, who exclaimed, "They are gone!" He had been struck by the way Gouvion clasped his hands as if elated by the family's escape.

Silly's testimony may have been orchestrated to incriminate Lafayette as an accomplice in the royal family's flight to Montmédy, but the queen denied any collaboration with the general. As usual, the queen was careful not to implicate anyone in her affairs.

Herman (to the witness): At what hour of the night did Lafayette leave the palace?

Silly: Within a few minutes of midnight.

Herman (to the queen): At what time did you depart?

Queen: As I already said, at a quarter to midnight.

Herman: Didn't you see Lafayette as you were leaving?

Queen: I saw his coach passing in the carousel.

Herman: Who furnished you with the famous carriage in which you departed with your family?

Queen: A foreigner.

Herman: Of what nationality?

Queen: Swedish.

Herman: Was it not Fersen, who resided in Paris at rue de Bacq?

Queen: Yes. [This answer would surely have created a commotion in the hall.]

Herman: Why did you travel under the name of a Russian baroness?

Queen: Because it was impossible in any other way to get out of Paris.

Herman: Who procured the passport for you?

Queen: It was demanded by a foreign minister.

Herman: Why did you leave Paris?

Queen: Because the king desired to leave.

At two o'clock in the afternoon, President Herman called an end to the first session of the court. Marie Antoinette motioned for Lagarde to approach her.[19]

"Did I speak with too much dignity in my voice?" she said.

"Madame, be yourself and you will be fine," he said. "But why do you ask?"

"Because I heard a woman in the audience say to her neighbor, 'See how proud she is!'"[20]

Ducoudray remarked that this conversation showed him that the queen still had hope and was still in control of herself (*bien maîtresse d'elle-même*). Despite all the commotion in the hall, she still heard everything that was said and knew when to keep her silence.

The queen was then escorted to her cell, where Lagarde and Ducoudray were allotted fifteen minutes to consult with their client. The queen asked them if they thought any of the testimonies received thus far could be used against her.

The defenders told her that up until this moment they did not believe the testimonies of the witnesses to be damaging; they were just "excessively ridiculous."

When Marie Antoinette saw the name "Pierre Manuel" on the list of witnesses summoned to the Tribunal, she said, "In that case, I am only fearful of Manuel."[21] But she did not fear his testimony; she feared only his lies.

FOURTH WITNESS WITH DAMAGING TESTIMONY

After a two-hour break, the court resumed with the testimony of Pierre-Joseph Terrasson. Employed in the office of the minister of justice, Terrasson stated that upon the royal family's return from Varennes, he saw the queen descend from her carriage at the Tuileries Palace. He claimed that she then glanced vindictively at the National Guards who escorted her, as well as at nearby citizens. This spiteful glance suggested to him that she was vengeful. And soon afterward, he reminded the court, the massacre at the Champ de Mars took place.[22]

Terrasson continued with testimony that the queen had indeed influenced the former king on his sanctioning of different decrees.

Herman (to the queen): Do you have any comments on the testimony of the witness?

Queen: I've said that I have never assisted in the king's council.

The court next called Pierre Manuel, who had been escorted from his prison cell in the Conciergerie to the Tribunal by two gendarmes.[23] Manuel had not been kind in words or deeds with respect to the royal family, but he had argued for saving the king, among other caprices, which eventually led to his imprisonment at the hands of the revolutionaries.[24]

As deputy of the Commune, Manuel had gone to the Temple prison several times to implement the Commune's decrees. Marie Antoinette feared Manuel's testimony; she knew that he was a charismatic and volatile speaker who might easily damage her reputation even further.

Manuel first testified that he had never had any rapport or conversation with the widow of the former king while he was on duty at the Temple. President Herman was clearly frustrated as he tried to wheedle an unfavorable testimony from the witness.

Herman: You have been a police administrator?

Manuel: Yes.

Herman: In this situation you must have had some connection with the royal court?

Manuel: It was the mayor [Jérôme Pétion] who had a connection with the court.* For my part, I was, I may almost say, always at La Force prison, where, from motives of humanity, I did as much good as possible for the prisoners.

Herman: Did Louis Capet at that time highly commend the Administration of Police?

Manuel: The Administration of Police was divided into five branches, of which there was one of subsistence, and it was upon this branch that Louis Capet bestowed so many commendations.

Herman: Have you any details to give with respect to the day of June 20?

Manuel: On that day I did not leave my post, as the people might have been alarmed at not finding one of their principal magistrates. I went into the Tuileries garden and spoke with different citizens, but I did not discharge any municipal function.

Herman: Tell what you know about what happened in the palace in the night between August 9 and 10.

---

*Jérôme Pétion, former mayor of Paris and the first president of the National Convention, was removed from power after a coup d'état by the more radical party of Jacobins.

Manuel: I did not choose to leave the post where the people had placed me. I remained all night at the bar of the Commune.

Herman: You were intimate with Pétion; he must have told you what had happened?

Manuel: I was his friend both from the ties of office and esteem, and if I had conceived him capable of deceiving the people and of being a party in the coalition of the palace, he would have lost my esteem. He had, however, told me that those in the palace desired to reestablish the royal authority.

Herman: Do you know that the masters of the palace had given orders to fire upon the people?

Manuel: I knew it from the post commander, an excellent republican, who came to inform me of it. Upon hearing this, I immediately notified the general of the armed force. And he expressly forbade me, as a deputy of the Commune, to fire upon the people.

Herman: How does it happen that you, who have just declared that in the night of August 9 you never left the post where the people had placed you, have since abandoned the honorable function of legislator, to which their confidence had called you?

Manuel: When I saw disturbances excited in the bosom of the National Convention, I retired. I adopted the principle of Thomas Paine, my master, in republicanism. My intentions were always pure.

Herman: What! You call yourself a good republican? You say you love equality, and yet you paid tribute to Pétion as if he were royalty?

Manuel: It was not to Pétion, who was only president for fifteen days, but to the president of the National Convention, that I wished to pay tribute.

Marie Antoinette must have sighed with relief. Manuel's testimony did not damage her reputation as she had feared. In fact, it was not unfavorable to her case at all. Perhaps Manuel refused to testify, having been imprisoned by his fellow revolutionaries.

President Herman had even more difficulty with the next witness, Jean Sylvain Bailly, a former mayor of Paris in dishonor for his role in the Champ de Mars massacres. Bailly immediately protested that the accusations against Marie Antoinette were unfounded and the facts contained in the indictment about the young Louis Charles were "absolutely false."[25]

Furthermore, he stated that there had been a rumor about the flight of the royal family to Montmédy some days before it occurred. He had communicated this to Lafayette, recommending that he take all necessary measures to prevent the escape. Bailly was obviously trying to distance himself from the unpopular general.

Herman (to the witness): At the time of the revision of the Constitution of 1791, were you not connected with Lameth, Barnave, Desmeunier, Chapellier,* and other famous conspiring revisionists, or rather men bribed by the royal court to strip the people of their real rights and leave them only the shadow of freedom?

Bailly: Lafayette was reconciled with them, but I was not, for I had never been connected with them.

Herman: It appears that you were very connected with Lafayette and that your opinions were much the same?

Bailly: My intimacy with him related to his office, and as to the rest, my opinion was at that time the general one.

Herman: You say you have never been present at any meeting, but how did it happen that, at the moment when you appeared before the Constitutional Assembly, Charles Lameth drew the answer you had already written from under his desk? That proved the existence of a criminal conspiracy. Did you likewise receive the orders of Antoinette to massacre the best patriots?

Bailly: No, I did not go to the Champ de Mars until after receiving an order from the General Council of the Commune.

Herman: The patriots assembled in the Champ de Mars with the permission of the municipality of Paris; they had made their declaration to the register and had obtained their receipt. Why did you hoist against them the infernal red flag?

Bailly: The council came to their resolution in consequence of two men having been murdered in the Champ de Mars. The subsequent accounts were more and more alarming. The council had been deceived and was determined to employ an armed force.

Herman: Were not the people, on the contrary, deceived by the municipality? Was it not the municipality that provoked the assembly of the people in order to collect the best patriots together and then have them murdered?

---

*Although strong supporters of revolution, Alexandre de Lameth, Antoine Barnave, Jean-Nicholas Desmeunier, and Jean le Chapellier were less radical than their counterparts, often angering Robespierre and the Jacobins.

Bailly: No, certainly not.

Herman: What did you do with the dead—that is, the patriots who were assassinated?

Bailly: The municipality, having drawn up the procès-verbal, transported the dead to the court of the military hospital at Gross-Caillou.

Herman: How many were they?

Bailly: The number was ascertained and rendered public in the procès-verbal, which was published at the time by the municipality; there might have been twelve or thirteen.

One of the jurors then spoke up. He informed the Tribunal that he was at the Champ de Mars with his father at the time the massacre began, and he saw seventeen or eighteen persons of both sexes killed near the river where he stood. "We could only escape death ourselves by wading up to our chins," he said.

Bailly was silent on the matter, but President Herman was not finished with him. Before letting him step down from the jury box, Herman turned to the subject of the unsworn priests. He aimed to show that by allowing unsworn priests into the Tuileries, Bailly had not fulfilled his duties as mayor.

Herman (to the queen): What was the number of priests you had in the palace?

Queen: We had none about our persons but the priests who said mass.

Herman: Had they taken the oaths?

Queen: The law allowed the king to choose whom he pleased.

FIFTH WITNESS WITH DAMAGING TESTIMONY

The second witness called earlier in the day, Roussillon, had stated that considerable sums were remitted to the emperor. This information, he said, was obtained from a good citizeness who was immediately summoned to the Tribunal. She was a domestic named Reine Millot, who told Roussillon that Marie Antoinette had sent the incredible sum of 200 million francs to her brother, Emperor Joseph of Austria, to fight the Turks and then come to her aid in France.[26]

The courtroom broke out in laughter. That the domestic had heard this news from the duke de Coigny was preposterous. The duke de Coigny was one of the nobles who had emigrated with the royal princes when the French Revolution broke out, and he had also joined the émigré army against the French republic.

Reine Millot also testified that the queen had formed a plot to assassinate the duke of Orléans, and the king, being acquainted with it, had ordered her searched immediately. "When two pistols were found on her person," Millot said, "the king had her confined to her own room for a fortnight."

Queen: It is possible I might have received an order from my husband to remain a fortnight in my apartment, but this was not the case.

Millot: I know further that in the first days of October 1789, some ladies of the court distributed white cockades to diverse persons at Versailles.

Queen: I remember having heard that, one or two days after the feast of the body-guards, some women distributed these cockades, but neither I nor my husband was the author of similar disorders.

Herman (to the queen): What steps did you pursue to punish these women after you were acquainted with this circumstance?

Queen: None at all.

SIXTH WITNESS WITH DAMAGING TESTIMONY

Jean-Baptiste Labenette wasted no time in revealing that he agreed with all the charges contained in the indictment. He then added that three persons had come to assassinate him at the instigation of Marie Antoinette. When President Herman heard the grave accusation, he asked the strangest of questions.[27]

Herman (to the queen): Did you ever read the *Orator of the People*?
Queen: No, never.

Louis Fréron's newspaper, *L'orateur du peuple*, violently attacked coun-terrevolutionaries, especially Marie Antoinette. Perhaps Herman was insinu-ating that the queen targeted those who were behind these attacks.

Herman next called François Dufresne, who had guarded Marie Antoinette's cell until the Carnation Plot. He was present in the cell when Rougeville brought the queen the carnation. He knew that the flower concealed a note containing the following words: "What are you doing here? We have men and money at your service."[28]

Marie Barassaint, the wife of Warden Richard, testified that the guard named Jean Gilbert had told her that their prisoner had received the carnation from a person brought there by police administrator Jean-Baptiste Michonis. Madame Richard, worried that she might be compromised, gave the message to Michonis, who said he would never bring another visitor into the widow Capet's cell.[29] Warden Toussaint Richard was called to the jury box and said that he knew the prisoner because she had been put under his guard since the beginning of August. He was not interrogated further.[30]

Marie Devaux Harel, known in the prison simply as the "woman Harel," testified that she had been with the prisoner for forty-one days at the Conciergerie. She had neither seen nor heard anything except a person coming one day with Michonis who gave the prisoner a note folded up in the petals of a carnation. She added that she was then working and saw the same person call again in the course of that day.[31]

Queen: He came twice in the course of a quarter of an hour.

Herman (to the witness): Who placed you with the widow Capet?

Harel: Michonis and Jobert.

Marie Antoinette's former guard Jean Gilbert swore to the facts heard concerning the Carnation Plot. He added that the queen had complained to the guards about the meals she was receiving but would not complain to the administrators. On that account, Gilbert had called Michonis, who was nearby in the women's prison yard with Rougeville, in order to relay the message. When Michonis returned to the cell, Gilbert heard the queen say to him, "Then I shall not see you anymore."[32]

The guard heard Michonis reply, "Oh, pardon me, I shall always be a municipal officer, and in that position I shall have a right to see you." Gilbert then added that the queen said she was greatly obliged to Rougeville.

Queen: I am under no other obligation to him other than that he was near me on June 20.

The queen was referring to June 20, 1792, when Rougeville helped lead the royal family from the Tuileries Palace to the National Assembly for their safety.

It was eleven o'clock in the evening when President Herman adjourned the court until the next morning. After fifteen hours of proceedings, the queen would have one more day to face her accusers. Her lawyer Lagarde noted that, although she sipped very little soup in the recess and was exhausted by her hemorrhaging, the queen had remained dignified and energetic throughout the day:

> That one could realize, if possible, all the fortitude the queen must have had to endure the fatigue of a such a long and horrible proceeding; on show before an audience; having to fight to defend herself against bloodthirsty monsters with traps set for her; and at the same time keep a demeanor worthy of herself.[33]

As Lieutenant de Busne escorted the queen back to her cell, she became faint. "I can no longer see," she said. "I am exhausted; I cannot walk."

The lieutenant offered her his arm out of respect and helped her down the slippery steps of the staircase to her room. He paid for such a display of kindness the following morning when he was arrested.

À SAVOIR . . .

Meteorologist's Report[34]

On October 15, Marie Antoinette awakened to a chilly, rainy morning for the second day of interrogations. The meteorologist recorded a temperature of ten degrees (about fifty degrees Fahrenheit) with winds from the north. The sky cleared up during the afternoon, but the queen returned later in the evening to a cell much colder than the night before.

12

THE REVOLUTIONARY TRIBUNAL—DAY TWO

"Yesterday I did not know the witnesses. I knew not what they were to depose against me, and nobody has produced against me any positive evidence."

—Marie Antoinette, last statement
to the Revolutionary Tribunal

Paris
October 15, 1793

Marie Antoinette wore the same black dress to the Tribunal as she had the day before, and she must have arrived in the hall before eight o'clock in the morning. The son of the old apothecary Jacques Antoine Lacour delivered the queen's medicinal potion every morning at nine o'clock; on this morning, however, Lacour gave the orders to send the bottle a few minutes before eight, but the queen had already left her cell.[1]

Nor was the queen seated in the same chair on this day; she was instead given an easy chair of sculpted wood covered with velour. During the first several hours of her trial, she tapped her fingers upon the arm of the chair with an "appearance of unconcern," as if she were playing the piano.[2]

The first witness called on the second day was Charles Henri d'Estaing, a vice admiral, who was escorted from his prison cell at Sainte Pélagie to testify against Marie Antoinette. D'Estaing had supported revolutionary ideas but was eventually convicted for his role during the days of October 1789 as well as his aristocratic background.[3]

D'Estaing testified that he had known the queen ever since she first arrived in France and that he even had reason to file a complaint against her. After he returned from fighting in the American Revolutionary War, the queen kept him from being compensated for his services abroad.* However, he said he would nevertheless tell the truth, which was that he had nothing at all to say with respect to the charges of her indictment.

Hoping to get some useful testimony from D'Estaing, Tribunal president Martial Joseph Armand Herman first questioned him about October 5 before turning to the Champ de Mars massacre.

Herman: Were you at the palace [Versailles] that day?

D'Estaing: Yes.

Herman: What did you hear at the palace?

D'Estaing: I heard the counselors of the royal court tell the queen that the people of Paris were coming to massacre her and that it was necessary she should depart. Upon which she replied with great firmness, "If the Parisians come hither to assassinate me, I shall fall at the feet of my husband; I will not take flight myself."

Queen: That is true. They wished to prevail on me to depart alone because, they said, I was the only one exposed to danger.

Herman (to D'Estaing): Have you any knowledge of the entertainments given to former royal guardsmen?

D'Estaing: Yes.

Herman: Do you know that they then cried out "Vive le roi" and "Vive la famille royale"?

D'Estaing: Yes.

Herman (to the queen): Did you not give entertainments to the National Guard of Versailles on their return from Paris, where they had been to fetch muskets?

Queen: Yes.

---

*Louis XVI actively supported the North American colonists, who were seeking their independence from France's enemy, Great Britain.

SEVENTH WITNESS WITH DAMAGING TESTIMONY

Antoine Simon, a former cobbler, was employed at the time as mentor to Marie Antoinette's young son, Charles Louis Capet. Simon stated that he had known the accused since he became a guard at the Temple when the royal family arrived on August 10 the previous year. He also stated that during the time that the former king and his family had the liberty to walk in the prison gardens, they were well informed of everything that happened in Paris and the rest of France.[4] In other words, the royal family had a network of informants and spies.

Herman: Have you any knowledge of the intrigues that took place at the Temple while the accused was there?

Simon: Yes.

Herman: Who were the administrators who communicated with her?

Simon: Little Capet told me that Toulan, Pétion, Lafayette, Lepître, Beugnot, Michonis, Vincent, Manuel, Leboeuf, and Dangé* were the persons for whom his mother had the greatest fondness and that the latter had taken him in his arms and said to him in the presence of his mother, "I sincerely wish that you were in your father's place [throne]."

Queen: I have seen my son playing quoits in the garden with Dangé, but I never saw the latter take him in his arms.[†]

Herman (to the witness): Do you know that, while the administrators were with the accused and her sister-in-law, the little Capet and his sister were shut up in the tower?

Simon: Yes.

Herman: Do you know that the little Capet was treated as a king, especially at the table?

Simon: I know that his mother and aunt gave precedence to him at the table.

Herman (to the queen): Have you not signed orders for receiving money from the treasurer of the Civil List?

---

*Toulan, Pétion, Lafayette, Lepître, Beugnot, Michonis, Vincent, Manuel, Leboeuf, and Dangé were all government officials or police administrators.

†Quoits was a game similar to pitching horseshoes.

Queen: No.

Herman. Your denial will become useless in a moment or two. Orders signed by your own hand have been found among the papers of Septeuil.* Two orders were indeed deposited in the hands of the committee, but they are at present mislaid, that commission being dissolved, but you will hear the witnesses who saw them.

EIGHTH WITNESS WITH DAMAGING TESTIMONY

François Tisset was employed without a salary at the Committee of Public Safety of the municipality when the royal family was taken to the Temple on August 10, 1792. He testified that when ordered to arrest Septeuil, the treasurer of the former royal Civil List, he did not find him at his residence. However, among Septeuil's papers he found two drafts for the sum of eighty thousand livres signed by Marie Antoinette and a note for two million signed by Louis.[5]

Queen: I desire that the witness will mention the dates of the drafts of which he speaks.

Tisset: One of them was dated August 10, 1792. The date of the other I do not remember.

Queen: I never gave such drafts, and how could I give any on August 10, when we went at eight o'clock in the morning to the National Assembly?

Herman (to the queen): Did you not, that day, when in the box of the *logographe*[†] in the assembly, receive money from those who were around you?

Queen: It was not in the box of the *logographe* but during the three days we remained at the Feuillants[‡] that, being without money, as we had not carried any with us, we accepted that which was offered to us.

Herman: How much did you receive?

Queen: Twenty-five louis d'or, the same which were found in my pockets when I was conducted from the Temple to the Conciergerie. Considering this debt as sacred, I

---

*Jean-Baptiste Tourteau de Septeuil was Louis XVI's valet de chambre and treasurer of the Civil List, the annual funds allotted for the king's household by the legislature.

†The *logographe* was a separate space in the National Assembly, also called the reporters' box.

‡This was the former monastery of the Feuillant monks on the rue Saint-Honoré near the National Assembly.

kept them untouched, in order that I might return them to the person from whom I received them, in case I should see her.

Herman: What is the name of that person?

Queen: The Dame Auguel [Auguié].*

The slightest mark of sympathy for the royal family since August 10 had been cause for suspicion. Madame Auguié, one of the queen's ladies-in-waiting, did indeed give the queen twenty-five gold coins on August 11 in the Feuillants convent. Confirming this, however, the queen had no idea that she was exposing Madame Auguié to any danger.[6]

The Committee of General Security immediately called for Madame Auguié's arrest, but at the moment when the gendarmes arrived at her residence, she jumped out of her apartment window and killed herself.[7]

The next witness, Jacques François Lepître, stated that he saw the accused at the Temple while he was on duty as commissioner of the provisional municipality, but he never had any particular conversation with her. As hard as President Herman tried, he was unable to retrieve any damaging information from this witness against the queen.[8]

Herman (to the witness): Did you never converse with her on politics?

Lepître: Never.

Herman: Did you not enable her to learn the news by sending a town crier every day to shout the *Journal de soir* near the tower of the Temple?

Lepître: No.

Herman (to the queen): Have you any observations to make on the declaration of the witness?

Queen: I never had any conversation with the witness. On the other hand, there was no necessity for engaging town criers to approach the tower; I heard them sufficiently every day when they passed through the nearby streets.

A small packet was then presented to Marie Antoinette. She declared that it was the same on which she had put her seal when she was removed from the Temple to the Conciergerie. After opening the packet, the registrar Fabricius declared the contents:

*Madame Auguié's name was misspelled in the trial transcript as "Auguel."

Fabricius: A packet of hair of different colors.

Queen: It is locks of hair of my children, dead and alive,* and that of my husband.

Fabricius: Another packet of hair.

Queen: It comes from the same individuals.

Fabricius: A paper, on which are cyphers.

Queen: It is a table for teaching my son arithmetic.

Fabricius then noted that there was also a small packet of papers of little importance such as washwomen's bills. However, there was a small green-beaded notebook in which was written the names of different persons on parchment. President Herman asked the queen to identify them.

Herman: Who is the woman Salentin?

Queen: It is she who, for a long time, has been charged with all my affairs.

Herman: Who is Mademoiselle Vion?

Queen: It is she who had the care of what belongs to my children.

Herman: And the Dame Chaumette?

Queen: It was she who succeeded the young woman Vion.

Herman: What is the name of the woman who took care of your lace?

Queen: I do not know her name. She was employed by the women Salentin and Chaumette.

Herman: Who is Bernier, whose name is found here?

Queen: He is the physician who attended to my children.

Fouquier-Tinville ordered that Salentin, Vion, and Chaumette be brought immediately before the Tribunal and that the physician Bernier be summoned to appear.

Fabricius continued to give an inventory of the items found under seal: a small purse with scissors, needles, and silk thread; a small mirror; a gold ring; a paper on which were two golden hearts with initials; another paper on which was a prayer; and a portrait of a woman.

---

*Marie Antoinette had four children. Princess Sophia died when she was eleven months old; Prince Louis Joseph died at the age of three.

Herman (to the queen): Whose portrait is this?

Queen: Madame Lamballe.*

Fabricius added that there were two more portraits of women, a roll of gold coins, and a small piece of cloth on which was found a flaming heart with an arrow.

Herman: Who are the persons whom these portraits represent?

Queen: Two ladies with whom I was educated in Vienna.

Herman: What are their names?

Queen: The ladies de Mecklenbourg and Heste.

Herman: And the roll of twenty-five louis d'or?

Queen: These are the louis d'or lent to me while we were at the Feuillants.

Herman: A small piece of cloth, on which is a flaming heart pierced with an arrow?

Prosecutor Antoine Quentin Fouquier-Tinville requested that Jacques René Hébert examine that heart and declare whether he knew it to be the same one he had found at the Temple. Hébert replied, "This heart is not that which I found at the Temple, but it resembles it."

Fouquier-Tinville then noted that among all the accused who had been brought before the Tribunal as conspirators—and on whom the law had done justice—most had carried these counterrevolutionary symbols on their persons.

Hébert remarked that he also did not know if Salentin, Vion, and Chaumette were ever employed at the Temple to serve the prisoners, but the queen spoke up: "They were there in the beginning."

Another witness who did no damage whatsoever to Marie Antoinette's case was Jean-Frédéric de la Tour-du-Pin, Louis XVI's minister of war. In fact, he showed deference to Marie Antoinette, at times addressing her as "your majesty" (*votre majesté*). Perhaps he was unaware that prosecutor Fouquier-Tinville abhorred the use of royal titles long since abolished.[9]

---

*Marie Thérèse Louise de Savoie-Carignan, the princess of Lamballe, was Marie Antoinette's confidante. She was killed during the September massacres of 1792.

Herman: Did you not assist at the entertainments of the palace [banquet for the Flanders regiment]?

Tour-du-Pin: I never, as I may say, frequented the royal court.

Herman: Were you not present at the entertainment of the former guards?

Tour-du-Pin: I could not be present; at that epoch I had the command in Burgundy.

Herman: What! Were you not minister at that time?

Tour-du-Pin: I never was minister; nor would I have accepted it, if those then in office had made me an offer of such an appointment.

Herman (to the witness Laurent Lecointre): Do you know the witness present to have been a minister of war in 1789?

Lecointre: I know this witness was never minister. He who was minister at that time is present here now and is going to be examined.

Herman (to Tour-du-Pin): Were you the minister on October 1?

Tour-du-Pin: Yes, I was.

Herman: You no doubt at the time heard of the feast of the former Gardes-de-Corps?

Tour-du-Pin: Yes, I did.

Herman: Were you not minister in the month of June 1789 when the troops arrived at Versailles?

Tour-du-Pin: No, I was then deputy of the assembly.

Herman: The royal court apparently laid you under restrictions in naming you minister of war?

Tour-du-Pin: I do not think the court did.

Herman: Were you at the former king's council on October 5, 1789?

Tour-du-Pin: No, I was not.

Herman: Was d'Estaing there?

Tour-du-Pin: I do not know.

D'Estaing (interrupting): Well then, my sight on that day was better than yours, for I remember perfectly well having seen you there.

Perhaps seeing that the interrogation was going nowhere, President Herman turned to the queen and addressed the subject of her Petit Trianon.

Herman: Have you not abused the influence you had over your husband in asking him continually for drafts on the public treasury?

Queen: I never did so.

Herman: Where did you then get the money to build and fit out the Petit Trianon, in which you gave feasts, of which you were always the goddess?

Queen: There was a fund destined for that purpose.

Herman: This fund was then very considerable because the Petit Trianon has cost enormous sums.

Queen: It is possible that the Petit Trianon may have cost immense sums, perhaps more than I wished. This expense was incurred inch by inch; in fact, I desire more than anyone that every person may be informed what has been done there.

Herman: Was it not at the Petit Trianon that you saw for the first time the wife of La Motte?*

Queen: I never saw her.

Herman: Was she not your victim of the affair of the famous necklace?

Queen: How could she be so, as I do not know her?

Herman: So you persist in denying that you ever knew her?

Queen: My intention is not to deny; I only speak the truth and shall persist in so doing.

Herman: Was it not you who caused ministers and other civil and military officers to be named to their posts?

Queen: No.

Herman: Had you not a list of the persons for whom you wished to get positions?

Queen: No.

Herman: Did you not force the ministers of finance to give you money, and some of them refusing to do so, have you not threatened them with all your resentment?

Queen: No, never.

Herman: Have you not been pleading with Minister Vergennes† to send 6 million to the king of Bohemia and Hungary [her brother]?

Queen: No.

---

*The Necklace Affair was a scandal caused by the comtesse de la Motte at the court of Versailles.

†Charles Gravier, Comte de Vergennes, was Louis XVI's foreign minister.

NINTH WITNESS WITH DAMAGING TESTIMONY

Jean François Mathey had been a guard in the Temple and testified that on hearing the song "Oh! Thou Wilt Remember Thy Returning from Varennes," he asked the young Louis Charles if he remembered returning from that place. The child answered, "Oh, yes, I remember it well."[10]

When Mathey asked him how his family carried him away when they fled the capital, he answered, "They took me out of my bed when asleep, and they dressed me in girl's clothes, saying, 'Come, you are going to Montmédy.'"

Herman: Did you not observe during your residence in the Temple a familiarity between some members of the committee and the prisoners?

Mathey: Yes, I even heard Toulan say one day to the prisoner, at the time of the new elections for the new municipality, "Madame, I wasn't reelected because I'm a Gascon." Another day I saw Jobert hand some medallions to the prisoner, and the daughter of Capet let one fall to the ground and broke it.

Queen: I have to observe that there were three medallions, and that which fell on the floor and was broken was the portrait of Voltaire; of the other two, one represented Medea and the other some flowers.

Herman (to the queen): Did you not give a gold snuffbox to Toulan?

Queen: No, neither to Toulan nor to anyone else.

Hébert observed that a justice of the peace had brought him a statement signed by two clerks of the Committee of Taxation, of which Toulan was the chief, clearly proving that he had bragged about receiving the snuffbox in the office.

TENTH WITNESS WITH DAMAGING TESTIMONY

The next witness with damning testimony was Jean-Baptiste-Olivier Garnerin, who stated that he had been commissioned to examine and record the papers found in the house of Septeuil, where he found a draft for eighty thousand livres signed by Marie Antoinette for her favorite, the duchess of

Polignac. He also found a draft relating to Monsieur Lazaille and another document proving that the queen had sold her diamonds to aid the emigrant aristocrats and royals.[11]

Herman: Do you have anything to say about the testimony of this witness?

Queen: I persist in saying that I never gave nor signed any drafts.

Herman: Do you know Lazaille?

Queen: Yes, I do.

Herman: How did you know him?

Queen: I know him to be a naval officer, and I have seen him at court.

Garnerin: I have to add that all the papers of which I spoke were carried to the Committee of General Security, where they must still be.

The witness Tisset interrupted. He asked President Herman to interrogate Citizen Garnerin to see if he remembered having seen among the receipts found at Septeuil's any purchases of sugar, coffee, and corn. They amounted to two million livres.

Herman (to Garnerin): You just now heard the question. Be so good as to answer it.

Garnerin: I know nothing of this business. At the same time it is notorious that there were plenty of forestallers all over France to buy up any article in order to enhance the price of it and thereby to disgust the people with the Revolution and liberty.

Herman (to the queen): Have you any knowledge of the immense forestalling of commodities made by order of the court to starve the people and compel them to demand again for reinstatement of the former government, which was so favorable to tyrants?

Queen: I have no knowledge whatsoever of any forestallings.

ELEVENTH WITNESS WITH DAMAGING TESTIMONY

Charles-Eléonore Dufriche-Valazé, former delegate to the National Assembly, testified that among the papers found at Septeuil's, he noticed two relating to the prisoner. The first was a draft, or rather a receipt, signed by her for ten or twenty thousand livres, as near as he remembered. The other was a letter in which Minister Septeuil begged the former king to communicate to Marie Antoinette the campaign, recently presented to him, to carry on considerable trade in corn, sugar, and coffee.[12]

Herman (to Valazé): Why did you not speak of the vouchers when you made your report to the convention?

Valazé: I did not mention them because I thought it superfluous to speak in the trial of Louis Capet about the expenses of Antoinette.

Herman: Do you know what became of these two vouchers?

Valazé: I believe that all the vouchers have now been returned to the Committee of General Security.

Herman (to the queen): What have you to answer to the statements of this witness?

Queen: I know nothing, neither of the check nor of the letter he mentions.

Fouquier-Tinville (to the queen): It seems to be proved, notwithstanding your denials, that through your influence over the former king, your consort, you made him do what you pleased.

Queen: There is a vast difference between advising an action and executing it.

Fouquier-Tinville: You mean to say that, from the declaration of the witness, it results that the ministers so well knew your influence over Louis Capet that one of them desired of him to communicate to you the plan of the campaign that he had presented to him a few days earlier. The consequence of which is that you were the master over his [the king's] feeble character, and you could make him do anything wicked.

Queen: I never knew him to have that character of which you are speaking.

The next witness, Nicholas Leboeuf, claimed to have no knowledge of the facts relating to the indictment. "If I had observed anything," he said, "I should have made you acquainted therewith."[13]

Herman: Did you ever converse with Louis Capet?

Leboeuf: No.

Herman: Did you not, when you were on duty in the Temple, enter into conversation on political affairs with your colleagues and the prisoners?

Leboeuf: I frequently conversed with my colleagues, but we did not speak of politics.

Herman: Did you frequently address Louis Charles Capet?

Leboeuf: Never.

Herman: Did you not offer him *Le nouveau Télémaque* to read?*

Leboeuf: No.

Herman: Have you not manifested a desire to be his governor?

Leboeuf: No, never.

Herman (to the queen): Do you declare that you never had any private conversation with the witness?

Queen: I never spoke to him.

Thus far, Marie Antoinette was holding up well with her questioning. "At about two o'clock," Rosalie wrote, "I heard some persons talking about the sitting; they said, 'Marie Antoinette will obtain her freedom—she has answered very well—they will only banish her.'"

The next witness, Augustin Germain Jobert, a municipal officer and police administrator, also declared that he had no knowledge whatsoever of any of the facts contained in the indictment against the queen.[14]

Herman (to the witness): Have you not, during your time of service in the Temple, had some meetings with the prisoner?

Jobert: No, never.

Herman: Did you not show her one day something curious?

Jobert: I have, in fact, shown medallions in wax allegorical to the Revolution to the widow Capet and her daughter.

Herman: Was there not a man's portrait among them?

Jobert: I do not believe there was.

Herman: For instance, the portrait of Voltaire?

Jobert: Yes, but I have some five thousand of that sort in my house.

---

*This is a curious question from Herman because *The Adventures of Telemachus* was also used to educate the young future King Louis XVI by his mentor Paul-François de Quélen Vauguyon.

Herman: Why was the picture of Medea among the number? Did you mean it as an allusion to the prisoner?

Jobert: It was all chance because I have so many of them. They are all articles from England in which I trade and sell to merchants.

Herman: Have you any knowledge that from time to time you and other administrators had private meetings with the prisoner?

Jobert: I know nothing of it.

Herman: And so you persist in saying that you never had any private meetings with the prisoner?

Jobert: Yes.

Herman (to the queen): Do you persist in saying that you never had any communication with the previous two witnesses?

Queen: Yes.

Herman: Do you equally persist that Bailly and Lafayette did not cooperate with your flight the night of June 20?

Queen: Yes.

Herman: I must tell you that you find yourself in contradiction with your son's declaration.

Queen: It is very easy to make an eight-year-old child say anything that one wishes.

Herman: But one sole declaration was not sufficient. He was made to repeat it at different times, and it was always the same.

Queen: Well, then, I deny the fact.

Herman: Since your detention in the Temple, didn't you have your portrait painted?

Queen: Yes, a pastel.

Herman: Were you not locked up with the painter, and didn't you use the portrait as a pretext to receive news about what was happening in the assemblies and the conventions?

Queen: No.

Herman: What was the name of the painter?

Queen: It was Coëstier, a Polish painter who has been in Paris for twenty years.

Herman: Where does he live?

Queen: Rue du Cocq-Saint-Honoré.

This questioning of the queen was insightful because it revealed that she had given her consent for a portrait, a pastel, to be made "since she was in the Temple." From the context of the question, it appeared that Herman was referring to the Conciergerie, where many visitors had accompanied Michonis to see the queen. Also, the artist was more than likely Alexandre Kucharski. Although the registrar wrote "Coëstier," he could have misunderstood the pronunciation of the foreign artist's name. Moreover, the queen gave the artist's address as rue du Cocq-Saint-Honoré, and Kucharski was known to live on this street.[15] Given this information, the last portrait of Marie Antoinette appears to have been made in the Conciergerie and not in the Temple.

Antoine-François Moyle was next called. He testified that he had once visited the king at the Temple and had twice visited the women prisoners there. He never spoke to them and never noticed anything out of the ordinary.[16]

Herman: Do you have anything to say about the testimony of the witness?

Queen: I can only say that I have never had any conversation with the witness.

The next witness, Renée Sévin, known as the "woman Chaumette," testified that she had known the accused for six years. She had served as a lady-in-waiting but had no knowledge of any charges against the queen. She had seen, however, the king review his guards on August 10.[17]

Herman (to the witness): Were you at the palace [Tuileries] at the time of the flight to Varennes?

Sévin: Yes, but I didn't know about it.

Herman: In what part of the palace did you sleep?

Sévin: At the far end of the Flore Pavilion.

Herman: Did you hear the alarms sound on the night of August 9?

Sévin: No, I was sleeping in the attic.

Herman: What! You were sleeping in the attic, and you didn't even hear the alarm?

Sévin: No, I was ill.

Herman: And how was it that you were present at the review of the king's guards?

Sévin: I had been up since six o'clock in the morning.

Herman: What! You were sick, but yet you were up at six o'clock?

Sévin: It was because of the noise.

Herman: During the review, did you hear cries of "Vive le roi" and "Vive la reine!"?

Sévin: I heard cries of "Vive le roi" on one side and "Vive la nation!" on the other.

Herman: Did you see the extraordinary assembly of the king's guards on the night before?

Sévin: I didn't go downstairs to the court.

Herman: But to take your meals, you must have surely gone downstairs.

Sévin: I didn't leave my room. A servant brought my meal.

Herman: But at least the servant told you what was happening.

Sévin: I didn't have any conversation with him.

President Herman was surely exhausted after interrogating Madame Sévin; he had a difficult time getting any information from the witness. There was likely, however, some levity in the Tribunal hall upon hearing the rather amusing question-and-answer session.

Herman next called Jean-Baptiste Vincent, a mason who had worked at the Temple, but he had never had any communication with the queen, and he was excused.[18]

The architect Nicolas-Marie-Jean Beugnot was then called. He stated that although his colleagues called him to take a look at the prisoners when he was there, he never once forgot to refrain from any communications with them, especially with the accused.[19]

Herman: You never locked up the little Capet and his sister in a tower while you and your colleagues had a conversation with the accused?

Beugnot: No.

Herman: Didn't she have you procure the means to know the news by town criers?

Beugnot: No.

Herman: Didn't you overhear the accused give Toulan a gold box?

Beugnot: No.

Queen: I never had any communication with the witness.

Former police administrator François Dangé next testified that he had been in the Temple many times but had no meetings with the prisoners; nor did he have to have any meetings.[20]

Herman: Didn't you ever take the little Capet on your knees? Didn't you tell him that you wished he were in his father's place?

Dangé: No.

Herman: Since the accused has been imprisoned, haven't you been able to secure entrance into the prison for many of your friends?

Dangé: No.

Herman: Did you ever hear that there were many who were escorted into the Conciergerie?

Dangé: No.

Herman: What is your opinion of the accused?

Dangé: If she is guilty, she must be judged.

Herman: Do you believe her to be a patriot?

Dangé: No.

Herman: Do you believe she wants a republic?

Dangé: No.

Throughout most of the day the crowd expressed no emotion, favorable or unfavorable. However, those gathered occasionally asked Marie Antoinette to stand up so that they could better see her.[21]

"When will the people be tired of my sufferings?" she said on one occasion after returning to her seat.

Worn down by the questioning and not having eaten much since the day before, the queen indeed showed signs of weakening. She asked for a glass of water, but no one stirred. Finally, Lieutenant Louis-François de Busne fetched a beverage and presented it to her with the same respect as if she were still queen at Versailles. He would soon pay dearly for this act of kindness.[22]

At four o'clock in the afternoon, President Herman called for an hour's recess. The warden told Rosalie, "The sitting is suspended for an hour, and the accused will not come downstairs. They have asked for some soup, so go up quickly."[23]

Rosalie immediately took some soup that she had kept ready for the queen up to the Tribunal hall. As she was entering the room, one of the police commissioners stopped her. An ugly little man named Labuzière took the soup out of her hands and gave it to his mistress, a gaudily dressed young lady.[24]

"This young woman wishes to see the widow Capet," Labuzière said to Rosalie, "and this will be a good opportunity for her."

His mistress immediately hurried off with the soup, spilling half of it on her way to the queen.

Rosalie objected, but the police commissioner was a man too powerful to disobey. Rosalie was mostly worried about what the queen would think when she received her soup from the hands of a stranger.[25]

After the recess Jean-Baptiste Michonis next testified. He said he knew the accused because he—along with his colleagues—had transferred her from the Temple to the Conciergerie on August 2.[26]

Herman (to the witness): Haven't you secured entry for someone to the chamber of the accused since she has been in this prison [Conciergerie]?

Michonis: Pardon me. I secured the entry of one named Giroux, a pension owner; another one of my friends, a painter; an administrator in public works; and another friend of mine.

Herman: You surely secured entry for other persons.

Michonis: Here's the fact, because I want to tell the whole truth here. On the day of Saint Peter [June 29], I dined at Monsieur Fontaine's residence in good company. One of the guests, Madame Dutilleul, invited Fontaine to dine at her home in Vaugirard and to bring me. When I arrived for the dinner, there were many guests, and after dinner the conversation turned to the widow Capet in the Conciergerie. Someone said she had changed greatly and that her hair was all white. I replied that her hair was graying, but she was doing quite well. A citizen who was present showed interest in seeing the prisoner, and I promised to grant his wish. The day after I escorted the gentleman to the prison, Madame Richard asked me, "Do you know the person whom you brought here yesterday?" I told her that I only knew him from dining with him at my friend's home. Madame Richard then told me that he was formerly a chevalier of Saint-Louis. At the same time, she gave me a piece of paper with writing done by pricking holes with a needle. I told her, "I swear I will never bring anyone here again."

Herman: Didn't you tell the accused that your position with the Commune was perhaps ending?

Michonis: Yes, I told her about it.

Herman: What did she say?

Michonis: She said, "We will not see you again?" and I added, "Madame, I'm still a municipal officer, and I can still visit you from time to time."

Herman: You, a police administrator! How could you have broken the rules by introducing an unknown to the accused! You didn't know that a great number of schemers would do anything to seduce administrators?

Michonis: It wasn't he who asked to see the widow Capet; it was I who offered it to him.

Herman: How many times did you dine with him?

Michonis: Two times.

Herman: What is this individual's name?

Michonis: I don't know.

Herman: How much did he promise you or give you for the satisfaction of seeing Antoinette?

Michonis: I never received any retribution.

Herman: While he was in the prisoner's cell, didn't you see him make any gesture?

Michonis: No.

Herman: Haven't you seen him since?

Michonis: I only saw him one time.

Herman: Why didn't you have him arrested?

Michonis: That was another mistake that I made in this regard.

At this point a juror spoke up and informed President Herman that he thought that Madame Sophie Lebon Dutilleul should be arrested as a suspect and a counterrevolutionary.

Then another witness, Pierre-Edouard Bernier, was called to the jury box. He said that he had known the accused for fourteen or fifteen years, having been her children's physician.[27]

Herman: Weren't you the doctor of Louis Capet's children in 1789, and in that capacity, didn't you overhear the reason for the assembly of the troops at Versailles and in Paris?

Bernier: No.

Witness Hébert interrupted the interrogation to add that Bernier was often at the Temple in the first days of the detention of the Capet family. He noted that these frequent visits were suspicious, especially when Bernier approached the children with all the baseness of the ancient regime. The doctor assured the court that this was done with "decorum, not baseness" (*bienséance, et non bassesse*).[28]

The next witness, Lieutenant Claude-Denis Tavernier, testified that while on guard on the night of June 20, he saw Lafayette arrive in the courtyard. He said that he saw the general turn red in the face when he heard that the Capet family had been arrested in Varennes.[29]

Lieutenant Jean-Maurice-François Lebrasse of the gendarmerie stated that he had known the queen for four years.[30] He had no knowledge of the charges in the indictment except for what he heard one evening in the Conciergerie about the Carnation Plot.[31]

The painter Joseph Boze then stated that he had known the accused for almost eight years. He had painted the king's portrait but had never spoken to the queen.[32]

TWELFTH WITNESS WITH DAMAGING TESTIMONY

The usher Didier Jourdheuil declared that he found a stack of papers at the residence of Louis Auguste d'Affry in the month of September 1792.* Among these papers was a note penned by Marie Antoinette that read, "Can we count on our Swiss? Will they put on a bold front when it is time?"[33] The queen quickly denied it.

Queen: I never wrote to d'Affry.

---

*D'Affry was the military governor of Paris until the National Assembly asked him to choose between the governorship and serving as colonel of Louis XVI's Swiss Guard. He chose the Swiss Guard in order to protect the royal family, especially at the Tuileries on August 10, 1792.

Fouquier-Tinville then interrupted, saying that he had been involved in the case against d'Affry a year earlier and had seen the letter of which the witness spoke. However, because the trial had been suspended, the letter was confiscated with d'Affry's other papers.

Pierre Fontaine, the wood merchant, was then called. He declared himself ignorant of every charge of the accusation, knowing the prisoner only by reputation and having no connection with the former court.[34]

Herman: How long have you known Michonis?

Fontaine: About fourteen years.

Herman: What is the name of the individual who dined with you in company with Michonis?

Fontaine: His name is Rougeville. I do not remember anything about him, but he was introduced to me by Madame Dutilleul.

Herman: How do you know that lady?

Fontaine: I once met her with another woman on the boulevards. We entered into a conversation and drank coffee together. Since that time, she has often dined at my residence.

Herman: She hasn't revealed any secrets to you?

Fontaine: Never.

Herman: What are the names of the deputies who were found with Rougeville and Michonis?

Fontaine: There was only one.

Herman: Do you know what has become of Rougeville?

Fontaine: No.

THIRTEENTH WITNESS WITH DAMAGING TESTIMONY

The final witness who testified negatively against Marie Antoinette was Michael Gointre, an employee of the Ministry of War. He said he had read the indictment against the queen but was surprised not to find any mention of the forged revolutionary notes called assignats. He was referring to the discovery of five million livres in forged assignats in Passy near Paris in 1789.[35] It was rumored, and later found to be true, that the émigrés had been counterfeiting assignats to flood France with them and thereby cause economic turmoil.[36]

Herman must have become frustrated or simply exhausted as midnight approached, because he haphazardly switched from one topic to another as if frantic to make any charge stick.

Herman (to the queen): On your marriage with Louis Capet, did you not conceive the project of reuniting Lorraine with Austria?

Queen: No.

Herman: You bear its name?

Queen: Because we ought to bear the name of our country.

Gointre: I request, Citizen President, that the accused declare whether, on the day the people did her husband the honor of decorating him with the red bonnet, there was not held a nocturnal council in the palace, where the destruction of Paris was resolved and where it was decided to hang posters by Esmenard.*

Queen: I do not know that name.

Herman: Did you not, on August 9, 1792, give your hand to Captain Tassin de l'Etang to kiss, saying to his battalion, "You are brave fellows, and of good principles; I will forever count on your fidelity"?

Queen: No.

Herman: Why did you, who had promised to bring up your children for the principles of the Revolution, teach them nothing but errors, in treating, for instance, your son with a respect that might make it believed that you thought of seeing him one day the successor of the former king his father?

Queen: He was too young to speak to on that subject. I placed him at the head of the table to give him myself what he wanted.

Herman: Have you anything to add to your defense?

Queen: Yesterday I did not know the witnesses. I knew not what they were to depose against me, and nobody has produced against me any positive evidence. I finish by observing that I was only the wife of Louis XVI, and it was my duty to conform myself to his will.

---

*The poet Joseph-Alphonse Esmenard was implicated in the hanging of public signs and was allegedly paid with funds from the Civil List to defame the republicans.

The clock struck midnight when President Herman announced that interrogations were closed. Thirteen witnesses had given scathing but vague testimonies against the queen; however, none of them could back up their statements with any evidence. Alleged drafts for millions of livres with Marie Antoinette's signature had disappeared, and witnesses could not swear to the exact amounts or where they could be located. Nor could letters written by the queen be presented, but witnesses assured the jury that they had known the persons who had seen them.

On the other hand, twenty-six witnesses had said nothing unfavorable about the queen. In fact, several witnesses contradicted earlier testimonies against her. One witness, Tour-du-Pin, angered prosecutor Fouquier-Tinville by addressing Marie Antoinette as "queen" and not "widow Capet." He even dared to bow with respect in front of the former queen of France before he entered the jury box.*

Marie Antoinette leaving the tribunal hall

---

*Jean-Frédéric de la Tour-du-Pin had recently been imprisoned for his royal affiliations; he would be guillotined seven months later on April 28, 1794.

À SAVOIR . . .

Meteorologist's Report[37]

Marie Antoinette complained of the cold in her cell on the night of October 15. She covered her feet with her cushion to keep them warm.

The temperature would be five degrees (about forty-five degrees Fahrenheit) on Wednesday morning, October 16, when the queen awoke. The weather in Paris, on that day, will forever be known as "cold and cloudy."

OCTOBER 16, 1793— COLD & CLOUDY

Marie Antoinette at trial

13

THE QUEEN'S
LAST RITES

"Antoinette, hear the sentence of the jury."

—Martial Joseph Armand Herman,
president of the Revolutionary Tribunal

Paris
October 16, 1793

Just minutes after midnight on October 16, President Herman addressed the queen's defense team: "Within a quarter of an hour, the debates will end; prepare your defense for the accused."[1]

As Tronçon-Ducoudray and Chauveau-Lagarde left the hall, Antoine Quentin Fouquier-Tinville stood and faced the jury. He cursed the royal court's past evil conduct and Marie Antoinette's incessant maneuvers against liberty, a notion that, in his estimation, "displeased her to such an extent that she wanted to see its total destruction at any price."[2]

Lagarde and Ducoudray hastily discussed the plan of their closing statements for the queen's defense. Lagarde would concentrate on the accusations of Marie Antoinette's conspiracy with the foreign powers; Ducoudray would focus on her alleged conspiracy with enemies within French borders. With only a few minutes remaining, the lawyers quickly leafed through their notes before they were recalled to the Tribunal hall. They were not permitted to communicate with their client before addressing the court.

The *Moniteur*, one of the most prominent newspapers during the Revolution, reported that the defense had only "solicited clemency from the Tribunal."[3] The newspaper was insinuating that the defense lawyers did not defend the queen because they believed her to be guilty. However, nothing could have been further from the truth. Lagarde wrote in his memoirs that he and Ducoudray never once forgot their obligation to the queen, and they fought the accusations with every weapon at their disposal. "We pled for more than three hours," argued Lagarde. The *Bulletin of the Revolutionary Tribunal* concurred: "This defense was very extensive and presented with as much zeal as eloquence."[4]

Lagarde was first to give his closing statement and concentrated on the queen's alleged conspiracies with France's enemies. More specifically, he focused on the following accusations: (1) squandering of the finances by sending funds to her brother, Emperor Joseph of Austria, (2) intelligence given to the late king's brothers exiled in Germany, and (3) military cooperation with the nation's enemies, leading to the disastrous retreat of the French army from Belgium.[5]

Lagarde first complained to the judges that he and his colleague were not given the time necessary to inspect all the case documents before undertaking the defense against such grievous accusations. He then addressed the retreat from Belgium, arguing that it was the work of the general who commanded the army—not the queen.

As for the intelligence given to the king's brothers in Germany and to the queen's brother in Austria, Lagarde reminded the court that not a trace of any alleged political correspondence between the queen and the foreign powers had been presented as evidence.

Lagarde finally addressed the misappropriation of finances with the utmost zeal; it was, after all, the most pressing charge brought against the queen. Lagarde called it "frivolous" because prosecutor Fouquier-Tinville had "relied only on his own statement and the more absurd hearsay of the domestic woman named Millot."[6]

Reine Millot had caused cackles in the court when she referred to the duke of Coigny as the count of Coigny, and even if she had recognized the duke, it would have been a breach of court etiquette for her to speak to him at all, let alone about such an important matter as the queen's gift of millions of livres to her brother.

When Fouquier-Tinville announced that he would bring in a draft for a "good sixty or eighty thousand francs" signed by the queen for Madame de Polignac, he assured the court that it would have written proof of the alleged embezzlement of funds. However, despite a court order to find the draft at the Committee of General Security (where it was last seen), the search was unsuccessful. But that was not a problem, said the prosecutor; he had himself seen it, and that was all that was necessary.

Lagarde then reminded the jurors that Fouquier-Tinville's statement was thus the only evidence submitted to the court of the queen's embezzlement and that the prosecutor could not be both accuser and witness at the same time.

After addressing all the charges against Marie Antoinette, Lagarde concluded that he had demonstrated beyond a doubt that any evidence to uphold them was "ridiculously absent."[7]

"I pled for nearly two hours," he wrote. "I was famished."

Marie Antoinette thanked Lagarde profusely and, noticing how fatigued he appeared, she said, "How tired you must be, Monsieur Chauveau-Lagarde! I am sensitive to all your troubles!"[8]

Lagarde had not simply asked the court for clemency; he had defended the queen, and he was surely gratified by her kind recognition of his efforts. The session was then suspended for a few minutes before Ducoudray gave his statement addressing the alleged conspiracies within France.

Ducoudray died before Lagarde's memoirs were published in 1816, and he left no account of his closing statement to the Tribunal, but Lagarde remembered that Ducoudray had spoken with great talent and dignity.[9]

When Ducoudray finished his one-hour statement, Lagarde began to approach the queen, but a gendarme stopped him. It was three o'clock in the morning, and the queen was removed from the hall.

President Herman then took the floor to give instructions to the jurors. He told them that the widow of Louis Capet was not only the former king's accomplice but also the "instigatrice of all the great tyrant's crimes."[10] She conspired not only with France's enemies, especially her brother Joseph

II of Austria, but also with the enemies within France's territories. In sum, Herman wanted her to be judged as the queen of France, an enemy of the new republic.[11]

> This trial, citizens of the jury, is not one of those where a single fact, a single crime, is submitted to your conscience and your knowledge. You have to judge the entire political life of the accused ever since she came to sit by the side of the last king of the French; but you must, above all, fix your deliberation upon the maneuvers that she never for an instant ceased to employ to destroy the rising liberty.

Herman would have liked, if he had found the time and resources, to invoke the names of all the French who had lost their lives at the Champ de Mars, on the frontiers, at La Vendée, and in the cities of Marseilles, Lyons, and Toulon. "Their deaths were the consequence of the infernal maneuvers of this modern Medici," he said, referring to the cunning Italian noblewomen who were once queens of France, Catherine and Marie de' Medici.[12]

He would also have brought the fathers, mothers, wives, and infants of the deceased patriots before the court. "All those families, in tears and despair," he said, "would have accused Antoinette of having snatched from them everything that was most dear to them in the world, and the deprivation of which renders life insupportable."[13]

Herman then focused on a statement made by the queen that she had earned the confidence of Louis Capet, the former king of France. The witness Charles-Eléonore Dufriche-Valazé had testified not only that she was consulted in political affairs but that the late king desired that she be consulted upon a plan of treacherous action, a plan whose object, however, was unclear to Valazé.[14]

Herman struggled when he brought up the subject of Marie Antoinette's alleged payment of millions of livres to her brother, but he did not dare mention the witness by name. That would have reminded the jury of the domestic Millot's ludicrous testimony; instead, he assured the jury that the charge was genuine:

> One of the witnesses, whose precision and ingenuity are remarkable, has told you that the late duke of Coigny had revealed that Antoinette had sent the

emperor, her brother, 200 million in 1788 to enable him to carry on the war that he then waged against the Turks. Since the Revolution, a draft of between sixty and eighty thousand livres, signed Antoinette and drawn upon Septeuil, has been given to the woman Polignac, then an emigrant; and a letter from La Porte, Italy, recommended to Septeuil not to leave behind the least trace of that gift. Lecointre of Versailles told you, as an eyewitness, that since the year 1779, enormous sums had been expended at court for the fêtes of which Marie Antoinette was always the idol.[15]

Herman did not give the exact amount of the draft given to Madame de Polignac, the queen's favorite; it could not be ascertained due to lack of evidence. Nor could the prosecutor present any documents to prove any of the other outlandish expenditures.

Herman concluded with a long list of offenses: (1) Marie Antoinette had always shown an "air of rebellion" against the sovereignty of the people; (2) she was found with an insignia of a heart in her possession, a sign of the counterrevolution; (3) she showed her son, after the death of his father, all the respect due a king, such as serving him first at the head of the table; and (4) she conspired with the former chevalier de Rougeville while imprisoned in the Conciergerie.

"The French nation accuses Antoinette!" said Herman. "All the political events prove evidence against her!"[16]

Curiously, Herman made no mention of the horrific accusations of the young Louis Charles. Was Herman confident that the jury would deliver a guilty verdict without it? Or was he hesitant to refresh the jurors' memory of the queen's emotional plea: "I appeal to the hearts of all mothers who are present in this room"?

Herman then concluded with four questions that the jury was required to answer:

1. Is it proved that there existed maneuvers and private intelligence with powerful foreign states and other external enemies of the republic; such maneuvers and intelligences tending to furnish them assistance in money and to give them ingress into the French territory for the purpose of facilitating the progress of their arms?

2. Is Marie Antoinette convicted of having cooperated with those maneuvers and of having communicated those intelligences?
3. Did a plot and conspiracy exist to start a civil war in the French homeland?
4. Is Marie Antoinette convicted of having had a share in that plot and that conspiracy?

The jurors all rose in silence and withdrew to an adjoining room, causing the candles to flicker in the overcrowded hall. After deliberating for almost an hour, they returned to the Tribunal hall. It was four o'clock in the morning, and Herman warned the audience to abstain from any outbreaks of emotion when the verdict would be given:[17]

> If the citizens who compose the audience were not liberal men, and of consequence capable of feeling all the dignity of their state, I ought perhaps to recall to their memory that at the moment when the national justice is about to declare the law, reason and morality impose upon them the greatest silence and forbid every mark of condemnation; and that a person, of whatever crimes they may be convicted by the law, is then only entitled to pity and humanity!

As soon as Marie Antoinette was brought back into the hall, Fouquier-Tinville demanded that, in conformity with the penal code, the accused "be punished with death" for conspiring with the enemies of France and for plotting to "trouble the state with a civil war."[18]

President Herman called upon Marie Antoinette to declare whether she had any objection to the sentence demanded by the prosecutor. Marie Antoinette shook her head in silence; she had nothing more to say.

When Herman asked her lawyers whether the queen should be put to death for her crimes, Lagarde remained silent. Ducoudray stood, however, and said, "Citizen President, the declaration of the jury being precise, and the law formal in this respect, I announce that my professional duty with regard to the widow Capet is terminated."[19]

How could the queen have interpreted Ducoudray's short statement? Why did the lawyer not object to the prosecutor's plea for the death penalty, or why did he not ask Marie Antoinette to make a final statement? Was he

Marie Antoinette listening to her sentence

apprehensive of possible criminal charges for defending the queen? Or did he fear the perception that he was too closely allied to the fallen queen or that he might even be a royalist? All of these questions have crossed historians' minds, but a more rational explanation might have been Ducoudray's disgust for the revolutionary system of justice. He was certainly aware that the Tribunal expected a condemnation, not a judgment.

At almost half past four in the morning, Herman gathered the ballots of his colleagues and pronounced the following sentence:

> The Tribunal, after the unanimous declaration of the jury, in conformity to the laws cited, condemns the said Marie Antoinette of Lorraine and Austria, widow of Louis Capet, to the penalty of death, her goods confiscated for the benefit of the republic, and this sentence shall be executed at the place de la Révolution.*

---

*The statue of Louis XV was torn down, and the place Louis XV was renamed the place de la Révolution.

When Marie Antoinette heard the sentence, she showed no emotion, but Lagarde said he and Ducoudray could not hear it without dismay.[20] "The queen, sitting alone, listened calmly," he said, "and we could only realize that something had just taken place in her soul, something of a revolution that was very remarkable.

"She did not give any sign of fear, indignation, or weakness," he continued. "It appeared she was annihilated by surprise."

Lagarde and Ducoudray were arrested on the spot in the presence of their client. She did not speak a word to them. She rose from her chair and crossed the hall without uttering a sound or making any gesture. When she arrived alongside the barrier where the spectators were seated, "she raised her head majestically."[21]

Lagarde and Ducoudray were taken to the Luxembourg Palace and questioned separately to determine whether Marie Antoinette had provided them with any documents or communicated any significant information during the trial. The lawyers had nothing to disclose; they were released the same day by court order.

Charles-Henri Sanson was present at the queen's trial, and after the jury's deliberation he knocked on prosecutor Fouquier-Tinville's door. When he entered, he found himself in the presence of the prosecutor, Herman, two judges, and Fabricius. The prosecutor immediately asked Sanson if all the preparations for the feast (*fête*) were ready.[22]

"My duty was to await the decisions of the justices and not anticipate them," said Sanson dryly, only aggravating the prosecutor.

"May I have an order to procure a closed carriage similar to that in which the king was taken to the guillotine?" asked Sanson, but his request infuriated Fouquier-Tinville.

"You yourself deserve to perish on the scaffold for daring to make such a suggestion, and a cart is quite good enough for the Austrian!" said the prosecutor.

However, the judges reminded Fouquier-Tinville that the Committee of Public Safety would have to be consulted on such an important decision. When the committee could not give an opinion on the matter, Maximilien Robespierre sent a message to Fouquier-Tinville that the prosecutor had "the power to act as he thought fit."

When Marie Antoinette arrived in her cell, she asked Warden Bault for a pen and paper.* He complied, and she sat down to write a letter to Élisabeth, the late king's sister. She began with the date and time, October 16 at four-thirty in the morning.

I write to you, my sister, for the last time. I have been condemned, not to an ignominious death—that only awaits criminals—but to go and rejoin your brother. Innocent as he, I hope to show the same firmness as he did in his last moments. I grieve bitterly at leaving my poor children; you know that I existed but for them and you—you who have by your friendship sacrificed all to be with us. In what a position do I leave you! I have learned, by the pleadings on my trial, that my daughter is separated from you. Alas, poor child—I dare not write to her for she would not receive my letter; I know not even if this may reach you.[23]

Marie Antoinette immediately separated herself from any wrongdoing in her testament. She was not being punished; rather, she was being reunited with her husband, and she was leaving the responsibility for her children in Élisabeth's hands. It was not clear in the trial's proceedings why the queen believed her daughter had been separated from her aunt, but this presumption explains why the letter was addressed only to Élisabeth. And if the queen thought this letter would not reach Élisabeth, a possible reason for writing it may have been to convince herself that her children would grow up together.

But this was a fantasy; she knew too well that her son had already been separated from his family—both physically and mentally. She also knew that the young uncrowned king would never sit on the throne of France, let alone be in a position to take revenge on his family's captors.

Receive my blessing for both. I hope one day, when they are older, they may rejoin you and rejoice in liberty at your tender care. May they both think on what I have never ceased to inspire them with! May their friendship and mutual confidence form their happiness! May my daughter feel that at her age she ought always to aid her brother with that advice with which the greater

---

*The historians Edmond and Jules Goncourt claimed that the queen was taken not back to her cell but to a holding cell for the condemned near the entrance.

experience she possesses, and her friendship, should inspire her! May my son, on his part, render to his sister every care and service which affection can dictate! May they, in short, both feel, in whatever position they may find themselves, that they can never be truly happy but by their union!

Let them take example by us. How much consolation has our friendship given us in our misfortunes, and in happiness to share it with a friend is doubly sweet. Where can one find any more tender or dearer than in one's own family? Let my son never forget the last words of his father. I repeat them to him expressly: "Let him never attempt to avenge our death."

Another possible reason for writing this letter may have been to allow Marie Antoinette to reiterate the absurdity of the charges of which her young son had accused her. She could only "hope" that the child, obviously brainwashed, would one day be in a condition to know better.

I must now speak to you of a matter most painful to my heart. I know how much trouble this child must have given you. Pardon him, my dear sister; think of his age and how easy it is to make a child say what one wishes and what he even does not comprehend. A day will arrive, I hope, when he will the better feel all the value of your kindness and affection for them both.

The queen next addressed her spirituality. She told Élisabeth that she did not know if she would have her last rites because she would not accept the services of a sworn priest. During the Terror, the clergy was required to take an oath to the constitution, literally "cutting them off from communion with the Church." Those priests who did not take the oath either emigrated or went into hiding.[24]

It still remains to me to confide to you my last thoughts. I had desired to write them from the commencement of the trial; but, exclusively of their not permitting me to write, the proceedings have been so rapid that I should really not have had the time. I die in the Catholic, Apostolic, and Roman religion; in that of my fathers; in that in which I have been bred and which I have always professed, having no spiritual consolation to expect, not knowing if priests of this religion [unsworn] still exist here—and even the place in which I am would expose them too much, were they once to enter it.

I sincerely ask pardon of God for all the errors I may have committed during my life. I hope that in his kindness he will accept my last vows, as well as those I have long since made, that he may vouchsafe to receive my soul in his mercy and goodness. I ask pardon of all those with whom I am acquainted, and of you, my sister, in particular, for all the trouble which, without desiring it, I may have caused you. I forgive all my enemies the evil they have done me.

The queen concluded her letter with touching farewells to her friends and family, but she ended it with a peculiar note—still uncertain of her spiritual salvation.

I say here adieu to my aunts and to all my brothers and sisters. I had friends, and the idea of being separated forever from them and their sorrows causes me the greatest regret I experience in dying. Let them, at least, know that in my last moments I have thought of them. Adieu, my good and kind sister! May this letter reach you! Think of me always! I embrace you with all my heart, as well as those poor dear children. My God, how heartrending it is to quit them forever! Adieu! Adieu! I ought no longer to occupy myself but with my spiritual duties. As I am not mistress of my actions, they may bring me perhaps a priest. But I here protest that I will not tell him one word and that I will treat him absolutely as a stranger.

When Marie Antoinette finished the letter, she repeatedly kissed each page, folded it without sealing it, and gave it to Warden Bault.* The gendarme standing guard outside the cell must have observed this; when Bault left the queen, the guard confiscated the letter and took it to Fouquier-Tinville. Élisabeth would never receive her sister-in-law's last testament.†

Soon after Bault's departure, a young guard then entered the queen's cell and announced, "I've been ordered not to leave you until all is finished."[25]

After praying, the queen lay down on her bed and slept, or tried to sleep because at five o'clock in the morning the general alarm was sounding throughout Paris. By seven o'clock the armed forces were on foot, with can-

---

*Marie Antoinette did not sign this letter written entirely in her own hand. But the last page bears the five following signatures: A. Q. Fouquier, Lecointre, Legot, Guffroy, and Massieu.

†The authorities may not have wanted the queen's testament published; royalist sentiment was revived when Louis XVI's testament was circulated just days after his execution.

nons placed in all the squares and on all the bridges from the Conciergerie to the place de la Révolution.

When Rosalie received word that the queen of France was doomed, she fled to her room, stifling her cries and sobs. At seven o'clock, Warden Bault ordered her to go down to the queen and inquire if she would like something to eat. When Rosalie entered the queen's cell, she found two candles burning and the young guard sitting in the corner. The queen was dressed in black, lying down with her face turned toward the window, her head resting on her hand.

"Madame," Rosalie said with a trembling voice, "you did not eat anything the night before and almost nothing yesterday. Will you have something this morning?"

Tears rolled down the queen's cheeks. "My child," she said, resigned to her fate, "I no longer need anything; everything is over for me."

"But, madame, I have some broth for you on the stove," said Rosalie.

Recovering herself, and perhaps out of compassion for her servant, the queen said, "Well, Rosalie, bring me some of your broth."[26]

When Rosalie went to fetch the bouillon, she discovered that the Commune had given orders that the queen not be allowed any food at all.* Although Marie Antoinette had been condemned to death, the Commune still wanted to show the people of Paris a woman weakened by terror and stripped of her noble pride.[27]

When Rosalie returned an hour later, the queen asked her for help dressing. The queen first stepped between the bed and the wall to hide her body from the guard's view as she let her black dress drop to the floor. When the young guard approached the queen to watch more closely, Marie Antoinette immediately put her scarf over her shoulders.

"In the name of decency, Monsieur" she said, "allow me to change my linen in private."

"I cannot consent," the guard replied. "I have orders to keep an eye on all of your movements."[28]

The queen sighed. She removed her bloodstained chemise, replacing it with a clean one. In addition to the long trial and her hunger over the past

---

*Stories about the queen's breakfast differ among historians. The Goncourts wrote that the queen asked for chicken, of which she ate a wing.

few days in the cold, dank cell, the queen's hemorrhaging had exhausted her even further.

She then put on her white negligee and draped a large muslin scarf over her shoulders, tying it under her neck. After the queen had arranged her white mourning cap on her head, Rosalie watched as she carefully rolled up the bloody chemise and tucked it into one of its sleeves. The queen looked around and found a small crack in the wall in which she hid the tattered garment.

Rosalie was too distressed to bid Marie Antoinette adieu. The queen sat trembling from the October cold when Rosalie left the cell.

A sworn priest named François Girard arrived next. The former curé of Saint-Landry demanded to hear her confession, but the queen refused.[29]

"You are guilty," said the priest.

"Ah, sometimes careless," said the queen. "Never guilty."[30]

"But madame," said the priest, "what will be said when it becomes known that in your last moments you refused to accept the means of grace provided by the church?"[31]

"I thank you," she said, "but my religion forbids me to accept the forgiveness of God through a priest who is of another persuasion.[32]

"You may tell such persons who speak to you on the subject," she continued, "that divine compassion has taken care to procure them for me."

Marie Antoinette was insinuating that she had already received, or would still receive, her last rites. Yet her letter to Élisabeth contradicted this when she wrote that she had "no spiritual consolation to expect, not knowing if priests of this religion still exist here—and even the place in which I am would expose them too much, were they once to enter it."[33]

If she had truly received communion by an unsworn priest in the Conciergerie, why would she not have told her sister-in-law? First, she would have implicated the priest and those who had helped her receive his services—bringing upon them a certain death sentence. Knowing that the queen was always fearful of endangering the lives of others, Élisabeth would have understood Marie Antoinette's message.

On the contrary, at the end of the letter, the queen wrote, "I ought no longer to occupy myself but with my spiritual duties." She was telling Élisabeth, or whoever else would read the letter, that her utmost concern was now for her salvation, even though she would not acknowledge a sworn priest. Was she possibly telling Élisabeth that she had made other arrangements to fulfill her spiritual duties? According to the historian Alphonse de Lamartine, the answer is yes.[34]

Mademoiselle Fouché, the pious woman who had introduced the Abbé Magnin into the queen's cell at the time Toussaint Richard was warden, approached Warden Bault with details of the secret visits of the priest to the queen's cell. Taking advantage of the new warden's goodwill, Abbé Magnin and Mademoiselle Fouché procured the same privilege. Furthermore, they asked permission to celebrate the Holy Mass in the dungeon cell.

"Calm yourself, my dear Monsieur Bault," said Mademoiselle Fouché. "Just provide two small candlesticks, and we will care for everything else."

According to the unlikely story, the religious pair smuggled a silk chasuble (liturgical vestment worn by the priest), some cloths to cover the table for an altar, a silver chalice that could be dismantled, the sacred stone, a small missal (text of prayers), and cruets to celebrate the service in the queen's cell. The famous painting by Alexandre Menjaud presented the scene with Mademoiselle Fouché and two gendarmes also attending the ceremony.

It is an unlikely picture, for several reasons. First, after the Carnation Plot, the two guards François Dufresne and Jean Gilbert had been replaced with new guards for increased security. One of these guards, Lieutenant Louis-François de Busne, was known to be secretly loyal to the queen, but it is doubtful that any additional guards would have risked participating in such an elaborate ceremony. Second, it is doubtful that the fearful warden, the Abbé Magnin, and Mademoiselle Fouché could have successfully smuggled everything they needed into the prison unnoticed. Finally, this was the Conciergerie, a prison manned by guards at every *guichet* and, outside the queen's window, by ferocious dogs, as well as by some fifteen administrators and even a police spy *en permanence*.[35]

This is not to say that the priest could not have assisted the queen. He may have been able to enter the prison as a vendor or dressed as a National Guardsman. After all, he was good at disguises; known as Monsieur Charles, he entered homes at great risk to his life to give Mass during the Terror.

If Abbé Magnin's memoirs can be trusted, the story had been greatly exaggerated. He claimed that he did enter the Conciergerie, but only with host wafers hidden under his cloak. If we can believe the words of a dying man, he did indeed have communion with the queen:[36]

> I am now very near the grave, and when a man has come to that, he does not wish to be guilty of falsehood. It's true, I gave the Sacred Host to the Queen with my own hands, and one of my chief pleasures in my old age is the remembrance of that act for which so many good people were associated to pray, and had sought my devoted cooperation and ministry. I should have been unworthy of my position as a Priest if I had hesitated one instant in fulfilling this duty, and accepting the honour and danger of it.[37]

Marie Antoinette receiving communion from the Abbé Magnin with Mademoiselle Fouché and the two "kind" guards attending

Although it is unlikely that Mademoiselle Fouché and the two guards participated, Mademoiselle Fouché could have indeed arranged the meeting with Warden Bault, as she was known for her good works in the prisons of Paris.[38]

By ten o'clock in the morning, the streets from the Conciergerie to the place de la Révolution were heavily patrolled. The jailer Louis Larivière had just entered the queen's cell. He was the son of Mère Larivière, the woman who had served the queen when she first entered the Conciergerie. Warden Bault had told him to go to the queen's cell, pick up any cups or glasses on the table, and wait for him there, most likely to inform him of what had occurred in his absence.[39]

When the queen saw the jailer, she said, "Larivière, you know that they are going to put me to death? Tell your good mother that I thank her for her care of me, and that I entreat her to pray for me."[40]

Minutes later, as the queen kneeled in prayer at her bed, another gendarme entered the cell, soon followed by the judges and the registrar Fabricius. The queen rose to receive them.

Jacques René Hébert spoke first. "Listen to your sentence."

As a peculiar mark of respect, the four officials removed their hats, more as a sign of Tribunal etiquette than as any show of respect for the queen. However, both Larivière and Warden Bault's wife remarked that the men did seem struck by the queen's majestic appearance.

"It is not necessary to read it," said the queen. "I know the sentence too well."

"That is of no consequence," said one of the judges. "It must be read to you again."

The queen remained silent as Fabricius read the sentence. When he finished, the executioner Sanson entered the cell, approached the queen, and said, "Hold out your hands."

The queen lost her composure for a moment and started back. "Will my hands be tied?" she said. "The king's hands were not tied."*

"Do your duty!" the judges ordered Sanson.

---

*The queen was not entirely right. Louis's hands were not fastened until he had reached the scaffold.

Sanson seized the queen's hands and bound them "tightly" behind her back. He was preparing the queen for the last toilette (*dernière toilette*) that prisoners endured before going to the scaffold. However, the historians Edmond and Jules Goncourt reported that the queen had already cut her own hair before Sanson arrived.[41] Their version is unlikely because the queen would never have been allowed to use a pair of scissors; she was not even allowed to have a needle to mend her socks. Madame Bault confirmed that Sanson cut the queen's hair and that the queen, looking back, saw the executioner place the locks of hair in his pocket.

"This I saw," said Madame Bault, "and I wish I had never seen that sight."[42]

The queen was ready to leave the prison, where she had spent the past seventy-six days. Besides the white peignoir that she normally used as a morning gown and her shawl (*fichu de mousseline*), she still had the small linen cap on her head; however, she had removed the black widow's ribbon. In fact, she may have been ordered to remove it to avoid any perception of her still being in mourning.*

The cap's cords, falling to the sides, were tied in a loose knot over her breast. She must have realized that her last moments were near because she had arranged her cap so that it could be easily removed.

À SAVOIR . . .

The Queen's Dog

Marie Antoinette's dog, Thisbé, never gave up hope, remaining outside the prison gates day after day, always waiting for an opportunity to slip through the carefully guarded entrance.[43]

It was never known what happened to the little dog, but a story circulated in the neighborhood that a kind and good-natured young milliner named Madame Arnaud picked the faithful dog up and took her home. However,

---

*According to Mercier (Nouveau Paris) the queen had a cup of chocolate and a small roll before departing, and she was not permitted to remove her bonnet.

the milliner was frightened that neighbors would think her a royalist for caring for the queen's pet, so she took Thisbé to her sister's home near the Pont Saint-Michel, where the dog was shut up in a room.[44]

It was rumored that the "queen's dog," as Thisbé was called, grieved for its mistress, not being able to be near her. The dog refused to eat or drink and became so vicious that it was not safe to approach. Finally one evening, after howling pitifully for many hours, Thisbé ended its life by plunging through an open window into the Seine River, which flowed by the house.[45]

14

THE ROUTE OF
THE FATAL TUMBRIL

*"Antoinette, along the road, looked with indifference at the
armed force, which numbered more than thirty thousand men
and formed a double line along the streets."*

—Esq. Michael Adams, *New Royal
Geographical Magazine*, 1794

*Paris
October 16, 1793*

When eleven o'clock in the morning struck, the tumbril stood ready
at the gates of the Palace of Justice. It was an open cart with a single
white horse, and its only seat was the wooden plank of its floor. Earlier that
year, Louis XVI had been driven to the place de la Révolution in a covered
coach fit for a king. Marie Antoinette's cart, however, would lack the luxury
of even some straw.[1]

All the streets were closed to carriages from the Conciergerie leading to the
place de la Révolution. Spectators were already gathering in the windows, on
the roofs, and in the trees to catch a glimpse of the former queen of France. A
crowd of angry women pressed against the gratings of the barred gates of the
palace; they waited impatiently to curse the *Autrichienne* ascending the steps
from the dungeon to the palace courtyard known as the Cour du Mai.[2]

The executioner and his assistant, the priest Girard, and prison guards
escorted the queen from her cell—where guards had kept watch over her

night and day—through the adjoining chamber to a long, somber corridor. The entourage passed the chamber where prisoners were washed before being incarcerated. If the queen had looked to the right, she would have seen the grating in a triangular area, where prisoners often said good-bye to loved ones. As she passed along the corridors, she saw several other prisoners in the Conciergerie and bid them farewell.

One of the prisoners, Madame Caron,[*] overheard the queen say, "Oh, I'm thirsty."[3] She hastened to fill a small cup of water and gave it to the queen, who took a long drink.[4]

The cortege soon passed by the grated gate leading to the rue de Paris on the left. Low-arched windows overlooking the courtyard illuminated this part of the Conciergerie, but a few steps later the corridor turned into a narrow and dark passageway, lit only by a lantern on the wall. At the end of the corridor the queen was escorted to a *guichet*, the same one that she had entered through seventy-six days earlier. A hand painted in black indicated that this was the exit (*sortie*).[5]

Guichet *in the hallway of the Black Hand,
through which the queen passed on October 16*

---

[*]Madame Caron was to be executed soon after the queen, but she was granted a stay of execution due to her pregnancy. When she became blind after an accident at the Conciergerie, her sentence was commuted, and she was set free.

The queen was then led through this macabre doorway, called the Black Hand (*Main Noire*), into a small courtyard, just steps away from the staircase leading up to the Cour du Mai, where the tumbril awaited. When she saw it, she paused, taken aback to discover that she would not be driven to the scaffold in a more decent carriage. Was this queenly pride? Or did she wonder whether she was so hated that she was denied a covered coach to the scaffold like the former king of France? He had not been well liked either, so was she disliked even more?

Not necessarily. More likely, the Revolution had advanced considerably since the execution of the queen's husband in January. The king's hands had not been tied on his way to the scaffold, but the incensed spectators gathered in the courtyard were not at all disappointed to see the queen's hands tied behind her back. Sanson even made a point of displaying the cords to the crowd.[6]

Undaunted, the queen walked to the small ladder at the back of the cart. Sanson took her elbow to help her up the three or four rickety steps; she

Marie Antoinette departing for the scaffold
(Bibliothèque Nationale Française)

thanked him with a nod and then sat down on the wooden plank. When Sanson saw that she was facing the horse, he told her to turn around with her back to the animal.[7]

The priest Girard, to whom she had refused to confess, sat next to her, while Sanson stood behind her. Both Sanson and his assistant had their hats in their hands. "The only people who behaved with decency on that occasion," the historians Goncourt wrote, "were the executioners."[8]

"This is the moment, madame, to arm yourself with courage," said the priest.[9]

Marie Antoinette in the tumbril

"Courage?" she said. "I have so long served an apprenticeship in it that it is not likely to fail me today."

The priest persisted, but she silenced him. She firmly repeated that she was "not of his religion, that she died professing that of her husband, and that she should never forget the principles so oft instilled in her."[10]

How things had changed. Twenty-three years earlier, the Archduchess Marie Antoinette departed Vienna in a magnificent coach to become the queen of France. The fourteen-year-old princess sat "sunk back in her carriage; her face bathed in tears; hiding her eyes with her handkerchief; several times putting her head out to see yet again this Palace of her Fathers, whither she was to return no more." There was an "audible sound of wail" in the streets and avenues of Vienna.[11]

When Marie Antoinette arrived in Paris for the first time on June 8, 1773, she was jubilantly greeted. The governor of Paris said, "Madame, you see before you two hundred thousand lovers."

And the press of the day showered the dauphine with compliments about her strawberry blond hair, her captivating blue eyes, and her majestic poise. The artist Madame Louise-Elisabeth Vigée-le Brun, who had painted portraits of Marie Antoinette, once wrote that although the queen's lips were rather full, "the remarkable beauty of her face was in its coloring, its expression." Le Brun had never seen so brilliant a complexion, "for her skin was so transparent that it hardly took a shadow."[12]

But on this gloomy, overcast day in the streets of Paris, the thirty-seven-year-old queen's hair was completely white; she was pale, and her eyes were red and swollen but dry. Despite the care she had taken in her morning toilette, the coarse linen of her dress and its wrinkled pleats made her unrecognizable as the former queen of France.

As the wooden cart slowly moved along, someone in the crowd cried out, "The queen must be made to drink long of death."

The queen bit her lower lip for a moment "as a person who suppressed the utterance of acute suffering."[13]

The queen could not have known that a loyal supporter had just attempted to save her life and failed. The count de Linange had requested permission from the convention to leave for Vienna to offer the queen's release in exchange for Austria's neutrality. The same tactic had also been used, unsuccessfully, to save the king. Unfortunately, the convention did not reply to this request regarding the queen.[14]

Numerous detachments of soldiers on horses and on foot accompanied the tumbril along its route. François Hanriot, Charles-Philippe Ronfin, and Servais Beaudouin Boulanger, generals of the revolutionary army who followed the cart, were preceded by their staff officers. The queen seldom cast her eyes upon the populace; with a cold indifference, she beheld the great armed force of thirty thousand men lining the streets in double ranks.[15]

At ten minutes past eleven, Grammont, one of General Ronfin's assistants, led the way, prancing on horseback with his sword drawn and inciting the crowd to insult the queen.* Grammont had also placed the "lowest of rabble" at various points along the tumbril's route to shout at her; he even cursed the crowd for not being more violent.[16]

Amid the roar, the queen's cart passed through the magnificent grated gates of the Palace of Justice and turned north on the rue de Palais toward the Money Changers' Bridge (pont au Change). After crossing the bridge, the cart turned to the west and crawled along the quai de la Mégisserie, an area where tanners kept their shops, before turning north on the rue de la Monnaie.[17]

The rue de la Monnaie ended at the rue Rivoli but continued on as the rue du Roule. At this intersection a new cavalry unit took lead of the cavalcade along the street of grand residences with large balconies. However, the cobblestone street was rutted and bumpy, and the queen was unable to support herself with her hands tightly bound. She struggled to move somewhat closer to the middle of the cart to keep her balance.[18]

"These aren't the cushions from your Trianon!" someone cried out.[19]

Surrounded by the outraged crowd, the cart next turned west onto the rue Saint-Honoré, and whenever people saw the tumbril, they yelled, "Here comes Sanson's cart! Let's go look! Let's go look!"[20]

Municipal officers informed the owners of the grand residences on the rue Saint-Honoré that their absence—or failure to cheer—would be duly noted.

---

*Guillaume-Antoîne Nourry, called Grammont, had quit the theater to become more involved in politics. He assisted at the massacre of royalists at Orléans and Versailles, and he is said to have even drunk wine from the skull of one of his victims.

They were also expected to drape the facades of their homes with republican tricolor streamers for the occasion, as was required along the entire route.[21]

The turn onto the narrower rue Saint-Honoré was made more difficult by the pressing and intoxicated crowd that had been paid to accompany the tumbril on the rue du Roule. The clocks struck half past eleven, and a penetrating fog on the cold October morning darkened the streets. Some spectators remarked that it gave the street a solemn, mourning cast. All the while, the queen's look remained fixed.[22]

Because the rue Saint-Honoré was narrow, spectators filling the windows and balconies of its residences could see Marie Antoinette up close. But they would not have recognized the woman who was once the queen not only of France but also of European fashion, who relied on the services of her milliner, Mademoiselle Rose Bertin, and her hairdresser, Léonard Autié.

In fact, Mademoiselle Bertin's shop, Le Grand Mogul, was located on the rue Saint-Honoré between the rue Champfleuri and rue du Chantre.* But the famous milliner would not have been watching the queen's cart pass by from her balcony; she had moved her business to London to serve numerous noble customers who had fled the Terror. Nor was Léonard, the queen's famous coiffeur, present; he was assisting the king's brothers who were in exile in Germany.[23]

Another establishment that the queen might have recognized on the rue Saint-Honoré was the pharmacy of Madame Derosne's sons, who served Louis XVI and Marie Antoinette. Among the medicines prescribed to the royal family were finely ground pearls and coral; they were very expensive but quite in vogue.[24] These pharmacists, once loyal servants who attentively cared for the king, the queen, and the royal children, may very well have been watching from their balconies.

When Marie Antoinette's cart passed the Protestant temple called the Oratoire, the queen noticed a young child in his mother's arms about the same age as her son, Louis Charles. The child sent her a kiss with his hand, and despite her insensitivity to the crowd's affronts, the queen's eyes filled with tears. The sight of this little blonde head likely reminded her of the boy

---

*Both of these streets have since disappeared; Bertin's shop was near the spot where the entrance to the Louvre is now located.

torn from her arms only a few months earlier.[25] This was perhaps the only time that the queen was brought to tears along the dreary route.

An ever-growing crowd awaited the tumbril when it arrived at the Royal Palace (*Palais-Royal*) and the Château d'Eau. The queen remained stoic, "like a statue," amid the savage cries of the men and women with their fists in the air.* According to a relative of the Vicomte Charles-Henri Desfossez who took part in the procession, "The queen's hair was cropped around her neck, her cheeks were flushed, her eyes were bloodshot, and her eyelashes remained stiff and still."[26] Other witnesses noticed the bloodshot eyes, but they may not have been caused by tears. The queen had suffered insomnia since the beginning of her trial, she was in poor health, and she had been breathing poor air in her dungeon cell.

When Marie Antoinette saw the entrance of the Royal Palace, witnesses claimed she appeared troubled, and her face reddened. Perhaps the sight of the palace triggered painful memories. Her husband's cousin Louis Philippe II, head of the House of Orléans, lived there. A prince with antiroyalist sentiments, he had voted in favor of the death sentence for the queen's husband.

The growing mob and its raging threats against the queen made the cart's passage down the rue Saint-Honoré increasingly difficult. But the queen remained calm. Perhaps she had prepared herself for the fury; she was certainly expecting it. In prison, she had once asked one of the gendarmes, "Do you believe the people will let me go to the scaffold without tearing me to pieces?"[27]

After leaving the Royal Palace, the cart passed the rue de l'Échelle to the Church of Saint-Roch. On the night of June 20, 1791, the royal family had escaped through this street from the Tuileries, only to be arrested the next day in Varennes. Returning to Paris under heavy guard, the family was met by a revolutionary crowd in aberrant silence; the people loathed them. Today the spectators were cheering the queen on her way to the scaffold.

During the Revolution, the Church of Saint-Roch was often the scene of shootings, which left their marks on its facade. For several minutes the queen's cart halted here where the women who had marched on Versailles on October 5, 1789, gathered on the church steps. They wore red bonnets and

---

*The Château d'Eau was demolished during the last empire.

carried pikes; one by the name of Rose Lacombe led the group with a banner reading, "Here's the vile tyrant whom we hunted right in front of us!"[28]

Grammont had organized this demonstration, and on his signal the queen was showered with insults. Rising in his stirrups and brandishing his sword, the former actor cried out, "Here she is, the infamous Antoinette, my friends; she's screwed, my friends! We are going to give you her head!"[29]

The queen was unmoved by the hateful cries when the cart finally jolted forward. Her looks wandered over the facades of the buildings and the people on the balconies. She never spoke, but she occasionally motioned to Girard that she suffered from her hands being tied too tightly. To comfort her, the priest would support her left arm with his hand.[30]

Minutes later the queen's cart passed the famous Hôtel de Noailles, one of the most magnificent hotels of Paris. Passing under its windows the queen surely would have remembered those who had lived there in much happier times and whom she had received in the splendid salons and gardens of Versailles or her Petit Trianon.[31]

But the queen's cart did not travel far. Between the rue de la Sourdière and the Vendôme Square, the cavalcade stopped again on Grammont's orders. Here stood the Jacobin Club, whose door displayed a banner that the queen had difficulty reading. It appeared that she leaned toward the priest to ask about the message, which said, "Republican army atelier to strike down tyrants!" (*Atelier d'armes républicanes pour foudroyer les tyrans*).[32]

And Grammont did not forget to bring his chorus of slanderers, mostly prostitutes and "infamous women." They pointed at the queen and shouted, "Here is Madame Veto, with her f**king crane's neck; only the guillotine can make her atone for her arrogance!"[33]

After the cart continued down the rue Saint-Honoré, it passed the Feuillants Convent, formerly a royal monastery. This large stone structure opposite the place Vendôme would also have been painful to revisit. Louis XVI and his family were housed there after their arrest a year earlier on August 10, before their transfer to the Temple prison.

Traveling further, the queen's cart passed the residence of Maximilien Robespierre, the leader of the revolutionary government, between the rue de Castiglione and the rue Duphot. Tribunal judges could have very easily watched the queen's passage to the place de la Révolution from the windows of his house. Ironically, Robespierre would soon be jailed in the Conciergerie—in the same cell where Marie Antoinette had been held.

Here the queen heard a woman cry out, "Death to the Austrian!" She glanced at the woman with brief contempt before noticing a former lady-in-waiting in the midst of a gathering of commoners. The queen was unaware that many of these commoners were actually hairdressers and barbers who had conspired to rescue her. The movement headed by Jean-Baptiste Basset and Catherine Fournier, however, had been infiltrated by the police and thwarted long before its planned execution on this day.[34]

Nearby, in the rue Saint-Honoré, the painter Jacques-Louis David, a friend of Robespierre, watched the convoy pass slowly beneath his window at the Jullien residence.[35] From this vantage point he sketched in pen a portrait of Marie Antoinette being conducted to the scaffold. Despite having been a painter for King Louis XVI and very well compensated for his creations, he became one of the most fanatical revolutionaries of the time. Did his hatred for royalty guide his hand as he sketched his former queen?

Finally, the cart turned south onto the rue Royale, then called the rue de la Révolution. At this intersection the queen looked up at a certain residence in which, supposedly, a disguised unsworn priest, the Abbé Puget, was waiting with a crucifix in his hands to absolve her of her sins *in articulo mortis.** Certain spectators noticed

Sketch of Marie Antoinette on the tumbril by Jacques-Louis David

the queen lower her forehead, close her eyes, and "collect herself under the

---

*According to the *Souvenirs de la marquise de Créquy*, the queen first looked toward the Hôtel de Coislin but did not recognize anyone. Quickly turning her head toward the Guarde-Meuble, she saw Puget, and her face lit up. He was standing on a pile of rocks with a crucifix in his hands.

invisible hand that blessed her." Unable to use her tied hands, she made the sign of a cross upon her breast with three movements of her head.[36]

If Marie Antoinette did not receive a priest's blessing as the tumbril turned onto the rue Royale, she may very likely have received it at the place de la Révolution. It was a little known fact that there existed "guillotine chaplains" (*aumôniers de la guillotine*) at this time to ensure unfortunate victims the consolation of their religion. Seven priests were organized to take turns accompanying the carts from the Conciergerie to the foot of the scaffold, each serving one day a week; executions also took place on Sundays.[37]

It was said that most victims knew they could count on the assistance of a priest either en route in the tumbril or at the scene of the execution. Spectators watching the cart destined for the place de la Révolution often noticed the victims tilting their heads in prayer, and they would remark, "There's one who is making his act of contrition!"[38]

When carts bearing the condemned arrived at the scaffold, a priest was placed as close as possible, but behind the National Guards. When the executioner seized the first victim, the priest gave a general absolution. All the spectators were forced to remove their hats at that time, allowing the more powerful to see better in the last rows. The priest would take advantage of this etiquette to make a sign of the cross unseen behind his hat.[39]

The priest was not restricted to giving a general absolution. A Parisian newspaper noted that, if he saw that all the convicts were honorable men—which was almost always the case—he would give individual absolution to the victims as they climbed the rungs of the fatal ladder.[40]

About this time, unbeknownst to the queen, gravediggers in the crypt of Saint-Denis, by order of the convention, were opening the coffin of the first dauphin, who had died of tuberculosis four years earlier. Marie Antoinette's second child, Louis Joseph-Xavier, was being removed from his coffin and thrown into the common quicklime pit of Saint-Denis.[41]

À SAVOIR . . .

Sanson Obituary[42]

The Executioner of Louis XVI—Mr. Sanson, the public executioner, was remarkable for the horrible task he had to perform in 1793; when, by virtue of his office, he had to bind the hands of Louis XVI and, afterward, place the monarch's head under the guillotine. He was the third of his name who had filled the same functions and who has left a son and grandson. He had acquired some property, had become an elector, was a well-informed man, was fond of the arts, and passed most of his evenings in playing on the piano.

Mr. Charles-Henri Sanson, however, was unable to serve as executioner on October 16. His son Henry would take his place.

15

THE "NATIONAL RAZOR"

"Alas! My troubles will soon be over, but yours are only just beginning."

—Marie Antoinette, overheard by
Siméon Despréaux, Cour du Mai[1]

Paris
October 16, 1793

It was twelve o'clock when the tumbril passed between two National Guard warehouses that form the northern border of the place de la Révolution at the end of the rue Royale. The cavalcade approached the pedestal where a Statue of Liberty stood.* Nearby, a wooden platform had been erected some two meters high and enclosed on three sides by railings.†

A ladder's top step was joined to the open side of the platform. In all the sketches of the scene, the guillotine stood eerily with its two parallel beams reaching upward to the blade at the crossbar—like a sinner raising his arms to heaven.

The crowds no longer hurled insults at Marie Antoinette as the cart rattled to a stop on the bumpy ground of the square; curiosity must have replaced

---

*This eighteenth-century statute, not to be confused with Bartholdi's gift to the United States, was destroyed after the Revolution.

†The queen's scaffold was not erected in the same place as that for Louis XVI. Hers was closer to the Tuileries gardens and only thirty meters from the Statue of Liberty.

ferocity. In the balconies near the square, members of the Commune were reunited to watch the queen ascend the scaffold and to draw up the minutes (*procès-verbal*) of the execution—just as they had done for King Louis XVI.[2]

It could not have been a difficult task for the officials to prepare this document; they had only to fill in the blanks on a preprinted form. Documenting the events on the place de la Révolution had become a common event by this time.

This was the queen's final public appearance. She had endured over two and a half months of suffering in the dungeons of the Conciergerie, and her journey to the place de la Révolution had also been long and grueling. When her eyes turned left to the gardens of the Tuileries Palace, she became emotional and grew much paler. All the blood "had left her cheeks and lips," one observer recorded.[3]

She had visited this grand palace for the first time twenty years earlier, on June 8, 1773, as the radiant dauphine of France, bathing in the enthusiastic cries of the Parisians. She and her family had more recently spent almost three years under house arrest here until August 10, 1792, when the royal family was forced to seek shelter in the National Assembly from the violent Parisian mobs. This had marked the end of the monarchy, and the family was imprisoned in the medieval Temple fortress.[4]

The queen's daughter, Princess Marie-Thérèse, recorded in her memoirs what was about to take place at the place de la Révolution. She even attested, "This memoir contains the truth."[5] But the princess was not present at the execution that morning; she was still locked up in the Temple with her aunt and younger brother.

Arriving at the truth about what really happened at the scaffold on that cold October morning has been a difficult task for any historian. There have been many conflicting stories about Marie Antoinette's comportment, her health, and her state of mind. One truth must be recognized, however; it has never been possible to know the thoughts of the dying. Unless shared in the final moments, the thoughts of the dying will always remain a mystery.

"She went to death with courage amid the insults that unhappy people threw at her; her courage did not desert her on the cart or on the scaffold," said Marie-Thérèse. "She showed courage in death just as she did in life."[6]

In pretending to attend the event, the princess may have wanted to control her mother's narrative. Or did she want to "save" her in the eyes of history? Was it truly a brave queen who arrived at the scaffold? She was certainly exhausted from the long days at the Tribunal and the lack of sleep, perhaps hungry and thirsty, and weakened by the bouts of hemorrhaging she suffered. But was she courageous? Or had she just completely given up all hope?

Four "witnesses" told a different story about the queen's composure. The first, Lafont d'Aussonne, wrote, "At the sight of the scaffold, Marie Antoinette closed her eyes, the pallor of death covered her face, and her head fell on her chest. She had ceased to exist."[7]

The second, Monsieur Claude-François Beaulieu,* wrote that the widow Capet's courage and strength abandoned her, and "it was necessary to carry her to the fatal plank where she was put to death." However, Beaulieu was not present; he was still incarcerated in the Conciergerie on this day. Also, there's no credible evidence or corroborating account of the queen fainting on the scaffold.[8]

Thomas Lapierre, an entrepreneur of military convoys, confirmed Beaulieu's claims in his article in the *Revue respective*:

Marie-Antoinette, the bitch, had as beautiful an end as the pig Godille, our butcher [King Louis XVI]. She stood on the scaffold with incredible firmness as well as all along the rue Saint-Honoré. She had gone through Paris looking at everyone with contempt and disdain, but wherever she passed, the real sans-culottes did not fail to cry 'Vive la République!' and 'Down with tyranny!' The slut had the strength to go to the scaffold without flinching, but when she saw the medical examiners, she fainted.[9]

Lapierre, however, was not present either; he, too, was imprisoned on the day of the queen's execution. He may very well have read Jacques-René Hébert's account of the event in *Père Duchêsne* before writing his own, because their language was very similar.[10]

---

*Beaulieu covered the debates in the National Assembly in his paper, *News of Paris*. He was imprisoned in the Conciergerie for his royalist opinions.

Hébert was the most determined to describe the queen's cowardice in the face of death:"The bitch was audacious and insolent to the end, but her legs gave away beneath her at the last moment. She undoubtedly feared a more terrible punishment after death than that which she was about to suffer."[11]

Other contemporary tabloids, however, reported that the queen did indeed face death with the utmost bravery. The *Glaive vengeur de la Républic française* reported, "She stepped on the scaffold with courage."[12] And the *Moniteur* reported, "She mounted the scaffold with enough courage."[13]

The following verse published in the *Révolution en vaudeville* also spoke to the queen's strength:

Against the widow Antoinette,
France gave only one cry;
She underwent the same test
As the sire her husband! (repeat)
To quell this former queen,
The iron blade did not succeed.
Her majesty sovereign
Showed herself just as firm!

As Marie Antoinette climbed the steps to the scaffold, Grammont excited the crowds: "The infamous *Autrichienne*, she's screwed!" And the crowd roared its approval and agreement.[14]

After the long procession from the Conciergerie, the queen must not have wanted to prolong her suffering and angst any longer. She climbed the steps quickly—so quickly that she lost a high-heeled yellow patent leather shoe on her way up.* And when stepping onto the scaffold, she accidentally stepped on Sanson's foot.[15]

Marie Antoinette quickly turned around and said, "Sir, I beg your pardon; I did not do it on purpose." History would record these innocuous sentences as her last words.[16]

---

*A young man waiting underneath the scaffold picked up the shoe and sold it the same day for one gold coin. It was a small, yellow patent leather shoe with a pointed toe.

Marie Antoinette at the place de la Révolution
(Bibliothèque Nationale Française)

Monsieur Louis Marie Prudhomme, certainly not a royalist, interpreted this brief moment quite differently. He claimed that the queen had planned this little scene so that she would be remembered kindly in the journals of history, adding, "Pride never leaves some people until their death."[17]

He argued that such chicanery was typical behavior of the royals. They would commit the most revolting crimes and injustices during their reigns but, when they met death, ask forgiveness for some small injustice, as if this would excuse a lifetime of transgressions against their people.[18]

Marie Antoinette stood, ironically, in the foreground of the Statute of Liberty and prayed fervently for a few moments while the executioner Sanson and his assistant made their final preparations. The woman who had at one time worn the crown of France now wore but a widow's cap, but she still held her head high, lifting her eyes up to the heavens.

She then threw her cap off with a movement of her head, as if she were finally in control of her destiny. One account even reported that she addressed Sanson, saying, "Make haste."[19]

Another account described a forgiving and graceful queen who fell to her knees and cried out, "Lord, enlighten and touch my tormentors. Good-bye forever, my children. I go to join your father."[20]

The most incredible and unlikely account was that of Prince Charles-Joseph de Ligne, who claimed to have heard from a good source that the "unfortunate and beautiful queen was already dead in her cart, where she

Scaffold at the foot of the Statue of Liberty

had drowned in her blood, her misfortunes, and her heartaches, having finished her days en route before reaching the scaffold."[21]

What is the truth?

To be sure, the queen was alive when the executioners grabbed her from behind, thrust her rapidly against the upright wooden plank, and tied her to it. They then tipped the plank over and pushed her neck through the hole of the wooden "lunette" that held her head in place. The executioner pulled the cord, and the steel-on-steel screeching of the falling blade ended with a clank.

It was a quarter past twelve when Marie Antoinette died in the thirty-eighth year of her life. The executioner Sanson lifted the blood-streaming head by its hair and showed it to the crowd from the four different corners of the scaffold. Customarily, however, the heads of victims were only displayed from the open side of the scaffold. Even in death the queen was treated more venomously than most.

The doleful silence accorded to those whose heads had fallen was refused to the former queen of France. At the sight of the blood and the convulsively twitching eyelids, the crowd roared, "Vive la Républic!" Hats flew into the air.[22]

Executioner showing the queen's head to the people

Journalists scurried off to write their accounts of the event. Some were hideously joyful, unable to hide their glee, such as Hébert, whose funeral oration in an issue of his *Père Duchêsne* read, "The greatest of all joys of the Father Duchesne was, after seeing with his own eyes, the head of the *veto femelle* [Madame Veto] separated from her damn crane neck and great anger against both devil's advocates who dared defend this monkey."[23]

In his pamphlet, Hébert wrote that he could not fathom how the two devil's advocates, Tronçon-Ducoudray and Chauveau-Lagarde, had ever had the audacity to defend Marie Antoinette. It was his fellow revolutionaries, however, who had assigned them to represent the queen.

How could it be that she found a bugger bold enough to defend her? However, two palace brawlers had the audacity; one of them pushed the effrontery to say that the nation owed her too much to punish her and declared that without her, without the crimes alleged against her, we would not be free! I cannot f**king conceive how one can accept a prostitute's thighs, the lure of a villain's spoils, a gold box, a watch, or diamonds to betray their conscience and try to throw dust in the eyes of jurors.

Have I not seen these devil's advocates not only thrashing about like hell in holy water to prove the innocence of the monkey but daring to mourn the death of the traitor Capet [Louis XVI] and tell the judges it was enough to have punished the big pig, but they should be merciful with his f**king wife!

A young man underneath the scaffold, who had dipped his handkerchief in the queen's blood and pressed it close to his heart, wiped his bloodstained hands on his jacket. His actions did not escape the troops nearby, and he was instantly apprehended. He had a carnation between his teeth, and the portraits of Louis XVI and Marie Antoinette were found on his person.[24]

Witnesses in the crowd considered him a counterrevolutionary and demanded that he be executed on the spot. The soldiers spared him from the crowd's fury, bringing him before the administrators of the Seine department.

The man was Antoine-François Maingot, a thirty-one-year-old junk dealer and gendarme of the Thirty-Third Division. He explained that it was impossible for him to go about his professional activities as a result of the call to arms of all citizens, and he had accompanied his father to attend the execution.[25]

He claimed that the crowd had pushed him under the scaffold and that, like many others, he had stepped in the blood at its base. Because he had been carrying images of the royals and a carnation, the magistrates sent Maingot before the Revolutionary Tribunal. Despite his implausible explanations, he was set free.

It was indeed a close call, because he had certainly been an accomplice of the last conspiracy to save the queen. And his loyalty certainly motivated him to collect some drops of Marie Antoinette's blood for a relic.

The fact that blood ran below the scaffold was additional proof that Marie Antoinette had certainly been alive at the time of her execution. A cadaver does not bleed profusely; the body's circulation of blood ends when the heart stops beating. The *Abréviateur universel* confirmed that the queen had been alive: "A considerable amount of blood collected after the execution was thrown into the sewer on the site."[26]

The chief executioner in 1793 was the fifty-four-year-old Charles-Henri Sanson. He had been dissatisfied with his macabre duties ever since the execution of Louis XVI earlier that year. Although he would not officially resign from his post until 1795, he found the execution of the king so repugnant that he had turned over his duties to his son Henry in early 1793.[27]

The heir apparent to the Sanson dynasty had been Charles-Henri's youngest son Gabriel, but he had died in 1792 when he accidentally fell from the scaffold while displaying a severed head to the crowd.

It was Henry Sanson who actually executed Marie Antoinette, despite the declaration of his son Clément-Henri, the sixth and last in the long line of family executioners, all called "Sanson." According to Clément's *Mémoires des Sanson*, his grandfather, Charles-Henri, was the queen's executioner. However, this was not true. In fact, Clément did not even write the book; he had sold the rights to his memoirs for thirty thousand francs to a ghostwriter.[28]

The ghostwriter took the liberty to claim that the queen had said, "Merci, Monsieur, merci!" to thank the executioner for his assistance when she stepped down from the tumbril at the place de la Révolution. He also omitted the fact that the queen had stepped on the executioner's foot. These were grave mistakes for the amateur; it was well documented that the queen had descended from the cart on her own without any assistance and that she did indeed step on the executioner's foot.[29]

Whether Marie Antoinette met her death fearlessly or not, she had wished to be brave to the very end. In her last testament—written to Élisabeth the very same morning—she said she wanted to face death as honorably as her husband: "Innocent like him, I hope to show the same firmness in my last moments. I am calm, as one is when one's conscience reproaches one with nothing."[30]

Marie Antoinette's death would not be shameful.

À SAVOIR . . .

Dr. Joseph-Ignace Guillotin[31]

The following cold, mechanical description of Doctor Guillotin's machine was presented to the National Assembly in Paris on March 7, 1792. The assembly decreed universal use of the new contraption on March 20.

> Considering the structure of the neck, the spine is the center, consisting of several bones including connecting tissues. There is thus no joint to look for, and it is not possible to be assured of a prompt and perfect separation by entrusting it to an agent whose application may differ physically and morally. It is necessary, for the certainty of the process, to depend upon an invariable mechanical means, by which we can also determine the force and effect.
>
> This is what is done in England: the body of the criminal is lying face down between two posts barred from above by a cross, upon which an axe is dropped on the neck by means of a latch. The back of the instrument should be strong enough and heavy enough to act effectively; we know that its strength increases due to the height from which it falls. It is easy to build such a machine whose effect is unmistakable.
>
> [Signed] Antoine Louis, Permanent Secretary of the Academy of Surgery

"Gentlemen, with my little machine there I can shave off your heads by dozens without any of you feeling a twitch of pain!" said Doctor Guillotin. "Only conceive, gentlemen, the pleasure of dying without pain!"[32]

THE ABSURDITY

Dinner plate commemorating the execution of Marie Antoinette

16

THE UNFORTUNATES
AND THE
SOLE SURVIVORS

"Being confined for thirteen months without seeing anyone that I know, I trembled in fear that I might compromise him [Jean-Baptiste Michonis]."

—Marie Antoinette, Revolutionary Tribunal[1]

Paris
October 16, 1793

Thousands of Parisians were executed as enemies of the Revolution during the Reign of Terror, a period that lasted a little over two years, from May 31, 1792, to July 27, 1794. During this frenzied time, debtors paid their debts by informing on their creditors, criminals denounced their prosecutors and judges, husbands found a way to rid themselves of their wives, priests were indicted for not abjuring their vows, and those who sympathized with the royals were easily compromised and assured a tumbril to the scaffold.[2]

Much blood was carelessly shed during the Terror, but revolutionaries may have thought it necessary to quell hostile factions to avoid the bloodshed of civil war and anarchy throughout France. The Revolutionary Tribunal became the most effective tool for judging the enemies of the Revolution, and whether conducted fairly or not, trials generally produced a guilty verdict.

Two trials and subsequent executions during the Terror differed from most due to the exceptional backgrounds of the prisoners. On January 21, 1793, nine months before his wife was sent to the guillotine, Louis XVI was led from his cell in the Temple and quickly driven to the place de la Révolution. As during the queen's journey, there must have been last-minute plots to rescue the king, but there was no concrete evidence that any effort was made.

Louis XVI had generally been considered morally upright and honest; he loathed bloodshed, but his weakness led to his downfall. He had willingly accepted numerous concessions to give his people more power, but many of his advisers, including the queen, were just as incompetent as he in reforming the government. At a time when France needed a strong leader, Louis was a shy and awkward monarch.[3]

Marie Antoinette, on the other hand, was in many ways stronger and more intelligent than her husband. Moreover, she was in a good position to exert power over him. And that she did, especially after the royal family was removed from Versailles and put under house arrest at the Tuileries Palace. Until the family was sent to the Temple three years later, Louis remained apathetic and depressed, unable to face the problems of his time.[4] And problems were inching closer and closer outside the walls of his palace.

After the execution of Louis XVI, Marie Antoinette was almost forgotten in the Temple until the country's outrage at the foreign coalition's success on France's borders. The northern town of Valenciennes had just been surrendered—for which the queen was blamed.

After being removed from her children and sent to the Conciergerie, the queen simply submitted to the revolutionaries' will. She suffered emotionally from being separated from her children and physically from both insomnia and hemorrhaging for seventy-six days in her dungeon cell.

During the grueling trial, the evidence produced against the queen was unfounded, at times obscene, and mostly based on hearsay. It has since been discovered that she actually was guilty of treason, but this evidence did not exist at the time and could never have been produced by prosecutor Antoine Quentin Fouquier-Tinville at the trial. The queen had also destroyed many incriminating letters and documents before the insurrection at the Tuileries. Still, after one hour's deliberation, the jury found her guilty. She was executed only hours later.

During her trial as well as her long imprisonment, Marie Antoinette often stated that her biggest fear was compromising her friends or anyone who showed loyalty to her and her family. "I had friends," she said in her last testament, remembering without a doubt those from her more carefree days at Versailles as well as those who risked their lives to free her and her family in prison.

One very special friend was Count Hans Axel von Fersen, who was deeply pained when he heard the news of her execution from his friend, the duke of Deux-Ponts, who wrote, "Today we received the terrible news that these barbarians, these bloody French servants, ended the unhappy life of our dear and respectable queen."[5]

"The queen of France, the model queen and woman is no more!" wrote Fersen. "My heart is cruelly torn; only time will weaken the vivacity of my pain."[6]

Unlike many of Marie Antoinette's closest friends and family, the man who had risked his life to help the royal family on their unsuccessful flight to Varennes did not suffer the guillotine's blade. Fersen would be murdered during a riot in the streets of Stockholm on June 20, 1810. He died fighting for the ideals for which he had lived.[7]

Not everyone, however, was aware that the queen had been taken to the place de la Révolution to be guillotined on the morning of October 16. In the Temple Louis Charles's caretaker Antoine Simon, municipal guards, and employees of the prison did not inform Élisabeth and the children of the queen's death, out of either charity or indifference.[8]

Simon knew that Marie Antoinette would be found guilty, but he did not know the exact day that the execution would take place. On the morning of October 16, he thought he heard a slight murmur outside, a confused noise that usually announced some unusual movement in the capital. However, the prisons were so crowded and the public prosecutor so overloaded with criminal cases that it was nearly impossible to establish the identity of those condemned to die.[9]

Simon was the Temple servant who had received the dauphin in his quarters at half past ten o'clock on the night the young Louis Charles was torn from the queen's arms. For two days the child did not accept any food from Simon and rarely spoke to him. If he did speak, he took an insolent kingly air: "I wish to know," said the child, "what law it is by which you are ordered to separate me from my mother and keep me in prison. Show me the law, I wish to see it!"[10]

"Hold thy tongue, Capet; thou art impertinent," said Simon to put the other guards at ease.[11]

Simon was not violent with the child at first, but when Louis Charles refused the gift of a small musical instrument called a "Jew's harp," the caretaker became enraged. "Your she-wolf of a mother and bitch of an aunt play on the piano," he said. "You must accompany them on the Jew's harp; what a fine row that will make!"[12]

When Louis Charles pushed the toy aside and swore he would never play on it, Simon struck the child for his ingratitude. When government officials made inquiries as to the manner in which Simon was fulfilling his duties caring for the child, they discovered that he was not following the secret instructions given to him.[13]

Simon had believed that he was required to make the Capet boy a good little citizen, remove the "royal stain" from his brow, and make him wear the revolutionary cap instead of a crown.

"Citizens, what do you decide about the wolf-cub?" Simon asked the officials. "He has been taught to be insolent, but I shall know how to tame him.[14]

"So much the worse if he sinks under it!" he continued. "I don't answer for that. After all, what do you want done with him? Do you want him transported?"

"No," answered the officials.

"Killed?"

"No."

"Poisoned?"

"No."

"But what, then?"

"We want to get rid of him!"

Louis XVI had made the young prince promise that he would never avenge his father's death were he to become king. But the child would never be crowned, and within two years the Revolution was able to "get rid" of the young prince.

Louis Charles, uncrowned Louis XVII, at the age of eight

The true heir to the throne of France perhaps suffered the most during the social convulsions of the French Revolution. During his fifteen months of solitary confinement in the Temple, his food was pushed through an opening in the cell door: "No one entered the cell; it was never aired or cleaned, and nothing was ever removed from it. His bedding was never changed during all this time, nor was his person cared for in any manner!"[15]

The cell was overrun with rats and mice attracted by decaying food and human waste. The scabies-infested child also became prey to insects before dying.[16] Louis XVII, the second son of Louis XVI, died on June 9, 1795. He was ten years old.*

Ironically, or perhaps fittingly, Antoine Simon, the rogue of the Temple who had made the young uncrowned king drink wine, learn to curse like a republican, and comply with Jacques René Hébert's charges of incest against his mother, was himself guillotined at the place de la Révolution in 1794, along with Maximilien Robespierre, the leader of the revolutionary movement.[17]

It should be remembered that not all revolutionaries were hostile to the royals. There were men and women working in the prisons and even in the republican government who sympathized with the queen and her family; in fact, they were ready to risk their lives for Marie Antoinette. Two of them, Jacques François Lepître and François Adrien Toulan, had been won over by the royal family even before the death of Louis XVI. The two guards served as messengers between the queen and Élisabeth and their friends outside the prison walls. Toulan had even conceived the first plan to rescue the queen, Madame Élisabeth, and the children—a plan that almost succeeded in March 1793.[18]

By the time another plan to rescue the royal family was devised two months later, Toulan had been relieved of his service at the Temple. A colleague in the prison had denounced him and others, although the plot was never discovered. However, Toulan would eventually pay for his devotion to his queen.

As a memento of her gratitude, the queen had given Toulan a small gold box, one of the few trinkets she still possessed. When it was found at Toulan's residence and its history was ascertained, he was convicted of the sole offense of having and valuing a relic of his sovereign. For this offense he was guillotined on June 30, 1794.[19]

Another of the queen's friends among the commissioners was Jean-Baptiste Michonis, who also feared that the danger to the queen's life was growing every day. He conspired with Baron Jean Pierre de Batz to rescue

---

*Louis Charles Capet's body was thrown into a common grave and never found. His heart, however, had been stolen and preserved by one of the doctors before the body was interred.

the queen and her family from the Temple, a plot that also failed but was not detected.

Michonis later attempted to save the queen again when she was incarcerated in the Conciergerie. He and the chevalier de Rougeville were able to relate to the queen all the details of their more daring plot scheduled to take place on the night of September 2. Warden Toussaint Richard, his wife, and Madame Marie Harel were all in on the conspiracy.

The chevalier de Rougeville was able to flee, but Michonis was caught and convicted of treason and aiding the foreign powers. He was guillotined on June 17, 1794.

Each of the plans to save Marie Antoinette could very easily have succeeded if all had not been interrupted by random circumstances at the last minute.[20] And the queen paid dearly for the failed attempts. After the Carnation Plot, new gendarmes were selected from among the most hard-core revolutionaries and placed night and day at the door of the queen's new and more secure cell. They had orders not to speak to her and not to answer if she spoke to them.[21]

The chevalier de Rougeville was never convicted for his part in the conspiracy, but he was later imprisoned for other political crimes. When caught relaying information to the Russian emperor Alexander, he was arrested, convicted, and shot by a firing squad on March 10, 1814.[22]

Warden Richard and his wife had strict orders for the imprisonment of the queen when she first arrived at the Conciergerie, but they treated her with the utmost kindness. Instead of serving her the coarse prison fare, Madame Richard prepared wholesome meals for the queen, did her best to provide some comfort in the dungeon cell, and secretly relayed news about her sister-in-law and children in the Temple.

It was Madame Richard who introduced Michonis and the chevalier de Rougeville into the prison to announce the plans for the queen's escape. When the plot was discovered, Warden Richard and his wife were both removed from their posts in the Conciergerie, immediately arrested with their son, and thrown into prison. They were later released and allowed to return to work in the prisons of Paris.[23] The Committee of General Security was unable to make any charge against them in the Michonis affair.[24]

Madame Richard, praised by most prisoners for her kindness, was murdered in 1796 by a desperate convict maddened by a sentence of twenty
years in irons. At the moment when Madame Richard handed him a bowl of
soup, he stabbed her in the heart with a knife. She died within a few minutes
of the attack.[25]

Warden Bault and his wife, formerly caretakers in La Force prison, eagerly
sought to assume Richard's duties in the Conciergerie after the Carnation
Plot; they too were determined to ease the queen's meager existence. Although ordered to give their prisoner only bread and water, the Baults followed the example of their predecessors and carefully prepared food bought
fresh from nearby vendors.

Marie Antoinette never drank wine, but the fetid water of the Seine River
did not agree with her. Madame Bault accordingly had the pure water of
Arcueil brought to her every day. Many persons from outside the prison forwarded little delicacies to the fallen queen with the Bault's permission. The
women of the Halles marketplace, for example, privately sent her presents of
fruits and flowers.

These indulgences were indeed a dangerous gesture on the part of the
Bault family. Warden Bault was once severely reprimanded for simply hanging an old piece of tapestry on the damp walls of Marie Antoinette's dungeon
and for requesting a warmer cover for the queen. Madame Bault was not allowed in the queen's cell, but her daughter was permitted to help the queen
make her bed and clean her room. She also combed the queen's hair every
morning and mended the two old gowns to which the queen of France's
wardrobe had been reduced.[26]

In 1822 Madame Bault wrote an account of her service to the queen in the
Conciergerie, but it has been difficult to validate some of her claims.* After
all, she was never allowed in the queen's cell. Also, she never mentioned
Rosalie Lamorlière in her memoirs; this is surprising because Rosalie had
helped cook, serve the queen's meals, and clean since the queen's first day
in the Conciergerie.[27]

---

*It is unknown if Madame Bault's account of her first days in the Conciergerie is accurate,
but it is the only account and has been trusted by most French authors who have written
about this period.

Rosalie was also the last person to tend to Marie Antoinette's belongings. After the queen was removed from the Conciergerie, the first bailiff of the Tribunal, accompanied by three or four colleagues, approached Rosalie in the warden's office and ordered her to follow them to the queen's dungeon. He allowed Rosalie to collect the tiny mirror and box that had belonged to her, but he ordered her to wrap the other objects belonging to the queen in a bed sheet. Rosalie was also ordered to fold the bundle up in the straw mattress lying on the floor; she later said she had no idea how she ever managed to do it.[28]

The following inventory of the queen's effects gave an indication of the poverty into which the princess had fallen at the time of her death: fifteen fine linen chemises lined with small lace, a cape made of material called "raz de Saint-Maur," two negligees of the same material, a sheath and petticoat with large stripes, five corsets of fine linen, a cotton robe, a jacket, undergarments, four handkerchiefs, two pairs of black stockings, slippers, a belt, a small chiffon scarf, a sponge, three pairs of shoes, a box of powder, a skirt hoop, and a small tin of ointment.

The following effects were yet to be sent to the washwoman: a set of sheets, a gray cotton towel, twenty-four handkerchiefs, and six linen scarves.[29]

When the officials removed the mattress with the queen's possessions, Rosalie said they took the last remnants in the Conciergerie belonging to "the best and the most unfortunate princess that ever existed!"

Rosalie, the kind soul, was found in the Incurable of the Rue de Sevres, a home for the sick, in 1825. Marie Antoinette's daughter, Marie-Thérèse, then the duchesse d'Angoulême, had placed her there, but the faithful servant of the last queen of France "languished in the most sensitive deprivation" with an annual pension of only two hundred francs provided by the queen's daughter.[30]

The guard Jean Gilbert, who was also involved but not charged in the Carnation Plot, married the sister of the jailer Louis Larivière, whose mother had first served as the queen's domestic in the Conciergerie. After Gilbert testified in the queen's trial, he was promoted to officer of the gendarmerie. Gilbert was a gambler, however, and after losing all of his company's money in a game, he killed himself with a gunshot to the head in a fit of depression.[31]

Others who played a role in the queen's trial did not fare well either. The witness Jacques René Hébert was followed to the guillotine by prosecutor Fouquier-Tinville, along with twenty others accused of conspiring with the allied powers. Their executions took place on March 24, 1794, only months after that of Marie Antoinette.

Four days before Marie Antoinette was executed, revolutionary spies had discovered another conspiracy to rescue the queen while on her journey in the tumbril to the scaffold. The plot was vast, including over five hundred conspirators. It was suspected, but never proved, that the chevalier de Rougeville and Baron Jean Pierre de Batz were involved or had helped plan this last escape attempt, but it too failed. The young barber Jean-Baptiste Basset and Madame Catherine Fournier were convicted and guillotined; Fournier's fourteen-year-old son was sentenced to twenty years in prison.[32]

The queen would have been devastated to discover that so many people, friends and foes alike, had been punished at the place de la Révolution. More distressing would have been the news about her sister-in-law Élisabeth.

The friendship between Marie Antoinette and Élisabeth had grown stronger in the last days of their lives, while they were imprisoned in the Temple. Perhaps the piety of Élisabeth, a devout Catholic, influenced the queen in her turn toward spirituality in the Conciergerie. There is no evidence that she had been so occupied with religion at any time before then.[33]

On May 9, 1794, Élisabeth was moved to the Conciergerie from the Temple, where she had cared for her niece since the queen's departure. She was convicted of conspiracy and condemned to death, along with twenty-three other men and women, on May 10.

Élisabeth Capet in the Temple

Élisabeth was remembered for helping these anxious prisoners through the ordeal, praying with them in the carriage to the scaffold.[34] Several of the prisoners were known to Élisabeth when she was Madame Élisabeth at the court of Versailles. As the procession crossed the Pont Neuf, the scarf covering Élisabeth's head fell off; bareheaded, the princess "attracted the notice of many who might not otherwise have noticed the calm sweetness of her countenance."[35]

A bench had been placed at the foot of the scaffold, just in case any of the condemned fainted while waiting their turn. Madame Anne Emmanuel de Crussol, who had known the princess, bowed low and respectfully asked permission to be kissed.

"Certainly," said Élisabeth, "and with all my heart."

Every woman who followed received the kiss, and every man bowed reverently to her when he passed. While Élisabeth waited her turn, however, a person below cried out, "Very fine to bow to her; she is done for, like the Austrian."

Only from these crude remarks did Madame Élisabeth perhaps learn that Marie Antoinette had met the same fate that would now be hers.[36]

Élisabeth's niece, Princess Marie-Thérèse Charlotte of France, the eldest of Louis XVI and Marie Antoinette's children, would thus become the sole Capet to survive the Temple. During her imprisonment there, the child never learned what had happened to her family; she wrote the following words on the wall of her chambers:

> Marie-Thérèse Charlotte is the most unhappy person in the world. She can obtain no news of her mother; nor be reunited with her, though she has asked it a thousand times. Live, my good mother! whom I love well, but of whom I can hear no tidings. O my father! watch over me from heaven above. O my God! forgive those who have made my parents suffer.[37]

In late August 1795, Marie-Thérèse was finally told about her family. When Madame Renée de Chanterenne, her female companion, informed her of each of their fates, the distraught princess cried out, "What—even my aunt?" The news left her gasping in a torrent of weeping.[38]

Princess Marie-Thérèse

Only once the Terror was over was Marie-Thérèse allowed to leave France. She was liberated from the Temple on December 18, 1795, the eve before her seventeenth birthday. Exchanged for a political prisoner, she was taken to Vienna, her mother's birthplace.*

After years of exile, Marie-Thérèse finally returned to Paris when her uncle became King Louis XVIII in 1815 and the monarchy was restored in France. Some twenty-five years had passed since its abolition, when France had drowned in the blood of the Terror and witnessed the executions of King Louis XVI and Queen Marie Antoinette.[39]

Marie-Thérèse married her cousin, the duke of Angoulême, and was unofficially the queen of France for twenty minutes in 1830. She died in 1851 at the age of seventy-two without any children, leaving the martyred King Louis XVI and Marie Antoinette with no descendants.†

---

*The prisoner was Nicolas-Marie Quinette, captured by the Austrians in April 1793.

†Marie-Thérèse was technically queen of France for the period between her father-in-law's signing of his abdication of the crown and her husband's reluctant signing of the same document.

À SAVOIR . . .

Madame Élisabeth of France

"Have courage and faith in the mercy of God," said Madame Élisabeth to the other condemned as they stepped up to the scaffold. Orders had been given that Louis XVI's youngest sister would be executed last, in the hopes that "the twenty-three heads falling before her eyes might perhaps break her courage."[40]

It did not. Élisabeth stepped onto the scaffold, and although the executioner offered his hand, she accepted no help, looking up to the sky with a crucifix in her hand. When she was tied to the fatal plank, her kerchief fell to the ground, revealing a silver medal of the immaculate conception of the Virgin on her bare bosom. When the executioner reached for it, his duty being to remove any sign of piety, Madame Élisabeth said her last words: "In the name of your mother, sir, cover me."[41]

Until then, an execution had not been watched with such solemnity, and there were no cries of "Vive la République!" in the place de la Révolution when the guillotine's blade fell. Afterward, the quieted spectators went about their way.

Élisabeth's body was placed in a common grave at the cemetery of Monceaux—together with the other twenty-three bodies.[42]

17

LA CIMETIÈRE
DE LA MADELEINE

*"On the 18th of January 1815, the commissioners appointed
by the king [Louis XVIII] to search for the sacred remains of
their late majesties Louis XVI and the Queen Marie Antoinette, arrived, at eight o'clock in the morning, at the ancient
cemetery of the Madeleine on the rue d'Anjou."*

—Charles-Henry Dambray, chancellor of France[1]

Paris
The Restoration

Marie Antoinette was to be the last queen of France when she was be-
headed at the onset of the First Republic of France, which lasted until
the declaration of Napoleon's First Empire in 1804.[2] When the allied powers forced Napoleon to abdicate ten years later, on April 11, 1814, he was
exiled to Elba, an island in the Mediterranean off the coast of Italy.

The long years of the Bourbons' exile thus ended with the emperor's
abdication and the first Bourbon restoration. Louis XVIII ascended to the
throne of France twenty-one years after the death of his brother Louis XVI
and nineteen years after the death of his nephew Louis XVII.

On May 3 the new king, called "The Desired" (Louis le Désiré), made
his entry into Paris, accompanied by Duchess Marie-Thérèse of Angoulême,
Louis XVI and Marie Antoinette's daughter and the sole Capet survivor
of the Temple. However, the people took little interest in the homecoming

except when they saw Napoleon's Imperial Guard in the procession and cried out, "Long live the Imperial Guard!" (*Vive le Garde impériale!*).[3]

The people must have been amused by the corpulence of the new king and the appearance of these forgotten personages who were coming to take possession of the Tuileries Palace. Louis XVIII immediately set out to steer a middle course between liberals and ultra-royalists during his reign.[4] He also attempted to suppress the many men who pretended to be Marie-Thérèse's long-lost younger brother, Louis XVII. These pretenders not only raised questions about the validity of Louis XVIII's claim to the throne but also distressed Marie-Thérèse.*

But the celebration did not last long. Within months Napoleon was able to gather support to escape from Elba on February 26, 1815. When he landed on the French mainland two days later, he shouted, "If there be amongst you a soldier who would kill his general, his emperor, let him do it now! Here I am!"[5]

But the troops responded, "Vive l'empereur!" And they followed Napoleon to Paris. On March 20, Louis XVIII had already fled the capital. Curiously, Marie-Thérèse, who was in Bordeaux at the time, remained in France to rally the support of the local troops. Although they agreed to defend her, they refused to enter into a civil war with Napoleon's troops.

Napoleon ordered his troops to arrest Marie-Thérèse, his wife's second cousin, but she had already agreed to leave France, believing her cause to be lost.† Her bravery caused Napoleon to remark that she was the "only man in her family."[6]

Napoleon would govern for a period called the Hundred Days before his forces were crushed by the duke of Wellington at the Battle of Waterloo on June 18, 1815. When the defeated emperor returned to Paris, he found that both the legislature and the people had turned against him. He abdicated on June 22, and the House of Bourbon was restored for a second time.

The more things change, the more things remain the same.‡ Louis XVIII returned again to the throne, this time not as *Le Désiré* but as *L'inévitable*.

---

*These fears were not put to rest until 2000, when DNA testing proved that the heart interred at Saint-Denis was that of Louis-Charles.

†Napoleon had married Marie-Antoinette's great-niece, Marie Louise.

‡Plus ça change—plus c'est la même chose.

The Parisians perhaps felt that they had deserted their lawful king, having previously received Napoleon with open arms. Moreover, they must have felt humiliated after defeat by their despised enemy at Waterloo.[7]

Naturally, the royalists were intoxicated with their success.[8] Marie-Thérèse, however, found her return from exile emotionally draining. Although greeted by two hundred ladies dressed in white with white lilies, she was still distrustful of the many Frenchmen who had supported either the republic or Napoleon.[9] She made pilgrimages to both the site where her brother had died and the Madeleine cemetery where her parents were buried.

Louis XVIII soon decreed that the remains of the late king and queen should be disinterred and laid to rest in the Basilica of Saint-Denis, the ancient burial place of the royal families of France. However, the remains of the martyred royals first needed to be found; it was thus necessary to find those persons who could give information about the royal burials in the Madeleine to ascertain their precise spots.[10]

François Silvani Uenard, formerly rector of the Church de la Madeleine, gave testimony that he had remained at the door of the church on the day King Louis XVI was executed until the body of the king was turned over to him. Then, accompanied by the municipals, he went to an area in the cemetery near the rue d'Anjou, where he asked for a moment of silence.

The king's body was dressed in a white waistcoat, grey silk breeches, and matching stockings. After the recitation of prayers, the clothes were removed before the body was placed in the coffin, which was then deposited in a grave about ten feet from the wall. After a quantity of quicklime was thrown in by order of the government, the coffin was closed and covered with a layer of lime, upon which some earth was added and beaten down firmly.

Another witness, Judge Antoine Lamaignère, testified that although not present at the king's interment, he arrived at the spot the moment after the body had been covered with lime. He could only concur that the king was buried in the spot marked by Pierre-Louis-Olivier Descloseaux, who lived nearby at the time; registrar Jean-Richard-Eve Yaudremont confirmed this.

Dominique-Emmanuel Danjou, son-in-law of Descloseaux, deposed that he had witnessed the interments of both the king and the queen. He saw them placed in coffins without lids, and the graves were then filled up with quicklime and earth. The king's head had been separated from his body and was placed between his legs. Danjou said he had never lost sight of the spot, which he regarded as sacred. Upon the purchase of the grounds by his father-in-law, the walls were heightened, and the space in which the bodies of the king and queen were interred was surrounded by a hedge, near which several cypresses and willows were planted.

After the interrogation of other witnesses, it was decreed that the remains of the king and queen would be exhumed and conveyed to Saint-Denis on January 21, 1815, the anniversary of the king's death. Chancellor Dambray oversaw the committee to find the exact spot where the royals were buried:

On the 18th of January, 1815, we, Charles-Henry Dambray, chancellor of France; the count de Blacas, minister of the king's household; M. le Bailli de Crussol, knight; M. de la Fare, bishop of Nancy and chief almoner to the duchess of Angoulême; and M. Phillipe Distel, his majesty's surgeon, commissioners appointed by the king to search for the sacred remains of their late majesties Louis XVI and the Queen Marie Antoinette, repaired, at eight o'clock in the morning, to the ancient cimetière de la Madeleine on the rue d'Anjou.

Cimetière de la Madeleine

Pierre-Louis-Olivier Descloseaux lived near the cemetery of the Madeleine and noted the names of all those buried with their locations. The cemetery had been closed on March 25, 1794, for health reasons; the neighborhood complained of the stench of decaying bodies.

Descloseaux purchased the grounds in 1802 and marked all the graves with plants and shrubs. On June 4, 1814, Descloseaux prepared a document listing all those buried in the cemetery during the Revolution. Of the list of 1,343 persons interred, the king of France was number 24 and the queen of France was number 107.[11]

Monsieur Joly, the gravedigger of the Madeleine cemetery, reported that he buried the body of Louis XVI in a deep grave on January 23, 1793; the head was separated from the trunk, and the corpse was without shoes and hat. Nine months later Joly buried Marie Antoinette's body in an obscure corner of the same cemetery, but only after finding it lying in the grass almost two weeks after her execution.* The last task of Martial Joseph Armand Herman in the Tribunal's case against the widow Capet was to secure payment to Joly for the burial expenses.[12]

During the Terror, the guillotine never rested. Nearly every day the cart brought one or more baskets full of headless corpses to the cemetery on the rue d'Anjou. The gates opened, the cart drove into the enclosure, and there— hidden by the walls—the gravediggers carried on their "horrible work . . . not so much seen as imagined by the people of the neighborhood."[13]

Upon the return of the Bourbons, Marie-Thérèse's first wish was to visit the sacred spot where her parents had been interred. The Madeleine cemetery was no longer used as a burial ground, but for a considerable time the cemetery was still closely guarded in case any attempt should be made to remove the bodies of the royal victims. The church had long been demolished by the time of Marie-Thérèse's visit, and the cemetery had been sold to Descloseaux, owner of the neighboring house.†

---

*G. Lenotre bases the two-week delay for the queen's burial on Joly's date of October 25. However, if the date was written "25 vendémiaire," according to the French Republican calendar, the date would have been October 16. This is a more likely scenario, being the same day that the queen was executed; however, this invoice was not received by Herman until two weeks later, on November 1 (11 brumaire l'an II). The question arises whether Joly would have waited two weeks for payment.

†M. Descloseaux was living at number 48 rue d'Anjou in 1815.

Descloseaux took it upon himself to make improvements to the cemetery. He restored and raised the walls, closed up the entrance on the rue d'Anjou, and made a new one from his private garden. He also covered the ground with a new layer of turf and planted an orchard, marking the alleyways of the old burial ground with trees.[14]

Descloseaux assigned graves in certain spots to the famous to the best of his ability, marking the places with shrubs and trees and crosses. A hedge separated the spots where the royal remains of Louis XVI and Marie Antoinette were buried; above it arose willows and cypresses. A small mound with a cross marked the grave of the king.[15]

As a sign of Descloseaux's fidelity to the monarchy, his family carefully collected flowers that blossomed upon the royal graves and sent them annually, with leaves of the cypress trees, to Duchess Marie-Thérèse of Angoulême in exile.[16] When she met Descloseaux for the first time, she said, "I did not expect to find such faithful Frenchmen. Good old man, you have religiously preserved the ashes of my parents; your family will be blessed."[17]

Marie-Thérèse frequently went to the cemetery. On her last visit she was accompanied by Monsieur, the count of Artois, the king's brother, who took off his cordon of the order of Saint Michael and presented it to Descloseaux in the king's name as a sign of gratitude. Louis XVIII also granted him a pension, perhaps because Descloseaux had already gifted the property to the king.[18]

By coincidence, Louis XVI and Marie Antoinette were surrounded by many of their most devoted friends and some of their bitterest enemies in the cemetery. At their feet lay five hundred of the Swiss Guards who perished on August 10, 1792, while protecting their sovereigns as mobs of Parisians besieged the Tuileries. Nearby also lay many notable revolutionaries, including Danton, Hébert, Chaumette, Gorsas, and Bailly. The cemetery of the Madeleine was used for burials until March 24, 1794.[19]

According to the memoirs of Paul François Barras, however, the last of all the condemned who filled and closed up the deeply dug common grave were Maximilien Robespierre himself and several members of the Paris Commune.[20]

Descloseaux took great care to preserve the remains that he had voluntarily taken it upon himself to protect. During the absence of the House of Bourbon from France, a few of the royal family's loyal followers were occasionally admitted to visit the spot that the owner was frequently solicited to sell.

In 1810, an unknown wealthy person had offered to purchase the orchard at any price that Descloseaux desired. The prospective buyer also proposed to trade a grand hotel in Paris or an estate in the country, but Descloseaux remained steadfast: "Sir, none of your proposals can ever be acceded to. In purchasing this ground I knew the treasure it possessed, and no offers shall make me alienate it.[21]

"I will seize my musket to punish anyone," he continued, "who dares attempt to deprive me of the sacred deposit of which I have constituted myself the guardian. I will restore it to none but the family for whom alone I preserved it; and no vile motive of interest shall ever induce me to yield."

As soon as Descloseaux learned that Louis XVIII planned to exhume the bodies of Louis XVI and Marie Antoinette, he gave the king the names of those who might be able to furnish more accurate information with regard to the exact location of the original graves. Consequently, Louis XVIII appointed Charles-Henry Dambray, the chancellor of France, to provide a report of all the circumstances that preceded, accompanied, and followed the burial of King Louis XVI and Queen Marie Antoinette.

On January 18, 1815, Chancellor Dambray's committee arrived at the home of Descloseaux, which adjoined the cemetery. There they were greeted by Descloseaux, his son-in-law Danjou, and several other members of his family, who escorted the officials into the orchard and pointed out the area in which Danjou had seen the bodies of the king and queen interred.

The workers first searched for the body of Marie Antoinette, in order that the remains of the king might be discovered with greater certainty; they believed that her remains had been deposited nearer the wall, toward the rue d'Anjou. After the workers had opened a space ten feet in length by five or six feet in breadth and five feet deep, they found a bed of quicklime ten or eleven inches deep.

In the Madeleine cemetery, most of the bodies of Sanson's victims had been rapidly destroyed by quicklime, which the municipals of Paris had required be put in the pits with the bodies.* The officials ordered the workers

---

*The guillotined were buried in the Madeleine cemetery from August 1792 to March 1794. They were afterward taken to the Mousseaux (also called the Errands) cemetery.

to remove the quicklime with the greatest care. Underneath, an outline of a coffin about five feet, six inches in length appeared.

A number of bones were found in the coffin, but most had disintegrated into dust. A skull, however, was found intact, and its position indicated that it had been severed from the body. When the workers produced a woman's stocking,* two elastic garters, and some hair, Monsieur Charles Louis de Barentin, who was eighty years old, clasped his hands and kneeled in prayer. He believed that they belonged to Marie Antoinette. Another official, the prince de Poix, burst into tears, uttered a cry, and fell fainting to the ground.[22]

The workers placed these items in a chest and locked it up. In another chest they deposited what they thought to be the queen's bones mixed with earth and quicklime. The opening in the ground was then covered with thick planks of wood. The party then turned its search to the body of the king.

Unable to find the remains of the king before nightfall, the party suspended its search until the following day. The two chests were moved into Descloseaux's home, where they were covered with a pall and surrounded with lighted candles. The priests of the king's chapel spent the night there praying. The gates of the cemetery were locked, and a guard was stationed on the cemetery grounds.[23]

Early the next morning, on January 19, 1815, the officials watched as the workers dug a deep trench nearer the wall and discovered some earth mingled with quicklime and several small pieces of board, similar to that used for coffins. They then discovered the bones of a man with the skull covered with quicklime and placed between the bones of the legs. The group carefully searched for fragments of clothes, but none were discovered. The workers collected all the remains and placed them in a cloth before enclosing them in a chest that was then taken inside and placed beside of the other two chests. The priests continued to pray over the two bodies.

On January 20, the officials were joined by other nobles appointed by Louis XVIII to observe the remains being removed from the chests and placed in lead coffins. Upon the lids were fastened gold plates, with the following inscriptions: "Here is the body of the most high, excellent prince,

---

*This stocking was similar to the ones provided to the queen in the Conciergerie by the sisters of the charity of Saint-Roch.

Louis XVI, by the grace of God, King of France and Navarre" and "Here is the body of the most high, excellent princess, Marie-Antoinette-Josèphe-Jeanne de Lorraine, Archduchess of Austria, wife of the most high, excellent prince, Louis XVI, by the grace of God, King of France and Navarre."[24]

On January 21, 1815, the remains of Louis XVI and Marie Antoinette were conveyed to the Basilica of Saint-Denis. Early in the morning, all the regiments of Paris had formed a double line from the rue d'Anjou to Saint-Denis. At eight o'clock, Monsieur, the king's brother, accompanied the duke of Angoulême from the Tuileries Palace to Descloseaux's house. They laid the first stone of a chapel upon the spot where the royal remains had been discovered.[25]

The coffins were then carried to the funeral carriage by twelve of the Guards de la Manche,* and the procession moved forward ostentatiously in the following order:

1. A detachment of gendarmes
2. The colonel of the king's regiment of hussars and its trumpeters
3. The colonel of the king and queen's regiment of light infantry
4. The governor of the first military division, attended by his staff
5. A detachment of the National Guards, on horseback and on foot
6. A lieutenant general attended by the staff of the National Guards
7. A captain and officers of the king's guards and grenadiers on horseback
8. Officers of the king's household in three carriages drawn by eight horses
9. A detachment of fusiliers of the king's guards, headed by its officers and band
10. A detachment of the king's guards, it officers, trumpets, and cymbals
11. High personages, appointed by the king, in eight carriages
12. The duke of Angoulême and the duke of Berry
13. Four heralds and the king at arms, on horseback
14. The grand master of the ceremonies on horseback and four light horsemen

---

*The Gardes de la Manche (Guards of the Sleeve) was an elite detachment of the king's personal guard.

15. Two gentlemen ushers, on horseback
16. The funeral coach: at the wheels were the captains of the four Red Companies; on the sides were six Guards de la Manche. It was escorted to Saint-Denis by thirty of the Hundred Swiss Guards, headed by their captain.
17. The equerry of the king's stables, on horseback
18. The captain of the bodyguards
19. A detachment of gendarmes of the king's guards and Movsirun's guards
20. The carriage of Monsieur, the king's brother
21. A detachment of the National Guards on horseback, and
22. A squadron of the king's dragoons.[26]

A detachment of artillery joined the procession at the barrier Saint-Denis and followed it, firing minute guns, and a regiment of the king's chasseurs lined the road from Paris to Saint-Denis. The cold was so intense that none of the unfortunate soldiers would likely ever forget the belated funeral of Louis XVI and Marie Antoinette.

The drums and musical instruments were covered with black serge (woolen fabric), and the arms and colors of the troops were ornamented with black crepe. At first, a solemn silence prevailed among the crowd that thronged the streets and through which the procession passed, but the behavior of the populace soon became anything but reverent.

The solemnity was at times interrupted when the crowds ridiculed the "quaint costumes and the medley of mourning emblems." At one point along the route, hostile cries mingled with laughter when the plume-bedecked roof of the hearse became entangled in the chains of a street lamp and an ill-natured jester shouted, "À la lanterne!"

It was a cry reminiscent of the dark days of the Revolution, but despite the accident, the pageant proceeded in safety.[27]

Upon reaching Saint-Denis at twelve o'clock in the afternoon, the Guards de la Manche took the bodies from the coach and carried them into the church, where they were received by the clergy. They were then placed upon a lofty tomb of state in the middle of the choir. After retiring for a few minutes, Monsieur, the count of Artois, entered the church, followed by the

*Funeral coach transferring the remains of Louis XVI
and Marie Antoinette to the Basilica of Saint-Denis
(Bibliothèque Nationale Française)*

duke of Angoulême and other princes, who occupied the stalls on the right nearest the altar. The duchess of Orléans and other princesses entered the opposite stalls. Next to the princes sat additional members of the royal family whom the king had appointed to support the pall when the coffins were carried to the vault.

Duchess Marie-Thérèse of Angoulême and King Louis XVIII did not attend.

In fact, Marie-Thérèse's own inclination would have been to allow her parents to rest undisturbed, but she sacrificed her personal feelings and reluctantly consented to the transfer of the remains from the Madeleine cemetery to Saint-Denis.[28]

When everyone had taken their places, the service commenced. The princes and princesses, followed by the grand master and master of the ceremonies, approached the altar to present their offerings, after which the bishop of Troyes delivered a funeral oration. Once the absolution was pronounced, the bodies were lowered into the royal vault, where Monsieur and his two sons descended and prostrated themselves on the coffins of their royal relatives.

As the door of the crypt opened to receive the remains of Louis XVI and Marie Antoinette, the roar of guns was heard, and all the bells of Paris began to toll. Salutes of artillery had been decreed to fire at the moment when the procession set out from Paris, during the service at Saint-Denis, and when the bodies were lowered into the vault.[29]

The vault where the remains of the king and queen of France were laid had been set apart for more than two centuries as the burial place of the House of Bourbon. It was located in the very center of the crypt under the choir of the basilica.[30]

At two o'clock the ceremony was finished.

À SAVOIR . . .

Basilica of Saint-Denis

Louis XVIII ordered that every year, on January 21, a service for the repose of the soul of Louis XVI would be celebrated in all the churches of his kingdom. Also, the royal court and all civil and military authorities would be in mourning, the courts of justice would not sit, and all theaters would be closed.[31]

The king also invited the bishops of the kingdom to celebrate the anniversary of the death of Marie Antoinette, but in a more restrained manner:

> We want no speech or eulogy delivered except for the reading from the pulpit of the touching and sublime letter that was miraculously found, where this princess, hours before her death, expressed all the feelings of religion inspired by a most Christian queen and the most tender of mothers.[32]

To this day, Mass has been celebrated in memory of Queen Marie Antoinette every year in October at the Church of Saint-Germain l'Auxerrois in the first arrondissement of Paris.

EPILOGUE

During the seventy-six days that Queen Marie Antoinette languished in the Conciergerie, she was perceived and treated as a political hostage. Maximilien Robespierre and the revolutionary leaders had not decided on her fate; they had only voted on setting a date for the Revolutionary Tribunal as a means of preventing the allied powers from marching onto French soil. The surrender of the former queen of France to Austria could have purchased the neutrality of certain Italian states, but negotiations stalled.[2]

The use of Marie Antoinette for political purposes was nothing new; she had been a pawn on the chessboard of diplomacy since her days playing in the gardens of the magnificent Schönbrunn Palace in Vienna. The marriage of the fourteen-year-old Austrian princess to the future Louis XVI of France was arranged by her mother, Empress Maria Theresa, to strengthen the alliance with Austria's longtime enemy. The empress could not have imagined that she had sacrificed her youngest daughter's life for the failed Franco-Austrian alliance. And, fortunately, Maria Theresa did not live long enough to receive the news that Marie Antoinette had been held in a dungeon for two and a half months until her severed head and body were thrown into a common grave at the cemetery of the Madeleine.

But the use of Marie Antoinette as a political pawn did not end in a vault at the Basilica of Saint-Denis. When Louis XVIII ordered the kingdom to celebrate the anniversary of her death on October 16 every year, the royalists used the occasion to violently call for "a rebellion of twenty-five years to be expiated by absolute obedience." The royalists suggested that those involved in the conviction of Marie Antoinette and her husband should be brought to justice, only incensing the slumbering passions of the men of the Revolution.[3]

Louis XVIII may have used the entombment of the royal couple's bones in Saint-Denis to help en-

Archduchess Marie Antoinette

dorse his claim to the throne, but there was soon doubt as to whether the bones in the crypt actually belonged to the last queen of France. Contemporary historians argued that the mandated quicklime would have devoured the bones beyond recognition. And it was well known that quicklime was used at the time; its use was closely monitored due to the neighborhood's complaints about the stench of decaying bodies coming from the cemetery.[4]

Moreover, it was not completely improbable that Pierre-Louis-Olivier Descloseaux was actually a charlatan—like many others who exploited the gullible Bourbons at the onset of the restoration. After all, Monsieur Descloseaux did generously give the cemetery to them, later receiving a hefty annual pension in return for his perceived loyalty.

If the quicklime had not reduced the royal bones to dust, as some had speculated, it was also possible that the queen's bones were intermingled with those of thousands of other cadavers interred in the same unmarked common graveyard during the Terror. One historian even argued that Robespierre's bones had been taken for those of the royal victims.[5]

Even if the bones of Marie Antoinette were actually found, were they truly the remains of a criminal who deserved the executioner's blade? Emperor Napoleon had given this question considerable thought. "Although this Louis XVI did not deserve his misfortune; so is the lot of kings. Their lives belong to everyone; an assassin, a conspiracy, a cannon ball, such are the risks they take."[6]

But did Marie Antoinette, an Austrian princess, deserve her misfortune: months of slow anguish in the gloomy dungeons of the Conciergerie; a horrific and gruesome ride on the back of an open cart amid a howling mob; and the wooden plank at the place de la Révolution?

Napoleon thought not: "The queen's death was a crime worse than regicide." It was a crime absolutely unjustifiable, since it had no pretext whatsoever to offer as an excuse; a crime eminently impolitic, since it struck down "a foreign princess, the most sacred of hostages; a crime cowardly beyond measure, since the victim was a woman who possessed only honors without any power."[7]

And the hatred of Marie Antoinette did not end with her death. The queen's enemies distributed pamphlets around Paris, saying that the Statue of Liberty at the foot of the scaffold turned its head and smiled when the blade of the guillotine fell—a place just a few steps from the gardens of the Tuileries where her children once played.[8]

The last queen of France. Marie Antoinette was a rather attractive and lively image. Though naturally thoughtless, she was a kindhearted woman with mostly good intentions. Indeed, she detested the etiquette of the rigid court, but she was also too ostentatious in her taste for privacy at her Petit Trianon, which only alienated her from the courtiers of Versailles. These were allies dearly missed in the troubling times on the horizon.

An excellent example of Marie Antoinette's thoughtlessness was her sleigh rides on the boulevards of Paris. Wrapped in a fur-lined velvet cloak with gold braid, she was a "delight for any eye," according to her chambermaid. But her timing was harshly criticized; the poorest of her subjects were freezing to death on the streets at the time.[9]

Such thoughtlessness was always a pretext for slander, but Marie Antoinette's conduct generally appeared to be an innocent diversion from the "wearisome monotony of court life."[10] One cannot forget that her husband, though at times strong-willed, was pathetically weak, and she soon became his closest adviser, only rousing the people's animosity against her even more.

By all accounts the queen behaved courageously during the attacks on Versailles and the Tuileries and against the royal family in general. Despite the public's outcries about her coldness, she was always more concerned about the welfare of her husband and her children than herself. While captive in the Temple prison with her family and servants, she remained dignified under the most trying circumstances. During the harsh conditions of her seventy-six-day imprisonment in the Conciergerie and her trial, Marie Antoinette exhibited a moral strength that seemed to astonish—and irritate—her bitterest enemies.

One ally that has received little attention in history was Marie Antoinette's little dog, Thisbé, which brought the queen some comfort in the Temple prison and followed her to the Conciergerie. According to one of many rumors circulating, the grieving Thisbé did not end its life by jumping into the Seine River; rather, it actually escaped from the home of the milliner Madame Arnaud through a door that was accidentally left open. Thisbé then found its way back to the Conciergerie.[11]

Portrait of Marie Antoinette

When the dog arrived at the prison, the tumbril for the guillotine was just leaving, with its mistress sitting between the priest and the executioner. Thisbé followed the cart, jolting over the stony pavement until it arrived at the scaffold among the sans-culottes and guardsmen.

When the queen's head fell, there was a moment of silence and then the loud, agonizing howl of a dog. In an instant, a guard's bayonet had pierced its heart.

"So perish all that mourn an aristocrat," the guard cried out.[12]

Another rumor circulated, however, that when Marie Antoinette learned about her little dog waiting outside the Conciergerie, she asked Madame Bault to care for it. After the queen's death, Madame Bault adopted Thisbé and cared for it for several years until giving it to the duchess de Charost.*

When the duchess was forced to hastily leave Paris for political reasons, she was heartbroken to see Thisbé, in the confusion of the departure, run out into the street and get struck by another coach. Her valet de chambre put Thisbé in a small oak coffin and buried the "queen's dog" at the foot of a sycamore tree in a garden on the rue de Bourbon.

According to legend, this occurred, coincidentally, on October 16.[13]

Thisbé?

Not only were there different stories about the queen's dog, but there were a multitude of conflicting accounts about the queen's life, especially during the seventy-six days of her imprisonment in the Conciergerie. These have been addressed in as much detail as possible for a better picture of what might have actually happened from the night of August 1 until the morning of October 16, 1793.

But it will be the readers' task to decide whether the imprisonment and punishment of this sovereign, mother, and devout Christian were just and deserving or odious and cruelly administered, and if I have presented the queen's misfortune as fairly as possible with the sense of dignity and respect due any human being.

Will Bashor
Paris, October 2015

---

*The duchess of Charost was the daughter of Louise-Élisabeth de Croÿ de Tourzel, the last governess to Marie Antoinette's children.

ACKNOWLEDGMENTS

Five years ago, when I began research for my book *Marie Antoinette's Head: The Royal Hairdresser, the Queen, and the Revolution*, I was astonished to find that very little had been written about the queen's frightful incarceration in the Conciergerie. From this discovery came the idea to reanimate the dungeons of the ancient prison where the queen was kept in a state of terror and apprehension for over two months.

I wish to express my gratitude to the Bibliothèque Nationale de France for its support of my research. Without help finding certain images from the eighteenth century, I surely would have missed some of the richness of the story. I am also grateful to Éditions Honoré Champion for permission to use a number of original lithographs from *La dernière année de Marie-Antoinette*, published in 1907, which has added immeasurable depth to each chapter.

I am especially grateful to my editors Susan McEachern, Audra Figgins, and Jen Kelland for their support, direction, and invaluable advice. And I would like to thank my friends Lisa Howell and Jon Sternfeld for motivating me at times when I was most doubtful of my ability to get these pages written.

It goes without saying that I would not have finished this book without my family's support. These pages are dedicated to my grandmother's memory, my mother's love, and my brother's unconditional amity. Thank you for giving me the opportunity to realize my dreams.

LIST OF ILLUSTRATIONS
AND CREDITS

A ll illustrations found in *Marie Antoinette's Darkest Days* originate from a variety of sources, including books, newspapers, and archived government documents. Many have been reprinted from the collections of the Bibliothèque Nationale de France and Éditions Honoré Champion. Any unidentified illustrations have long been in the public domain due to their age; however, I will make every attempt to identify their creators for future editions.

PROLOGUE

Storming of the Bastille. *Attack on the Bastille, July 14, 1789.* Adolphe Thiers, *History of the French Revolution* (London: A. Fullerton, 1845). Work in the public domain; copyright has expired in countries copyrighting works for life plus one hundred years or less.

Execution of Louis XVI. *Hinrichtung Ludwig XVI von Frankreich.* Hector Fleishmann, *Das Wissen des 20. Jahrhunderts* (Rheda: Bildungslexikon, 1931).

INTRODUCTION

Towers of the Temple prison. *Les tours et la rotunde du Temple.* Andr Marty, *La dernière année de Marie-Antoinette* (Paris: Honoré Champion, 1907).

Separation of Louis Charles from his family. *Adieux de Marie Antoinette, à son fils.* Anonymous. (ark:/12148/cb402481821). Bibliothèque Nationale Française.

Young Louis Charles, his jailer Antoine Simon, and Madame Simon. *Simon le cordonnier.* Jean-Louis Prieur. (ark:/12148/btv1b6950174w). Bibliothèque Nationale Française.

PART I

Marie Antoinette taken to the Conciergerie. *The persecuted queen hurried at the dead of night.* Mariano Bovi. (ark:/12148/btv1b6949923v). Bibliothèque Nationale Française.

CHAPTER 1

Separation of Marie Antoinette from her family. *Abschied der Königin Marie Antoinette.* J. F. Bolt. (ark:/12148/btv1b6949922f). Bibliothèque Nationale Française.

Door of the queen's cell at the Conciergerie. *Porte de la prison de la reine.* Gustave Armand Henri, comte de Reiset, *Modes et usages au temps de Marie-Antoinette: 1790–1793* (Paris: Firmin-Didot et Cie, 1885).

CHAPTER 2

Request for clothing. *Demand par la reine de vêtements.* André Marty, *La dernière année de Marie-Antoinette* (Paris: Honoré Champion, 1907).

Portraits of Marie Antoinette by Kucharski and Prieur. *Portrait de Marie Antoinette.* Alexandre Kucharski. André Marty, *La dernière année de Marie-Antoinette* (Paris: Honoré Champion, 1907); La reine à la Conciergerie. Jean-Louis Prieur. (ark:/12148/btv1b69417740). Bibliothèque Nationale Française.

CHAPTER 3

Conciergerie floor plan in 1793. Author's rendition based on archived documents and eyewitness accounts.

Archway on the Cour du Mai leading to the prison entrance. *Les Girondins conduits au supplice.* Charles-Aimé Dauban, *La démagogie en 1793 à Paris* (Paris: Henri Plon, 1868).

Marie Antoinette's first cell. *Marie Antoinette.* Charles Francis Horne, *Workmen and Heroes* (Paris: S. Hess, 1894).

Eighteenth-century depiction of the Conciergerie. *Les Frères Agasse allant au supplice.* Prieur et Berthault, *Collections des tableaux historiques de la révolution française* (Paris: Pierre Didot, 1798).

CHAPTER 4

The queen of France in her last prison. *La reine de France, dans sa dernière prison.* Forsell after Deseine. (ark:/12148/btv1b6949927h). Bibliothèque Nationale Française.

Rosalie attending to the queen. *Marie Antoinette, le matin de son exécution.* Charles Desire Dupeuty, *Le magasin pittoresque* (Paris: Jouvet et Cie Éditeurs, 1907).

PART II

Allegorical depiction of Marie Antoinette in the Conciergerie. *Plan de la cellule.* André Marty, *La dernière année de Marie-Antoinette* (Paris: Honoré Champion, 1907).

CHAPTER 5

King Louis XVI's farewell to his family in the Temple with Cléry in background. *Louis XVI's farewell to his family.* Jacques-Antoine Dulaure,

Esquisses historiques des principaux évènements *de la révolution* (Paris: Baudouin Frères, 1823).

CHAPTER 6

Hallway of Marie Antoinette's cell (*Chambre de Conseil*). *Le couloir de la chambre de conseil.* G. Lenotre, *Le vrai chevalier de maison-rouge* (Paris: Perrin, 1905).

"I am kept in sight. I cannot talk to anyone. I trust you. I will come." *Facsimile du billet troué d'*épingles. André Marty, *La dernière année de Marie-Antoinette* (Paris: Honoré Champion, 1907).

Marie Antoinette in her cell. *La reine à la Conciergerie.* Adolphe Thiers, *Histoire de la Révolution* (Paris: Furne et Cie, 1841).

CHAPTER 7

Marie Antoinette's new cell (16) as of September 11, 1793. Author's rendition based on archived documents and eyewitness accounts.

Marie Antoinette's new cell. Author's rendition based on "Plan de la cellule." André Marty, *La dernière année de Marie-Antoinette* (Paris: Honoré Champion, 1907).

CHAPTER 8

The iron chest. *Correspondance royale trouvée dans l'armoire de fer.* Chez Depeuille. (ark:/12148/btv1b84116867). Bibliothèque Nationale Française.

PART III

Arraignment of the Widow Capet. *Acte d'accusation.* André Marty, *La dernière année de Marie-Antoinette* (Paris: Honoré Champion, 1907).

CHAPTER 9

Antoine Quentin Fouquier-Tinville (1746–1795). *Fouquier-Tinville.* Albert Maurin, *Galerie historique de la Révolution française: 1787 à 1799* (Paris: Au Bureau de la Société des Travailleurs Réunis, 1848).
Signature of the abused and inebriated Louis Charles. *Louis Charles Capet.* Alcide de Beauchesne, *Louis XVII: His Life, His Suffering, His Death, the Captivity of the Royal Family in the Temple* (Paris: Beauchesne, 1853).
Marie Antoinette's brother, Holy Roman Emperor Joseph II. *Joseph II, Holy Roman Emperor.* H. G. Moke, *Geïltustreerde geschiedenis van België* (Brussels: Hubert, 1885).

CHAPTER 10

Satirical depiction of Marie Antoinette. *Harpie femelle.* Jean Marie Mixelle, 1784. (ark:/12148/btv1b84104103). Bibliothèque Nationale Française.

CHAPTER 11

Marie Antoinette appeals to the mothers in the audience. *La veuve Capet devant le tribunal.* André Marty, *La dernière année de Marie-Antoinette* (Paris: Honoré Champion, 1907).

CHAPTER 12

Marie Antoinette leaving the tribunal hall. *Marie Antoinette après sa condamnation.* Robert Bingham, *Oeuvre de Paul Delaroche* (Paris: Goupil, 1858).

PART IV

Marie Antoinette at trial. *Marie Antoinette devant le tribunal.* Louis Jean Joseph Blanc, *Histoire de la Révolution française* (Paris: Docks de la Librairie, 1878).

CHAPTER 13

Marie Antoinette listening to her sentence. *Trial of Marie Antoinette.* John S. Abbott, *The French Revolution of 1789* (New York: Harper & Brothers, 1859).

Marie Antoinette receiving communion from the Abbé Magnin with Mlle. Fouché and the two "kind" guards attending. *Marie Antoinette in the Conciergerie.* Louis François de Robiano de Borsbeekt, *Marie-Antoinette à la Conciergerie: fragment historique* (Paris: Badouin Frères, 1902).

CHAPTER 14

Guichet in the hallway of the "Black Hand," through which the queen passed on October 16. *Ancien greffe.* Gustave Armand Henri, comte de Reiset, *Modes et usages au temps de Marie-Antoinette: 1790–1793* (Paris: Firmin-Didot et Cie, 1885).

Marie Antoinette departing for the scaffold. *Journée de 16 octobre.* Pieter Hendrik Jonxis, 1794. (ark:/12148/btv1b6949940c). Bibliothèque Nationale Française.

Marie Antoinette in the tumbril. *L'exécution de la reine.* Hector Fleishmann, *Les femmes et la Terreur* (Paris: Charpentier et Fasquelle, 1910).

Sketch of Marie Antoinette on tumbril by Jacques-Louis David. *La reine dans la charrette.* André Marty, *La dernière année de Marie-Antoinette* (Paris: Honoré Champion, 1907).

CHAPTER 15

Marie Antoinette at the place de la Révolution. *Journée de 16 octobre.* Isidore-Stanislas Helman, 1793. (ark:/12148/btv1b6949961j). Bibliothèque Nationale Française.

Scaffold at the foot of the Statue of Liberty. *La veuve Capet à la guillotine.* André Marty, *La dernière année de Marie-Antoinette* (Paris: Honoré Champion, 1907).

Executioner showing the queen's head to the people. *Fin tragique de Marie Antoinette*. André Marty, *La dernière année de Marie-Antoinette* (Paris: Honoré Champion, 1907).

PART V

Dinner plate commemorating the execution of Marie Antoinette. *Soucoupe à la guillotine*. André Marty, *La dernière année de Marie-Antoinette* (Paris: Honoré Champion, 1907).

CHAPTER 16

Louis Charles, uncrowned Louis XVII, at the age of eight. *Louis XVII at the age of eight*. Arnould Galopin et al., *The King Who Never Reigned: Being Memoirs upon Louis XVII* (New York: J. McBride Company, 1909).

Élisabeth Capet in the Temple. *Madame Élisabeth*. Albert Maurin, *Galerie historique de la Révolution française: 1787 à 1799* (Paris: Au Bureau de la Société des Travailleurs Réunis, 1848).

Princess Marie-Thérèse. *Marie-Thérèse-Charlotte de France*. G. Lenotre, *La fille de Louis XVI, Marie-Thérèse-Charlotte de France* (Paris: Perrin, 1908).

CHAPTER 17

Cimetière de la Madeleine. *Cimetière de la Madeleine*. André Marty, *La dernière année de Marie-Antoinette* (Paris: Honoré Champion, 1907).

Funeral coach transferring the remains of Louis XVI and Marie Antoinette to the Basilica of Saint-Denis. *Vue du char funèbre*. Chez Basset. (ark:/12148/btv1b6949987s). Bibliothèque Nationale Française.

EPILOGUE

Archduchess Marie Antoinette. *Marie-Antoinette, en buste*. Jean Baptiste Charpentier. (ark:/12148/btv1b530281719). Bibliothèque Nationale Française.

MARIE ANTOINETTE'S DARKEST DAYS

Portrait of Marie Antoinette. *Marie-Antoinette.* Author's collection. Lithograph by Ducarme; original by Michel Garnier (Paris: Blaisot, 1825).

Thisbé? *Le dernièr compagnon.* G. Lenotre, *La fille de Louis XVI, Marie-Thérèse-Charlotte de France* (Paris: Perrin, 1908).

NOTES

AUTHOR'S NOTE

xii   "The Parisians are frogs": Edme Théodore Bourg Saint-Edme, *Répertoire général des causes célèbres françaises, anciennes et modernes* (Paris: Louis Rosier, 1834), 195. "Les Parisiens sont des grenouilles qui ne font que coasser."

xii   "Madame Deficit": Anonymous, *Etrennes aux fouteurs ou Le calendrier des trois sexes* (Paris: 1793), 3. "Depuis qu'une autrichienne en ru, a tout venant montre le cu."

xii   "All the crimes committed": Kate Field, "Ristori as Marie Antoinette," *McBride's Magazine* 1 (1868): 175.

PROLOGUE

xiii   "It is at the same time amazing": Maria Theresa, Comte Florimond-Claude de Mercy-Argenteau, and Marie-Antoinette, "Marie Antoinette to Maria Theresa," in *Correspondance secrète entre Marie-Thérèse et le Comte de Mercy-Argenteau avec les lettres de Marie-Thérèse et de Marie-Antoinette* (Paris: Firmin Didot Frères, 1874), 2:342. "J'ai fait de mon mieux pendant tout le temps du voyage pour répondre aux empressements du peuple, et quoiqu'il y ait eu beaucoup de chaleur et de foule, je ne regrette pas ma fatigue, qui d'ailleurs n'a pas dérangé ma santé. C'est une chose étonnante et bien heureuse en même temps d'être si bien reçu deux mois après la révolte et malgré la cherté du pain, qui malheureusement continue."

xiii   The artificially high cost of grain: A. Gazier, "La Guerre des Farines," in *Mémoires de la Société de l'histoire de Paris et de l'Île-de-France* (Paris: H. Champion, 1880), 6:1.

xiv   "I'm too fond of war": Christophe-Michel Roguet, *Louis XIV* (Paris: Librairie Militaire, 1869), 428. "Vous allez être bientôt roi d'un grand royaume. Ce que je vous recommande le plus fortement est de n'oublier jamais les obligations que vous avez à Dieu; souvenez-vous que vous lui devez tout ce que vous êtes. Tâchez de conserver la paix avec vos voisins. J'ai trop aimé la guerre, ne m'imitez pas en cela, non plus que dans les trop grandes dépenses que j'ai faites."

xiv   "Care for your people as soon as you can": Roguet, *Louis XIV*, 428. "Prenez conseil en toute chose et cherchez à connaître le meilleur pour le suivre toujours. Soulagez vos peuples le plus tôt que vous pourrez et faites ce que j'ai eu le malheur de ne pas faire moi-même."

xiv   When on his deathbed: Arsène Houssaye, *Louis XV* (Paris: Bibliothèque Charpentier, 1890), 23.

xiv   Although this book does not focus exclusively: Maxime de la Rocheterie, *Histoire de Marie-Antoinette* (Paris: Perrin, 1890), 560. "Expose qu'examen fait de toutes les pièces transmises à l'accusateur public, il en résulte qu'à l'instar des Messaline, Brunehaut, Frédégonde et Médicis, que l'on qualifiait autrefois de reines de France, et dont les noms, à jamais odieux, ne s'effaceront pas des fastes de l'histoire, Marie-Antoinette, veuve de Louis Capet, a été, depuis son séjour en France, le fléau et la sangsue des Français."

xiv   In fact, the press was calling: de la Rocheterie, *Histoire de Marie-Antoinette*, 553. "On cherche midi à quatorze heures pour juger la tigresse d'Autriche, et l'on demande des preuves pour la condamner, tandis que, si on lui rendait justice, elle devrait être hachée comme chair à pâté."

xiv   "Where the monarch is feeble-minded": Lord John Russell, "The Causes of the French Revolution," *Quarterly Review* 49 (1833): 167.

xv   The French people knew very little of America: Alexander Hill Everett, *Remarks on Article IX in the Eighty-Fourth Number of the North American Review* (Boston: Perkins, Marvin, and Company, 1834), 10.

INTRODUCTION

2   Amid laughter and murmurs: Philippe-Joseph-Benjamin Buchez and Pierre-Célestin Roux-Lavergne, eds., *Histoire parlementaire de la Révolution française ou journal des assemblées nationales, depuis 1789 jusqu'en 1815* (Paris: Paulin, 1886), 23:445–46. "Il est étonnant qu'après la mort de Louis Capet on nous établisse encore les valets-de-chambre de sa femme (ris et murmures), oui, les valets-de-chambre; car sans doute c'est pour vider son pot de chambre qu'on nous y envoie; il est temps qu'on relève le conseil-général de ce fardeau, et que sa responsabilité cesse; il est temps que la table d'Antoinette ne soit plus si somptueusement servie; il est scandaleux qu'on voie encore au Temple huit cuisiniers; qu'on l'envoie à la Conciergerie ou à la Force."

2   Louis Charles was often found sitting on a cushion: Alcide de Beauchesne, *Louis XVII: His Life, His Suffering, His Death, the Captivity of the Royal Family in the Temple* (New York: Harper & Brothers, 1858), 2:44. When the municipal Bernard saw the child sitting at the table, he remarked, "I never saw chair or table either given to prisoners; straw is good enough for them."

2   The legal majority of a king of France: W. T. Brande and G. W. Cox, *A Dictionary of Science, Literature and Art* (London: Longman, Green, and Company, 1875), 2:545. "Minority: The royal authority, in hereditary monarchies, never dies; and when a sovereign deceases leaving a successor below age, it passes immediately to the person or persons whom the constitution has invested with the authority of regent; as it also does when a king becomes subject to any other incapacity. The term of royal Minority is variously regulated by the constitution of different countries. The legal majority of a king of France was fixed at fourteen by an ordinance of Charles V., which has been since followed in that country; but, as a year commenced is reckoned as accomplished, the actual period at which a king of France begins to govern is the age of thirteen years and a day."

2   "I have great hope": Edme Théodore Bourg Saint-Edme, *Répertoire général des causes célèbres françaises, anciennes et modernes* (Paris: Louis Rosier, 1834), 265.

2   "Charles I died on the scaffold": Bourg Saint-Edme, *Répertoire général des causes célèbres françaises, anciennes et modernes*, 102. Pierre-François Réal: "Louis n'était presque plus à craindre. . . . [M]ais son fils, cet enfant intéressant encore appuyé par une antique prévention, ne le comptez-vous pour rien? Croyez-moi, c'est un otage qu'il faut conserver avec soin. . . . Je ne dis plus qu'un mot: Charles Ier périt sur l'échafaud mais son fils remonta sur le trône."

3   To put such fears to rest: Marie-Thérèse Charlotte, duchesse d'Angoulême, *Journal de Marie-Thérèse de France, duchesse d'Angoulême, 5 octobre 1789–2 septembre 1792* (Paris: Firmin-Didot, 1893), 105.

3   Then, when necessary, the convention could present: Francis Nettement, *Histoire populaire de Louis XVII* (Paris: C. Dillet, 1868), 275. "S'il arrivait, disaient-ils, que, dans quelque mouvement populaire, les Parisiens se portassent au Temple pour proclamer roi Louis XVII, nous leur montrerions un petit bambin dont l'air stupide et l'imbécillité les forceraient à renoncer au projet de le placer sur le trône."

4   Locks and bolts clanked: Clara Tschudi, *Marie Antoinette* (London: Swan Sonnenschein, 1902), 269–71.

4   And then he proceeded to read: Maxime de la Rocheterie, *The Life of Marie Antoinette* (New York: Dodd, Mead and Company, 1906), 333–35. This decree was signed by Jean Bon Saint-André, Jacques-Alexis Thuriot, C. A. Prieur, Marie-Jean Hérault de Séchelles, Robert Lindet, Bertrand Barrère, Georges Couthon, Louis Antoine de Saint-Just, and Maximilien Robespierre.

5   Two officers seized Marie-Thérèse: Marie-Thérèse Charlotte de France Angoulême, *Madame Marie-Thérèse-Charlotte de France, fille de Louis XVI, relation du voyage de*

Varennes, et récit de sa captivité à la tour du Temple (Paris: Auguste Vaton, 1852), 76. "Ma mère leur dit qu'ils n'avoient donc qu'à la tuer, avant de lui arracher son enfant: et une heure se passa ainsi en résistance de sa part, en injures, en menaces de la part des municipaux, en pleurs et en défenses de nous tous. Enfin, ils la menacèrent si positivement de le tuer ainsi que moi, qu'il fallut qu'elle cédât encore, par amour pour nous."

5   The officers began to lose patience: de Beauchesne, *Louis XVII*, 2:62. The following is an extract of the register of the Temple relating to the seizure of Louis Charles. The term "consideration" may be considered ironical: "We may observe, moreover, that the separation was carried on with all the consideration that could be expected in such circumstances, the magistrates of the people having shown as much kindness as was compatible with the severity of their functions. (Signed) Eudes, Gagnant, Abnaud, Veron."

5   "Be good, patient and truthful": de la Rocheterie, *The Life of Marie Antoinette*, 335.

6   We know only that the child: de Beauchesne, *Louis XVII*, 67. "We only know that the child wept long, that he remained for hours seated on a chair in the darkest corner of the room, and that Simon had great difficulty in gaining a few brief answers to the questions that he imperiously put to him, swearing and smoking his pipe as he spoke."

6   "Mamma, mamma": Maria C. Bishop, *The Prison Life of Marie Antoinette and Her Children, the Dauphin and the Duchesse d'Angoulême* (London: Kegan Paul, Trench & Company, 1893), 280.

7   But the convention found the request: Henriette Simon-Viennot, *Marie-Antoinette devant le dix-neuvième siècle* (Paris: Librarie d'Amyot, 1843), 2:320.

7   In the days to follow: de Beauchesne, *Louis XVII*, 92.

7   He called for the convention to adopt: Louis Pierre Anquetil and Paul Delaure Lacroix, *Histoire de France depuis le temps les plus régulés jusqu'à la Révolution en 1789* (Paris: Dufour et Mulat, 1850), 233. Among the other measures, (1) all individuals of the Bourbon family were to be deported outside the territory of the republic, with the exception of the two children of Louis XVI and those members of the family who were already in captivity, (2) Élisabeth, sister of Louis XVI, was to be deported after the judgment of Marie Antoinette, and (3) expenses for the two children of Louis XVI were to be reduced to only what was necessary for food and maintenance.

CHAPTER 1: TRANSFER FROM THE TEMPLE PRISON

11   By eight o'clock in the evening: G. Lenotre, *The Last Days of Marie Antoinette* (London: William Heinemann, 1908), 144. "At eight o'clock in the evening matches were distributed in the artillery-park that occupied the court . . . and the troops were astir throughout the night."

11   "From the time he came": G. Lenotre, *The Daughter of Louis XVI: Marie-Thérèse-Charlotte de France, Duchesse d'Angoulême* (London: John Lane, 1908), 169.

12   At two o'clock in the morning: A. Eymery, *Procès de Louis XVI, de Marie-Antoinette, de Marie-Élisabeth et de Philippe d'Orléans; discussions législatives sur la famille des Bourbons* (Paris: Delaunay, 1821), 445. "Marie-Antoinette est envoyée au Tribunal extraordinaire. Elle sera transportée sur-le-champ à la Conciergerie."

12   The queen embraced her daughter: Eymery, *Procès de Louis XVI, de Marie-Antoinette, de Marie-Élisabeth et de Philippe d'Orléans*, 445.

12   In all, they took a gold ring: Ronald Gower, *Last Days of Marie Antoinette: An Historical Sketch* (London: Kegan Paul, Trench & Company, 1885), 19.

12   Only a handkerchief and a small bottle: Alphonse de Lamartine, *History of the Girondists* (New York: Harper & Brothers, 1848), 3:140.

13   Only an inscription on the prison wall: Edmond de Goncourt and Jules de Goncourt, *Histoire de Marie-Antoinette* (Paris: G. Charpentier, 1879), 433. "27 mars 1793, quatre pieds dix pouces trois lignes. Trois pieds deux pouces."

13   As the queen passed: M. C. O'Connor Morris, *The Prisoners of the Temple; or Discrowned and Crowned* (London: Burns and Oates, 1874), 93–94.

14   Once the paperwork was complete: Alcide de Beauchesne, *Louis XVII: His Life, His Suffering, His Death, the Captivity of the Royal Family in the Temple* (New York: Harper & Brothers, 1858), 2:112. "En sortant, elle se frappa la tête au guichet, faut de penser à se baisser."

14   "No, nothing can hurt me now": Marie-Thérèse Charlotte de France Angoulême, *Madame Marie-Thérèse-Charlotte de France, fille de Louis XVI, relation du voyage de Varennes, et récit de sa captivité à la tour du Temple* (Paris: Auguste Vaton, 1852), 79. "Oh! non, répond-elle, rien ne peut me faire du mal desormais."

14   A few lights glimmered: Henriette Simon-Viennot, *Marie-Antoinette devant le dix-neuvième siècle* (Paris: Librarie d'Amyot, 1843), 2:322.

14   Once on the Île de la Cité: Augustus J. C. Hare, "Walks in Old Paris," *Good Words and Sunday Magazine* 28 (1887): 617. "The ground now covered by the hospital was covered till the present century, by a labyrinth of little streets and curious buildings. Between the Rue de la Lanterne and Rue de la Juiverie (both swallowed up in the Rue de la Cité) the Rue de Marmousets ran eastwards to the cloister of Notre-Dame." See also Félix Lazare, "Cité," in *Dictionnaire des rues et monuments de Paris* (Paris: Au Bureau de la Revue Municipale, 1855), 278–79.

15   Even though the entrance was barely lit: Lafont d'Aussonne, *Mémoires secrets et universels des malheurs et de la mort de la reine de France* (Paris: A. Philippe, 1836), 39. Readers must be wary when reading Lafont d'Aussonne's works; however, his interview with Louis Larivière appears credible because it does not conflict with other accounts with respect to the queen's dress, her first cell, or the summoning of Larivière's mother to attend to the queen as her waiting woman.

15   "The most infected dungeon": Christophe Félix Louis Ventre de la Touloubre Montjoie, *Histoire de Marie-Antoinette-Josèphe-Jeanne de Lorraine, archiduchesse*

d'Autriche, reine de France (Paris: Lepetit, 1814), 460. "Voici littéralement la réponse qu'on lui fit: 'Le cachot le plus infect, quelques bottes de paille pour lit, voilà tout ce qu'il lui faut.'"

15 According to one, she was confined: William Forsythe, *Marie Antoinette in the Conciergerie* (London: Society for Promoting Christian Knowledge, 1867), 14.

15 Another reported her temporarily lodged: Montjoie, *Histoire de Marie-Antoinette-Josèphe-Jeanne de Lorraine, archiduchesse d'Autriche, reine de France*, 463. The queen was temporarily placed in Richard's office until daybreak, when she was moved to the Salle de Conseil. This is confirmed by the Goncourts.

16 When he angrily inquired: Goncourt and Goncourt, *Histoire de Marie-Antoinette*, 435.

16 In fact, it was so teeming: Gower, *Last Days of Marie Antoinette*, 15.

16 These were turbulent times: Eliakim Littell, "The Conciergerie," *Living Age* 205 (1895): 581.

16 Muddy slime covered the floor: John S. C. Abbott, *History of Maria Antoinette* (New York: Harper & Brothers, 1868), 294.

17 It appeared that the "most pestilential": Gower, *Last Days of Marie Antoinette*, 15.

17 According to General Custine's daughter-in-law: John G. Cochrane, "Marquis de Custine's Russia," *Foreign Quarterly Review* 31 (1843): 428.

17 It was filled with "moans": Philippe Edmé Coittant, *Almanach des prisons, ou anecdotes sur le régime intérieur de la Conciergerie* (Paris: Chez Michel, 1795), 22.

17 "The Conciergerie! What an abyss!": Imbert de Saint-Amand, "La dernière année de Marie-Antoinette," *Correspondant* 117 (1879): 628. "La Conciergerie! quel abîme!"

17 "From hour to hour the chimes slowly": Gower, *Last Days of Marie Antoinette*, 13–14.

18 The butt of the prisoner's jokes: Barthélemy Maurice, *Histoire politique et anecdotique des prisons de la Seine, contenant des renseignements entièrement inédits sur la période révolutionnaire* (Paris: Guillaumin, 1840), 209.

18 When the official visitors departed: Goncourt and Goncourt, *Histoire de Marie-Antoinette*, 434.

18 Whenever the Seine River rose: Augustus Hare, *Walks in Paris* (New York: Routledge and Sons, 1888), 270–72.

19 The queen's cell was furnished: Maria C. Bishop, *The Prison Life of Marie Antoinette and Her Children, the Dauphin and the Duchesse d'Angoulême* (London: Kegan Paul, Trench & Company, 1893), 30.

19 She then earnestly looked: Anna L. Bicknell, *The Story of Marie Antoinette* (New York: Century Company, 1898), 304.

19 Her manner, according to Rosalie: Bishop, *The Prison Life of Marie Antoinette and Her Children*, 30–31.

19 At the main gate, the little dog: Jacques Delille, *La pitié* (Paris: Giguet et Michaud, 1805), 158.

20 However, the radical Jacques René Hébert: Lenotre, *The Last Days of Marie Antoinette*, 148. "He said: 'I have promised Antoinette's head, and I shall go and cut it off myself if there is any delay about giving it to me. I have promised it in your name to the sansculottes who demand it, to those without whom you would cease to exist.'"

20 After Marie Antoinette spent the first night: Montjoie, *Histoire de Marie-Antoinette-Josèphe-Jeanne de Lorraine, archiduchesse d'Autriche, reine de France,* 156.

20 She was therefore relocated: William Guthrie, *A New Geographical, Historical, and Commercial Grammar* (London: G. G. and J. Robinson and J. Mawman, 1801), 474.

21 Poem by Antoine de Rivarol: M. le comte César du Bouchet, *Les adieux de Marie-Antoinette d'Autriche, reine de France* (Paris: Lerouge, 1814), 23. "La reine de France à la Conciergerie" by M. de Rivarol:

Veuve et mère au midi de mes tristes année,
Levant mes yeux éteints vers la divinité,
Mes yeux, car de leurs fers mes mains sont enchaînées,
Je meurs dans la captivité.
Je meurs; et dans ces lieux où l'horreur m'environne,
Tout est passé pour moi, le temps seul est veste;
Il verra mes cheveux, sur un iront sans couronne,
Blanchir dans la captivité.
Rends-moi mes deux enfants, ô peuple sans clémence!
Ou destin de leur mère ils n'ont point hérité;
Je te pardonne tout, si parfois leur enfance,
Console ma captivité.
Mais tout est sourd pour moi; l'univers m'abandonne.
Dans le fond d'un cachot, par le crime habité,
La fille des Césars tombe du haut d'un trône,
El périt en captivité.
Je ne vois près de moi qu'une garde inhumaine,
Et dans chaque regard un forfait médité;
Au-delà de ces murs, qu'une pitié lointaine
Pour ma triste captivité.
Quelquefois au sommeil si ma douleur succombe,
Ciel! Quel jour s'offre à moi! Quelle horrible clarté!
Quel fantôme s'avance, et, soulevant sa tombe,
Vient troubler ma captivité!
C'est mon époux! C'est lui! J'entends sa voix plaintive:
D'où viens-tu, cher époux, dans ce lieu détesté?
Mais je lui parle eu vain; son ombre fugitive
Me laisse à ma captivité.

CHAPTER 2: THE QUEEN'S DUNGEON CELL

23   "If Marie Antoinette's qualities were her own": Eugêne Pottet, *Histoire de la Conciergerie du Palais de Paris* (Paris: Quantin, 1895), 175. Quote from M. de la Rocheterie, *Dix ans dans la vie d'une reine*: "Si les qualités de Marie-Antoinette furent bien d'elle-même, ses défauts furent surtout de son entourage et de son temps."

23   "I hope she won't disappoint me": Pottet, *Histoire de la Conciergerie du Palais de Paris*, 40.

23   Later in the morning Marie Antoinette awoke: Maxime de la Rocheterie, *The Life of Marie Antoinette* (New York: Dodd, Mead and Company, 1906), 341.

23   The two new guards: H. Schütz Wilson, *History and Criticism* (London: T. Fisher Unwin, 1896), 34. Quote attributed to Paul Gaulot: "Une espèce de poissarde dont elle se plaignait fort."

24   The duke of Penthièvre was Louis XVI's cousin: G. Lenotre, *La captivité et la mort de Marie-Antoinette* (Paris: Perrin et Cie, 1902), 355. Louis Larivière was a pastry chef in 1825 when he recounted his memories of Marie Antoinette's last hours to Lafont d'Aussonne. The writings of d'Aussonne have normally been considered unreliable, but the historian Lenotre noted that he cited the writer's interview with Larivière with the most confidence: "Nous croyons qu'on peut lui accorder toute confiance."

24   She then added that ever since: Lafont d'Aussonne, *Mémoires secrets et universels des malheurs et de la mort de la reine de France* (Paris: A. Philippe, 1836), 40.

24   He was not sure if the queen: d'Aussonne, *Mémoires secrets et universels des malheurs et de la mort de la reine de France*, 40.

25   No doubt they feared: Laure Junot, *Memoirs of Celebrated Women of All Countries* (London: Edward Churton, 1834), 299.

25   This medallion contained a lock: G. Lenotre, *Paris révolutionnaire* (Paris: Perrin et Cie, 1896), 246.

25   And they found their accomplice: Lenotre, *Paris révolutionnaire*, 366.

25   In fact, the queen distrusted her: G. Lenotre, *Le vrai chevalier de maison-rouge, A. D. J. Gonzze de Rougeville, 1761–1814* (Paris: Perrin et Cie, 1907), 93. "La reine avait témoigné de la confiance à la vieille; elle ne jugea pas l'autre aussi favorablement: aussi presque jamais ne lui adressait-elle la parole."

25   And Barassin occasionally visited: Eliakim Littell, "The Conciergerie," *Living Age* 205 (1895): 595.

25   The French journalist Claude-François Beaulieu: Littell, "The Conciergerie," 595.

26   Knowing that Barassin had discharged: Schütz Wilson, *History and Criticism*, 58.

26   "She wears a black dress": de la Rocheterie, *The Life of Marie Antoinette*, 341.

26   In fact, the queen implored Madame Richard: Gustave Armand Henri, comte de Reiset, *Modes et usages au temps de Marie-Antoinette* (Paris: Librairie Firmin Didot, 1885), 2:341.

26 When the queen opened the package: Maria C. Bishop, *The Prison Life of Marie Antoinette and Her Children, the Dauphin and the Duchesse d'Angoulême* (London: Kegan Paul, Trench & Company, 1893), 31.

27 "Madame," said the queen: William Forsythe, *Marie Antoinette in the Conciergerie* (London: Society for Promoting Christian Knowledge, 1867), 17.

27 Rosalie would preserve these: Imbert de Saint-Amand, "La dernière année de Marie-Antoinette," *Correspondant* 117 (1879): 206.

27 "Citizen Colleagues, Marie Antoinette has charged me": Goncourt and Goncourt, *Histoire de Marie-Antoinette*, 435. "Citoyens collègues, Marie Antoinette me charge de lui faire passer quatre chemises et une paire de souliers non numérotés, dont elle a un pressant besoin."

28 The queen now had two gowns: Edmond de Goncourt and Jules de Goncourt, *Histoire de Marie-Antoinette* (Paris: G. Charpentier, 1879), 435.

28 Using the long pieces of thread: Alphonse de Lamartine, *History of the Girondists* (New York: Harper & Brothers, 1848), 3:146.

28 On one occasion Barassin removed the chamber pot: Henriette Simon-Viennot, *Marie-Antoinette devant le dix-neuvième siècle* (Paris: Librarie d'Amyot, 1843), 2:339. "Dans ces circonstances, dit Rosalie, madame me priait de brûler quelques grains de genièvre pour changer l'air."

28 Some of the women in the courtyard begged: Forsythe, *Marie Antoinette in the Conciergerie*, 30.

29 When the queen first observed this: Saint-Amand, "La dernière année de Marie-Antoinette," 634.

29 When Madame Richard and Rosalie left the room: Émile Campardon, *Marie-Antoinette à la Conciergerie* (Paris: Chez Jules Gay, 1864), 185. "Qu'elle se garderait bien de ramener son fils dans le cachot."

29 She read *Un voyage à Venise*: Lenotre, *La captivité et la mort de Marie-Antoinette*, n. 109.

29 Reading was a common pastime: François-Alphonse Aulard, "Mémoires de la dépenses de la veuve Capet à la Conciergerie," *Révolution française* 48 (1905): 169. "Pour loyer de livres 16."

29 "She has a big appetite": Aulard, "Mémoires de la dépenses de la veuve Capet à la Conciergerie," 178. "Antoinette se lève tous les jours à sept heures et se couche à dix heures. Elle appelle ses deux gendarmes messieurs; sa femme de chambre madame Harel. Les administrateurs de police et ceux qui l'approchent officiellement lui disent madame. Elle mange avec beaucoup d'appétit; le matin, du chocolat et un petit pain; à dîner, de la soupe et beaucoup de viande: poulets, côtelettes de veau et de mouton. Elle ne boit que de l'eau, ainsi que sa mère, dit-elle, qui ne but jamais de vin. Elle a quitté la lecture des révolutions d'Angleterre et lit actuellement le voyage du jeune Anacharsis. Elle fait sa toilette elle-même, avec cette coquetterie qui n'abandonne point une femme au dernier

soupir. Sa chambre donne sur la prison des femmes, mais celles-ci n'ont point l'air de prendre garde au voisinage d'une ci-devant reine."

30   Even dead bodies: Antoine Augustin Parmentier, *Dissertation sur la nature des eaux de la Seine* (Paris: Buisson, 1787), 30.

30   Her sister-in-law Élisabeth: Maxime de la Rocheterie, *Histoire de Marie-Antoinette* (Paris: Perrin, 1890), 2:534.

30   When Rosalie nodded: Joseph Durieux, *Près de la reine Marie-Antoinette* (Paris: Les Éditions de France, 1933), 146. The prisoner was the doctor Edmond Saint-Léger of Saint-Domingue who was later acquitted in 1794.

30   This was quite a change: Goncourt and Goncourt, *Histoire de Marie-Antoinette*, 432.

30   He was certainly referring to the beheading: Edme Théodore Bourg Saint-Edme, *Répertoire général des causes célèbres françaises, anciennes et modernes* (Paris: Louis Rosier, 1834), 268.

31   The delay gave the queen's supporters: A. C. Sabatié, *Le Tribunal révolutionnaire de Paris* (Paris: P. Lethielleux, 1914), 57–58.

31   "If you were ever happy": Anne Louise Germaine de Staël, *Réflexions sur le procès de la reine* (Paris: Anonymous, 1793), 5–6. "Oh! vous, femmes de tous les pays, de toutes les classes de la société, écoutez-moi avec l'émotion que j'éprouve; la destinée de Marie Antoinette contient tout ce qui peut toucher votre coeur, si vous êtes heureuses, elle l'a été; si vous souffrez, depuis un an, depuis plus long-tems encore toutes les peines de la vie ont déchiré son cœur; si vous êtes sensibles, si vous êtes mères, elle a aimé de toutes les puissances de l'âme, et l'existence a pour elle encore le prix qu'elle conserve, tant qu'il peut nous rester des objets qui nous sont chers."

32   During the time that Marie Antoinette was incarcerated: Hillaire Belloc, *Marie Antoinette* (New York: Doubleday, Page, and Company, 1909), 488. Belloc states that the painting was "presumably sketched at the Temple." However, the title infers that it was possibly painted in the Conciergerie, and this is confirmed in Prosper Dorbec, "Le portrait dans la Révolution," *Revue de l'art ancien et moderne* 21 (1907): 140.

32   He later painted the queen's last portrait: It is doubtful that Kucharski painted the queen's portrait in the Temple; it was prohibited. See "Une Lettre du représentant de Don Carlos," *Légitimité* 16–18 (1898): 183. "No guard at the Temple or otherwise may draw anything and if anyone is caught in contravention of this decree, he will immediately be put under arrest."

33   As poor as this image is: Ronald Gower, *Iconographie de la reine Marie-Antoinette* (Paris: A. Quantin, 1883), xv. "Ce portrait, gravé au moment le plus critique de l'existence de la Reine, après le retour de Varennes, ne fut pas le dernier qui fut fait de Marie Antoinette. Pendant les jours qui précédèrent sa mort, un artiste bien peu connu, Prieur, grava sans talent la Reine à la Conciergerie. Dans cette planche naïvement fidèle, on reconnaît encore les traits que Moreau le Jeune nous a, le premier, appris à connaî-

tre; le malheur, les veilles et les pleurs ont altéré ce visage; un embonpoint qui est de la boursouflure plutôt que de la santé a modifié les lignes principales de la face; un voile de veuve couvre les rares cheveux qui ont résisté à tant d'angoisses et de misères; tout attachement à la vie a disparu de ce visage autrefois souriant etradieux; la Reine attend la mort avec fermeté, sans défaillance et sans effroi; tout ce qu'elle aimait au monde lui a été ravi; son sacrifice est fait, elle est prête à la mort. Quelque médiocre que soit cette image, elle offre un intérêt puissant, parce que l'on sent que son auteur a été naïf et vrai."

CHAPTER 3: THE HORRORS OF THE CONCIERGERIE

35   "The whole prison, from crowdedness": John Aldolpus, "Biographical Memoirs of the French Revolution," *Monthly Review* 31 (1800): 71.

35   Every cell contained as many beds: William Chambers and Robert Chambers, *Chambers's Journal* 12 (1850): 186.

35   Prisoners who could afford a bed: Anonymous, "Inedited Facts Respecting the French Revolution of 1789," *Monthly Chronicle* 7 (1841): 104.

35   This would have been relatively expensive: Will Bashor, *Marie Antoinette's Head: The Royal Hairdresser, the Queen, and the Revolution* (Guilford, CT: Lyons Press, 2013), 109. It is a difficult task to ascertain a dollar value for the French livre in 1793 due to the fluctuations in its value at the time. There were twenty sous in a livre, and the livre was worth approximately $4.

36   Chamber pots added such an infectious stench: Charles-Aimé Dauban, *Les prisons de Paris* (Paris: Plon, 1870), 145.

38   "If you didn't bump your nose": Dauban, *Les prisons de Paris*, 142.

38   All the *guichets* throughout the prison: Dauban, *Les prisons de Paris*, 142.

40   "Nobody has a better memory": Hector Fleischmann, *Behind the Scenes in the Terror* (New York: Brentano's, 1915), 32–34. "Besides the warden and turnkeys, there is an old turnkey who wanders up and down the corridors, inspecting those who go in or out. When there is any uncertainty, vigilant words are heard issuing from the arm-chair: 'Allumez le miston!' (allumez is slang for 'look sharply at' and miston is slang for an 'individual'). The turnkey repeats the phrase to his comrades who are on duty at the gates. Whenever a new prisoner enters, the turnkeys are advised to 'allumez le miston,' so that he may be generally known, and be unable to make himself out as a stranger."

40   "I couldn't see any more": Comte Jacques-Claude Beugnot, *Mémoires du Comte Beugnot, ancien ministre* (Paris: E. Dentu, 1868), 160. "Le jour de mon entrée, ajoute-t-il, deux hommes attendaient l'arrivée du bourreau. Ils étaient dépouillés de leurs habits et avaient déjà les cheveux épars et le col préparé. Leurs traits n'étaient point altérés. Soit avec ou sans dessein, ils tenaient leurs mains dans la posture où ils allaient être attachés, et

s'essayaient à des attitudes fières et dédaigneuses. Leurs regards lançaient le mépris sur tout ce qui les approchait, et je jugeai par quelques mots qui leur échappaient par intervalles, qu'ils n'étaient pas indignes du sort qu'ils éprouvaient. Quel spectacle présentait le lieu où ces malheureux attendaient leur dernière heure ! Des matelas étendus sur le plancher indiquaient qu'ils y avaient passé la nuit, qu'ils avaient déjà subi le long supplice de cette nuit. On voyait, à côté, les restes du dernier repas qu'ils avaient pris; leurs habits étaient jetés çà et là, et deux chandelles, qu'ils avaient négligé d'éteindre, repoussaient le jour pour n'éclairer cette scène que d'une lueur funèbre. Je détaillais l'horreur de ce sépulcre animé, quand la porte s'ouvrit avec bruit; je vis paraître des gendarmes, des guichetiers, des bourreaux. Je n'en vis pas davantage: j'éprouvai un saisissement subit; il me semblait que tout mon sang venait de se glacer dans mon cœur; et je tombai sur une banquette du greffe, poursuivi par cet appareil de la mort."

40   The condemned were then escorted: Beugnot, *Mémoires du Comte Beugnot*, 160.

41   They make a mistake: Beugnot, *Mémoires du Comte Beugnot*, 36.

42   "There then fell an instant's silence": Beugnot, *Mémoires du Comte Beugnot*, 37.

42   Those who paid the *pistole*: Pierre Jean-Baptiste Nougaret, *Histoire des prisons de Paris et des départements: contenant des mémoires rares et précieux* (Paris: Courcier, 1797), 2:15–16.

43   Like many other prisoners: Dauban, *Les prisons de Paris*, 147.

43   Formerly, they had estimated their fortune: Anonymous, "Inedited Facts Respecting the French Revolution of 1789," 105.

44   It was impossible to purify: Beugnot, *Mémoires du Comte Beugnot*, 198.

44   "He made his fortune": Fernand Engerand, *Ange Pitou* (Paris: Leroux, 1899), 54. "Une odeur cadavéreuse, témoigne Ange Pitou, infectait en y entrant; l'un avait la figure couverte de boutons et d'ulcères, un autre les lèvres bouffies et noires comme du charbon, deux ou trois autres moribonds étaient dans le même lit. Un sale coquin, nommé Pierre, condamné à dix ans de fers, était notre infirmier depuis la mort de la Reine, à qui il avait servi de valet de chambre. Il faisait sa fortune au milieu de la putréfaction, car la plupart des malades étaient sans connaissance et soigneusement dévalisés."

44   In fact, the invalids had to wait: Yves Pouliquen, *Félix Vicq d'Azyr, les lumières et la Révolution* (Paris: Odile Jacob, 2009), 186.

44   To save even more time: Beugnot, *Mémoires du Comte Beugnot*, 106.

44   "He's much better today": H. Wallon, "Le Terreur," *Le correspondant* 86 (1872): 805.

45   This would not happen immediately: Wallon, "Le Terreur," 805.

45   Dr. Thierry had been one of Marie Antoinette's: François Victor Mérat de Vaumartoise, "Éthers," in *Dictionnaire universel de matière médicale, et de thérapeutique* (Paris: Société Belge de Librairie, 1837), 2:235. Liqueur Hofmann was an ether by-product with drops of fresh wine oil.

45   "Calming potion composed of lime water": Maurice Bouvet, "Les apothicaires royaux," *Revue d'histoire de la pharmacie* 72 (1931): 15–32.

45 "Both of these incompetents": Gustave Laurent, "Quelques notes sur les dernières années du chirurgien Souberbielle, le médicin de Robespierre," *Revue historique de la Révolution française* 15 (1923): 56.

46 "Here's some chicken": Eugêne Pottet, *Histoire de la Conciergerie du Palais de Paris* (Paris: Quantin, 1895), 192.

46 "She separated the bones": Pottet, *Histoire de la Conciergerie du Palais de Paris*, 200.

46 She was thinner, graying: Pouliquen, *Félix Vicq d'Azyr*, 187.

46 The broth was made every morning: Joseph Durieux, *Près de la reine Marie-Antoinette* (Paris: Les Éditions de France, 1933), 193.

46 "The broth was called": Durieux, *Près de la reine Marie-Antoinette*, 193.

47 "When at the guillotine": Anonymous, "Inedited Facts Respecting the French Revolution of 1789," 106.

47 When Girey-Dupré reached the scaffold: Adolphe Granier de Cassagnac, *Histoire des Girondins et des massacres de septembre* (Paris: E. Dentu, 1860), 1:107:

Pour nous, quel triomphe éclatant!
Martyrs de la liberté sainte, L'immortalité nous attend.
Dignes d'un destin si brillant,
À l'échafaud marchons sans crainte; L'immortalité nous attend.
Mourons pour la patrie,
C'est le sort le plus beau, le plus digne d'envie!

48 The victim then had to fall: Beugnot, *Mémoires du Comte Beugnot*, 106.

CHAPTER 4: KINDHEARTED SOULS

49 "About three o'clock in the morning": John Aldolpus, "Biographical Memoirs of the French Revolution," *Monthly Review* 31 (1800): 71.

49 During the restoration of the Bourbon monarch: G. Lenotre, *The Last Days of Marie Antoinette* (London: William Heinemann, 1907), 150.

49 Because Rosalie was illiterate: Duchesse Laure Junot d'Abrantès, *Mémoires sur la restauration ou souvenirs historiques sur cette époque, la révolution de juillet et les premières années du règne de Louis-Philippe 1er* (Paris: L'Henri, 1836), 486.

49 However, if Lafont d'Aussonne omitted some: Lenotre, *The Last Days of Marie Antoinette*, 150.

50 The historian Émile Campardon also concurred: Émile Campardon, *Marie-Antoinette à la Conciergerie* (Paris: Chez Jules Gay, 1864), v.

50 Biographer Léon de la Sicotière admitted: Léon de la Sicotière, *Bio-bibliographie de la reine Marie-Antoinette* (Paris: Dupray de la Mahérie, 1863), 162.

MARIE ANTOINETTE'S DARKEST DAYS

50   When Lafont d'Aussonne interviewed Rosalie: Henriette Simon-Viennot, *Marie-Antoinette devant le dix-neuvième siècle* (Paris: Librarie d'Amyot, 1843), 325.

50   He added that his theater: Lenotre, *The Last Days of Marie Antoinette*, 152.

50   Madame Richard had also worked: Lenotre, *La captivité et la mort de Marie-Antoinette* (Paris: Perrin et Cie, 1902), 227.

51   Noticing that the queen did not have a drawer: James de Chambrier, *Marie-Antoinette, reine de France* (Paris: Lebigre-Duquesne, 1868), 2:427–28.

51   The decree dryly added: de Chambrier, *Marie-Antoinette, reine de France*, 2:432.

51   She blushed to loan the queen: Simon-Viennot, *Marie-Antoinette devant le dix-neuvième siècle*, 328–29.

51   Madame Harel then gave the two ends: Marie, comtesse de Villermont, *Histoire de la coiffure féminine* (Paris: Renouard, 1892), 726.

52   When they asked what type of foods: Jean-Baptiste Cléry, *La captivité de Louis XVI* (Paris: J. Casterman, 1848), 209.

52   "Here, take the most beautiful": Clara Tschudi, *Marie Antoinette* (London: Swan Sonnenschein, 1902), 276.

52   One was "La Carmagnole": Jules Maurel, Marie Escudier, and Leon Escudier, *La France musicale* (Paris: César Bajat, 1838), 9:29. "La Carmagnole":

Madame Veto avait promis,
Madame Veto avait promis.
de faire égorger tout Paris,
de faire égorger tout Paris.
Mais son coup a manqué,
grâce à nos canoiners.

Refrain:
Dansons la Carmagnole
Vive le son,
Vive le son,
Dansons la Carmagnole
Vive le son du canon.

Monsieur Veto avait promis
D'être fidèle à son pays,
Mais il y a manqué,
Ne faisons plus quartié.
Refrain

Antoinette avait résolu
De nous faire tomber sur le cul;

Mais le coup a manqué
Elle a le nez cassé.
Refrain

53   When he asked how she was: Tschudi, *Marie Antoinette*, 426.

54   Moreover, they were denied the services: Jean-Baptiste B. Sauvan and Jean Philippe Schmit, *Histoire et description pittoresque du Palais de Justice de la Conciergerie et de la Sainte Chapelle de Paris* (Paris: G. Engelmann, 1825), 44.

54   If caught, priests were imprisoned: Philip Schaff and Samuel Macauley Jackson, *A Religious Encyclopaedia; or Dictionary of Biblical, Historical, Doctrinal, and Practical Theology* (New York: Funk & Wagnalls, 1891), 3:2042.

54   According to her biographer G. Lenotre: G. Lenotre, *Paris rvolutionnaire* (Paris: Perrin et Cie, 1896), 46.

54   When Madame Antoinette-Marie Adélaïde de Quélen: Gustave Armand Henri, comte de Reiset, *Modes et usages au temps de Marie-Antoinette* (Paris: Librairie Firmin Didot, 1885), 2:173–74.

54   In fact, Mademoiselle Fouché: Charles G. Herbermann, "Reverend Simon Fouché," in *Historical Records and Studies* (New York: United States Catholic Historical Society, 1916), 9:181.

55   Unable to smuggle the abbé out: "Reverend Simon Fouché," 9:181.

55   They went quickly on their way: Herbermann, "Reverend Simon Fouché," 9:182.

55   It is not known if Dufresne and Gilbert: Herbermann, "Reverend Simon Fouché," 9:183.

55   Mademoiselle Fouché was ecstatic: Louis-François Robiano de Borsbeek, "Souvenirs de Mlle. Fouché," in *La captivité et la mort de Marie-Antoinette: les Feuillants—le Temple—la Conciergerie* (Paris: Perrin, 1902), 309.

55   Warden Richard kept his word: Lenotre, *La captivité et la mort de Marie-Antoinette*, 311.

56   She needed to adopt: Lenotre, *The Last Days of Marie Antoinette*, 184.

56   Religion alone can give you: Lenotre, *La captivité et la mort de Marie-Antoinette*, 312.

56   Mademoiselle Fouché also arranged: Lenotre, *The Last Days of Marie Antoinette*, 185.

57   Mademoiselle Fouché also sent: Lenotre, *The Last Days of Marie Antoinette*, 185.

57   In turn, the queen never failed: Louis Sifrein Joseph Foncrosé de Salamon, *Unpublished Memoirs of the Internuncio at Paris during the Revolution, 1790–1801* (Boston: Little, Brown, and Company, 1896), 263.

57   "How kind you are": de Salamon, *Unpublished Memoirs*, 263.

57   She added that the queen was especially attracted: Lenotre, *The Last Days of Marie Antoinette*, 177.

59   Before the queen's transfer to the Conciergerie: Hans Axel von Fersen, *Diary and Correspondence of Count Axel Fersen: Grand-Marshal of Sweden, Relating to the Court of France* (London: Heinemann, 1902), 292.

60 Mercy flatly told him: Hans Axel von Fersen, *Le Comte de Fersen et la cour de France* (Paris: Librairie de Firmin-Didot et Cie, 1878), 2:85. "La réponse du prince de Cobourg au comte de Mercy est pitoyable; elle roule toujours sur l'idée d'aller avec l'armée à Paris, et sur l'impossibilité d'une pareille entreprise."

61 This is the only known depiction: Knowles, *The Twentieth Century* 59 (1906): 999.

61 "There is a difference between holding a brave front": Knowles, *The Twentieth Century* 59:1000.

CHAPTER 5: ROYALIST SUPPORTERS

65 "It will be a disgrace": Maria C. Bishop, *The Prison Life of Marie Antoinette and Her Children, the Dauphin and the Duchesse d'Angoulême* (London: Kegan Paul, Trench & Company, 1893), 151.

65 After the king was executed: Paul Gaulot, *A Conspiracy under the Terror: Marie Antoinette-Toulan-Jarjayes* (London: Chatto & Windus, 1904), 61.

66 But after spending two days: G. Lenotre, *The Last Days of Marie Antoinette* (London: William Heinemann, 1907), 106.

66 He was often heard cursing: Lenotre, *The Last Days of Marie Antoinette*, 107.

66 Even more remarkable was how Toulan managed: Marie-Thérèse Charlotte de France Angoulême, *Journal de Marie-Thérèse de France, duchesse d'Angoulême, 5 octobre 1789–2 septembre 1792* (Paris: Firmin-Didot, 1893), 156.

66 He would never see his family: Will Bashor, *Jean-Baptiste Cléry: Eyewitness to Louis XVI and Marie-Antoinette's Nightmare* (Philadephia: Diderot Press, 2011), 197.

66 "After my death, you will give this seal": Bashor, *Jean-Baptiste Cléry*, 197.

66 "How much it has cost me": John S. C. Abbott, *History of Maria Antoinette* (New York: Harper & Brothers, 1868), 280.

66 Before Cléry left the Temple: Bashor, *Jean-Baptiste Cléry*, 197.

67 Risking his life, Toulan tricked: Jean Eckard, *Mémoires historiques sur Louis XVII, roi de France et de Navarre* (Paris: H. Nicolle, 1818), 152–53.

67 She decided to convey the precious souvenirs: Gaulot, *A Conspiracy under the Terror*, 131.

67 "Here are the ring, the seal, and the packet of hair": Gaulot, *A Conspiracy under the Terror*, 131–32.

68 The gifts recognized that the princes: Gaulot, *A Conspiracy under the Terror*, 137.

68 "I trust neither her nor her husband": Clara Tschudi, *Marie Antoinette* (London: Swan Sonnenschein, 1902), 260.

68 Jarjayes welcomed Toulan: Tschudi, *Marie Antoinette*, 261.

69 He was always punctual: Tschudi, *Marie Antoinette*, 261.

69 Consequently, not all members of the family: Tschudi, *Marie Antoinette*, 261.

70 "We are, indeed, encompassed": Tschudi, *Marie Antoinette*, 262.

70 "And I, Madame," said Toulan: Tschudi, *Marie Antoinette*, 262.

70 "But nothing could give me pleasure": M. Adolphe Huard, *Mémoires sur Marie-Antoinette* (Paris: Martin-Beaupré, 1865), 202–5. "Nous avons fait un beau rêve, voilà tout; nous y avons beaucoup gagné, en trouvant encore dans cette occasion une nouvelle preuve de votre dévoûment pour moi. Ma confiance en vous est sans bornes; vous trouverez, dans toutes les occasions, en moi, du caractère et du courage, mais l'intérêt de mon fils est le seul qui me guide; et quelque bonheur que j'eusse éprouvé à être hors d'ici, je ne peux pas consentir à me séparer de lui. Au reste, je reconnais bien votre attachement dans tout ce que vous m'avez dit hier. Comptez que je sens la bonté de vos raisons pour mon propre intérêt, et que cette occasion peut ne plus se rencontrer; mais je ne pourrais jouir de rien en laissant mes enfants, et cette idée ne me laisse pas même de regret."

70 But the government's clampdown: Tschudi, *Marie Antoinette*, 262.

70 Toulan and Lepître had been removed: Edmond de Goncourt and Jules de Goncourt, *Histoire de Marie-Antoinette* (Paris: G. Charpentier, 1879), 388.

71 With Michonis and Cortey now at his disposal: Maxime de la Rocheterie, *The Life of Marie Antoinette* (New York: Dodd, Mead and Company, 1906), 1:331.

71 But it was never implemented: Charles Duke Yonge, *The Life of Marie Antoinette, Queen of France* (London: Harper & Brothers, 1876), 447.

71 Cortey would also include some thirty other men: Alcide de Beauchesne, *Louis XVII: His Life, His Suffering, His Death, the Captivity of the Royal Family in the Temple* (New York: Harper & Brothers, 1858), 2:53.

72 Arriving at the Temple, Simon said: de Beauchesne, *Louis XVII*, 2:54. Beauchesne is the only source who explains that the anonymous note was given to Simon by an unknown gendarme.

72 When told that he must immediately report: de la Rocheterie, *The Life of Marie Antoinette*, 1:332.

73 If Simon had not received the anonymous note: Gaulot, *A Conspiracy under the Terror*, 160.

73 "It would be a breach": de Beauchesne, *Louis XVII*, 2:46.

73 But there would be other plots: Lady Charlotte Walpole Atkyns, *Madame Atkyns et la prison du Temple, 1758–1836* (Paris: Perrin et Cie, 1905), 20.

73 The English couple remained: Frédéric Barbey, *Une amie de Marie-Antoinette: Madame Atkyns et la prison du Temple* (Paris: Perrin et Cie, 1905), 84.

74 Lady Atkyns then safely returned: Barbey, *Une amie de Marie-Antoinette*, 84.

74 A closer look at the brave actress's correspondence: Barbey, *Une amie de Marie-Antoinette*, 61.

75 "It will be a disgrace": Bishop, *The Prison Life of Marie Antoinette and Her Children*, 151.

75   Though all plans thus far had failed: G. Lenotre, *A Gascon Royalist in Revolutionary Paris: The Baron de Batz, 1792–1795* (London: Dodd Mead and Company, 1910), 46–50.

75   There is no mention of breakfast: François-Alphonse Aulard, "Mémoires de la dépenses de la veuve Capet à la Conciergerie," *Révolution française* 48 (1905): 169. "Soixante-quatorze jours de nourriture, café pour déjeuner, pour dîner, soupe, bouilli, un plat de légumes, poulet et dessert; dans d'autres jours, canard et pâté, pour lesdits soixante-quatorze jours, à raison de 15 livres chaque jour fait 1.110 1 (livres). Plus quarante et un jours de nourriture à la femme qui était auprès de ladite Capet, a raison de 3 livres chaque jour fait1.23 l. Plus deux matelas, dont un de crin, l'autre de laine, un lit de sangle, un traversin, une couverture, un fauteuil en canne servant de garde-robe, le tout ensemble et en loyer suivant les quittances 54 1. Pour un bidet en basane rouge garni de sa seringue, le tout neuf, pour servir à ladite veuve Capet 60 l. Pour loyer de livres 16 l. Pour deux bonnets, 7 livres chaque 14 l. Ruban et soie pour garniture d'un jupon 3 l. 16 s (sous). Ruban pour ses souliers et ses cheveux 18 s. Une bouteille d'eau pour ses dents 3 l. 12 s. Pour blanchissage 22 1. Total 1.407 l. 6 s."

CHAPTER 6: THE CARNATION PLOT

77   He passed through Warden Toussaint Richard's office: Antoine-Denis Bailly, *Choix d'anecdotes, anciennes et modernes, recueillies des meilleurs auteurs: contenant les faits les plus intéressants de l'histoire en général; les exploits des héros; traits d'esprit; saillies ingénieuses, bons mots, etc.* (Paris: Poncelin, 1803), 4:197.

78   The Tuileries, the palace where the family: Bailly, *Choix d'anecdotes*, 4:197.

78   From there she would be taken: James de Chambrier, *Marie-Antoinette, reine de France* (Paris: Lebigre-Duquesne, 1868), 2:395.

78   The chevalier was also a wealthy man: G. Lenotre, *Le vrai chevalier de maison-rouge, A. D. J. Gonzze de Rougeville, 1761–1814* (Paris: Perrin et Cie, 1907), 106.

79   It is unknown how Rougeville: Lenotre, *Le vrai chevalier de maison-rouge*, 102.

79   Michonis proudly spoke: Lenotre, *Le vrai chevalier de maison-rouge*, 103.

80   In fact, Michonis joined the two: Lenotre, *Le vrai chevalier de maison-rouge*, 104.

80   When Michonis insisted: Lenotre, *Le vrai chevalier de maison-rouge*, 104.

80   She was so weak: Maxime de la Rocheterie, *The Life of Marie Antoinette* (New York: Dodd, Mead and Company, 1906), 345.

81   When she stooped down: Jean-Baptiste Cléry, *Journal de Cléry* (Paris: Baudouin Frères, 1824), 314.

81   "Don't you know the danger": Lenotre, *Le vrai chevalier de maison-rouge*, 145. "Malheureux, me dit-elle, votre témérité me fait frémir! Savez-vous à quel danger vous vous exposez en pénétrant dans mon séjour affreux!"

82   There was also an offer: Lenotre, *Le vrai chevalier de maison-rouge*, 146.

82   Finally, Rougeville reported years later: Lenotre, *Le vrai chevalier de maison-rouge*, 110.

83   "I've just seen a chevalier": William Forsythe, *Marie Antoinette in the Conciergerie* (London: Society for Promoting Christian Knowledge, 1867), 19.

84   When he returned to his post: Forsythe, *Marie Antoinette in the Conciergerie*, 19–20.

85   The Committee of General Security: Émile Campardon, *Marie-Antoinette à la Conciergerie* (Paris: Chez Jules Gay, 1864),

85   "But, not wishing to have nothing": Léon Lecestre, "Les tentations d'évasion de Marie Antoinette," *Revue des questions historiques* 39 (1886): 554. "Mon Colonel, dans un poste aussi délicat, je manquerais absolument à mon devoir de ne pas vous instruire sur des rescues qu'il pourrait survenir par des entrevues de gens suspects qui s'introduisent chez la femme Capet. Enfin, pour vous mettre au fait et ne point me compromettre, ni mon camarade, ni le corps en entier, voici dans mon âme et conscience l'exacte vérité. L'avant-dernière fois que le citoyen Michonis est venu ici, il y est venu avec un particulier, dont l'aspect a fait tressaillir la femme Capet, qui m'a déclaré être un ci-devant chevalier de Saint-Louis, mais qu'elle tremblait qu'il ne fût découvert, et qu'elle était bien surprise de la manière qu'il avait pu parvenir jusqu'à elle. Elle m'a de même déclaré qu'il lui avait fait tenir dans ce même jour un oeillet, dans lequel il y avait un billet, et qu'il devait revenir le vendredi suivant. De plus, sa femme de chambre étant à jouer une partie de cartes avec moi, la femme Capet a profilé de cette occasion pour écrire avec une épingle un papier qu'elle m'a remis, à dessein de le remettre au certain quidam. Mais, ne voulant point avoir rien à me reprocher sur la place et les devoirs que j'avais à remplir, je me suis transporté aussitôt chez le concierge, à la femme duquel je lui ai remis le billet et fait absolument le rapport aussi exact que j'ai l'honneur de vous le présenter."

85   "You will only hasten my end": Henriette Simon-Viennot, *Marie-Antoinette devant le dix-neuvième siècle* (Paris: Librarie d'Amyot, 1843), 2:335.

85   Only later did paleographer Adam Pilinski: Eugêne Pottet, *Histoire de la Conciergerie du Palais de Paris* (Paris: Quantin, 1895), 180.

86   At four o'clock in the afternoon: Lenotre, *Le vrai chevalier de maison-rouge*, 306.

87   The questions were at times demeaning: Pierre Turbat, *Procès des Bourbons: contenant des détails historiques sur la journée du 10 août 1792, les évènements qui ont précédé, accompagné et suivi le jugement de Louis XVI; les procès de Marie-Antoinette, de Louis-Philippe d'Orléans, d'Élisabeth et de plusieurs particularités sur la maladie et la mort de Louis-Charles, fils de Louis XVI; l'échange de Marie-Charlotte, et le départ des derniers membres de la famille pour l'Espagne* (Hamburg: Turbat, 1798), 2:202–33.

90   "It was of Lafayette's assistant": George Lillie Craik and Charles MacFarlane, *Pictorial History of England: Being a History of the People, as Well as a History of the Kingdom* (London: C. Knight, 1843), 2:640.

94 *Le chevalier de maison-rouge*: C. E. Meetkerke, "Plot of the Pink," *Argosy* 63 (1897): 423.

94 "I would venture to ask": J. Lucas-Dubreton, *La vie d'Alexandre Dumas père* (Paris: Gallimard, 1923), 169. The author confirms that Dumas had originally titled the work *Le chevalier de Rougeville*, but changed the title to *Le chevalier de maison-rouge* after receiving a complaint from the son of the Marquis de Rougeville.

94 Dumas immediately replied: Maria C. Bishop, *The Prison Life of Marie Antoinette and Her Children, the Dauphin and the Duchesse d'Angoulême* (London: Kegan Paul, Trench & Company, 1893), 39.

95 Dumas, still feeling bound: G. Lenotre, "Le fils du chevalier de maison-rouge," *Revue politique et littéraire* 4 (1894): 568.

CHAPTER 7: THE QUEEN'S NEW CELL

97 "Every day and at every moment": Jules Janin, "The Queen's Gray Hair," *Living Age* 133 (1877): 367.

97 Now he faced the deputies: Pierre Turbat, *Procès des Bourbons: contenant des détails historiques sur la journée du 10 août 1792, les évènements qui ont précédé, accompagné et suivi le jugement de Louis XVI; les procès de Marie-Antoinette, de Louis-Philippe d'Orléans, d'Élisabeth et de plusieurs particularités sur la maladie et la mort de Louis-Charles, fils de Louis XVI; l'échange de Marie-Charlotte, et le départ des derniers membres de la famille pour l'Espagne* (Hamburg: Turbat, 1798), 211–14

98 But he was adamant: Turbat, *Procès des Bourbons*, 212.

100 In the meantime, the deputies questioned: Turbat, *Procès des Bourbons*, 214.

101 But Michonis explained: Turbat, *Procès des Bourbons*, 215.

102 "If you need three hundred pounds": Turbat, *Procès des Bourbons*, 216.

103 He had never mentioned: Léon Lecestre, "Les tentations d'évasion de Marie Antoinette," *Revue des questions historiques* 39 (1886): 563.

103 "She's hardly changed": Turbat, *Procès des Bourbons*, 217–18.

103 The deputies found it necessary: Turbat, *Procès des Bourbons*, 220.

104 This would prevent him: Turbat, *Procès des Bourbons*, 221.

104 The next deposition: Turbat, *Procès des Bourbons*, 222.

106 Moreover, they were likely dissatisfied: Turbat, *Procès des Bourbons*, 223.

109 He also wrote his superiors: Lecestre, "Les tentations d'évasion de Marie Antoinette," 563.

109 Rougeville had hastily fled: Lecestre, "Les tentations d'évasion de Marie Antoinette," 563.

109 If she did not mean it: Turbat, *Procès des Bourbons*, 223.

109 It was obvious that the queen: Turbat, *Procès des Bourbons*, 229–33.

113 The note had changed hands: Turbat, *Procès des Bourbons*, 2:223.

113 Indeed, they had failed: Maxime de la Rocheterie, *The Life of Marie Antoinette* (New York: Dodd, Mead and Company, 1906), 346.

114 Rougeville later related his failed attempt: Hans Axel von Fersen, *Diary and Correspondence of Count Axel Fersen: Grand-marshal of Sweden, Relating to the Court of France* (London: Heinemann, 1902), 301.

114 "The attempt to escape failed": von Fersen, *Diary and Correspondence of Count Axel Fersen*, 301.

115 This would allow the citizen: de la Rocheterie, *The Life of Marie Antoinette*, 347.

115 "Every day and at every moment": de la Rocheterie, *The Life of Marie Antoinette*, 347.

118 Two additional bolts: de la Rocheterie, *The Life of Marie Antoinette*, 348.

118 If so, this cell would at least: Eugène Pottet, *Histoire de la Conciergerie du Palais de Paris* (Paris: Quantin, 1895), 187–88.

CHAPTER 8: TIGHTENED SECURITY

119 When the queen asked for an English cotton cover: Jules Janin, "The Queen's Gray Hair," *Living Age* 133 (1877): 367.

119 In fact, they looked forward: G. Lenotre, *La captivité et la mort de Marie-Antoinette* (Paris: Perrin et Cie, 1902), 279.

120 He kept his head covered: Jan ten Brink, *Slachtoffers en helden der Fransche Revolutie* (Amsterdam: Funke en van Santen, 1875), 29.

120 A sentinel was placed: G. Lenotre, *The Last Days of Marie Antoinette* (London: William Heinemann, 1908), 158.

120 The deputies told him: Lenotre, *The Last Days of Marie Antoinette*, 189.

121 They immediately corrected: Lenotre, *The Last Days of Marie Antoinette*, 188.

121 Out of the blue, the queen said: William Forsythe, *Marie Antoinette in the Conciergerie* (London: Society for Promoting Christian Knowledge, 1867), 29.

122 He was even reprimanded: Maxime de la Rocheterie, *Histoire de Marie-Antoinette* (Paris: Perrin, 1890), 549.

122 He rushed forward: Forsythe, *Marie Antoinette in the Conciergerie*, 32.

122 "In God's name, Rosalie": Forsythe, *Marie Antoinette in the Conciergerie*, 29.

123 "You deserve the guillotine?": James de Chambrier, *Marie-Antoinette, reine de France* (Paris: Lebigre-Duquesne, 1868), 442.

123 "So much kindness, gentleness": de Chambrier, *Marie-Antoinette, reine de France*, 442.

123 Bault clenched the gift: de la Rocheterie, *Histoire de Marie-Antoinette*, 350.

123 Bault could sometimes give: de la Rocheterie, *Histoire de Marie-Antoinette*, 349.

124 Bault is pronounced: Clara Tschudi, *Marie Antoinette* (London: Swan Sonnenschein, 1902), 280. "Bon vaut mieux que beau."

124 The noise and swearing were eliminated: Eliakim Littell, "The Conciergerie," *Living Age* 205 (1895): 206.

124 This only fueled the clamor: G. Lenotre, *Le vrai chevalier de maison-rouge, A. D. J. Gonzze de Rougeville, 1761–1814* (Paris: Perrin et Cie, 1907), 163–65.

125 "In public and in private": Henri Alexandre Wallon, *Histoire du Tribunal révolutionnaire de Paris* (Paris: Librairie Hachette et Cie, 1880), 1:307. "On répand avec éclat dans le public une grande conspiration de Marie-Antoinette, Michonis, l'administrateur de police, s'est chargé pour elle d'un bouquet qui renfermait un billet portant ces mots: 'Soyez tranquille, j'ai de l'argent et des hommes tout prêts.' En public et en particulier, les citoyens paraissent indignés de ce nouveau complot, et je crois le moment favorable pour presser le jugement de cette reine orgueilleuse et éternellement conspiratrice, qui ne cesse de mettre sa tête en balance avec celle de tous les Français."

125 Rosalie attributed the hemorrhaging: Tschudi, *Marie Antoinette*, 275.

126 They argued that the queen: de Chambrier, *Marie-Antoinette, reine de France*, 416.

126 "We aim to judge the Austrian": de Chambrier, *Marie-Antoinette, reine de France*, 445.

126 "The f**king bitch": de Chambrier, *Marie-Antoinette, reine de France*, 416.

126 He claimed that such an act: de Chambrier, *Marie-Antoinette, reine de France*, 416.

127 He soon "groaned": Horace Viel-Castel, *Marie-Antoinette et la Révolution française* (Paris: Techener, 1859), 315–17.

127 "This political act and humanity": Viel-Castel, *Marie-Antoinette et la Révolution française*, 316.

128 "But until now, no evidence": de Chambrier, *Marie-Antoinette, reine de France*, 447.

129 "My own family does not come here": Lafont d'Aussonne, *Mémoires secrets et universels des malheurs et de la mort de la reine de France* (Paris: A. Philippe, 1836), 342.

130 Their plan was to assemble: Henri Alexandre Wallon, *Le Tribunal révolutionnaire: 10 mars 1793–31 mai 1795* (Paris: E. Plon, 1899), 1:324.

130 He said that three-quarters: Forsythe, *Marie Antoinette in the Conciergerie*, 35.

130 At first sight, Fersen found the chevalier: Hans Axel von Fersen, *Diary and Correspondence of Count Axel Fersen: Grand-marshal of Sweden, Relating to the Court of France* (London: Heinemann, 1902), 302.

131 Such a long conversation: von Fersen, *Diary and Correspondence of Count Axel Fersen*, 302.

CHAPTER 9: PROSECUTOR FOUQUIER-TINVILLE

135 He only needed information: Alphonse Dunoyer, *The Public Prosecutor of the Terror, Antoine Quentin Fouquier-Tinville* (New York: Putnam & Sons, 1913), 39.

136 The plot failed due to its extensive network: Maxime de la Rocheterie, *The Life of Marie Antoinette* (New York: Dodd, Mead and Company, 1906), 351.

136   Catherine Fournier's fourteen-year-old son: Bureau Central, *Réimpression de l'Ancien moniteur depuis la réunion des États-Généraux jusqu'au consulat, mai 1789–novembre 1799* (Paris: Au Bureau Central, 1841), 18:231.

136   And he conducted his investigation: Dunoyer, *The Public Prosecutor of the Terror*, 39–40.

137   The president of the convention: M. Adolphe Huard, *Mémoires sur Marie-Antoinette* (Paris: Martin-Beaupré, 1865), 221.

138   Hébert and Chaumette were actually responsible: Edmond Biré, *Journal d'un bourgeois de Paris pendant la Terreur* (London: Chatto & Windus, 1896), 5:325.

138   Although he was under the care: G. Lenotre, *The Dauphin (Louis XVII): The Riddle of the Temple* (Toronto: Doubleday, Page and Company, 1921), 122.

138   In any event, due to change of doctors: Lenotre, *The Dauphin (Louis XVII)*, 122.

138   Having set the tone: Lenotre, *The Dauphin (Louis XVII)*, 146.

138   The following morning, Simon made him drink: Phoebe Allen, *The Last Legitimate King of France: Louis XVII* (New York: J. M. Dent & Sons, 1912), 41.

140   When she fearfully asked: Marie-Thérèse Charlotte, duchesse de Angoulême, *Mémoires de Marie-Thérèse, duchesse d'Angoulême* (Paris: Au Bureau de la Mode Nouvelle, 1858), 73–74.

140   Chaumette then questioned her: Alfred Nettement, *Vie de Marie-Thérèse de France, fille de Louis XVI*, Vol. 1 (Paris: J. Lecoffre, 1872), 121. "Chaumette m'interrogea ensuite sur mille vilaines choses dont on accusait ma mère, je répondis avec vérité que cela n'était pas, mais une fausse calomnie. Ils insistèrent beaucoup, mais je me tins toujours sur la négative, qui était la vérité."

141   She also denied knowledge: Pierre Turbat, *Procès des Bourbons: contenant des détails historiques sur la journée du 10 août 1792, les évènements qui ont précédé, accompagné et suivi le jugement de Louis XVI; les procès de Marie-Antoinette, de Louis-Philippe d'Orléans, d'Élisabeth et de plusieurs particularités sur la maladie et la mort de Louis-Charles, fils de Louis XVI; l'échange de Marie-Charlotte, et le départ des derniers membres de la famille pour l'Espagne* (Hamburg: Turbat, 1798), 326.

141   "Yes, it is true": Turbat, *Procès des Bourbons*, 326.

141   Marie-Thérèse said she did not notice: Turbat, *Procès des Bourbons*, 241.

142   When questioned again: Turbat, *Procès des Bourbons*, 242.

143   When asked who had taught him: G. Lenotre, *La captivité et la mort de Marie-Antoinette* (Paris: Perrin et Cie, 1902), 48.

143   Daujon also said: Lenotre, *The Dauphin (Louis XVII)*, 152.

143   The prince was, after all, as impulsive: Lenotre, *The Dauphin (Louis XVII)*, 153.

144   It was dark, and the two candles: Edme Théodore Bourg Saint-Edme, *Répertoire général des causes célèbres françaises, anciennes et modernes* (Paris: Louis Rosier, 1834), 325.

144   The queen was actually only thirty-seven: Bourg Saint-Edme, *Répertoire général des causes célèbres françaises, anciennes et modernes*, 325–37.

147 If Marie Antoinette wanted peace: Charles Alan Fyffe, "Declaration of Pillnitz," in *A History of Modern Europe* (London: Cassell, Petter, Galbin & Company, 1880), 1:4–5.

151 "From an examination made": François Guizot, Henriette Witt, and Hazeltine Mayo, *France* (New York: P. F. Collier, 1902), 6:169.

152 When the newspapers reported: Louis Viardot, *An Illustrated History of Painters of All Schools* (London: Sampson, Low, Marston, Searle, & Rivington, 1877), 387.

152 Because Brutus was the heroic defender: Viardot, *An Illustrated History of Painters of All Schools*, 387.

CHAPTER 10: THE INDICTMENT, THE JURY, AND THE WITNESSES

153 She had held her composure: Nicolas-Louis Achaintre, *Histoire de Marie-Antoinette, archiduchesse d'Autriche, reine de France et de Navarre, rédigée d'après les mémoires et les traditions les plus authentiques* (Paris: Picard, 1824), 399.

153 I will defend my life: M. Adolphe Huard, *Mémoires sur Marie-Antoinette* (Paris: Martin-Beaupré, 1865), 224.

154 The scene was so heartbreaking: Lafont d'Aussonne, *Mémoires secrets et universels des malheurs et de la mort de la reine de France* (Paris: A. Philippe, 1836), 26. "Le 12 d'octobre, deux heures environ après son coucher, les juges du Tribunal vinrent lui faire subir le grand interrogatoire, et le lendemain, quand j'entrai chez elle, pour faire son lit, je la vis qui se promenait rapidement dans sa pauvre cellule. J'avais le coeur brisé, je n'osai point porter mes regards sur elle."

154 The next day, on October 13: Huard, *Mémoires sur Marie-Antoinette*, 224–37.

154 The opening language of the document: J. Elder, *The Accusation, Trial, Defence, Sentence, and Execution, of Marie Antoinette, Late Queen of France* (Edinburgh: J. Elder, 1793), 1–73.

155 The Parisian newspapers sensationalized: George Long, *France and Its Revolutions: A Pictorial History, 1789–1848* (London: C. Knight, 1850), 63.

156 The National Guards who organized: Long, *France and Its Revolutions*, 307.

156 White cockades representing the monarchy: Maxime de la Rocheterie, *The Life of Marie Antoinette* (New York: Dodd, Mead and Company, 1906), 33.

156 This comment not only angered: de la Rocheterie, *The Life of Marie Antoinette*, 33.

157 However, rumors of this: John S. C. Abbott, *The Life of Marie Antoinette, Queen of France* (London: Sampson Low, 1850), 158.

157 She only sought intervention: Maxime de la Rocheterie, *Marie-Antoinette et l'émigration: d'après des documents inédits* (Paris: Charles Douniol, 1875), 76.

158 Although the French National Guard: John S. C. Abbott, *History of Maria Antoinette* (New York: Harper & Brothers, 1868), 156.

158 The family was then escorted: Abbott, *History of Maria Antoinette*, 149.

159 Believing that his majesty: Abbott, *History of Maria Antoinette*, 214.

159 "The Queen was the only man": Maria C. Bishop, *The Prison Life of Marie Antoinette and Her Children, the Dauphin and the Duchesse d'Angoulême* (London: Kegan Paul, Trench & Company, 1893), 39.

160 General Lafayette and the National Guard: Alphonse de Lamartine, *History of the Girondists* (New York: Harper & Brothers, 1848), 217.

160 The exact numbers of dead: de Lamartine, *History of the Girondists*, 217. "Leurs feuilles, un moment abandonnées, s'envenimèrent de toute la peur qu'ils avaient éprouvée. Elles couvrirent de ridicule et d'exécration les noms de Bailly et de la Fayette."

161 The country's deep deficit: Luise Mühlbach, *Marie Antoinette and Her Son* (London: Chesterfield Society, 1867), 71–75.

161 Even the king felt: de la Rocheterie, *The Life of Marie Antoinette*, 336.

162 Although Marie Antoinette had instituted: de la Rocheterie, *The Life of Marie Antoinette*, 337.

162 "If I had known it": de la Rocheterie, *The Life of Marie Antoinette*, 338.

163 The indictment was thus accusing: James Rodger Miller, "George III," in *The History of Great Britain* (Philadelphia: Thomas Davis, 1844), 383.

163 A year earlier, on August 1: Adolphe Thiers, *History of the French Revolution* (London: G. Vickers, 1845), 1:124.

163 Just a few hundred volunteer soldiers: William Cobbett, "War against France," *Cobbett's Political Register* 27 (1815): 557.

164 It is doubtful that she carried: de la Rocheterie, *The Life of Marie Antoinette*, 361.

164 "The gunners are not willing": de Lamartine, *History of the Girondists*, 63.

165 A bloody massacre: de Lamartine, *History of the Girondists*, 64.

166 The bailiff added: J. de Boffe, *Procès de Marie-Antoinette, de Lorraine-d'Autriche, veuve Capet, du 23 du premier du mois, l'an 2 de la République* (London: J. De Boffe, 1793), 14.

166 The five judges appointed: G. Lenotre, *Tribunal of the Terror* (London: W. Heinemann, 1909), 71.

166 The brutal crime made the family: Imprimerie Nationale, *Journal des débats et des décrets, ou Récit de ce qui s'est passé aux séances de l'assemblée nationale depuis le 17 juin 1789, jusqu'au premier septembre de la même année* (Paris: Baudouin, 1794), 57:83.

166 The members of the Tribunal: Eliakim Littell, "The Conciergerie," *Living Age* 205 (1895): 589.

167 As a juror of the Tribunal: Lenotre, *Tribunal of the Terror*, 94. Note Renaudin's writing: "Renaudin tinvite à fair paraître dent l'affaire de Duporte du Tertres comme témoin le citoyen Mouchet comendent on segond de la section des gardes françaises rue des Poullye, no 207; de plus, Boullanjé géneral de larmé révolutionnaire et Merlin de tyonviles [*sic*] député à la Convention."

167 Dr. Souberbielle had nothing more to say: Paul-Louis-Balthasar Caffe, "Souberbielle," *Journal des connaissances médicales* 8 (1846).

167 But Souberbielle was such a revolutionary: Lenotre, *Tribunal of the Terror*, 94.

167 Besnard had been accused: Lenotre, *Tribunal of the Terror*, 94.

167 The fourth juror, Claude Besnard : M. Dubuisson, *L'art du limonadier* (Paris: Chez Galland, 1804), 5.

168 Accordingly, Ganney called: Lenotre, *Tribunal of the Terror*, 94.

169 At the trial of Louis XVI: de la Rocheterie, *The Life of Marie Antoinette*, 359.

169 Jean-Baptiste Lapierre: Émile Campardon, *Marie-Antoinette à la Conciergerie* (Paris: Chez Jules Gay, 1864), 102–7. Jean-Baptiste Lapierre was an adjutant general of the Fourth Legion; Antoine Roussillon was a surgeon, a gunner, and a naturalist who was one of the first judges of the Tribunal, where he presided for four months; Jacques René Hébert was a substitute procurer of the Commune; Abraham Justin Silly was a public recorder in Paris; Joseph Terrasson was a secretary of correspondence; Pierre Manuel was an ex-procurer of the Commune of Paris and deputy of the National Convention; Jean Silvain Bailly, homme de lettres, was a former mayor of Paris; Jean-Baptiste Béguin was an attorney and a department deputy; Reine Millot was a domestic; Jean Baptiste Larenette was editor of the *Journal du diable*; and Honoré Nicolas Tarré was a hairdresser.

169 Fouquier-Tinville's list: Campardon, *Marie-Antoinette à la Conciergerie*, 102–7. François Dufresne, guard at the Conciergerie; Marie Anne Barassin, wife of Toussaint Richard, warden of the Conciergerie; Marie Devaux, the Woman Harel; and Jean-Guillaume Gilbert, gambler and guard at the Conciergerie.

169 The following articles of the Revolutionary Tribunal: Émile Campardon, *Le Tribunal révolutionnaire de Paris* (Paris: Henri Plon, 1866), 8.

CHAPTER 11: THE REVOLUTIONARY TRIBUNAL—DAY ONE

171 "Citizen, you are informed": Christophe Félix Louis Ventre de la Touloubre Montjoie, *Histoire de Marie-Antoinette-Josèphe-Jeanne de Lorraine, archiduchesse d'Autriche, reine de France* (Paris: Lepetit, 1814), 202.

172 "I know my insufficiency": Sydney Smith, "Tronson du Coudray," *Edinburgh Review* 95 (1852): 300.

172 His knees trembled: William Forsythe, *Marie Antoinette in the Conciergerie* (London: Society for Promoting Christian Knowledge, 1867), 45.

172 They returned to the queen's cell: *Tribunal révolutionnaire procès de Louis XVI, de Marie-Antoinette, de Marie-Élisabeth et de Philippe d'Orléans: discussions législatives sur la famille des Bourbons. Recueil de pièces authèntiques* (Paris: A. Eymery, 1821), 518.

173 "I trust that the Convention": Ronald Gower, *The Despatches of Earl Gower, English Ambassador at Paris from June 1790 to August 1792* (London: University Press, 1885), 103.

173 The prosecutor had simply ignored: Forsythe, *Marie Antoinette in the Conciergerie*, 45.

174 "The law prohibits any sign": M. Adolphe Huard, *Mémoires sur Marie-Antoinette* (Paris: Martin-Beaupré, 1865), 243.

174 "You swear, Citizen, and promise": Huard, *Mémoires sur Marie-Antoinette*, 244.

174 Her defenders would have only three: Montjoie, *Histoire de Marie-Antoinette-Josèphe-Jeanne de Lorraine*, 40.

174 When Herman turned to the queen: Huard, *Mémoires sur Marie-Antoinette*, 243.

175 "This is what you are accused": Huard, *Mémoires sur Marie-Antoinette*, 245

175 The convention had ignored: Le Baron Carl de Ketschendorf, *Archives juridiciaires: recueil complet des discussions législatives* (Paris: Libraire Polytechnique de Decq, 1869), 209.

177 His testimony was short: Ketschendorf, *Archives juridiciaires*, 211.

177 This happened, he said: Ketschendorf, *Archives juridiciaires*, 211.

178 In its pages was an emblem: Ketschendorf, *Archives juridiciaires*, 213.

181 Before President Herman proceeded: Ketschendorf, *Archives juridiciaires*, 214.

182 The other spectators: Montjoie, *Histoire de Marie-Antoinette-Josèphe-Jeanne de Lorraine*, 202.

182 After that he saw Lafayette: Montjoie, *Histoire de Marie-Antoinette-Josèphe-Jeanne de Lorraine*, 202.

183 Marie Antoinette motioned for Lagarde: Eugène Pottet, *Histoire de la Conciergerie du Palais de Paris* (Paris: Quantin, 1895), 208.

184 "Because I heard a woman": Pottet, *Histoire de la Conciergerie du Palais de Paris*, 208.

184 When Marie Antoinette saw the name: Émile Campardon, *Le Tribunal révolutionnaire de Paris* (Paris: Henri Plon, 1866), 128.

184 And soon afterward, he reminded: Ketschendorf, *Archives juridiciaires*, 216.

185 The court next called Pierre Manuel: Ketschendorf, *Archives juridiciaires*, 217.

185 Manuel had not been kind: John Adolphus, *Biographical Memoirs of the French Revolution* (London: T. Cadell, Jun. and W. Davis, 1799), 2:23.

186 Bailly immediately protested: Ketschendorf, *Archives juridiciaires*, 217.

188 She was a domestic named Reine: Ketschendorf, *Archives juridiciaires*, 219.

189 When President Herman heard: Ketschendorf, *Archives juridiciaires*, 220.

190 He knew that the flower: Ketschendorf, *Archives juridiciaires*, 220.

190 Madame Richard, worried that she might be compromised: Ketschendorf, *Archives juridiciaires*, 220.

190 He was not interrogated: É. Parret, *Marie-Antoinette devant le Tribunal révolutionnaire* (Lyon: Evrard, 1868), 41.

190   She added that she was then working: Ketschendorf, *Archives juridiciaires*, 220.

190   When Michonis returned: Ketschendorf, *Archives juridiciaires*, 220.

191   "That one could realize": M. Chauveau-Lagarde, *Note historique sur les procès de Marie-Antoinette d'Autriche, reine de France, et de Madame Élisabeth de France* (Paris: Gide, 1816), 11.

191   Meteorologist's Report: Gustave Armand Henri Comte de Reiset, *Modes et usages au temps de Marie-Antoinette* (Paris: Librairie Firmin Didot, 1885), 2:406.

CHAPTER 12: THE REVOLUTIONARY TRIBUNAL—DAY TWO

193   The son of the old apothecary: Lafont d'Aussonne, *Mémoires secrets et universels des malheurs et de la mort de la reine de France* (Paris: A. Philippe, 1836), 303.

193   During the first several hours: J. Elder, *The Accusation, Trial, Defence, Sentence, and Execution, of Marie Antoinette, Late Queen of France* (Edinburgh: J. Elder, 1793), 75.

193   D'Estaing had supported: Le Baron Carl de Ketschendorf, *Archives juridiciaires: recueil complet des discussions législatives* (Paris: Libraire Polytechnique de Decq, 1869), 221.

195   He also stated that during the time: Ketschendorf, *Archives juridiciaires*, 223.

196   However, among Septeuil's papers: Ketschendorf, *Archives juridiciaires*, 223.

197   Confirming this, however: Louis Mortimer-Ternaux, *Histoire de la Terreur, 1792–1794* (Paris: Michel Lévy Frères, 1863), 3:18.

197   The Committee of General Security: Mortimer-Ternaux, *Histoire de la Terreur*, 3:18.

197   As hard as President Herman tried: Ketschendorf, *Archives juridiciaires*, 224.

199   Perhaps he was unaware: Ketschendorf, *Archives juridiciaires*, 225.

202   The child answered: Ketschendorf, *Archives juridiciaires*, 228.

203   He also found a draft: Ketschendorf, *Archives juridiciaires*, 229.

204   The other was a letter: Alexandre Dumas, *Histoire de Louis XVI et Marie Antoinette* (Paris: Dufour et Mulat, 1853), 3:235.

204   "If I had observed anything": Mortimer-Ternaux, *Histoire de la Terreur*, 3:230.

205   The next witness, Augustin Germain Jobert: Mortimer-Ternaux, *Histoire de la Terreur*, 3:231.

207   Moreover, the queen gave the artist's address: Charles Adolphe Cantaluzène, "Kucharski, auteur des portraits de Marie-Antoinette," in *L'intermédiaire des chercheurs et curieux* (Paris: Benjamin Duprat, Libraire de l'Institut, 1908), 582. "Kucharsky demeurait, sous la Terreur, rue du Coq Saint-Honoré."

207   He never spoke to them: Mortimer-Ternaux, *Histoire de la Terreur*, 3:231.

207   She had seen, however: Dumas, *Histoire de Louis XVI et Marie Antoinette*, 3:241.

208   Herman next called Jean-Baptiste: Dumas, *Histoire de Louis XVI et Marie Antoinette*, 3:241.

208 He stated that although his colleagues: Dumas, *Histoire de Louis XVI et Marie Antoinette*, 3:241.

209 Former police administrator François: Dumas, *Histoire de Louis XVI et Marie Antoinette*, 3:233.

209 However, those gathered occasionally asked: Ronald Gower, *The Despatches of Earl Gower, English Ambassador at Paris from June 1790 to August 1792* (London: University Press, 1885), 110.

209 He would soon pay dearly: Gustave Armand Henri, comte de Reiset, *Modes et usages au temps de Marie-Antoinette* (Paris: Librairie Firmin Didot, 1885), 2:407.

210 They have asked for some soup: Laure Junot, *Memoirs of Celebrated Women of All Countries* (London: Edward Churton, 1834), 306.

210 An ugly little man: Junot, *Memoirs of Celebrated Women of All Countries*, 306.

210 Rosalie was mostly worried: G. Lenotre, *The Last Days of Marie Antoinette* (London: William Heinemann, 1907), 167.

210 He said he knew the accused: Ketschendorf, *Archives juridiciaires*, 233.

211 He said that he had known: Ketschendorf, *Archives juridiciaires*, 234.

212 The doctor assured the court: Chevalier de Langeac, *Journal de l'anarchie, de la terreur et du despotisme: ou chaque jour marqué par un crime, une calamité publique, une imposture, une contradiction, un sacrilège, un ridicule ou une sottise, et comme telle la doctrine des doctrinaires* (Paris: Chez Delaunay, 1821), 2:897.

212 He said that he saw the general turn red: Ketschendorf, *Archives juridiciaires*, 234.

212 Lieutenant Jean-Maurice-François Lebrasse: Dumas, *Histoire de Louis XVI et Marie Antoinette*, 3:247.

212 He had no knowledge: Ketschendorf, *Archives juridiciaires*, 234.

212 He had painted the king's portrait: Ketschendorf, *Archives juridiciaires*, 234.

212 "Will they put on a bold front": Ketschendorf, *Archives juridiciaires*, 234.

213 He declared himself ignorant: Ketschendorf, *Archives juridiciaires*, 235.

213 He was referring to the discovery: Gower, *The Despatches of Earl Gower*, 162.

214 It was rumored, and later: Gower, *The Despatches of Earl Gower*, 236.

216 Meteorologist's Report: de Reiset, *Modes et usages au temps de Marie-Antoinette*, 2:406.

CHAPTER 13: THE QUEEN'S LAST RITES

219 Just minutes after midnight: Christophe Félix Louis Ventre de la Touloubre Montjoie, *Histoire de Marie-Antoinette-Josèphe-Jeanne de Lorraine, archiduchesse d'Autriche, reine de France* (Paris: Lepetit, 1814), 207. "Sous un quart-d'heure les débats finiront; préparez votre défense pour l'accusée."

219 He cursed the royal court's past: Le Baron Carl de Ketschendorf, *Archives juridiciaires: recueil complet des discussions législatives* (Paris: Libraire Polytechnique de

Decq, 1869), 237. "Fouquier, accusateur public, prend la parole. Il retrace la conduite perverse de la ci-devant cour, ses machinations continuelles contre une liberté qui lui déplaisait, et dont elle voulait voir la destruction à tel prix que ce fût."

220 The *Moniteur*, one of the most prominent newspapers: "Tribunal Criminel Révolutionnaire," *Gazette Nationale, ou le Moniteur Universel* 36 (1793): 145. "Chauveau et Tronçon-Ducoudray, nommés d'office par le Tribunal, pour défendre Antoinette, s'acquittent de ce devoir et sollicitent la clémence du Tribunal. Ils sont entendus dans le plus grand silence."

220 "This defense was very extensive": *Bulletin du Tribunal révolutionnaire* 29 (October 28, 1793): "Les deux avocats ont plaidé avec autant de zèle que d'éloquence."

220 More specifically, he focused on the following: Ketschendorf, *Archives juridiciaires*, 242.

220 Lagarde called it "frivolous": Ketschendorf, *Archives juridiciaires*, 242.

221 After addressing all the charges: M. Chauveau-Lagarde, *Note historique sur les procès de Marie-Antoinette d'Autriche, reine de France, et de Madame Élisabeth de France* (Paris: Gide, 1816), 44. "La ridicule nullité des preuves."

221 "I am sensitive": Chauveau-Lagarde, *Note historique sur les procès de Marie-Antoinette d'Autriche*, 44.

221 Ducoudray died before Lagarde's memoirs: Chauveau-Lagarde, *Note historique sur les procès de Marie-Antoinette d'Autriche*, 44.

221 He told them that the widow: Ketschendorf, *Archives juridiciaires*, 237.

222 In sum, Herman wanted her to be judged: Ketschendorf, *Archives juridiciaires*, 237.

222 "Their deaths were the consequence": Ketschendorf, *Archives juridiciaires*, 238. "Et s'il eût été permis, en remplissant un ministère impassible, de se livrer à des mouvements que la passion de l'humanité commandait, nous eussions évoqué devant le jury national les mènes de nos frères égorgés à Nancy, au Champ de Mars, aux frontières, a la Vendée, à Marseille, a Lyon, à Toulon, par suite des machinations infernales de cette moderne Médicis!"

222 "All those families, in tears": Ketschendorf, *Archives juridiciaires*, 238.

222 The witness Charles-Eléonore Dufriche-Valazé: Alexandre Dumas, *Histoire de Louis XVI et Marie Antoinette* (Paris: Dufour et Mulat, 1853), 3:257.

223 "Since the Revolution, a draft of between sixty": Dumas, *Histoire de Louis XVI et Marie Antoinette*, 3:257. "L'un des témoins, dont la précision et l'ingénuité ont été remarquables, vous a déclaré que le ci-devant duc de Coigny lui avait dit, en 1788, qu'Antoinette avait fait passer à l'empereur son frère, deux cents millions, pour lui aider à soutenir la guerre qu'il faisait alors. Depuis la Révolution, un bon de soixante à quatre-vingt mille livres, signé Antoinette, et tire sur Septeuil, a été donné à la Polignac, alors émigrée, et une lettre de Laporte recommandait à Septeuil de ne pas laisser la moindre trace de ce don. Lecointre (de Versailles) vous a dit, comme témoin oculaire, que depuis l'année 1779 des sommes énormes avaient été dépensées à la cour, pour des fêtes dont Marie-Antoinette était toujours la déesse."

223 "All the political events": Dumas, *Histoire de Louis XVI et Marie Antoinette*, 3:239.

224 It was four o'clock in the morning: Dumas, *Histoire de Louis XVI et Marie Antoinette*, 3:239.

224 As soon as Marie Antoinette was brought back: Dumas, *Histoire de Louis XVI et Marie Antoinette*, 3:239. "Every maneuver or intelligence with the enemies of France, tending to facilitate their entrance into any part of the Empire, whether it be to deliver up to them Towns, Fortreffes, Ports, or Veffels, appertaining to France, or in furnishing them with succours in men, Money, Provisions, or Ammunition, or to favor in any manner the progress of their Arms on the French Territory, or against our Forces by Sea or Land, whether by corrupting the fidelity of the Officers, Soldiers, or other Citizens, towards the French Nation, shall be punished with Death."

224 Ducoudray stood, however, and said: Dumas, *Histoire de Louis XVI et Marie Antoinette*, 3:239.

226 When Marie Antoinette heard the sentence: Charles-Aimé Dauban, *Les prisons de Paris* (Paris: Plon, 1870), xi.

226 When she arrived alongside: Dauban, *Les prisons de Paris*, xi.

226 The prosecutor immediately asked Sanson: Clément Henri Sanson, *Memoirs of the Sansons* (London: Chatto and Windus, 1876), 2:51.

227 "Alas, poor child—": Sanson, *Memoirs of the Sansons*, 2:240. "16 octobre 1793, 4 h. 1/2 du matin. C'est à vous, ma soeur, que j'écris pour la dernière fois; je viens d'être condamnée, non pas à une mort honteuse, elle ne l'est que pour les criminels, mais à aller rejoindre votre frère; comme lui, innocente, j'espère montrer la même fermeté que lui dans ces derniers moments. Je suis calme comme on l'est quand la conscience ne reproche rien. J'ai un profond regret d'abandonner mes pauvres enfants. Vous savez que je n'existais que pour eux et vous, ma bonne et tendre soeur. Vous qui avez, par votre amitié, tout sacrifié pour être avec nous, dans quelle position je vous laisse 1 J'ai appris, par le plaidoyer même du procès, que ma fille était séparée de vous. Hélas! la pauvre enfant, je n'ose pas lui écrire; elle ne recevrait pas ma lettre. Je ne sais même pas si celle-ci vous parviendra. Recevez pour eux deux ici ma bénédiction. J'espère qu'un jour, lorsqu'ils seront plus grands, ils pourront se réunir avec vous et jouir en entier de vos tendres soins. Qu'ils pensent tous deux à ce que je n'ai cessé de leur inspirer, que les principes et l'exécution exacte de ses devoirs sont la première base de la vie, que leur amitié et leur confiance mutuelle en feront le bonheur; que ma fille sente qu'à l'âge qu'elle a, elle doit toujours aider son frère, par les conseils que l'expérience qu'elle aura de plus que lui et son amitié pourront lui inspirer; que mon fils, à son tour, rende à sa soeur tous les soins, les services que l'amitié peut inspirer; qu'ils sentent enfin tous deux que, dans quelque position où ils pourront se trouver, ils ne seront vraiment heureux que par leur union; qu'ils prennent exemple de nous: combien, dans nos malheurs, notre amitié nous a donné de consolation; et, dans le bonheur, on jouit doublement quand on peut le partager avec un ami; et où en trouver de plus tendre, de

plus cher que dans sa propre famille? Que mon fils n'oublie jamais les derniers mots de son père, que je lui répète expressément: qu'il ne cherche jamais à venger notre mort. J'ai à vous parler d'une chose bien pénible à mon coeur. Je sais combien cet enfant doit vous avoir fait de la peine (1); pardonnez-lui, ma chère soeur; pensez à l'âge qu'il a, et combien il est facile de faire dire à un enfant ce qu'on veut, et même ce qu'il ne comprend pas. Un jour viendra, j'espère, où il ne sentira que mieux le prix de vos bontés et de votre tendresse pour tous deux. Il me reste à vous confier encore mes dernières pensées. J'aurais voulu les écrire dès le commencement du procès; mais, outre qu'on ne me laissait pas écrire, la marche en a été si rapide que je n'en aurais réellement pas eu le temps, et que j'ai toujours professée; n'ayant aucune consolation spirituelle à attendre, ne sachant pas s'il existe encore ici des pretr.es de cette religion, et même le lieu où je suis les exposerait trop s'ils y entraient une fois, je demande pardon à tous ceux que je connais, et à vous, ma soeur, en particulier, de toutes les peines que sans le vouloir j'aurais pu vous causer. Je pardonne à tous mes ennemis le mal qu'ils m'ont fait. Je dis ici adieu à mes tantes et à tous mes frères et soeurs. J'avais des amis; l'idée d'en être séparée pour jamais et leurs peines sont un des plus grands regrets que j'emporte en mourant; qu'ils sachent du moins que, jusqu'à mon dernier moment, j'ai pensé à eux. Adieu, ma bonne et tendre soeur, puisse cette lettre vous arriver! Pensez toujours à moi. Je vous embrasse de tout mon coeur, ainsi que ces pauvres et chers enfants. Mon Dieu! qu'il est déchirant de les quitter pour toujours! Adieu, adieu! je ne vais plus m'occuper que de mes devoirs spirituels. Comme je ne suis pas libre dans mes actions, on m'amènera peut-être un prêtre; mais je proteste ici que je ne lui dirai pas un seul mot, et que je le traiterai comme un être absolument étranger."

228 Those priests who did not take the oath: E. Bowles, "A Last Communion in the Conciergerie," *The Month: A Magazine and Review* 12 (1870): 409–20.

229 Soon after Bault's departure: M. Adolphe Huard, *Mémoires sur Marie-Antoinette* (Paris: Martin-Beaupré, 1865), 269. "Déclarant qu'il avait ordre de ne la quitter que quand tout serait terminé."

230 Recovering herself, and perhaps out of compassion: Ronald Gower, *Last Days of Marie Antoinette: An Historical Sketch* (London: Kegan Paul, Trench & Company, 1885), 141.

230 Although Marie Antoinette had been condemned: Horace Viel-Castel, *Marie-Antoinette et la Révolution française* (Paris: Techener, 1859), 340.

230 "I cannot consent": Viel-Castel, *Marie-Antoinette et la Révolution française*, 343.

231 The former curé of Saint-Landry: Louis-François Robiano de Borsbeek, *Marie-Antoinette à la Conciergerie* (Paris: Baudouin Frères, 1824), 67.

231 "Ah, sometimes careless": Montjoie, *Histoire de Marie-Antoinette-Josèphe-Jeanne de Lorraine*, 211. "Ah! parfois légère, jamais coupable."

231 "But Madame," said the priest: de Borsbeek, *Marie-Antoinette à la Conciergerie*, 68.

231 "I thank you," she said: Clara Tschudi, *Marie Antoinette* (London: Swan Sonnenschein, 1902), 290.

231 Yet her letter to Élisabeth: Alphonse de Lamartine, *History of the Girondists* (New York: Harper & Brothers, 1848), 154.

232 According to the historian Alphonse de Lamartine: de Lamartine, *History of the Girondists*, 157.

232 Finally, this was the Conciergerie: Victor Pierre, "Marie Antoinette à la Conciergerie," *Revue des questions historiques* 47 (1890): 174.

233 If we can believe the words: Jean Guillaume Baron Hyde de Neuville, *Mémoires et souvenirs du baron Hyde de Neuville* (Paris: E. Plon, Nourrit et Cie, 1892), 90.

233 "I should have been unworthy": Bowles, "A Last Communion in the Conciergerie," 420.

234 Although it is unlikely: G. Lenotre, *La captivité et la mort de Marie-Antoinette* (Paris: Perrin et Cie, 1902), 321.

234 Warden Bault had told him to go: G. Lenotre, *The Last Days of Marie Antoinette* (London: William Heinemann, 1907), 242.

234 "Tell your good mother": Lenotre, *The Last Days of Marie Antoinette*, 242.

235 However, the historians Edmond and Jules: Edmond de Goncourt and Jules de Goncourt, *Histoire de Marie-Antoinette* (Paris: G. Charpentier, 1879), 438.

235 "This I saw," said Madame Bault: Gower, *Last Days of Marie Antoinette*, 148.

235 Marie Antoinette's dog: George Cockburn Harvey, *Famous Four-Footed Friends* (New York: Robert M. McBride and Company, 1916), 76.

235 However, the milliner was frightened: Harvey, *Famous Four-Footed Friends*, 76.

236 Finally one evening, after howling: C. O'C. E., "The Queen's Favourite," *Irish Monthly* 14 (1886): 391.

CHAPTER 14: THE ROUTE OF THE FATAL TUMBRIL

237 Marie Antoinette's cart: Ronald Gower, *Last Days of Marie Antoinette: An Historical Sketch* (London: Kegan Paul, Trench & Company, 1885), 152.

237 A crowd of angry women: Alphonse de Lamartine, *History of the Girondists* (New York: Harper & Brothers, 1848), 155.

238 One of the prisoners, Madame Caron: Gustave Armand Henri, comte de Reiset, *Modes et usages au temps de Marie-Antoinette* (Paris: Librairie Firmin Didot, 1885), 2:408. "Ah, que j'ai soif!"

238 She hastened to fill a small cup: Eliakim Littell, "The Conciergerie," *Living Age* 205 (1895): 590.

238 A hand painted in black: de Reiset, *Modes et usages au temps de Marie-Antoinette*, 414.

239 Sanson even made a point: Gower, *Last Days of Marie Antoinette*, 153.

240 When Sanson saw that she was facing the horse: Gower, *Last Days of Marie Antoinette*, 153.

240 "The only people who behaved": Edmond de Goncourt and Jules de Goncourt, *Histoire de Marie-Antoinette* (Paris: G. Charpentier, 1879), 438. "Il ne devait y avoir en ce jour de décent que les bourreaux."

240 "This is the moment, madame": Littell, "The Conciergerie," 590.

241 She firmly repeated: Maxime de la Rocheterie, *The Life of Marie Antoinette* (New York: Dodd, Mead and Company, 1906), 372.

241 There was an "audible sound of wail": Joseph Weber, *Mémoires concernant Marie-Antoinette, archiduchesse d'Autriche, reine de France* (London: G. Schulze & Company, 1809), 1:15–16.

241 Le Brun had never seen: Marie Louise Élizabeth Vigée-Lebrun, *Souvenirs de Mme Vigée le Brun* (Paris: Bibliothèque Charpentier, 1860), 1:44. "Mais ce qu'il y avait de plus remarquable dans son visage, c'était l'éclat de son teint. Je n'en ai jamais vu d'aussi brillant, et brillant est le mot; car sa peau était si transparente qu'elle ne prenait point d'ombre. Aussi ne pouvais-je en rendre l'effet à mon gré: les couleurs me manquaient pour peindre cette fraîcheur, ces tons si fins qui n'appartenaient qu'à cette charmante figure et que je n'ai retrouvés chez aucune autre femme."

241 The queen bit her lower lip: de Lamartine, *History of the Girondists*, 156.

242 Unfortunately, the convention did not reply: François-Xavier Feller, "Marie-Antoinette-Josèphe-Jeanne de Lorraine," in *Dictionnaire historique* (Paris: Chez Méguignon Fils Aîné, 1819), 3:190.

242 The queen seldom cast her eyes: Esq. Michael Adams, *The New Royal Geographical Magazine; or, A Modern, Complete, Authentic, and Copious System of Universal Geography* (London: Alexander Hogg, 1794?), 909.

242 Grammont had also placed: Gower, *Last Days of Marie Antoinette*, 155.

242 After crossing the bridge: de Reiset, *Modes et usages au temps de Marie-Antoinette*, 2:415.

242 She struggled to move: Abel Stevens, "The Two Prisoners of the Conciergerie," *National Magazine* 3 (1853): 237.

242 "These aren't the cushions: de Lamartine, *History of the Girondists*, 156.

242 "Let's go look!": de Reiset, *Modes et usages au temps de Marie-Antoinette*, 2:415.

243 They were also expected: de Reiset, *Modes et usages au temps de Marie-Antoinette*, 2:416.

243 All the while, the queen's look: de Reiset, *Modes et usages au temps de Marie-Antoinette*, 2:416.

243 Nor was Léonard: Émile Langlade, *Rose Bertin: The Creator of Fashion at the Court of Marie-Antoinette* (New York: Charles Scribner's Sons, 1913), 128.

243 Among the medicines prescribed: de Reiset, *Modes et usages au temps de Marie-Antoinette*, 2:417.

243 The sight of this little blonde: de Reiset, *Modes et usages au temps de Marie-Antoinette*, 2:418. "C'est presque en face de l'Oratoire qu'un enfant de l'âge du Dauphin, soulevé dans les bras de sa mère qui comprenait tous les sentiments maternels de la pauvre

Reine, lui envoya de sa petite main un baiser. Insensible aux outrages, Marie-Antoinette sentit alors ses yeux se remplir de larmes."

244 "The queen's hair was cropped": de Reiset, *Modes et usages au temps de Marie-Antoinette*, 2:419.

244 In prison, she had once asked: Thomas Campbell, "France in 1793," *New Monthly Magazine* 111 (1857): 375.

244 They wore red bonnets: Léon Lecestre, "Les tentations d'évasion de Marie Antoinette," *Revue des questions historiques* 39 (1886): 182.

245 "We are going to give you": de Reiset, *Modes et usages au temps de Marie-Antoinette*, 2:419.

245 To comfort her, the priest: Goncourt and Goncourt, *Histoire de Marie-Antoinette*, 486.

245 Passing under its windows: de Lamartine, *History of the Girondists*, 156.

245 It appeared that she leaned: de Reiset, *Modes et usages au temps de Marie-Antoinette*, 2:420.

245 They pointed at the queen: de Reiset, *Modes et usages au temps de Marie-Antoinette*, 2:421.

246 The movement headed by Jean-Baptiste: William Forsythe, *Marie Antoinette in the Conciergerie* (London: Society for Promoting Christian Knowledge, 1867), 35.

246 Nearby, in the rue Saint-Honoré: de Reiset, *Modes et usages au temps de Marie-Antoinette*, 2:421.

247 Unable to use her tied hands: Renée de Froulay de Créquy, *Souvenirs de la marquise Renée de Froulay de Créquy* (Paris: H. L. Delloye, 1842), 151.

247 Seven priests were organized: Edmond Biré, *Journal d'un bourgeois de Paris pendant la Terreur* (London: Chatto & Windus, 1896), 5:287.

247 Spectators watching the cart: Biré, *Journal d'un bourgeois de Paris pendant la Terreur*, 5:288.

247 The priest would take advantage: Biré, *Journal d'un bourgeois de Paris pendant la Terreur*, 5:288.

247 A Parisian newspaper noted: Jean Edme Auguste Gosselin, *Vie de M. Emery* (Paris: A. Jouby, 1861), 1:360.

247 Marie Antoinette's second child: Frank Crane, "The Unusual, Ghostly, Superstitioius, Queer," *Current Opinion* 4 (1890): 286.

248 Sanson Obituary: Clément Henri Sanson, "Les mémoires des Sanson," *Nouveau journal* 25 (1864): 1.

CHAPTER 15: THE "NATIONAL RAZOR"

249 "Alas! My troubles": Eugène Pottet, *Histoire de la Conciergerie du Palais de Paris* (Paris: Quantin, 1895), 216.

250 In the balconies near the square: Émile Campardon, *Le Tribunal révolutionnaire de Paris* (Paris: Henri Plon, 1866), 171. "Procès-verbal d'exécution de mort de la veuve Capet: Nous, Eustache Nappier, huissier audiencier du Tribunal, demeurant rue de la Parcheminerie, soussigné, nous nous sommes transporté à la maison de justice dudit Tribunal, pour l'exécution du jugement rendu par le Tribunal aujourd'hui contre la nommée Marie-Antoinette d'Autriche, veuve de Louis Capet, qui la condamne à la peine de mort pour les causes énoncées audit jugement; et de suite l'avons remise à l'exécuteur des jugements criminels et à la gendarmerie qui l'ont conduite sur la place de la Révolution de cette ville, où, sur un échafaud dressé sur ladite place, ladite Marie-Antoinette, veuve Capet, a, en notre présence, subi la peine de mort; et de tout ce que dessus avons fait et rédigé le présent procès-verbal pour servir et valoir ce que de raison, dont acte."

250 All the blood "had left her cheeks": Luise Mühlbach, *Marie Antoinette and Her Son* (London: Chesterfield Society, 1867), 213.

250 This had marked the end: Louis-Pierre Anquetil, *Histoire de France depuis les Gaulois jusqu'à la mort de Louis XVI* (Paris: Jubin, 1829), 11:461.

250 She even attested: Marie-Thérèse Charlotte de France Angoulême, *Relation de la captivité de la famille royale à la tour du Temple: publ. pour la 1ère fois dans son intégrité et sur un mss authentique* (Paris: Poulet-Malassis, 1862), 97. "Elle alla à la mort avec courage, au milieu des injures qu'un malheureux peuple egaré jettoit sur elle: son courage ne l'abandonna pas sur la charrette et sur l'échafaud. Elle en montra autant à sa mort que pendant sa vie."

250 "She showed courage in death": Marie-Thérèse Charlotte de France Angoulême, *Relation de la captivité de la famille royale à la tour du Temple*, 81. "Son courage ne l'abandonna pas sur la charrette, ni sur l'échafaud. Elle en montra autant à sa mort que pendant sa vie."

251 "She had ceased to exist": D. Cabanes, "Mort de Marie Antoinette," *Chronique médicale* 4 (1897): 730. "A la vue de l'échafaud, écrit Lafont d'Aussonne, les yeux de Marie-Antoinette se fermèrent, la pâleur de la mort couvrit son visage, sa téte tomba sur sa poitrine. Elle avait cessé d'exister. Une apoplexie foudroyante termina les jours de la reine et ce fut son triste cadavre et non pas elle-même que les républicains portèrent sur l'échafaud."

251 Also, there's no credible evidence: Cabanes, "Mort de Marie Antoinette," 730.

251 "The slut had the strength": Citoyen Lapierre, "l'exécution de Marie Antoinette," *Revue rétrospective: recueil de pièces intéressantes et de citations curieuses* 6 (1893): 72. "Marie-Antoinette, la garces, a fait une aussi belle fin que le cochon à Godille, charcutier de chez nous; elle a été à l'échafaud avec une fermeté incroyables, tout le Ion de la rues Saint-Honoré; enfin elle a traversé presque tout Paris en regardant le mondes avec mépris et dédain, mais partout où elle a passé, les vrais sans-culotte ne désésais de crier:

Vives la Républiques et à bas la tiranique! La coquines a eu la fermeté d'aller jusqu'à l'échafaud sans broncher, mais quand elle a vue la médecines à l'épreuve devant ces yeux, elle a tombé sans forces."

251   He may very well have read: Jacques René Hébert, "La plus grande joie du *Père Duchêsne* après avoir vu de ses propres yeux la tête du Veto femelle séparée de son col de grue et sa grande colère contre les deux avocats du diable qui ont osé plaider la cause de cette guenon," *Père Duchêsne* 299 (1793).

252   She undoubtedly feared: G. Lenotre, *La guillotine et les exécuteurs des arrêts criminels pendant la Révolution: d'après des documents inédits* (Paris: Perrin, 1893), 297.

252   The *Glaive vengeur*: H. G. Dulac, *Le glaive vengeur de la République française une et indivisible ou galerie* (Paris: Galletti, 1793), 116.

252   And the *Moniteur* reported: Eliakim Littell, "Lord Holland's Foreign Reminiscences," *Living Age* 29 (1851): 392. "Elle est montre ensuite sur l'échafaud avec assez de courage—à midi et un quart sa tête est tombée.—Moniteur, Oct. 26, 1793."

252   And the crowd roared: Littell, "Lord Holland's Foreign Reminiscences," 217.

252   And when stepping onto the scaffold: M. de Lescure, *La vraie Marie-Antoinette* (Paris: Librarie Parisienne, 1863), 590. "Monsieur, je vous demande excuse; je ne l'ai fais exprès."

252   History would record these: de Lescure, *La vraie Marie-Antoinette,* 590.

253   "Pride never leaves": L. M. Prudhomme, *Révolutions de Paris* (Paris: Rue de Marais, 1793), 96.

253   They would commit the most: Prudhomme, *Révolutions de Paris,* 97.

254   One account even reported: Hector Fleischmann, *La guillotine en 1793: d'après des documents inédits des Archives nationales* (Paris: Librairie des Publications Modernes, 1908), 218. "La voici, l'infâme Antoinette! Elle est foutue, mes amis!"

254   "I go to join your father": Fleischmann, *La guillotine en 1793,* 218.

254   The most incredible and unlikely account: Prince Charles-Joseph de Ligne, *Fragments de l'histoire de ma vie* (Paris: Plon, 1928), 295. "La reine d'à présent, hélas sans royaume, la femme de Louis XVIII (i), m'a assuré que la malheureuse et belle reine était morte dans la charrette où elle était noyée dans son sang, ses pertes, ses maux, ayant fini ses jours en chemin pour l'échafaud."

255   Hats flew into the air: Prince Charles-Joseph de Ligne, *Fragments de l'histoire de ma vie,* 295.

256   Journalists scurried off: Jacques René Hébert, "La plus grande joie du *Père Duchêsne* après avoir vu de ses propres yeux la tête du Veto femelle séparée de son col de grue et sa grande colère contre les deux avocats du diable qui ont osé plaider la cause de cette guenon": "Se peut-il qu'il se soit trouvé un bougre assez hardi pour la défendre! Cependant deux braillards de palais (les avocats défenseurs d'office, ont eu cette audace; l'un d'eux a poussé l'effronterie jusqu'à dire que la nation lui avait trop d'obligations pour

la punir et de soutenir que, sans elle, sans les crimes qu'on lui reproche, nous ne se-
rions pas libres! Je ne conçois pas, f . . . ! Comment l'on peut souffrir que des cuistres
de basoche, par l'appât des dépouilles des scélérats, pour une boîte d'or, une montre,
des diamants, trahissent leur conscience et cherchent à jeter de la poudre aux yeux des
jurés. N'ai-je pas vu ces deux avocats du diable, non seulement se démener comme des
diables dans un bénitier, pour prouver l'innocence de la guenon, mais oser pleurer la
mort du traître Capet et dire aux juges que c'était assez d'avoir puni le gros cochon,
qu'il fallait au moins faire grâce à sa saloperie de femme!"

256 He had a carnation: Ronald Gower, *Last Days of Marie Antoinette: An Historical Sketch*
(London: Kegan Paul, Trench & Company, 1885), 149–60.

256 He explained that it was impossible: Gustave Armand Henri, comte de Reiset, *Modes et
usages au temps de Marie-Antoinette* (Paris: Librairie Firmin Didot, 1885), 2:423.

257 The *Abréviateur universel*: de Reiset, *Modes et usages au temps de Marie-Antoinette*,
423.

257 Although he would not officially resign: Lenotre, *La guillotine et les exécuteurs des arrêts criminels pendant la Révolution*, 198.

257 In fact, Clément did not even write: Lenotre, *La guillotine et les exécuteurs des arrêts
criminels pendant la Révolution*, 198.

257 These were grave mistakes: Clément Henri Sanson, "Les mémoires des Sanson," *Nouveau journal* 25 (1864): 728.

258 "I am calm, as one is": Gower, *Last Days of Marie Antoinette*, 132.

258 Dr. Joseph-Ignace Guillotin: Auguste Dide, "Guillotin," *La Révolution française: revue
d'histoire moderne et contemporaine* 25 (1893): 455. "En considérant la structure du
cou, dont la colonne vertébrale est le centre, composée de plusieurs os, dont la con-
nexion forme des enchevauchures. de manière qu'il n'y a pas de joint à chercher, il
n'est pas possible d'être assuré d'une prompte et parfaite séparation, en la confiant à
un agent susceptible de varier en adresse, par des causes morales et physiques. Il faut
nécessairement, pour la certitude du procédé, qu'il dépende de moyens mécaniques
invariables, dont on puisse également déterminer la force et l'effet. C'est ce que l'on a
fait en Angleterre (1); le corps du criminel est couché sur le ventre, entre deux poteaux
barrés par le haut par une traverse, d'où l'on fait tomber sur le cou la hache convexe au
moyen d'une déclique. Le dos de l'instrument doit être assez fort et assez lourd, pour
agir efficacement comme le mouton qui sert à enfoncer des pilotis; on sait que sa force
augmente à raison de la hauteur d'où il tombe. Il est aisé de faire construire une pareille
machine dont l'effet est immanquable. Consulté à Paris le 7 mars 1792. Signé: Louis,
secrétaire perpétuel de l'Académie de chirurgie."

258 "Only conceive, gentlemen": George Lillie Craikhe and Charles MacFarlane, *Pictorial
History of England: Being a History of the People, as Well as a History of the Kingdom*
(London: C. Knight, 1843), 3:55.

CHAPTER 16: THE UNFORTUNATES AND THE
SOLE SURVIVORS

261 "Being confined for thirteen months": É. Parret, *Marie-Antoinette devant le Tribunal révolutionnaire* (Lyon: Évrard, 1868), 21.

261 During this frenzied time: Anonymous, *The Reign of Terror* (London: W. Simpkin and R. Marshall, 1826), 1:v.

262 At a time when France needed a strong leader: Imbert de Saint-Amand, *Marie Antoinette at the Tuileries, 1789–1791* (New York: Charles Scribner's Sons, 1898), 168.

262 Until the family was sent: Charles Duke Yonge, *Three Centuries of Modern History* (London: Longmans, Green and Company, 1872), 426.

263 One very special friend: Hans Axel von Fersen, *Le comte de Fersen et la cour de France* (Paris: Librairie de Firmin-Didot et Cie, 1878), 2:428. "Aujourd'hui nous recevons l'affreuse nouvelle que ces barbares, ces sanguinaires Français ont terminé la vie malheureuse de notre chère et respectable reine."

263 "My heart is cruelly torn": Gustave Armand Henri, comte de Reiset, *Modes et usages au temps de Marie-Antoinette* (Paris: Librairie Firmin Didot, 1885), 429.

263 He died fighting: de Reiset, *Modes et usages au temps de Marie-Antoinette*, 429.

263 In the Temple Louis Charles's caretaker: Alcide de Beauchesne, *Louis XVII: His Life, His Suffering, His Death, the Captivity of the Royal Family in the Temple* (New York: Harper & Brothers, 1858), 145.

263 However, the prisons were so crowded: de Beauchesne, *Louis XVII*, 145.

264 "Show me the law": Anne Severin, "A Life of Ten," *The Month* 10 (1869): 344.

264 "Hold thy tongue": Severin, "A Life of Ten," 344.

264 "You must accompany them": de Beauchesne, *Louis XVII*, 72.

264 When government officials made inquiries: de Beauchesne, *Louis XVII*, 72.

264 "He has been taught to be insolent": de Beauchesne, *Louis XVII*, 72.

265 His bedding was never changed: Anna L. Bicknell, *The Story of Marie Antoinette* (New York: Century Company, 1898), 239.

265 The scabies-infested child: Bicknell, *The Story of Marie Antoinette*, 327–31.

266 Ironically, or perhaps fittingly: de Beauchesne, *Louis XVII*, 71.

266 Toulan had even conceived: Anne Severin, "Marie Antoinette," *The Month* 6 (1867): 535.

266 For this offense he was guillotined: Charles Duke Yonge, *The Life of Marie Antoinette, Queen of France* (London: Harper & Brothers, 1876), 447.

267 Each of the plans to save Marie Antoinette: G. Lenotre, *Le vrai chevalier de maison-rouge, A. D. J. Gonzze de Rougeville, 1761–1814* (Paris: Perrin et Cie, 1907), 133.

267 They had orders not to speak: George Lillie Craik, *The Pictorial History of England during the Reign of George the Third: 1792–1802* (London: C. Knight, 1843), 3:349.

267   When caught relaying information: Lenotre, *Le vrai chevalier de maison-rouge*, 275–76.

267   They were later released: Julia Kavanagh, *Woman in France during the Eighteenth Century* (London: Smith, Elder & Company, 1864), 397.

267   The Committee of General Security: Émile Campardon, *Marie-Antoinette à la Conciergerie* (Paris: Chez Jules Gay, 1864), 36.

268   At the moment when Madame Richard handed him a bowl: Campardon, *Marie-Antoinette à la Conciergerie*, 36.

268   She also combed the queen's hair: Hector Fleischmann, *Behind the Scenes in the Terror* (New York: Brentano's, 1915), 33.

268   Also, she never mentioned Rosalie: Dame Bault, *Récit exact des derniers moments de captivité de la Reine, depuis le 11 septembre 1793 jusqu'au 16 octobre suivant* (Paris: C. Ballard, 1817).

269   Rosalie was also ordered: Lafont d'Aussonne, *Mémoires secrets et universels des malheurs et de la mort de la reine de France* (Paris: A. Philippe, 1836), 411. "Lorsqu'elle fut sortie de cette affreuse maison, le premier huissier du tribunal, accompagné de trois ou quatre personnes de son même emploi, vint me demander chez le concierge et m'ordonna de le suivre jusqu'au cachot. Il me laissa reprendre mon miroir et le carton. Quant aux autres objets qui avaient appartenu à Sa Majesté, il me commanda de les serrer dans un drap de lit. Ils m'y firent ployer jusqu'à une paille qui se trouva, je ne sais comment, sur le pavé de la chambre, et ils emportèrent cette misérable dépouille de la meilleure et de la plus malheureuse Princesse qui ait jamais existé!"

269   The following effects were yet to be sent: de Reiset, *Modes et usages au temps de Marie-Antoinette*, 423. "Quinze chemises de toile fine, garnies de petite dentelle; Un mantelet de raz de Saint-Maur; Deux déshabillés complets de pareille étoffe; Un fourreau a collet et un jupon de bazin des Indes à grandes rayes; Deux jupons de bazin à. petites rayes; Cinq corsets de toile fine; Une robe à collet en toile de coton; Une camisolle aussi à collet de pareille toile. Linges à blancher: Quatre mouchoirs de baptiste; Un jupon de buzin à petites rayes; Une serviette; Et onze chauffoirs (linge de propreté à l'usage des femmes); Une paire de draps; Deux paires de poches de coton; Une serviette de toile de coton grise; Vingt-quatre mouchoirs de baptiste; Six fichus de linon; Une coeffe de linon; Deux paires de bas de soye noire; Une paire de bas de fil; Onze paires de chaussons; Une ceinture de crespe; Un petit fichu de mousseline; Un autre fichu de crespe; Six serviettes de baptiste; Une grosse éponge fine; Une petite corbeille d'ozier; Une paire de souliers neufs; Et deux paires de vieux; Une boite à poudre en bois; Et une houpe de cigne; Une petite boite de pommade en fer-blanc."

269   Marie Antoinette's daughter, Marie-Thérèse: de Reiset, *Modes et usages au temps de Marie-Antoinette*, 423.

269   Gilbert was a gambler: Campardon, *Marie-Antoinette à la Conciergerie*, 107.

270   The young barber Jean-Baptiste: Campardon, *Marie-Antoinette à la Conciergerie*, vi.

270   There is no evidence: Élisabeth Guénard, *Histoire de Madame Élisabeth de France, soeur de Louis XVI* (Paris: Lerouge, 1802), 154.

271   Élisabeth was remembered: Guénard, *Histoire de Madame Élisabeth de France, soeur de Louis XVI*, 154.

271   As the procession crossed: M. C. O'Connor Morris, *The Prisoners of the Temple; or Discrowned and Crowned* (London: Burns and Oates, 1874), 146.

271   Only from these crude remarks: Morris, *The Prisoners of the Temple*, 146.

271   "O my God": Marie-Thérèse Charlotte, duchesse d'Angoulême, *Journal de Marie-Thérèse de France, duchesse d'Angoulême, 5 octobre 1789–2 septembre 1792* (Paris: Firmin-Didot, 1893), vi. "Marie-Thérèse-Charlotte est la plus malheureuse personne du monde. Elle ne peut obtenir de savoir des nouvelles de sa mère, pas même d'être réunie à elle quoiqu'elle l'ait demandé mille fois. Vive ma bonne mère que j'aime bien et dont je ne peux savoir des nouvelles. Ô mon père, veillez sur moi du haut du Ciel. Ô mon Dieu, pardonnez à ceux qui ont fait souffrir mes parents."

271   The news left her gasping: Joseph Turquan, *Madame Royale, the Last Dauphine* (New York: Brentano's, 1910), 58.

272   Some twenty-five years had passed: Alfred Nettement, *Vie de Marie-Thérèse de France, fille de Louis XVI* (Paris: J. Lecoffre, 1872), 1:165.

273   Orders had been given: Imbert de Saint-Amand, *Marie Antoinette and the End of the Old Régime* (New York: Charles Scribner's Sons, 1890), 151.

273   When the executioner reached for it: Alcide de Beauchesne, *La vie de Madame Élisabeth, soeur de Louis XVI* (Paris: Henri Plon, 1869), 230. "Au nom de votre mère, monsieur, couvrez-moi."

273   Élisabeth's body was placed: Morris, *The Prisoners of the Temple*, 147.

CHAPTER 17: *LA CIMETIÈRE DE LA MADELEINE*

275   On the 18th of January 1815: É. Parret, *Marie-Antoinette devant le Tribunal révolutionnaire* (Lyon: Évrard, 1868), 21.

275   Marie Antoinette was to be the last queen: Louis Antoine Fauvelet de Bourrienne, *The Life of Napoleon Bonaparte* (London: H. Colburn and R. Bentley, 1831), 3:333. "The Allied Powers having declared that Emperor Napoleon was the sole obstacle to the restoration of peace in Europe, Emperor Napoleon, faithful to his oath, declares that he renounces, for himself and his heirs, the thrones of France and Italy, and that there is no personal sacrifice, even that of his life, which he is not ready to do in the interests of France. Done in the palace of Fontainebleau, 11 April 1814."

275   However, the people took little interest: Frederick W. Hoffman, *A Sailor of King George: The Journals of Captain Frederick* (London: John Murray, 1901), 330.

276 Louis XVIII immediately set out: Eyre Evans Crowe, *History of the Reigns of Louis XVIII and Charles X* (London: Richard Bentley, 1854), 2:16.

276 "Here I am!": Ida Minerva Tarbell, *A Short Life of Napoleon Bonaparte* (New York: S. S. McClure Company, 1896), 204.

276 Her bravery caused Napoleon to remark: Tarbell, *A Short Life of Napoleon Bonaparte*, 409.

277 Moreover, they must have felt humiliated: Antoine de Saint-Gervais, *Histoire de Sa Majesté Louis XVIII, surnommé le Désiré: depuis sa naissance jusqu'au traité de paix de 1815* (Paris: P. Blanchard, 1816), 234.

277 Naturally, the royalists were intoxicated: George Long, *France and Its Revolutions: A Pictorial History, 1789–1848* (London: C. Knight, 1850), 533.

277 Although greeted by two hundred ladies: Clara Tschudi, *Marie Antoinette* (London: Swan Sonnenschein, 1902), 300.

277 However, the remains of the martyred royals: Anonymous, *The History of Paris: From the Earliest Period to the Present Day* (London: A. and W. Galignani, 1825), 3:375.

279 Of the list of 1,343 persons: Anonymous, *The History of Paris*, 3:375.

279 The last task of Martial Joseph Armand Herman: Eliakim Littell, "Memoirs of Marie Antoinette," *Living Age* 60 (1895): 37.

279 The gates opened, the cart drove: G. Lenotre, *The Last Days of Marie Antoinette* (London: William Heinemann, 1907), 267.

280 He also covered the ground: Anonymous, *The History of Paris*, 373.

280 A small mound with a cross: Anonymous, *The History of Paris*, 373.

280 As a sign of Descloseaux's fidelity: Anonymous, *The History of Paris*, 374.

280 "Good old man, you have religiously preserved": Anonymous, *The History of Paris*, 374.

280 Louis XVIII also granted him a pension: Anonymous, *The History of Paris*, 379.

280 The cemetery of the Madeleine: Littell, "Memoirs of Marie Antoinette," 268.

280 According to the memoirs of Paul François Barras: Hector Fleischmann, *Behind the Scenes in the Terror* (New York: Brentano's, 1915), 129.

281 "In purchasing this ground": Anonymous, *The History of Paris*, 373.

282 Another official, the prince de Poix: Lenotre, *The Last Days of Marie Antoinette*, 278.

282 The gates of the cemetery: Anonymous, *The History of Paris*, 377.

282 Upon the lids were fastened: Anonymous, *The History of Paris*, 378. "Ici est le corps du très-haut, très-puissant et très-excellent prince, Louis XVI. du nom, par la grâce de Dieu, roi de France et de Navarre; Ici est le corps de très-haute, très-puissante et très-excellent princesse, Marie-Antoinette-Josèphe-Jeanne de Lorraine, archiduchesse d'Autriche, épouse du très-haut, très puissant et très-excellent prince Louis XVI. du nom, par la grâce de Dieu, roi de France et de Navarre."

283 They laid the first stone: Anonymous, *The History of Paris*, 379.

284 The coffins were then carried: Anonymous, *The History of Paris*, 380.

284 It was a cry reminiscent: Joseph Turquan, *Madame Royale, the Last Dauphine* (New York: Brentano's, 1910), 171.

285 In fact, Marie-Thérèse's own inclination: Turquan, *Madame Royale*, 171.

286 Salutes of artillery: Edme-Louis Barbier, *Notice sur l'exhumation de leurs majestés Louis XVI, et Marie-Antoinette, archiduchesse d'Autriche* (Paris: Le Normant, 1815), 29.

286 It was located in the very center: L'Abbé Savornin, *Notice historique sur les faits et particularités qui se rattachent à la chapelle expiatoire de Louis XVI et de la reine Marie-Antoinette* (Paris: Vaton, 1864), 202–6.

286 Also, the royal court: Imbert de Saint-Amand, *The Duchess of Angoulême and the Two Restorations* (New York: Charles Scribner's Sons, 1894), 376.

286 "We want no speech or eulogy": Victor Pierre, "Marie Antoinette à la Conciergerie," *Revue des questions historiques* 47 (1890): 208.

EPILOGUE

287 "The first crime of the Revolution": François-René de Chateaubriand, *Oeuvres de Chateaubriand* (Paris: Dufour, Boulanger et Legrand, Éditeurs, 1863), 16:211.

287 The surrender of the former queen: Henri Martin, *A Popular History of France* (Boston: C. F. Jewett, 1877), 1:498. "This plan was a negotiation with Venice, Tuscany, and Naples, the three Italian States yet neutral, who were to pledge themselves to maintain their wavering neutrality, in consideration of a guaranty of the safety of Marie Antoinette and her family. Two diplomatic agents who afterward held high posts in France, Marat and Sémonville, were intrusted with this affair. As they were crossing from Switzerland into Italy, they were arrested, in violation of the law of nations, upon the neutral territory of the Grisons by an Austrian detachment (July 25). It might have been supposed that the Austrian government upon learning the object of their mission would hasten to release them; on the contrary, they were loaded with chains and sent to the pestilential dungeons of Mantna. The young Emperor Francis II, the most unfeeling of men, and his new minister Thugut, an unscrupulous and heartless intriguer, thought far more of drawing Naples, Florence, and Venice into their coalition, than of saving the lives of the aunt and cousins of the Emperor."

288 The royalists suggested: Anonymous, "Inedited Facts Respecting the French Revolution of 1789," *Monthly Chronicle* 7 (1841): 379.

288 And it was well known that quicklime: Alcide de Beauchesne, "Les derniers moments de Madame Élisabeth," *Revue des questions historiques* 5–6 (1868): 547.

288 One historian even argued: Hector Fleischmann, *Behind the Scenes in the Terror* (New York: Brentano's, 1915), 129. "He was so by my orders; it was I who commanded that he should be taken to the Place de la Révolution, and when his affair was over he should be thrown into the same grave as Louis XVI and Marie-Antoinette in

the Madeleine cemetery. I wanted in this way to give Robespierre a certain approximation to royalty because he was accused of having been disposed to it during the last moments of his power. Everyone knows also that Robespierre was the only person of this period who had been executed and thrown into the Madeleine cemetery, who wore buckles on his breeches and on his shoes; and as, I believe, a question has been raised about some trinkets of that kind among the things that were gathered together at the exhumation of the bodies of Louis XVI and Marie-Antoinette, since it is true that after Robespierre's death only some members of the Commune were interred there, it appears extremely probable that it was Robespierre himself with his buckles who was taken for the august victims."

289   "Their lives belong to everyone": F. Jeffries, "Marie Antoinette," *Gentleman's Magazine* 169 (1840): 600.

289   It was a crime absolutely unjustifiable: Maxime de la Rocheterie, *The Life of Marie Antoinette* (New York: Dodd, Mead and Company, 1906), 374.

289   The queen's enemies distributed: de la Rocheterie, *The Life of Marie Antoinette*, 374.

289   Wrapped in a fur-lined velvet cloak: Jeanne-Louise-Henriette Campan, *Memoirs of the Private Life of Marie Antoinette* (New York: Brentano's, 1917), 1:xxxvi.

289   Such thoughtlessness was always a pretext: Campan, *Memoirs of the Private Life of Marie Antoinette*, 1:xxxvi.

290   Thisbé then found its way: O'C. E., C. "The Queen's Favourite," *Irish Monthly* 14 (1886): 390.

290   "So perish all that mourn": O'C. E., C. "The Queen's Favourite," 391.

291   According to legend, this occurred: G. Lenotre, "Chiens Gentilshommes," *Revue historique de la question Louis XVII* 5–6 (1908): 180.

SELECTED BIBLIOGRAPHY

I am referencing the sources used in writing *Marie Antoinette's Darkest Days*, but this selected bibliography is not a complete record of all the books and sources that I have consulted.

Abbott, John S. C. *History of Maria Antoinette*. New York: Harper & Brothers, 1868.

———. *The Life of Marie Antoinette, Queen of France*. London: Sampson Low, 1850.

Abrantès, Duchesse Laure Junot de. *Mémoires sur la restauration, ou souvenirs historiques sur cette époque, la révolution de juillet et les premières années du règne de Louis-Philippe 1er*. Paris: L'Henri, 1836.

Achaintre, Nicolas-Louis. *Histoire de Marie-Antoinette, archiduchesse d'Autriche, reine de France et de Navarre, rédigée d'après les mémoires et les traditions les plus authentiques*. Paris: Picard, 1824.

Adams, Michael, Esq. *The New Royal Geographical Magazine; or, A Modern, Complete, Authentic, and Copious System of Universal Geography*. London: Alexander Hogg, 1794[?].

Adolphus, John. *Biographical Memoirs of the French Revolution*. 2 vols. London: T. Cadell, Jun. and W. Davis, 1799.

———. "Biographical Memoirs of the French Revolution." *Monthly Review* 31 (1800): 71.

Allen, Phoebe. *The Last Legitimate King of France: Louis XVII*. New York: J. M. Dent & Sons, 1912.

Angoulême, Marie-Thérèse Charlotte, duchesse de. *Journal de Marie-Thérèse de France, duchesse d'Angoulême, 5 octobre 1789–2 septembre 1792.* Paris: Firmin-Didot, 1893.

———. *Madame Marie-Thérèse-Charlotte de France, fille de Louis XVI, relation du voyage de Varennes, et récit de sa captivité* à la tour du Temple. Paris: Auguste Vaton, 1852.

———. *Mémoires de Marie-Thérèse, duchesse d'Angoulême.* Paris: Au Bureau de la Mode Nouvelle, 1858.

———. *Relation de la captivité de la famille royale à la tour du Temple.* Paris: Poulet-Malassis, 1862.

Anonymous. *Etrennes aux fouteurs ou le calendrier des trois sexes.* Paris: Unknown, 1793.

———. "Inedited Facts Respecting the French Revolution of 1789." *Monthly Chronicle* 7 (1841).

———. *The History of Paris: From the Earliest Period to the Present Day.* 3 vols. London: A. and W. Galignani, 1825.

———. *The Reign of Terror.* Vol. 1. London: W. Simpkin and R. Marshall, 1826.

Anquetil, Louis-Pierre. *Histoire de France depuis les Gaulois jusqu'à la mort de Louis XVI.* 15 vols. Paris: Jubin, 1829.

Anquetil, Louis Pierre, and Paul Delaure Lacroix. *Histoire de France depuis le temps les plus régulés jusqu'à la Révolution en 1789.* Paris: Dufour et Mulat, 1850.

Atkyns, Lady Charlotte Walpole. *Madame Atkyns et la prison du Temple, 1758–1836.* Paris: Perrin et Cie, 1905.

Aulard, François-Alphonse. "Mémoires de la dépenses de la veuve Capet à la Conciergerie." *La Révolution française* 48 (1905): 169.

Aussonne, Lafont d'. *Mémoires secrets et universels des malheurs et de la mort de la reine de France.* Paris: A. Philippe, 1836.

Bailly, Antoine-Denis. *Choix d'anecdotes, anciennes et modernes, recueillies des meilleurs auteurs: contenant les faits les plus intéressants de l'histoire en général; les exploits des héros; traits d'esprit; saillies ingénieuses, bons mots, etc.* 5 vols. Paris: Poncelin, 1803.

Bangs, Lemuel B., and William A. Hardaway. *An American Textbook of Genito-urinary Diseases, Syphilis and Diseases of the Skin.* Philadelphia: W. B. Saunders, 1898.

Barbey, Frédéric. *Une amie de Marie-Antoinette: Madame Atkyns et la prison du Temple.* Paris: Perin et Cie, 1905.

Barbier, Edme-Louis. *Notice sur l'exhumation de leurs majestés Louis XVI, et Marie-Antoinette, archiduchesse d'Autriche.* Paris: Le Normant, 1815.

Bashor, Will. *Jean-Baptiste Cléry: Eyewitness to Louis XVI and Marie-Antoinette's Nightmare*. Philadelphia: Diderot Press, 2011.

——. *Marie Antoinette's Head: The Royal Hairdresser, the Queen, and the Revolution*. Guilford, CT: Lyons Press, 2013.

Bault, Dame. *Récit exact des dernièrs moments de captivité de la reine, depuis le 11 septembre 1793 jusqu'au 16 octobre suivant*. Paris: C. Ballard, 1817.

Beauchesne, Alcide de. *La vie de Madame Élisabeth, soeur de Louis XVI*. Paris: Henri Plon, 1869.

——. "Les dernièrs moments de Madame Élisabeth." In *Revue des questions historiques*. Vol. 5. Paris: Librairie de Victor Palme, 1868.

——. *Louis XVII: His Life, His Suffering, His Death, the Captivity of the Royal Family in the Temple*. Vol. 2. New York: Harper & Brothers, 1853.

Belloc, Hillaire. *Marie Antoinette*. New York: Doubleday, Page, and Company, 1909.

Beugnot, Comte Jacques-Claude. *Mémoires du Comte Beugnot, ancien ministre*. Paris: E. Dentu, 1868.

Bicknell, Anna L. *The Story of Marie Antoinette*. New York: Century Company, 1898.

Biré, Edmond. *Journal d'un bourgeois de Paris pendant la Terreur*. 5 vols. London: Chatto & Windus, 1896.

Bishop, Maria C. *The Prison Life of Marie Antoinette and Her Children, the Dauphin and the Duchesse d'Angoulême*. London: Kegan Paul, Trench & Company, 1893.

Blanc, Louis. *Histoire de la Révolution française*. 12 vols. Paris: Langlois & Leclercq, 1857.

Bouchet, M. le Comte César du. *Les adieux de Marie-Antoinette d'Autriche, reine de France*. Paris: Lerouge, 1814.

Bourrienne, Louis Antoine Fauvelet de. *The Life of Napoleon Bonaparte*. 3 vols. London: H. Colburn and R. Bentley, 1831.

Bouvet, Maurice. "Les apothicaires royaux." *Revue d'histoire de la pharmacie* 72 (1931): 15–32.

Bowles, E. "A Last Communion in the Conciergerie." *Month* 12 (1870).

Brande, W. T., and G. W. Cox. *A Dictionary of Science, Literature and Art*. 3 vols. London: Longman, Green, and Company, 1875.

Buchez, Philippe-Joseph-Benjamin, and J. C. Pierre-Célestin Roux-Lavergne. *Histoire parlementaire de la Révolution française ou journal des assemblées nationales, depuis 1789 jusqu'en 1815*. Vol. 23. Paris: Paulin, 1886.

Bulletin du Tribunal révolutionnaire 29 (October 28, 1793).

Bureau Central. *Réimpression de l'Ancien moniteur depuis la réunion des* États-Généraux *jusqu'au Consulat (mai 1789–novembre 1799).* Vol. 18. Paris: Au Bureau Central, 1841.

Burns, E. "A Last Communion in the Conciergerie." In *The Month.* Vol. 1. London: Simpkin, Marshall, and Company, 1870.

Cabanes, D. "Mort de Marie Antoinette." In *Chronique médicale.* Vol. 4. Paris: Redaction et Administration, 1897.

Caffe, Paul-Louis-Balthasar. "Souberbielle." *Journal des connaissances médicales* 8 (1846).

Campan, Jeanne-Louise-Henriette. *Memoirs of the Private Life of Marie Antoinette.* New York: Brentano's, 1917.

Campardon, Émile. *Le Tribunal révolutionnaire de Paris.* Paris: Henri Plon, 1866.

———. *Marie-Antoinette à la Conciergerie.* Paris: Chez Jules Gay, 1864.

Campbell, Thomas. "France in 1793." *New Monthly Magazine* 111 (1857): 375.

Cantaluzène, Charles Adolphe. "Kucharski, auteur des portraits de Marie-Antoinette." In *L'intermédiaire des chercheurs et curieux.* Paris: Benjamin Duprat, Libraire de l'Institut, 1908.

Cassagnac, Adolphe Granier de. *Histoire des Girondins et des massacres de septembre.* Vol. 1. Paris: E. Dentu, 1860.

Chambers, William and Robert. *Chambers's Journal* 12 (1850).

Chambrier, James de. *Marie-Antoinette, reine de France.* 2 vols. Paris: Lebigre-Duquesne, 1868.

Chateaubriand, François-René de. *Oeuvres de Chateaubriand.* 18 vols. Paris: Dufour, Boulanger et Legrand, 1863.

Chauveau-Lagarde, M. *Note historique sur les procès de Marie-Antoinette d'Autriche, reine de France, et de Madame* Élisabeth *de France.* Paris: Gide, 1816.

Cléry, Jean-Baptiste. *Journal de Cléry.* Paris: Baudouin Frères, 1824.

———. *La captivité de Louis XVI.* Paris: J. Casterman, 1848.

Cobbett, William. "War against France." *Cobbett's Political Register* 27 (1815).

Cochrane, John G. "Marquis de Custine's Russia." *Foreign Quarterly Review* 31 (1843): 427–37.

Coittant, Philippe E. *Almanach des prisons, ou anecdotes sur le régime intérieur de la Conciergerie.* Paris: Chez Michel, 1795.

Conny, Félix de. *Histoire de la Révolution française de France.* Paris: Jeulin, 1838.

Craik, George Lillie, and Charles MacFarlane. *Pictorial History of England: Being a History of the People, as Well as a History of the Kingdom.* 8 vols. London: C. Knight, 1843.

Crane, Frank. *Current Opinion* 4 (1890).

Créquy, Renée de Froulay de. *Souvenirs de la marquise Renée de Froulay de Créquy.* Paris: H. L. Delloye, 1842.

Croker, John W. *Essays on the Early Period of the French Revolution.* London: John Murray, 1857.

Crowe, Eyre Evans. *History of the Reigns of Louis XVIII and Charles X.* 2 vols. London: Richard Bentley, 1854.

Dauban, Charles-Aimé. *Les prisons de Paris.* Paris: Plon, 1870.

De Boffe. *Procès de Marie- Antoinette, de Lorraine-d'Autriche, veuve Capet, du 23 du premier du mois, l'an 2 de la République.* London: J. De Boffe, 1793.

Delille, Jacques. *La pitié.* Paris: Giguet et Michaud, 1805.

Dide, Auguste. "Guillotin." *La Révolution française: revue d'histoire moderne et contemporaine* 25 (1893).

Dorbec, Prosper. "Le portrait dans la Révolution." *Revue de l'art ancien et moderne* 21 (1907).

Dubuisson, M. *L'art du limonadier.* Paris: Chez Galland, 1804.

Dulac, H. G. *Le glaive vengeur de la République française une et indivisible ou galerie.* Paris: Galletti, 1793.

Dumas, Alexandre. *Histoire de Louis XVI et Marie Antoinette.* Vol. 3. Paris: Dufour et Mulat, 1853.

Dunoyer, Alphonse. *The Public Prosecutor of the Terror, Antoine Quentin Fouquier-Tinville.* New York: Putnam & Sons, 1913.

Durieux, Joseph. *Près de la reine Marie-Antoinette.* Paris: Les Éditions de France, 1933.

Eckard, Jean. *Mémoires historiques sur Louis XVII, roi de France et de Navarre.* Paris: H. Nicolle, 1818.

Edgeworth de Firmont, M. *Des dernières heures de Louis Seize.* Paris: Baudouin Frères, 1825.

Elder, J. *The Accusation, Trial, Defence, Sentence, and Execution, of Marie Antoinette, Late Queen of France.* Edinburgh: J. Elder, 1793.

Engerand, Fernand. *Ange Pitou.* Paris: Leroux, 1899.

Everett, Alexander Hill. *Remarks on Article IX in the Eighty-Fourth Number of the North American Review.* Boston: Perkins, Marvin, and Company, 1834.

Eymery, Alexis. *Procès de Louis XVI, de Marie-Antoinette, de Marie-Élisabeth et de Philippe d'Orléans; discussions législatives sur la famille des Bourbons.* Paris: Delaunay, 1821.

F. G. A. "Procès de Louis XVI, roi de France suivi des procès de Marie-Antoinette, reine de France, de Madame Élisabeth, soeur du roi, et de Louis-Philippe duc d'Orléans." In *Ami du trône*. Paris: Lerouge, 1814.

Feller, François-Xavier. "Marie-Antoinette-Josèphe-Jeanne de Lorraine." In *Dictionnaire historique*. Vol. 3. Paris: Chez Méguignon Fils Aîné, 1819.

Fersen, Hans Axel von. *Diary and Correspondence of Count Axel Fersen: Grand-Marshal of Sweden, Relating to the Court of France*. London: Heinemann, 1902.

———. *Le Comte de Fersen et la cour de France*. 2 vols. Paris: Librairie Firmin-Didot et Cie, 1878.

Field, Kate. "Ristori as Marie Antoinette." *McBride's Magazine* 1 (1868).

Fleischmann, Hector. *Behind the Scenes in the Terror*. New York: Brentano's, 1915.

———. *La guillotine en 1793: d'après des documents inédits des Archives nationales*. Paris: Librairie des Publications Modernes, 1908.

Forsythe, William. *Marie Antoinette in the Conciergerie*. London: Society for Promoting Christian Knowledge, 1867.

Fuller, Horace W. "Old French Prisons." In *The Green Bag*. Boston: Boston Book Company, 1899.

Fyffe, Charles Alan. "Declaration of Pillnitz." In *A History of Modern Europe*. London: Cassell, Petter, Galbin & Company, 1880.

Gallois, M. Léonard. *Histoire de France*. Paris: Jubin, 1829.

Gaulot, Paul. *A Conspiracy under the Terror: Marie Antoinette-Toulan-Jarjayes*. London: Chatto & Windus, 1904.

Gazier, A. "La Guerre des Farines." In *Mémoires de la Société de l'histoire de Paris et de l'Île-de-France*, 6:1. Paris: H. Champion, 1880.

Goncourt, Edmond de, and Jules de Goncourt. *Histoire de Marie-Antoinette*. Paris: G. Charpentier, 1879.

Gosselin, Jean Edme Auguste. *Vie de M. Emery*. 2 vols. Paris: A. Jouby, 1861.

Gower, George Granville Leveson (Duke of Sutherland). *The Despatches of Earl Gower, English Ambassador at Paris from June 1790 to August 1792*. London: University Press, 1885.

Gower, Ronald. *Iconographie de la reine Marie-Antoinette*. Paris: A. Quantin, 1883.

———. *Last Days of Marie Antoinette: An Historical Sketch*. London: Kegan Paul, Trench & Company, 1885.

Guénard, Élisabeth. *Histoire de Madame Élisabeth de France, soeur de Louis XVI*. Paris: Lerouge, 1802.

Guizot, François, Henriette Witt, and Hazeltine Mayo. *France*. Vol. 6. New York: P. F. Collier, 1902.

Guthrie, William. *A New Geographical, Historical, and Commercial Grammar*. London: G. G. and J. Robinson and J. Mawman, 1801.

Hare, Augustus J. C. "Walks in Old Paris." *Good Words and Sunday Magazine* 28 (1887): 615–21.

———. *Walks in Paris*. New York: Routledge and Sons, 1888.

Harvey, George Cockburn. *Famous Four-Footed Friends*. New York: Robert M. McBride and Company, 1916.

Hatin, Eugène. *Bibliographie historique et critique de la presse périodique française, ou catalogue systématique et raisonné de tous écrits périodiques de quelque valeur publiés ou ayant circulé en France . . . précédé d'un essay historique et statistique sur la naissance et les progrès de la presse périodique dans les deux mondes par Eugène Hatin*. Paris: Librairie de Firmin-Didot Frères, Fils et Cie, 1866.

Hébert, Jacques-René. "La plus grande joie du *Père Duchêsne* après avoir vu de ses propres yeux la tête du Veto femelle séparée de son col de grue et sa grande colère contre les deux avocats du diable qui ont osé plaider la cause de cette guenon." In *Père Duchêsne*. No. 299. Paris: Girardin, 1793.

Herbermann, Charles G. "Reverend Simon Fouché." *Historical Records and Studies* 9 (1916): 180–90.

Hoffman, Frederick W. *A Sailor of King George: The Journals of Captain Frederick*. London: John Murray, 1901.

Houssaye, Arsène. *Louis XV*. Paris: Bibliothèque Charpentier, 1890.

Huard, M. Adolfe. *Mémoires sur Marie-Antoinette*. Paris: Martin-Beaupré, 1865.

Hyde de Neuville, Jean Guillaume Baron. *Mémoires et souvenirs du baron Hyde de Neuville*. Paris: E. Plon, Nourrit et Cie, 1892.

Imprimerie Nationale. *Journal des débats et des décrets, ou récrit de ce qui s'est passé aux séances de l'assemblée nationale depuis le 17 juin 1789, jusqu'au premier septembre de la même année*. Vol. 57. Paris: Baudouin, 1794.

Janin, Jules. "The Queen's Gray Hair." *Living Age* 133 (1877): 367.

Jeffries, F. "Marie Antoinette." *Gentleman's Magazine* 169 (1840).

Junot, Laure. *Memoirs of Celebrated Women of All Countries*. London: Edward Churton, 1834.

Kavanagh, Julia. *Woman in France during the Eighteenth Century*. London: Smith, Elder & Company, 1864.

Ketschendorf, Le Baron Carl de. *Archives juridiciaires: recueil complet des discussions législatives*. Paris: Libraire Polytechnique de Decq, 1869.

La Rocheterie, Maxime de. *Histoire de Marie-Antoinette*. 2 vols. Paris: Perrin, 1890.

———. *The Life of Marie Antoinette*. New York: Dodd, Mead and Company, 1906.

———. *Marie-Antoinette et l'émigration: d'après des documents inédits*. Paris: Charles Douniol, 1875.

La Sicotière, Léon de. *Bio-bibliographie de la reine Marie-Antoinette*. Paris: Dupray de la Mahérie, 1863.

Lamartine, Alphonse de. *History of the Girondists*. 3 vols. New York: Harper & Brothers, 1848.

Lamorlière, Rosalie. "La dernière prison de Marie-Antoinette." *Récits de grands jours de l'histoire* 4 (1897): 1–24.

Langeac, Chevalier de. *Journal de l'anarchie, de la terreur et du despotisme: ou chaque jour marqué par un crime, une calamité publique, une imposture, une contradiction, un sacrilége, un ridicule ou une sottise, et comme telle la doctrine des doctrinaires*. 3 vols. Paris: Chez Delaunay, 1821.

Langlade, Émile. *Rose Bertin: The Creator of Fashion at the Court of Marie-Antoinette*. New York: Charles Scribner's Sons, 1913.

Lapierre, Citoyen. "L'exécution de Marie Antoinette." *Revue rétrospective: recueil de pièces intéressantes et de citations curieuses* 6 (1893).

Laurent, Gustave. "Quelques notes sur les dernières années du chirurgien Souberbielle, le médicin de Robespierre." *Revue historique de la Révolution française* 15 (1923): 56–58.

Lazare, Félix. *Dictionnaire des rues et monuments de Paris*. Paris: Au Bureau de la Revue Municipale, 1855.

Lecestre, Léon. "Les tentations d'évasion de Marie Antoinette." *Revue des questions historiques* 39 (1886): 510–68.

Lenotre, G. *A Gascon Royalist in Revolutionary Paris: The Baron de Batz, 1792–1795*. London: Dodd Mead and Company, 1910.

———. "Chiens Gentilshommes." *Revue historique de la question Louis XVII* 5–6 (1908).

———. *The Daughter of Louis XVI: Marie-Thérèse-Charlotte de France, Duchesse d'Angoulême*. London: John Lane, 1908.

———. *The Dauphin (Louis XVII): The Riddle of the Temple*. Toronto: Doubleday, Page and Company, 1921.

———. *La captivité et la mort de Marie-Antoinette*. Paris: Perrin et Cie, 1902.

———. *La guillotine et les exécuteurs des arrêts criminels pendant la Révolution: d'après des documents inédits*. Paris: Perrin, 1893.

———. *Last Days of Marie Antoinette*. London: William Heinemann, 1907.

———. "Le fils du chevalier de maison-rouge." *Revue politique et littéraire* 4 (1894).

———. *Le vrai chevalier de maison-rouge, A. D. J. Gonzze de Rougeville, 1761–1814*. Paris: Perrin et Cie, 1907.

———. *Paris rvolutionnaire*. Paris: Perrin et Cie, 1896. ———. *Tribunal of the Terror*. London: W. Heinemann, 1910.

Lescure, M. de. *La vraie Marie-Antoinette*. Paris: Librarie Parisienne, 1863.

Ligne, Prince Charles-Joseph de. *Fragments de l'histoire de ma vie*. Paris: Plon, 1928.

Littell, Eliakim. "The Conciergerie." *Living Age* 205 (1895): 589.

———. "Lord Holland's Foreign Reminiscences." *Living Age* 29 (1851): 392.

———. "Marie Antoinette." *Living Age* 22 (1895): 206.

———. "Memoirs of Marie Antoinette." *Living Age* 60 (1895): 37.

Long, George. *France and Its Revolutions: A Pictorial History, 1789–1848*. London: Charles Knight, 1850.

Louis XVIII. "Lettre." In *L'intermédiaire des chercheurs et curieux*. Paris: Benjamin Duprat, Librairie de l'Institut, 1904.

Maria Theresa, Comte Florimond-Claude de Mercy-Argenteau, and Marie-Antoinette. "Marie Antoinette to Maria Theresa." In *Correspondance secrète entre Marie-Thérèse et le Comte de Mercy-Argenteau avec les lettres de Marie-Thérèse et de Marie-Antoinette*, 2:342–44. Paris: Firmin-Didot Frères, 1874.

Martin, Henri. *A Popular History of France*. 3 vols. Boston: C. F. Jewett, 1877.

Maurel, Jules, and Marie and Léon Escudier. *La France musicale*. Vol. 9. Paris: César Bajat, 1838.

Maurice, Barthélemy. *Histoire politique et anecdotique des prisons de la Seine, contenant des renseignements entièrement inédits sur la période révolutionnaire*. Paris: Guillaumin, 1840.

Meetkerke, C. E. "Plot of the Pink." *Argosy* 63 (1897).

Miller, James Rodger. "George III." In *The History of Great Britain*. Philadelphia: Thomas Davis, 1844.

Montjoie, Christophe Félix Louis Ventre de la Touloubre. *Histoire de Marie-Antoinette-Josèphe-Jeanne de Lorraine, archiduchesse d'Autriche, reine de France*. 2 vols. Paris: Lepetit, 1814.

Morris, M. C. O'Connor. *The Prisoners of the Temple; or Discrowned and Crowned*. London: Burns and Oates, 1874.

Mortimer-Ternaux, Louis. *Histoire de la Terreur, 1792–1794*. 8 vols. Paris: Michel Lévy Frères, 1863.

Mühlbach, Luise. *Marie Antoinette and Her Son*. London: Chesterfield Society, 1867.

Nettement, Francis. *Histoire populaire de Louis XVII.* Paris: C. Dillet, 1868.

———. *Vie de Marie-Thérèse de France, fille de Louis XVI.* 2 vols. Paris: J. Lecoffre, 1872.

Nougaret, Pierre Jean-Baptiste. *Histoire des prisons de Paris et des départements: contenant des mémoires rares et précieux.* 4 vols. Paris: Courcier, 1797.

O'C. E., C. "The Queen's Favourite." *Irish Monthly* 14 (1886).

Parmentier, Antoine Augustin. *Dissertation sur la nature des eaux de la Seine.* Paris: Buisson, 1787.

Parret, E. *Marie-Antoinette devant le Tribunal révolutionnaire.* Lyon: Évrard, 1868.

Pierre, Victor. "Marie Antoinette à la Conciergerie." *Revue des questions historiques* 47 (1890).

Pottet, Eugêne. *Histoire de la Conciergerie du Palais de Paris.* Paris: Quantin, 1895.

Pouliquen, Yves. *Félix Vicq d'Azyr, les lumières et la Révolution.* Paris: Odile Jacob, 2009.

Prudhomme, Louis Marie. *Les crimes des reines de France, depuis le commencement de la monarchie jusqu'à la mort de Marie-Antoinette, avec les pièces justificatives de son procès.* Paris: Bureau des Révolutions, 1793.

———. *Révolutions de Paris.* Paris: Rue de Marais, 1793.

Reiset, Gustave Armand Henri Comte de. *Lettres inédites de Marie-Antoinette et de Marie-Clotilde de France.* Paris: Librairie Firmin-Didot, 1876.

———. *Modes et usages au temps de Marie-Antoinette.* 2 vols. Paris: Librairie Firmin-Didot, 1885.

Robiano de Borsbeek, Louis-François. *Marie-Antoinette à la Conciergerie.* Paris: Baudouin Frères, 1824.

———. "Souvenirs de Mlle. Fouché." In *La captivité et la mort de Marie-Antoinette: les Feuillants—le Temple—la Conciergerie.* Paris: Perrin, 1902.

Roguet, Christophe-Michel. *Louis XIV.* Paris: Librairie Militaire, 1869.

Russell, Lord John. "The Causes of the French Revolution." *Quarterly Review* 49 (1833): 167.

Sabatié, A. C. *Le Tribunal révolutionnaire de Paris.* Paris: P. Lethielleux, 1914.

Saint-Amand, Imbert de. "La dernière année de Marie-Antoinette." *Correspondant* 117 (1879).

———. *The Duchess of Angoulême and the Two Restorations.* New York: Charles Scribner's Sons, 1894.

———. *Marie Antoinette and the End of the Old Régime.* New York: Charles Scribner's Sons, 1890.

———. *Marie Antoinette at the Tuileries, 1789-1791.* New York: Charles Scribner's Sons, 1898.

Saint-Edme, Bourg. *Répertoire général des causes célèbres françaises, anciennes et modernes.* Paris: Louis Rosier, 1834.

Saint-Gervais, Antoine de. *Histoire de Sa Majesté Louis XVIII, surnommé le Désiré: depuis sa naissance jusqu'au traité de paix de 1815.* Paris: P. Blanchard, 1816.

Salamon, Louis Sifrein Joseph Foncrosé de. *Unpublished Memoirs of the Internuncio at Paris during the Revolution, 1790-1801.* Boston: Little, Brown, and Company, 1896.

Sanson, Clément Henri. "Les mémoires des Sanson." *Nouveau journal* 25 (1864).

———. *Memoirs of the Sansons.* Vol. 2. London: Chatto and Windus, 1876.

Sauvan, Jean-Baptiste B., and Jean Philippe Schmit. *Histoire et description pittoresque du Palais de justice de la Conciergerie et de la Sainte Chapelle de Paris.* Paris: G. Engelmann, 1825.

Savornin, l'Abbé. *Notice historique sur les faits et particularités qui se rattachent à la chapelle expiatoire de Louis XVI et de la reine Marie-Antoinette.* Paris: Vaton, 1864.

Schaff, Philip, and Samuel Macauley Jackson. *A Religious Encyclopaedia; or Dictionary of Biblical, Historical, Doctrinal, and Practical Theology.* 3 vols. New York: Funk & Wagnalls, 1891.

Severin, Anne. "A Life of Ten." *Month* 10 (1869).

———. "Life of Marie Antoinette." *Month* 6 (1867).

Simon-Viennot, Henriette. *Marie-Antoinette devant le dix-neuvième siècle.* 2 vols. Paris: Amyot, 1843.

Smith, Sydney. "Tronson du Coudray." *Edinburgh Review* 95 (1852).

Staël, Anne Louise Germaine de. *Réflexions sur le procès de la reine.* Paris: Anonymous, 1793.

Stevens, Abel. "The Two Prisoners of the Conciergerie." *National Magazine 3* (1853).

Tarbell, Ida Minerva. *A Short Life of Napoleon Bonaparte.* New York: S. S. McClure Company, 1896.

Thiers, Adolphe. *History of the French Revolution.* 5 vols. London: G. Vickers, 1845.

Tribunal Révolutionnaire. *Procès de Louis XVI, de Marie-Antoinette, de Marie-Élisabeth et de Philippe d 'Orléans; discussions législatives sur la famille des Bourbons. Recueil de pièces authentiques.* Paris: A. Eymery, 1821.

———. *Procès de Marie-Antoinette, dite de Lorraine d'Autriche, veuve de Louis Capet: acte d'accusation, interrogatoire public, dépositions, confrontation des témoins au Tribunal révolutionnaire, et jugement.* Paris: Marchands de Nouveautés, 1793.

Troche, N. M. *La communion de la reine Marie-Antoinette.* Paris: Divry, 1863.

———. *Nouvelles preuves de la communion de la reine Marie-Antoinette.* Paris: Imprimerie Divry, 1864.

Tschudi, Clara. *Marie Antoinette.* London: Swan Sonnenschein, 1902.

Turbat, Pierre. *Procès des Bourbons: contenant des détails historiques sur la journée du 10 août 1792, les évènements qui ont précédé, accompagné et suivi le jugement de Louis XVI; les procès de Marie-Antoinette, de Louis-Philippe d'Orléans, d'Élisabeth et de plusieurs particularités sur la maladie et la mort de Louis-Charles, fils de Louis XVI; l'échange de Marie-Charlotte, et le départ des derniers membres de la famille pour l'Espagne.* 2 vols. Hamburg: Turbat, 1798.

Turquan, Joseph. *Madame Royale, the Last Dauphine.* New York: Brentano's, 1910.

Tytler, Sarah. *Marie Antoinette: The Woman and Queen.* London: Marcus Ward & Company, 1883.

Vaumartoise, François Victor Mérat de. "Éthers." In *Dictionnaire universel de matière médicale, et de thérapeutique.* Vol. 2. Paris: Société Belge de Librairie, 1837.

Viardot, Louis. *An Illustrated History of Painters of All Schools.* London: Sampson, Low, Marston, Searle, & Rivington, 1877.

Viel-Castel, Horace. *Marie-Antoinette et la Révolution française.* Paris: Techener, 1859.

Vigée-Lebrun, Marie Louise Élizabeth. *Souvenirs de Mme Vigée le Brun.* 3 vols. Paris: Bibliothèque Charpentier, 1860.

Villermont, Marie Comtesse de. *Histoire de la coiffure féminine.* Paris: Renouard, 1892.

Wallon, Henri. *Histoire du Tribunal révolutionnaire de Paris.* Vol. 1. Paris: Librairie Hachette et Cie, 1880.

———. "Le Terreur." *Correspondant* 86 (1872).

Weber, Joseph. *Mémoires concernant Marie-Antoinette, archiduchesse d'Autriche, reine de France.* 3 vols. London: G. Schulze & Company, 1809.

Wilson, H. Schütz. *History and Criticism.* London: T. Fisher Unwin, 1896.

Yonge, Charles Duke. *The Life of Marie Antoinette, Queen of France.* London: Harper & Brothers, 1876.

———. *Three Centuries of Modern History.* London: Longmans, Green and Company, 1872.

INDEX

Page references for illustrations are italicized.

off

190, 215, 219, 222–26, 262; jury
box, 167–68, 182, 188, 211, 215;
tribunal hall (*Salle de Liberté*), 173,
208–10, *215*, 219, 224, *225*. *See also*
Fouquier-Tinville, Antoine Quentin;
Fabricius, Nicolas-Joseph Pâris
Rhine River, 156
Richard, Marie Anne Barassin, 169
Richard, Toussaint, 15, 21, 23, 26, 32,
34, 38, 50–51, 66–67, 96–97, 103,
162, 232
Robespierre, Maximilien, 137, 167–68,
181, 226, 245–246, 280, 287
Rocheterie, Maxime de la, 23
Roederer, Pierre Louis, 165–65
Ronfin, Charles-Philippe, 242
Rougeville, chevalier Alexandre de,
190–91, 213, 267; Carnation Plot,
77–94; description, 78–79, 130;
disappearance, 109; meeting with
Fersen, 130; narration of, 114–15;
son of, 94–95; testimony of Fontaine
and, 104
Roussillon, Antoine, 169, 177–78, 188
Royal Palace (*Palais Royale*), 244

Saint-Denis, Basilica of, 247, 277–78,
283–85
Saint-Germain l'Auxerrois, Church of,
286
Saint-Honoré, rue de, 196, 206–7,
242–43, 245, 251
Saint-Louis, chevalier of, 78, 83, 86–
88, 91, 93, 98, 100, 102, 104–5,
210
Saint-Michel, Pont, 236
Saint-Roch: charity of, 56, 282;
church of, 244. *See also* Fouché,

Mademoiselle; Quélen, Antoinette-
Marie Adélaïde de
Sainte-Anne, rue, 121
Sainte-Pélagie prison, 119
Salamon, Monseigneur Louis Sifrein
de, 57
Salentin, Commissioner, 198
Sallatin, Madame, 12
Sambat, Jean-Baptiste, 168
Sanson, Charles-Henri, 226, 234–35,
239–42, 248
Sanson, Clément, 257
Sanson, Gabriel, 257
scaffold, 40–41, 47–48, 50, 226, 234–
35, *240*, *244*, 246–255
Seine River, 14, 16–18, 30, 41, 43, 236,
256, 268
Septeuil, Jean-Baptiste Tourteau, 196,
202–4, 223
Sévestre, Joseph Marie, 85
Sévin, Renée, 207–8
Silly, Abraham, 169, 182–83
Simon, Antoine, 6, 7, 72–73, 119,
138–43
Simon-Vouet, Madame, 57–59
smallpox, 78
Souberbielle, Dr. Joseph, 46, 167
Soupé, Dr. Louis, 138
La Souricière prison, 43
spies, 68, 97, 115, 136, 195, 270
Suard, juror, 168
Swiss Guards, 78, 148, 164, 280, 284

Tarré, Honoré Nicolas, 169
Tavernier, Lieutenant Claude-Denis,
212
Temple prison, 1, *3*, 6, 11–19, 26–30,
111, 123–26, 175, 179, 204–8, 243–

ABOUT THE AUTHOR

Will Bashor received his MA in French literature from Ohio University and his PhD in international studies from the American Graduate School in Paris. He lives downtown in Columbus, Ohio, and teaches at Franklin and Ohio Dominican universities. A member of the Society for French Historical Studies, he specializes in eighteenth-century French literature, culture, and history. His other publications include *Marie Antoinette's Head: The Royal Hairdresser, the Queen, and the Revolution*, which won the Adele Mellen Prize for Distinguished Scholarship and was a *New York Post* "Must-Read" book in 2015, and *Jean-Baptiste Cléry: Eyewitness to Louis XVI and Marie Antoinette's Nightmare*. Visit him at www.willbashor.com.